FIGHTING FOR THE CROSS

FIGHTING FOR
THE CROSS
CRUSADING TO THE HOLY LAND

❖

NORMAN HOUSLEY

YALE UNIVERSITY PRESS
NEW HAVEN AND LONDON

For information about this and other Yale University Press publications, please contact:
U.S. Office: sales.press@yale.edu   www.yalebooks.com
Europe Office: sales@yaleup.co.uk   www.yaleup.co.uk

Set in Adobe Caslon by IDSUK (DataConnection) Ltd
Printed in Great Britain by TJ International, Padstow, Cornwall

Library of Congress Cataloging-in-Publication Data

Housley, Norman.
    Fighting for the cross: crusading to the Holy Land/Norman Housley.
        p. cm.
    Includes bibliographical references and index.
    ISBN 978-0-300-11888-9 (ci: alk. paper)
    1. Crusades.   I. Title.
    D157.H69 2008
    909.07–dc22

                                                                        2008026775
A catalogue record for this book is available from the British Library.

10 9 8 7 6 5 4 3 2 1

For Alison, Carolyn, Jenny and Nick, my MA group without equal

CONTENTS

❖

ILLUSTRATIONS AND MAPS

16 Peter the Hermit leading his crusaders, from *Histoire Universelle, c.* 1286. (British Library, London/British Library Board. All rights reserved/The Bridgeman Art Library).

17 Frederick Barbarossa's death, illumination in *Liber ad honorem Augusti* by Petrus de Ebulo, 1195–6 (akg-images).

18 Philistines massacring the Israelites, historiated initial introducing I Kings, in a Latinate bible, Paris, *c.* 1245–50 (Morgan Library, New York, MS M.269 f.88).

19 Scythian women besieging their enemies, from *Histoire Universelle, c.* 1286 (Bibliothèque nationale, Paris/The Bridgeman Art Library).

20 Battle of the Christians and Saracens at Damietta, from the *Historia Major* by Matthew Paris, *c.* 1218 (Corpus Christi College, Cambridge/The Bridgeman Art Library).

21 Idealised representation of a knight confronting the vices (British Library Board. All rights reserved. MS Harley 3244, f.28).

22 Moat, bridge and main entrance gate, the Citadel, Aleppo, Syria (E Simanor/Robert Harding).

23 Walls of Constantinople (Francesca Yorke/Dorling Kindersley).

24 Battle between crusaders and Muslims, from *Le Roman de Godefroi de Bouillon* (Bibliothèque nationale de France, Paris/The Bridgeman Art Library).

25 Battle between crusaders and Khorezmians (Courtesy of the Master and Fellows of Corpus Christi College, Cambridge).

26 Arrival of Louis IX at Damietta, 1249, from *Vie et Miracles de Saint Louis* by Guillaume de Saint-Pathus (Bibliothèque nationale de France, MS Fr 5716. Sonia Halliday Photographs).

27 Siege of Antioch, from *Histoire d'outremer* by Guillaume de Tyr. (Bibliothèque municipale de Lyon, MS 828 f.83).

28 Bronze horses, St Mark's (Venice. R Sheridan/Ancient Art & Architecture Collection Ltd).

29 Thirteenth-century coin depicting John of Brienne (Ashmolean Museum, Oxford/The Bridgeman Art Library).

30 Crusading knights shown with pilgrim scrips, from *Le Roman de Godefroi de Bouillon*, 1337 (Bibliothèque nationale de France, MS Fr 22495 f.19).

31 Godfrey of Bouillon and his brother Baldwin I, from *Histoire d'outremer* by Guillaume de Tyr (Bibliothèque municipale de Lyon, MS 828 f.33).

32 Adhemar of Le Puy leads the barons on the First Crusade, from *Histoire d'outremer* by Guillaume de Tyr (Bibliothèque municipale de Lyon, MS 828 f.15v).

33 Christ with a dagger (British Library Board. All rights reserved, MS Royal 19 B15, f.37r).
34 Battle scene outside Antioch, from William of Tyre (British Library Board. All rights reserved, Yates Thompson 12 f.29/The Bridgeman Art Library).
35 A medieval reliquary (akg-images).
36 Christians threatened by Saracen monster, from the Oscott Psalter, 1260s (British Library Board. All rights reserved, MS Add. 5000 f.213).
37 Brutal treatment of non-combatants in European warfare (British Library Board, All rights reserved, MS Add. 15269 fol.178v).
38 The siege of Nicaea, from *Historia (et continuation)* by Guillaume de Tyr (Bibliothèque nationale de France, MS Fr 2630 f.22v).
39 Urban II preaches the First Crusade (The Walters Art Museum, MS 10137 f.1r).
40 Dome of the Rock, Jerusalem (Jon Arnold/JAI/Corbis).
41 Tiles from Chertsey Abbey, Surrey (The Trustees of the British Museum).
42 The martyrdom of St Vincent, from *Livre d'images de madame Marie, c.* 1285–90 (Bibliothèque nationale de France, MS nouv. acq. 16251 f.78).
43 Thirteenth-century map of Jerusalem (Uppsala University Library, MS C691).
44 Map of Acre by Marino Sanudo (Bodleian Library, University of Oxford, MS Tanner 190 f.207r).
45 Mosaic of Alexios I Komnenos, Hagia Sophia, Constantinople (Sonia Halliday Photographs).
46 Detail of cynocephali in the Pentecost relief, Sainte Marie-Madeleine, Vézelay, France (The Art Archive/Gianni Dagli Orti).
47 Hugh de Vaudemont embraced by his wife, from the cloister of the priory at Belval, Lorraine (Musée des Monuments Français, Paris/Lauros/Giraudon/The Bridgeman Art Library).
48 Relief of St George, church of St George, Fordington, Dorset (Conway Library, The Courtauld Institute of Art, London).
49 Holy Sepulchre Church, Northampton (Author's photograph).
50 Godfrey of Bouillon, from *Historia (et continuation)* by Guillaume de Tyr (Bibliothèque nationale de France, MS Fr 9084 f.20v).
51 Urban II preaching the First Crusade, from *Les Passages d'Outre-Mer* by Sebastian Mamerot de Soissons, *c.* 1490 (Bibliothèque nationale de France/Giraudon/The Bridgeman Art Library).
52 Engraving by Bernand de Montfaucon, after a painted window in the Abbey of St Denis, *c.* 1100 (Hulton Archive/Getty Images).

Plates

Maps

PREFACE AND
ACKNOWLEDGEMENTS

There are countless histories of the crusades to the Holy Land, but hardly any attempts have been made to describe what the practice of crusading meant for the men and women who engaged in it. This is astonishing because crusading generated a very large volume of eyewitness testimony. For generations the accounts that Geoffrey of Villehardouin and John of Joinville wrote about the Fourth and Seventh Crusades have been among the most widely read medieval texts. They deserve their fame because they're exceptionally vivid and personal memoirs. But Villehardouin and Joinville are just the tip of the iceberg. Narratives, letters, poems, songs, sermons and treatises give us the means to reconstruct to a remarkable degree both the lived experience of crusading and the state of mind of participants.

Wherever possible I've allowed these sources to speak for themselves, using translations when they exist. The crusades have always been well served by translators and in recent years there's been a welcome growth in translations that are both accurate and accessible. The surviving texts are complemented by an unusually large quantity of striking visual evidence, as the illustrations reproduced here should demonstrate. Diacritical marks in oriental place and personal names present a constant issue for historians of crusading and I've cut the Gordian knot by using none.

The people whose exploits and sufferings are described in this book all took the cross to fight for Jerusalem. Crusading was an extraordinarily diverse phenomenon and thousands took the cross to fight in areas of the medieval world that were far away from the Holy Land, against Muslims, pagans and heretics among others. But for various reasons their experience of crusading was different from that of the crusaders who fought in the East, so I've made no attempt to bring them into this book. Exceptionally, I have included some of the fighting in Iberia, because it took place when crusaders were travelling to the Holy Land. I've also been selective in my use of the evidence left by the settlers and military orders based in the East, because their experience and outlook were likely to be different from those of visiting crusaders.

I'm grateful to Yale University Press for commissioning this book, to Heather McCallum for much helpful advice on it, and to the Press's readers for their detailed comments. The book is the fruit of three decades of reading, talking, teaching and writing about the crusades, and I can't begin to list the hundreds of colleagues and students who have shaped my thinking about the subject. To all of them I'm grateful. But I want to single out for special thanks the series of PhD students supervised by Jonathan Riley-Smith whose theses I examined: Cassandra Chideock, Michael Lower, Christoph Maier, William Purkis, Rebecca Rist, Caroline Smith and Susanna Throop. Some of their theses have been published, and I hope that the others will soon join them. Between them these historians have made a fundamental contribution to how we should view the ideas and practices of crusading to the Holy Land. They've certainly taught me more than I can say.

Norman Housley
University of Leicester

Map 1 Europe and the crusades to the Holy Land, 1095–1291
Towns in italics show locations of attacks on Jews in 1096

Map 2 The Middle East at the time of the First Crusade, 1095–9

Map 3 The crusader states and their neighbours, 1099–1291

❖

CRUSADING IN THE EAST, 1095–1291[1]

Blessed are the warmakers – Urban II and the launching of the First Crusade

In August 1095 men bringing in the harvest in the Rhône valley witnessed the spectacular sight of a papal entourage on the move. Pope Urban II had crossed the Alps from Italy to visit his native land. It was a momentous journey because medieval popes rarely travelled outside Italy. Urban's itinerary was extensive and his agenda was packed, including the investigation of the French king's adultery. Yet this tour of southern and central France is remembered today for a single sermon that Urban preached in the open air at Clermont in the Auvergne on 27 November 1095. His subject was the holy city of Jerusalem, which had been captured by the Muslims in 638 during the first wave of Islamic conquests. The pope called on all Christians to liberate Jerusalem from the Muslims in the name of God. In so doing Urban brought into being the First Crusade, which achieved his goal in July 1099. But he did much more than that. The Muslims counter-attacked and the difficulty of holding on to Jerusalem compelled Urban II's successors to preach further crusades over a period that lasted almost two centuries. For this reason Urban's exhortation to the Catholic faithful outside the walls of Clermont ranks among the most significant sermons ever preached. This includes the Sermon on the Mount, whose message of non-resistance to evil (Matthew 5: 38–44) Urban dramatically reshaped. The pope's preaching at Clermont changed and in many cases destroyed the lives of countless thousands of people – men, women and children, Christian, Muslim and Jewish.

Hence it's frustrating that we know so little for certain about what Urban II actually said. We don't possess the text that he used, if indeed he used one. What we have are several reconstructed versions. True, some are by eyewitnesses, but all were written up *after* the triumph of 1099. There's also the inexplicable fact that in the middle of winter the news of the pope's appeal rippled out from Clermont to the far corners of the Catholic world, so that several armies were able to assemble in the spring of 1096 and begin their march eastwards. Given the speed of these events it's tempting to argue that the thousands who responded to the pope's appeal to 'take the cross' must have been expecting his call to arms, or something like it. It's highly likely that the pope was responding to a groundswell of popular anxiety about what was happening at Christianity's holiest shrines under Muslim occupation; there are even one or two indications that his summons of a big military effort to free Jerusalem was expected. As he made his way through southern France towards Clermont, Urban would have been able to gauge the mood of the faithful and he may even have started sketching out the format for a military expedition to the East that could achieve his aim. One of his predecessors, Gregory VII, had got this far in 1074. Urban's sermon at Clermont looks like a well-publicized attempt to test the waters, and judging by the letters that he wrote in the months that followed he was taken aback by the scale of the response that he either encountered at first hand or was told about. These letters show clearly that he was under a lot of pressure, trying to shape the crusade that was evolving, above all to address basic questions about who should take part in and preside over it.

Pilgrimage or war? The First Crusade's volatile character

Urban II's problem wasn't just coping with the extraordinary scale of the response; almost certainly he himself wasn't sure of what he had created. His preaching was like a chemistry experiment that created an inherently unstable compound. He had called for an armed pilgrimage, and it's certain that most of those who went on the First Crusade saw themselves first and foremost as pilgrims to Jerusalem. They'd made vows to worship at Jerusalem's sacred shrines, and they were carrying out one of Christianity's most ancient and popular devotional practices, earning forgiveness of sins through the public demonstration of sorrow, or penitence. But the military task facing these pilgrims was novel and extraordinary. The 'cross-bearers' (*crucesignati*) were marching to Palestine through the territory of the Byzantine empire, whose European lands extended from the Adriatic Sea to Constantinople. It's possible that the arrival of envoys sent by Constantinople's ruler Alexios I, appealing for western military help, triggered in Urban's mind the idea of launching the expedition. The crusaders could certainly rely on Alexios for friendly support and guidance. But most of the territory that Alexios's predecessors had ruled for centuries in Anatolia (Asia Minor) and northern Syria had recently been overrun by the Seljuq Turks, so hard fighting could be expected along the entire route leading from Constantinople to Jerusalem. Above all, the imposing Syrian fortress-city of Antioch would have to be recaptured from the Turks.

1 The Church of the Holy Sepulchre in Jerusalem, the spiritual focus for all crusaders and for many their military objective as well.

What made it possible even to contemplate such a challenging project was the emergence of leaders among those who took the cross. They had to sort this out for themselves. The first crusaders got nothing but rudimentary guidance from Urban and his court about how they should proceed, so they fell back on their own ideas to create armies that would be capable of achieving the task that the pope had set them. The first group of armies to depart depended on the leadership of charismatic individuals, men who called on their own religious conviction and force of character to keep control over their followers. The charismatics were epitomized by Peter the Hermit, who'd been one of the crusade's most successful preachers. These armies were followed by groups that coalesced around important territorial rulers who'd taken the cross – above all Godfrey duke of Bouillon, Raymond count of Toulouse, Robert duke of

Normandy and Robert count of Flanders. To a large extent it was these men, usually called 'princes', who gave Urban's programme the potential to succeed. He must have been mightily relieved that such an imposing group stepped forward.

Equally important was the fact that many of western Europe's finest fighting men, the knights (*milites*), took the cross. This was the case in the armies led by the charismatics as well as those commanded by the *principes*. The enthusiasm of the knights can't have been surprising given that their fighting skills and social obligations dragged them into constant warfare against other Christians. Churchmen never tired of warning them that shedding Christian blood would lead to an eternity of suffering. Urban II knew that these arms-bearers had a desperate desire to perform penance, and the armed pilgrimage to Jerusalem was preached as a guarantee of salvation. But two features of the response to his sermon almost certainly did worry him. The first was the popularity of his crusade among contemporaries who weren't fighting men, but had no intention of being left out. They couldn't be excluded given the fact that the crusade was a pilgrimage, but they had much less value than knights as combatants. We'll see that this conundrum at the heart of crusading was never fully resolved.

Urban's second concern was the way those who took the cross shaped his preaching to their own devotional needs. The Catholic faithful (the laity) didn't just embrace the idea that the pope launched into their world in November 1095, they customized it with their own values. Some of what they brought into it, such as an emphasis on the practice of vendetta, was repugnant to the Church. Other ideas, like their tendency to see Jesus Christ as a feudal lord and themselves as his vassals, obliged to recover his lost lands in Palestine, were more acceptable. In fact a lot of preachers found colourful analogies like these useful in getting their message across. Overall, a project created by pious intellectuals who were excited by the prospect of recovering Jerusalem, with the bonus of persuading violent men to do penance, was made more xenophobic and more muscular. With hindsight it's clear that this was essential to give the crusade the raw vitality to succeed in the face of almost unendurable suffering and setbacks. The pope came up with the concept but it was the laity that gave it life.

Alliance with Byzantium

In 1096 the first of these setbacks occurred when the initial wave of armies, those led by the charismatics, were shattered by defeat and disintegration. Although far from rabbles, they were less well supplied, equipped and disciplined than the armies of the princes. Three groups failed even to survive their march through the Balkans: they ran into trouble with the authorities *en route* and were driven back. Those groups that did reach Anatolia were cut to pieces in their first encounters with the Turks. It's possible that lessons were learnt from this, though the sheer speed of events and the slowness of communication didn't give much time for reflection or discussion; for in autumn 1096, less than twelve months after Urban II's sermon, the armies led by the princes, a cluster of forces that numbered some tens of thousands of men and women, marched eastwards. Some made their way through central Europe and others through Italy, and they converged outside Constantinople around Christmas 1096. This wasn't the assistance for which Alexios had appealed to Urban. Patiently the emperor worked out a series of agreements with individual princes. His primary goal was to safeguard his lands and subjects from violence at the hands of the crusaders as they marched through Anatolia; all being well, he might also use their armed strength to regain some of the territory that he'd lost to the Turks. Perhaps this could even include Antioch, which had only been lost to the Turks in 1085.

Initially this cautious plan worked well for Alexios, winning him the city of Nicaea in June 1097. But the crusaders weren't interested in conducting a war of systematic reconquest on behalf of their Byzantine allies. They were marching towards Jerusalem, and the further southwards they got, the more exposed Alexios's lines of communication would be. So from Nicaea onwards co-operation with Alexios became tenuous. By the time the crusaders reached northern Syria they'd started to get fractious and disillusioned with the Byzantines. In other respects, however, things went well. The march through Anatolia was rapid and efficient and it included an important victory over the Turks at Dorylaeum on 1 July 1097. A large number of fortified towns were captured and Baldwin of Boulogne, Godfrey of Bouillon's brother, seized Edessa, establishing the first of the crusader principalities. In the letters that they wrote home the crusaders were jubilant and self-confident, at times almost light-headed.

Trial by fire: Antioch

Then came the crusade's time of trial, the military operations conducted at and around Antioch in 1097–9. The siege of Antioch was the pivotal event in the First Crusade. In every sense, military, logistical, political and religious, it proved desperately demanding. It makes sense to regard it as the crucible in which armed pilgrimage was transformed into something new that we now call crusading. Urban II had regarded the military recovery of Jerusalem as such a grim and arduous prospect that it would earn the participants God's full forgiveness for all their sins. Theologically this was optimistic, even speculative. The purgative tribulations endured at Antioch mattered because they bore the pope out, and more importantly they impressed themselves on the minds of the crusaders themselves. The cry that went up when Urban II finished speaking at Clermont, *Deus lo volt* ('God wants this'), was vindicated not just by military victory but also by the fact that victory followed prolonged physical, mental and emotional suffering. The crusaders had to experience their Good Friday as well as their Easter Day.

The heart of the crusaders' dilemma at Antioch was military: the fortress was formidable, its garrison strong and ably commanded, and although Seljuq authority in the region was highly fragmented, the Turkish rulers of Aleppo, Damascus and Mosul all made separate attempts to relieve the besieged city. In the event Antioch was betrayed to the crusaders by one of its garrison's officers on 3 June 1098, in a deal that was brokered by a Norman prince called Bohemund of Taranto. Just two days after taking the city the crusaders were themselves besieged in it by Kerbogha, the governor of Mosul. Bohemund again played the leading role in the battle of Antioch (28 June 1098) in which Kerbogha's army was resoundingly defeated. Bohemund couldn't match his fellow princes in resources but his extraordinary skills coupled with his ambition enabled him to dominate this phase of the crusade. He'd set his sights on becoming the ruler of Antioch and he argued that his role in its betrayal entitled him to possession of the city and its territories. The other princes clung to the battered ideal of co-operation with the Byzantines, and the resulting stalemate lasted throughout the autumn and winter of 1098–9. The march southwards simply couldn't be resumed until the issue of Antioch's future was resolved. The crusaders had already been weakened by two periods of starvation, the first during their siege of Antioch and the second in the weeks when they'd been bottled up in the city by Kerbogha's army. Now they suffered a third period of starvation, which seems to have been the most severe of them all. Worst of all, the enemy now wasn't external but internal: the greed and bickering of their own leaders. Many despaired of a solution and the crusade came close to collapse.

'Wonderful in our eyes' – the capture of Jerusalem

The catalyst for movement was a revolt by the poor pilgrims. They knew that Raymond of Toulouse was the prince who was most susceptible to Jerusalem's attraction, and in January 1099 they exerted enough pressure on Raymond to make him initiate a march to the holy city. Bohemund remained as ruler of Antioch but the other princes joined the army, which after a reasonably easy march got to Jerusalem in June. The crusaders had now left the lands held by the Turks and entered a zone that was under the control of Egypt, which was ruled by the Fatimid dynasty. There was every expectation that the Fatimids would despatch a relief army so the capture of Jerusalem was urgent.

With the completion of their task in sight the crusaders set about this with infectious enthusiasm. The city was stormed on 15 July 1099, an event that set the seal on the collective mood of triumphalism that had been gathering pace throughout the southwards march from Syria. Contemporaries celebrated Jerusalem's recovery as nothing less than the work of God (Ps. 118:23–4), the clearest possible indication that the crusade was indeed his will.

There were key decisions that had to be made immediately about the future government of Jerusalem. A patriarch was chosen and Godfrey of Bouillon emerged from an obscure electoral process as Jerusalem's first secular ruler. The crusaders then defeated the Fatimid army at the battle of Ascalon on 12 August 1099. An exodus of the survivors ensued, though there were painfully few of them: it's likely that about 80 per cent of those who'd set out three years earlier had perished. Urban II had died in July 1099 but his successor Paschal II passed the news of Jerusalem's capture to the whole of Catholic Europe. The resulting excitement contributed a good deal towards the preaching of another expedition whose participants set out for the East in 1100 with the goal of reinforcing the settlers. The Turks in Anatolia were now alert to the threat posed by crusaders and aware of their opponents' military shortcomings. They defeated the newcomers comprehensively in a series of engagements in 1101, so little assistance reached those who'd stayed behind in the Holy Land. Nonetheless, the capture of Tripoli in 1109 meant that a cluster of important cities were in Christian hands and these formed the nuclei for four states: the kingdom of Jerusalem, the principality of Antioch, and the counties of Tripoli and Edessa. The Latin East was born.

The gestation of the Second Crusade

In most respects the states that the first crusaders founded in the East lived separate lives, quarrelling with each other just like states in Europe. But they also had shared interests as a group, and these made it certain that crusading would enjoy a long future. Circumstances forced their rulers to become adept at lobbying for help. All too few Christians could be persuaded to settle permanently in what they called *outremer* ('beyond the sea'). It's been estimated that the total number of knights owing military service to the Latin rulers of Palestine and Syria reached no more than 2,000. It followed that if these lands, and above all Jerusalem, were going to be defended against the Muslims, then their fellow Christians in the West would have to come out to the East to help them on a temporary basis. There was never any credible alternative to this military assistance taking the form of further crusading. The need was established twenty years after Jerusalem's capture, when a brief period of Christian belligerence fizzled out, and was followed by a powerful

Islamic counter-offensive. This stemmed not from Fatimid Egypt nor from the Seljuq heartland in Iraq but from a Turkish dynasty based at Mosul and Aleppo, whose first protagonist was the warlord Zengi. On Christmas Eve 1144 Zengi captured Edessa, which thus enjoyed the dubious honour of being both the first of the large cities to be captured by the Christians and the first to fall again into Muslim hands.

The news of Edessa's capture had some impact on popular feeling in the West, where its strategic importance was generally appreciated. In religious and cultural terms the time seemed right for the preaching of another great crusade. Contemporaries had grown up surrounded by reminders on stone, parchment and glass of what had been done by the first crusaders. Their zeal, sufferings and victories generated almost mythic admiration and they were regarded as 'the great generation' of their times. This was the case above all in France, where the summary title created for the First Crusade, 'God's deeds, acting through the French' (*Gesta dei per Francos*), enshrined proto-nationalist pride. Pope Eugenius III issued the first significant crusading encyclical, a letter intended for reading aloud to all the faithful. Like all papal bulls the encyclical is known by its opening words, *Quantum praedecessores*, a phrase that overtly references Eugenius's awareness of the challenging legacy that he'd inherited from Urban II. However, the Second Crusade got off to a false start. In the regions where the First Crusade had recruited most vigorously monarchy had been at a low ebb, so second-tier leadership by the princes had proved necessary. Thanks largely to good luck this had worked reasonably well; crucially, it had survived the storm and stress over who would rule at Antioch and Jerusalem. But kingship had now revived and the French looked to their king, Louis VII, to take the lead. For this he needed the support of his barons and initially they were lukewarm. For very good reasons they were worried about the destabilizing effect of a great expedition to the East. It was only in the spring of 1146 that their concerns were swept aside as collective enthusiasm caught them in its grip, together with the rest of France and many other regions of Europe.

St Bernard and the Second Crusade

What transformed the situation was the passionate advocacy of St Bernard, an abbot of the new Cistercian order who has a good claim to be the twelfth century's most influential churchman. To the preaching of the crusade Bernard brought new ideas as well as incredible stamina. Conscripting the Hebrew idea of a jubilee, he portrayed the crusade as a rare opportunity offered by God for Christians to win their salvation by personal effort. This he tied in with a deep devotion towards the Holy Land's shrines and a perception of their acute dependence on western protection. The overwhelming response to Bernard's own preaching showed that he was in tune with the thinking of the broad mass of the faithful, but there was no strategic reflection about the best way to harness this zeal so as to recover Edessa from Zengi. Remarkably, the Christian rulers in the Holy Land don't seem to have been consulted at all during the crusade's planning, and it's hard to work out what Louis VII expected to do in the East apart from fulfilling his vow as a pilgrim to worship in Jerusalem. The expedition that took shape closely resembled the First Crusade, especially in terms of

2 Speyer Cathedral, where St Bernard gave a crusade banner to Conrad III in December 1146.

its inclusive approach to who could take part, and its determination to follow the same route to the Holy Land as its predecessor. Nobody seems to have pointed out that the glorious victories of 1098 and 1099 had been preceded and followed by awful massacres in Anatolia in 1096 and 1101.

The crusade's prospects were already uncertain and they weren't helped by Bernard's decision that the German king, Conrad III, should be brought into the expedition's leadership alongside Louis VII. The prospects of these two monarchs working effectively together weren't at all good. Conrad took the cross in response to Bernard's 'honey-tongued' preaching at Christmas 1146 and his host assembled at Regensburg in May 1147. In its substantial size and mixed composition the German force resembled the French host that Louis led eastwards from Metz a few weeks later. Other groups also left for the East, including an army made up of people who'd taken the cross in the Low Countries, the Rhineland and England, who set sail from Dartmouth in May 1147. A sizeable naval contingent had been brought into the crusade's recruitment and possibly into its planning too. This marked a significant advance on the haphazard way in which seaborne reinforcements and supplies had been deployed during the First Crusade. The problem was that there weren't many other innovations to match it. Conservatism was the order of the day, and this has seldom if ever been a way to win wars.

The failure of the Second Crusade and the 'lost generation' of crusaders

What ensued was largely disastrous. The Dartmouth contingent stopped off in Portugal and assisted in the capture of Lisbon from the Moors in October 1147. This set a precedent for a series of similar campaigns in the peninsula by crusaders who were sailing to the Holy Land from ports in north-western Europe. In the East all was catastrophe. The Byzantine emperor Manuel, like his grandfather Alexios before him, placed the emphasis on safeguarding his capital. Byzantine assistance was offered only grudgingly, but what mattered far more was the energetic harassment of both the German and the French hosts by the Turks as the crusaders tried to make their way across Anatolia. The armies took different routes but it made little difference. Both suffered appalling losses. When Conrad and Louis met with the rulers of the Latin East at the port of Acre in June 1148 to discuss military options, the forces at their disposal were a pathetic remnant of what they'd set out with. Embarking on the recovery of Edessa was out of the question. Instead an attempt was made to take Damascus. If this had succeeded it's possible that the balance of power in Syria would have swung back in the Christians' favour. But for reasons which have always perplexed commentators the siege of Damascus was mismanaged and it had to be abandoned. Both Louis and Conrad returned home angry and humiliated.

The Second Crusade had failed miserably to deal with the Islamic threat. Thanks to the wave of optimism on which it had been launched, generated above all by St Bernard's preaching, there was a severe backlash against crusading generally. In part the backlash took the form of harsh criticism directed against the pope, Bernard and the returned crusaders, but a more dangerous expression was apathy. Pope after pope between 1150 and 1187 tried and failed to arouse the faithful in response to the growing pressure that the Muslims were exerting on the Holy Land. No European king or prince would take on the heavy responsibility of leading another big crusade to the East. In 1169 Nur ed-Din, Zengi's son, seized control over Egypt from the Fatimid dynasty. He'd brought about the Christians' strategic nightmare, the unification of Syria and Egypt. It soon became a religious unification as well as a political one, for Nur ed-Din ended the Shi'a caliphate in Egypt, enforcing Sunni orthodoxy. The crusader states were now all but encircled by Turkish armed might, and the apologists of the House of Zengi couched its escalating ambitions in the Middle East in terms of propaganda about the need to recover Jerusalem (Al Quds) from the Christian unbelievers.

This wasn't going to be easy, for while Catholics responded coolly towards crusading appeals, they still cared passionately about Jerusalem. Every year they flocked to its shrines as pilgrims, and once they'd discharged their pilgrim vows they sometimes took up arms to help out the settlers on campaign. Such assistance came in handy, but by the last quarter of the twelfth century more important military support was being provided by the religious military orders, the Knights Templar and Knights Hospitaller. Their members took monastic vows which committed them for life, providing assistance that was both continuous and reliable, from the settlers' viewpoint far preferable to intermittent help from pilgrims. There were never many professed members of the orders available for combat duty in the East – probably fewer even than the 2,000 or so knights owing service for their fiefs; but the masters of the orders had the financial means to hire a lot of mercenaries. So increasingly they shouldered the burden of maintaining and manning the castles which were starting to play a central role in defence. All in all, it looked as if the age of the great armed pilgrimages was over. Sheltered by their castles and bolstered by the military orders and occasional pilgrims-turned-warriors, the rulers of the crusader states could just about get by, so long as they were prudent and adroit in using their scanty resources to stave off the challenge posed by Muslim resurgence.

Disaster and recovery – Saladin and the Third Crusade

It was a Muslim who unwittingly gave crusading a new lease of life. This was Saladin, Nur ed-Din's lieutenant and from 1171 his governor of Egypt. When

Nur ed-Din died in 1174 Saladin successfully challenged his heirs for control of his extensive lands, announcing his goal of completing the process of driving out the Christians. He very nearly achieved it. In 1187 he managed to lure King Guy of Jerusalem into a reckless and indefensible gamble. Guy led on campaign almost his full military strength, including contingents from the county of Tripoli, and at the battle of Hattin on 3–4 July this large army was all but destroyed and Guy himself captured. In the course of the desperate fighting at Hattin the most sacred of the Holy Land's relics, a portion of the True Cross on which Christ had died, fell into Muslim hands. Saladin lost no time in capturing all of the ports south of Tripoli with the exception of Tyre, and on 2 October 1187 he occupied Jerusalem. News of these events, above all the loss of the True Cross and the fall of Jerusalem, achieved what nothing else since 1150 had been able to. Pope Gregory VIII issued what has a good claim to be the most impressive of all crusading encyclicals, *Audita tremendi*, and preparations immediately began for an enterprise to recover the Holy Land.

The situation in the East was catastrophic but the Catholic faithful rose to the challenge. The fifty years that followed Hattin were the high-water mark of the crusade's popularity. The social and geographical breadth of support that crusading commanded in these decades showed that it enjoyed deep and universal appeal. More problematic than recruitment was the question of who would lead a great crusade to recover Jerusalem, because this was tied up with disputes and rivalries between Christian rulers that were unending. Warfare between the kings of England and France was particularly trouble-some; if they weren't actually fighting they were getting ready to do so. None the less, the rulers of both kingdoms took the cross as did the Holy Roman Emperor Frederick I, whose red beard gained him the imposing nickname of 'Barbarossa'. This triumvirate constituted an unprecedented degree of commit-ment by western Europe's crowned heads, and it was accompanied by some reflective strategic thinking. One way to recover the Holy Land was by using the surviving Christian holdings in Lebanon and Syria, especially Tripoli and Antioch, as a springboard and this approach seems to have been favoured by Barbarossa, who also decided to march his troops to Syria via the customary overland route. Richard I of England and Philip II ('Augustus') of France decided to go by ship. Their destination was the port city of Acre, which King Guy had placed under siege in August 1189 following his release from Muslim captivity.

More than any other crusade, the Third was a mixture of disaster and triumph. Barbarossa's expedition suffered a truly tragic fate. Following a rela-tively easy march through the Balkans and a gruelling but successful crossing of Anatolia, the Germans reached the safety of Cilician Armenia only to lose their leader in a bizarre swimming accident on 10 June 1190. Demoralization, sickness and loss of purpose ate like acid into the German host, causing its slow disintegration. In future no crusade would try to reach the Holy Land by marching there. By contrast, the contingents that went eastwards by sea reached the East virtually intact, and with their assistance the siege of Acre was pressed with vigour in 1190–1. Saladin staged a massive effort to relieve his garrison but he couldn't save the city, which surrendered on 12 July 1191. By the skin of their teeth the Christians had survived the crisis unleashed by their defeat at Hattin, though both Jerusalem and the True Cross were still in Muslim hands.

It can't have surprised anybody that the exercise of joint command on crusade by Richard I and Philip II was riven by bickering, and the situation wasn't helped by their involvement in the fraught dynastic politics of the kingdom of Jerusalem. But Philip's early return to France, just weeks after Acre's capitulation, left Richard with a free hand to try to recover Jerusalem. He marched southwards to Jaffa and from there made two attempts to march inland, in the winter of 1191 and the summer of 1192. The strategic issues were complex and went beyond the recapture of the city. The king was persuaded by leaders of the settlers, including the masters of the military orders, that even if he managed to take Jerusalem it couldn't be held against a determined counter-attack. It was clear that the crusade had reached a stalemate. Richard toyed with the idea of invading Egypt but he also conducted lengthy negotiations with Saladin to try to work out a compromise. These were the most detailed talks that had ever been held between crusaders and Muslims and some imaginative ideas were tabled – at one point it was even suggested that Richard's sister Joan might marry Saladin's brother al-Adil. In the event all that proved possible was a truce. This was concluded in September 1192 and was painful for both sides: the Muslims retained Jerusalem, the Christians their string of ports along the Mediterranean coast. From these ports, as Saladin well knew, the Christians could both consolidate and expand their position whenever fresh help arrived from the West. This they did almost immediately, when a German crusade despatched by Barbarossa's son Henry VI in 1197 succeeded in reoccupying Sidon and Beirut.

Diversion – the Fourth Crusade and the Latin conquest of Constantinople

As crusading entered its second century, its success increasingly came to depend on two preconditions. One was its appeal to the Catholic faithful, because in the end everything depended on their willingness to contribute blood and treasure to the Holy Land's cause. The other was the ability and readiness of society's great lords, the authorities of Church and state, to provide an array of initiative, leadership and support. This was structure, without which zeal was helpless. Of course the two preconditions enmeshed with each other. Individuals would

3 Krak des Chevaliers, the great Hospitaller castle in Syria.

respond much more spontaneously to crusade preaching if they were optimistic about their chances of discharging their vows, while rulers (as after Hattin) could be pushed into action by public opinion and lobbying. The trouble was that warfare between those rulers always stood in the way of crusading. Despite this, for several decades the level of activity remained astonishing. Henry VI's forces had hardly returned before the new pope Innocent III proclaimed a crusade in 1198. This time no monarchs answered the pope's appeal but there was a cluster of crusading barons, similar to the group that had fought their way through to Jerusalem in 1099. They comprised the counts of Champagne, Blois and Flanders; following the death of their agreed leader Theobald of Champagne, Boniface the marquis of Montferrat joined the group in 1201 as the crusade's new commander.

This Fourth Crusade intended to bring about the recovery of Jerusalem by pursuing the strategy of attacking Muslim power in Egypt. This approach wasn't new: it had been advocated during the First and Third Crusades. However, it was now pursued with energy; above all the crusade's leaders contracted the services of a powerful Venetian fleet. But they miscalculated the numbers who would turn up and they weren't able to pay the full fee agreed with Venice. A series of diversions took place as crusaders and Venetians alike wrestled with their financial quandary. The first was to the Christian port of Zadar in Dalmatia, which the crusaders stormed in November 1202 on behalf of their Venetian allies. This gained them a delay in repaying their debt. They then sailed to Constantinople, where they planned to pay their debt in full by placing on the throne a Byzantine pretender, Alexios Angelos. Like all men in his position Alexios was boundlessly generous in his promises of support to his western supporters, but when they'd placed him in power, in July 1203, he found that he couldn't honour his promises. Nor did he think that he needed to. In November relations between Alexios IV and his erstwhile allies collapsed into open hostility.

This was a very different situation from that faced by the many earlier crusading armies that had pitched camp in the vicinity of Constantinople. The crusaders and Venetians, who'd supplied 200 ships including 60 galleys, were staring at bankruptcy and they felt betrayed and dishonoured by Alexios. During the winter of 1203–4 Alexios IV was himself overthrown, though this made little difference to the strategic scenario that had crystallized. There was no alternative to mounting another assault on Constantinople's walls. In April 1204 the crusaders stormed the city, proceeding to install a Latin emperor and patriarch there. As contemporaries recognized, this was a mirror image of what had happened in Jerusalem in 1099, but it was a very odd one. For this time it was a Christian city that had been taken and, it must be added, ruthlessly sacked. The crusaders never set eyes on the Holy Land for whose recovery they had taken their vows. Some stayed to defend Constantinople but most sailed for home. The Latin empire struggled to survive against heavy odds until 1261, when the Byzantine Greeks recaptured their capital and saw off the intruders from the West.

Warfare or diplomacy? The Fifth Crusade and Emperor Frederick II

Meanwhile the death of Saladin in 1193 had given the crusader states in Palestine and Syria a much needed breathing space. Saladin's lands were divided among his heirs, the Ayyubids, and they were soon immersed in constant quarrels which enabled the Christians to play one Muslim ruler off against the other. But Jerusalem remained in Islamic hands and the narrow coastal strip held by the Christians was vulnerable to attack. The situation remained fragile and the response of the faithful to this was highly emotional. This was demonstrated in 1212 by the popular surge of cross-taking tradition- ally called 'the Children's Crusade'. Contrary to its status in folklore, this was a 'popular' crusade like that led in 1096 by Peter the Hermit. The ambiguous Latin word *pueri* lies at the root of the idea of children setting out, and it's better translated as 'lads'. The crusade of the *pueri* wasn't sponsored by the Church, but just a year later Innocent III did launch another official crusade, and although he died in 1216 before the crusaders had set out, his successor Honorius III pushed the project ahead with vigour. The organization and co-ordination of Christendom's crusading efforts by the Church had reached their height: in 1215 the Fourth Lateran Council, the most glittering clerical assembly of the entire Middle Ages, passed legislation ('canons') that applied to the forthcoming crusade and to all future ones.

Some of the Fifth Crusade's participants took part in a lacklustre campaign in Palestine in 1217, but at its heart there lay an ambitious attempt to carry out the same strategy of attacking Egypt that had been envisaged for the Fourth Crusade. The reasoning was that Christian control of all Egypt would ensure the military recovery of Jerusalem; alternatively, if the sultan of Egypt lost enough land in the Nile delta he'd agree to hand Jerusalem back, together with sufficient territory to make the city's defence viable over the long term. In this way crusading commanders would avoid the strategic impasse that had frustrated Richard I in 1191–2. In May 1218 the crusaders landed near Damietta and laid siege to the port. Capturing Damietta was far from easy, but in November 1219 the town was finally occupied. Then, much like their predecessors at Antioch in 1098–9, the crusaders fell victim to bickering and inactivity. No kings from the West had joined the crusade's Egyptian phase and strong leadership was absent. The army's composition was also unusually fluid, because crusaders arrived and left for home in successive spring and autumn voyages or 'passages'. The sultan made two offers to return to the Christians all the land that they'd held before the battle of Hattin in exchange for their withdrawal from Egypt. The Muslims were even prepared to grant a truce lasting thirty years, which would have given their opponents the time needed to refortify all of their castles. Both offers were turned down. There's no doubt that the expedition was spectacularly misman-aged. When the decision was finally made to march up the Nile, in July 1221, the timing couldn't have been worse, for the crusaders were soon marooned and cut off from Damietta by the summer rise in the river's level. There was no alter-native to suing for peace, and the crusaders evacuated Egypt late in the summer.

One factor behind the Fifth Crusade's paralysis after capturing Damietta was the hope that the Holy Roman Emperor Frederick II would soon be joining the army with substantial reinforcements. The argument went that Frederick would become the crusade's natural commander, so it was unaccept-able to pre-empt his decisions. In reality Frederick, who had taken the cross when he was crowned in 1215, didn't arrive in the East until thirteen years later. In the past his expedition has been called the Sixth Crusade, though in most respects it makes more sense to regard the eight months that Frederick spent in Palestine as a belated episode in the Fifth Crusade. No crusade to date had so glaringly highlighted the destructive impact that political disputes in the West exerted on Catholic Europe's ability to assist the Holy Land. Frederick had quarrelled with the pope about a whole list of issues including his slowness in setting out for the East, and when he finally did sail there he'd been excommunicated. The emperor saw the Holy Land's salvation as lying in diplomacy rather than combat, and by siding with Egypt against Damascus he managed to recover most of Jerusalem (though not the Temple Mount), together with a corridor of land connecting the city with the coast. This wasn't a viable long-term solution because Jerusalem's walls had been demolished in 1219, demilitarizing the city.

The price that Frederick II paid for his achievements in the East was the alienation of some of the key players in the kingdom of Jerusalem's political affairs, including the Knights Templar and the patriarch of Jerusalem. The patriarch refused to be present when Frederick visited Jerusalem to wear his crown in the Church of the Holy Sepulchre, and the emperor's enemies stirred up the mob to hurl tripe at him when he embarked for the West at Acre in May 1229. More significant, though, was the fact that the emperor brought few crusaders with him; the short time that he spent in the East was no more than an interlude in his protracted battle of wills with the popes. The paradox was that Frederick was the most powerful monarch of his day. Ruler of lands that stretched from Sicily to the Baltic, in terms solely of resources he could have done an immense amount to help the Holy Land. In 1225 an attempt had even been made to link him to the kingdom of Jerusalem by marrying him to Yolande (Isabella) of Brienne, the heiress to the throne. Yet he did little. It would be wrong to blame either Frederick or his papal adversaries for the failure of these hopes, which were unrealistic. Frederick wasn't that different from many other European rulers in the mid-thirteenth century. These rulers sensed the significance that the Holy Land held for the Church and their subjects alike, and in part shared that esteem, but they weren't prepared to sacrifice to its alarmingly high demands the numerous other concerns of dynasty, honour and prestige. The Holy Land was always on the agenda but it never came first, and it needed to come first if it was to be saved.

The Seventh Crusade – Louis IX in Egypt and Palestine

Arguably there was one exception to this generalization and it was Frederick's near-contemporary, the king of France Louis IX. Throughout Europe enthusiasm for crusading and anxiety about the Holy Land remained forces to reckon with. There was ample proof of this in the 'Barons' Crusade' of 1239–41, an eclectic expedition made up of French and English participants commanded by Thibald count of Champagne, Peter count of Brittany and Richard earl of Cornwall. They conducted military operations in Palestine rather than Egypt, and like Frederick II in 1228–9 they worked with the grain of Ayyubid dynastic politics. As a result they achieved greater territorial gains than any crusade since the Third. But recovered land was illusory given the underlying imbalance of power that had characterized the status quo in the Middle East ever since Saladin's time. The fact was that only successful operations in Egypt had any chance of restoring the situation that had existed before Hattin. It was this task that Louis IX addressed. The king took the cross in 1244 as thanks to God for his recovery from an illness that had brought him close to death. News arriving from the East made it clear that his commitment was remarkably timely, because Jerusalem fell for the second (and last) time in the same year, while the sultan of Egypt inflicted a catastrophic defeat on the settlers and the military orders at Harbiyah (La Forbie).

Louis prepared his crusade with obsessive attention to detail. The army that embarked for the East in August 1248 was most likely the best equipped that had ever set out from France. The crusade's initial phase, following a winter spent on Cyprus, went well: Damietta, which had resisted the Fifth Crusade for so long, fell into French hands immediately in June 1249. But, like the fifth crusaders, Louis waited too long before taking his next step, which was to march on Cairo, 'the serpent's head'. His army stalled outside Mansurah and was cut off from Damietta by astute Turkish tactics. A painful retreat ended in wholesale capitulation. This was a defeat as massive as those inflicted on Louis VII and Conrad III during the Second Crusade, arguably worse because it included the king's own capture. Given Louis IX's renowned piety and dedication, these events created just as much disillusionment as the disasters of 1147–8. But Louis' resilience was breathtaking. His great-grandfather had stayed in the East for just a few months after the débâcle at Damascus. Louis IX sailed to Acre in May 1250 and lived continuously in the Holy Land for almost four years. The majority of his ransomed army had gone home, but the king's presence lifted morale in the Holy Land as nothing else could have. He also spent a large amount of money in refortifying the ports of Acre, Caesarea, Sidon and Jaffa. It fell far short of what had been hoped for in 1248, but it was better than nothing.

The emergence of the Mamluks

When Louis IX returned to France in 1254 it was apparent that half a dozen crusades, including two substantial invasions of the Nile delta, had failed to redress the radical dismemberment of Christian power in the Holy Land that was Saladin's lasting legacy to the Islamic cause. At best the 'Barons' Crusade', and the years that Louis IX spent in the Holy Land, had helped to shore up a building that was in constant danger of collapse. It had stayed upright mainly because the Ayyubid sultans of Egypt and Syria had lacked the will and incentive to demolish it. Fundamental upheavals affecting the whole Middle East now transformed this situation. In Egypt Louis' own crusade precipitated the overthrow of the Ayyubid dynasty in May 1250 by the slaves, or Mamluks, who'd long constituted its military elite. The sultans who emerged from the ranks of this privileged group showed an aggression towards the Christians in the Holy Land which was as dangerous and unrelenting as that of Saladin, if not more so.

In part this was because the sultans couldn't afford complacency. An even more fundamental development than the Mamluk seizure of power in Egypt was the arrival of the pagan Mongols. Originating in the steppe lands of Inner Asia, they had occupied Persia and Iraq, and pushing westwards into Syria they posed an enormous threat to Christians and Muslims alike. The Mamluks managed to stave off the Mongol attack at Ain Jalut in 1260 and Homs in 1281, but their greatest fear was a Mongol–crusader alliance which could destroy not just their own lordships but Islam itself. Moreover, following Ain Jalut and the retreat of the Mongols a power vacuum existed in Syria which the Mamluks hastened to fill. As at the time of Nur ed-Din in 1171, the ebb and flow of conquest had brought Egypt and Syria under the control of a single regime. It was a much more centralized form of government than Nur ed-Din's or Saladin's, and from the mid-1260s its sultans began systematically to besiege the remaining Christian castles and ports in Palestine and Syria. The increasingly grim news was communicated to the West, in time-honoured style, by a stream of tearful envoys bearing pathetic letters. Louis IX of France was still anxious about the fate of the Holy Land and he responded to the disasters by taking the cross for a second time in 1267. But Louis' crusade pursued the vain dream of winning Tunisia for the Christian faith by landing in North Africa. Here in August 1270 the century's greatest crusading king died of disease at the site of ancient Carthage.

The failure of the West

It's tempting to say that the hopes of the Holy Land expired with Louis at Carthage. Certainly the last twenty years of the crusading states pose a problem of explanation that's almost as perplexing as accounting for the First Crusade. Why did Catholic Europe fail to save its co-religionists in the East from being expelled by the Mamluks? The resources weren't lacking. Europeans in the late thirteenth century were more productive and advanced in almost every way than their ancestors had been two centuries earlier. The population was larger and more diverse, the economy more sophisticated, forms of government infinitely more effective. Yet although the West was presented with clear evidence that the Latin East was poised on the very edge of disaster, it couldn't produce an effort to match the First Crusade. This isn't the same as saying that

4 The siege of Acre in April–May 1291: its fall effectively spelled doom for the crusader states.

a repeat of that expedition was needed – far from it. Contemporaries were always referring nostalgically to the heady days of 1095–9, but in practice another armed pilgrimage would have been disastrous. It was one thing to defeat the quarrelling warlords of the Seljuq empire's western borderlands, quite another to take on the centralized and militarily proficient Mamluk sultanate. A massive investment of men, money and *matériel* was certainly called for, but it had to be accompanied by sustained control and strategic finesse.

If this wasn't the heart of the dilemma it was certainly a substantial part of it. In terms of its own political and military structures, Catholic Europe was simply not up to the task that now faced it. Crusading retained a strong grip on religious beliefs and practices. The days of its greatest popularity were over, but there were still many people, from popes and kings to townsfolk and peasants, who were willing to fight on or give money for a crusade to save what was left of the Holy Land. Catholics in the 1270s and 1280s don't seem to have shared the first crusaders' visceral attachment to the earthly Jerusalem, but they were just as anxious to save their souls and they were depressed by the prospect of Muslim occupation of the whole of Palestine and Syria. They had no desire to be considered less devout or less heroic than their ancestors. The trouble was that forging a workable military enterprise had become so much more problematic than at any point in the past. Organizationally, crusading had always been daunting. As we've seen, the first crusaders faced all the difficulties thrown up by a largely novel enterprise, while later crusading was damaged time and again by the West's internal squabbles. In the late thirteenth century warfare between Christians remained the biggest brake on effective crusading, but just as serious an obstacle was the emergence in the East of military agendas that were dispiriting in their demands and complexity.

So there was nothing to prevent the imbalance of power created by Saladin in 1187 on the field of Hattin finally reaching its logical conclusion. On 18 May 1291 the Mamluk forces broke through the walls of Acre. It was exactly a century since that city's recapture by the Third Crusade had spelled doom to Saladin's hopes, but this time there was no such reprieve. Acre's grand palaces, streets and docks witnessed scenes of terrible panic. Those Christians who couldn't afford the exorbitant prices charged for a few square feet on the last boats to leave port were either killed or enslaved. The remaining towns and castles soon capitulated to the Muslims. Although nobody wanted to believe it at the time, no future European generation would have the opportunity to fight for the cross in the Holy Land.

2

❖

THE CALL TO CRUSADE

'Take up your cross and follow me'

In 1195 Conrad of Wittelsbach, the archbishop of Mainz, appealed to the Germans to embark on a new crusade to the Holy Land. Despite the fact that just five years had passed since the German army that set out on the Third Crusade had disintegrated with appalling loss of life following Barbarossa's death in the River Saleph, Conrad enjoyed much success. Crusading was at the height of its popularity. The chronicler known as 'Pseudo-Ansbert' commented that nothing could hold the Germans back from responding anew to the call of the cross. He remarked with wonder that none of the many other acts of devotion that Christians could perform – fasting, vigils, prayers or almsgiving – could compete with crusading's appeal. These 'domestic sufferings' (*passiones domestice*) were held to be less effective than 'the passions of the holy journey', on which the Christian testified to his or her faith 'by hand and tongue'.[1]

This made crusading sound like a vocation, which it was; 'I believed, therefore I have spoken' (Ps. 116:10). But what drove the response was an aching sense of sinfulness coupled with near-despair about the believer's chances of achieving salvation. Both were brilliantly characterized in an image deployed by the great crusade preacher James of Vitry, who was a close contemporary of Conrad of Mainz and Pseudo-Ansbert. James described Christ's cross as 'the last plank for a shipwrecked world'.[2] It was just one in a string of analogies that James used to drive home the meaning of the cross in Christian thinking. But more than any other image, in a world that feared the perils of sea travel, it communicated the conviction that living was bound to involve sin, and that Christ's redeeming sacrifice was the believer's only chance of fending off sin's consequences. 'As a man swims in the manner of the cross and a ship sails in the manner of the cross and a bird flies in the manner of the cross, so you, too, cannot cross the sea of this world and reach the heavenly Jerusalem without the cross.'[3] This book is about religion, and more specifically about why generations of men and women between 1095 and 1291 believed that the surest way of reaching 'the heavenly Jerusalem' was by obeying Christ's command in Mark 8:34 to 'take up your cross and follow me'. So it makes sense to start by asking what the crusaders' cross meant to them, and why they thought that assuming it would save them.

'The fire will burn thee to the bare bane'

Save them from what? A crusade song composed in the late twelfth century commented bleakly on life's brevity that 'we have no tomorrow; nothing is more certain'.[4] After death no sinner could escape the just punishment of God. In the case of the unrepentant this meant an eternity in Hell, but even the souls of the repentant would have to suffer the anguish of pain in a 'middle place' located somewhere between Heaven and Hell. Unlike Hell it was subject to the rules of time and sinners were 'purged' of their evildoing, hence the name eventually given it of 'Purgatory'.[5] Irrespective of whether it was Hell or Purgatory, for most believers the afterlife would entail suffering worse than anything that could be imagined in this world. It would be 'a cruel and endless death, each day worse than the one before'.[6]

A few people were privileged to see it. Around 1131 the chronicler Orderic Vitalis narrated the story of a priest called Walchelin who witnessed a procession of tortured souls near Bonneval in Normandy on 1 January 1091, just four years before Pope Urban II preached the First Crusade. Knights, women, priests and monks all passed by the astonished priest, suffering excruciating torment as they did so. The weapons carried by the knights were red-hot, and the women, who in life had been sexually licentious, rode saddles 'studded with burning nails', on to which they constantly fell. One knight had deprived a family of its mill by applying merciless usury; his sentence was to carry a burning mill-shaft driven through his mouth. In this instance the torments of the afterlife were paraded before Walchelin, who was so shocked that he took a week to recover from his ordeal.[7] Other people had visions in which they were taken to Hell and given guided tours of its sites. In 1206 the Essex peasant Thurkill gave an account of almost Dantesque detail. It included the Infernal Theatre, where every Saturday night the souls of the damned were forced to re-enact the sins which had brought about their plight.[8] Like Walchelin's mill-shaft, Thurkill's bizarre theatricals illustrated both the horror awaiting people after death and the severely retributive character of the sufferings that had to be endured. Status would count for nothing. Walchelin's tormented included high-ranking aristocrats and men of the Church, and

Thurkill witnessed the soul of one of King John's barons transformed into a black horse so that a demon could cause him pain by riding him.[9]

Escape routes – penance, pilgrimage and crusade

Given the constant temptations to sin in a world where the devil never rested, escaping such a fate was extraordinarily difficult. Those who had fled the world for the cloister, the 'religious', had an infinitely stronger chance of escape than the laity; Walchelin's procession included monks, but there was a presupposition that monastic houses were arks of salvation and that the religious would make up the majority of the saved. Those dead who had repented of their sins could be released from their torment by the prayers and acts of charity of their living relatives or communities of religious. One of the suffering souls witnessed by Walchelin was his own brother Robert, who looked forward to being free of his torments in the near future. 'Remember me, I beg,' he asked Walchelin, 'help me with your prayers and compassionate alms.'[10]

The value of such intercession and works of mercy was a constant theme of the period. But it was clearly preferable to endure the punishment due for one's sins while still alive, through the operation of penance, one of the Church's seven sacraments. A powerful factor lying behind crusading's initial success was disarray in the Church's teaching about penance in the eleventh century. The truly contrite (that is, repentant) sinner who'd confessed was given penance (*poena*) to perform, but nobody was prepared to declare authoritatively that a penance imposed by a cleric was equivalent to the punishment that a just God would reckon to be appropriate. Hence the massive popularity of pilgrimage in this period. Whether assumed voluntarily or imposed by a priest after confession, pilgrimage was a penitential exercise that displayed contrition both before God and to society at large. And because pilgrimage centred on a journey to a particular shrine, the pilgrim enlisted the assistance of the saint whose relics were venerated there. It was taken for granted that such figures would intercede with God on the sinner's behalf and that God would listen to what they said.[11]

The vow to set out on crusade was an offshoot of the pilgrim's vow, and the best way to define crusade is as an 'armed pilgrimage' or 'penitential war'. Albert of Aachen and the chronicler of Monte Cassino described the first crusaders as 'pilgrim soldiers' (*peregrini milites*);[12] and Louis VII's expedition of 1147–9 was described as a 'sacrosanct', 'most famous' or 'renowned' pilgrimage.[13] Pseudo-Ansbert called Barbarossa's crusade 'the glorious army of Christ's pilgrims'.[14] Crusading's links with pilgrimage remained strong in the thirteenth century. Crusaders storming Constantinople in 1204 were 'pilgrims fighting for Paradise'.[15] John of Joinville, the great chronicler of

Louis IX's first crusade, called crusading 'the pilgrimage of the cross'.[16] The preacher Humbert of Romans could address a sermon 'to crusader pilgrims'.[17]

The channel of forgiveness

But in terms of spiritual reward there was a big difference between receiving the staff and 'wallet' (shoulder bag) of the intending pilgrim, and assuming the cross of the crusader. In the sermon quoted at the start James of Vitry referred to each Christian being 'signed with the cross from baptism alone'.[18] In a sense then all Christians were 'crusaders' (*crucesignati*). But although baptism saved Christians from original sin, it couldn't save them from the consequences of their own sinfulness. Only another *crucesignatio* could do that. It did it by forging an individual 'imitation of Christ' that simultaneously complemented and personalized the gift of forgiveness to all believers that was symbolized by baptism. So the crusader's pilgrimage outclassed all other pilgrimages, because Christ outclassed the saints. He was 'the saint of saints'.[19] People who took the cross were 'reborn of a new baptism of repentance'.[20]

All crusaders believed that discharging their vow guaranteed release from the terrors that otherwise would await them in the afterlife. But it's a remarkable feature of early crusading that the precise process by which this release occurred remains obscure. For several decades release was rooted in the protracted, dangerous and gruelling character of crusading. Crusaders were offering everything they had, including their own bodies, to Christ.[21] What more could a just God require than this? By about 1200 the Church had become more self-confident. It regarded itself as empowered to 'remit', or cancel, all of a contrite sinner's penance in exchange for the service that the crusader rendered. Technically it's only from this point onwards that we can describe the crusader as receiving an 'indulgence'.[22]

By the mid- to late thirteenth century this process of remission and the theology needed to underpin it were quite well advanced. But preachers like Odo of Châteauroux and Gilbert of Tournai, and poets like Thibald of Champagne and Rutebeuf, still preferred to characterize crusading as a supreme act of self-sacrifice, a practice entailing so much suffering that it must surely guarantee entry to Paradise.[23] The idea of imitating Christ was too powerful and affecting to lose. Above all, the crusader's cross was the key to Heaven. For the crusader 'dying here on earth will be a sort of door or entrance to the kingdom of Heaven and life without end'.[24] Angels would immediately carry the deceased person to Paradise, where he or she would enjoy the close company of God in what's been described as 'a pleasing combination of knightly camaraderie and eucharistic conviviality'.[25]

5 The chapel of St Helena in the Church of the Holy Sepulchre marks the spot where Constantine's mother discovered the True Cross.

Christ's tomb and the Catholic West

Crusading was first and foremost an act of devotion but it was also a form of warfare, and the link between these two defining features was the city of Jerusalem and its shrines.[26] By fighting for the earthly Jerusalem the crusader gained entry to the heavenly one.[27] The Church of the Holy Sepulchre in Jerusalem contained the *aedicula*, the little chapel built by the first Christian emperors around the remains of the stone tomb that was believed to have been Christ's.[28] The importance of this site for Christians couldn't be exaggerated, especially when they believed, as Catholics did, that the locations where God had worked wonders retained an aura of sanctity. When they worshipped in the Church of the Holy Sepulchre, at the completion of a crusade, Catholics were enacting a devotional intimacy with Christ that had no parallels, because they believed that what they'd achieved confirmed the promise of their Saviour's death on the cross.

But crusading acquired an additional dimension from Jerusalem's status and meaning for the whole of Christianity. It wasn't just an individual experience but a collective one as well. As Richard I put it in relation to his march from Acre to Jaffa in 1191, every crusader had a two-fold goal, 'pursuing

Christianity's cause and carrying out our vows'.[29] Much of the faith's historical consciousness, its *memoria*, was located at Jerusalem, a fact that was richly celebrated in the liturgy sung by the canons of the Holy Sepulchre during the annual feast of the city's liberation by the first crusaders.[30] The Holy Land was 'our heritage',[31] so it followed that 'the wound of this small country brought pain to all lands'.[32] One account of the Christian defeat at Hattin described Saladin's triumphant army 'devastating the Church'.[33] Jerusalem symbolized the Church that had been founded there by Christ. It was from this place, 'city of the living God, and our mother',[34] that the apostles had set out to convert the world. And in due course the wheel would come full circle, for Jerusalem would be the location for Christ's physical return, his *parousia*, when he would pass judgement on the living and the dead.

In theological terms this explained why only the Church could preach crusades. As the embodiment of God's saving purpose for his creation, the Church had the job of declaring that the time was right, in military and religious terms, for an expedition to take place that would enclose penitential devotion within the iron framework of warfare. In a world where churchmen knew at first hand what evils war caused, only a potent sense of the central role that Jerusalem occupied in the Church's mission could have overridden reservations about sanctifying bloodshed. A threat to Jerusalem was a threat to the Church. Repelling it took priority over everything else, so much so that in September 1187, as Saladin's army marched on the city, its leading ecclesiastic, the patriarch Heraclius, pre-empted papal authority by taking it upon himself to proclaim a crusade in Jerusalem's defence.[35]

Jerusalem, crusading and the Church – lessons of the Seventh Crusade

This cluster of ideas and beliefs about Jerusalem, the two-fold nature of crusading as an individual and collective experience, and the close relationship between crusading and the Church, were common to all the major expeditions. But it's especially revealing to view them functioning in the West's response to the loss of Jerusalem in 1244. Captured by the first crusaders in 1099, retaken by Saladin in 1187 and then partially regained under the terms of Frederick II's treaty with Egypt in 1229, Jerusalem was seized by the Khorezmian Turks in August 1244. Their sacking of the holy city was violent and brutal, according to one contemporary much worse than any of its predecessors.[36] In the Church of the Holy Sepulchre the Khorezmians damaged Christ's tomb and, in an action charged with symbolic meaning, they desecrated the tombs of the kings of Jerusalem. A few weeks later the Egyptians and Khorezmians inflicted a heavy defeat on the field army of the kingdom of Jerusalem and its Muslim allies of Damascus, at the battle of Harbiyah.[37]

This terrible sequence of disasters was all too reminiscent of what had occurred in 1187, when Saladin's defeat of the Christians at Hattin paved the way for his occupation of Jerusalem and threatened the crusader states with total annihilation. There was good reason to think that the West's response would follow the same course that it had in the aftermath of Saladin's *annus mirabilis*, and that another crusade would be preached by the Church with the goal of recovering Jerusalem. And up to a point they did. Even though he was at war with the emperor Frederick II, Pope Innocent IV proclaimed a crusade to recapture the holy city, sent clerics to preach the cross in many parts of Europe, and took a number of steps to raise money for the expedition. The Seventh Crusade, the fruit of Innocent's activity, was one of the most impressive that embarked for the East. But at the same time it revealed some of the inherent tensions and problems that beset this means of harvesting force from devotion.

Louis IX's leadership of the Seventh Crusade

In the first place, the Seventh Crusade illustrated in a crystal-clear way the extent to which the call to crusade had come to depend on important leaders stepping forward. What made the crusade possible was the fact that King Louis IX of France took the cross in December 1244. Louis couldn't have known about the disaster at Harbiyah when he took the cross, though he'd probably heard about the fall of Jerusalem. Throughout his life he felt exceptional devotion towards Jerusalem. The prospect of royal leadership held out in turn the prospect of a substantial expedition to the East; no other European ruler at this time was in the position to provide what Louis could. But his leadership depended on the French baronial elite agreeing to and following their king's example, and this was far from being a foregone conclusion. The English chronicler Matthew Paris told an anecdote about the bishop of Paris attempting to dissuade the king from carrying out his vow on the ground that France would be vulnerable to attack during his absence. Louis' response was to remove the cross from his clothing and hand it to the bishop, then ask for its return. He was making the point that he took the cross in full knowledge of the perils that it entailed.[38] But the king still had to win over his barons.

In October 1245 a papal legate, Odo of Châteauroux, helped to gain the approval of France's great lords at an assembly convened at Paris. Odo and other preachers of the crusade enjoyed the backing of the crusading decrees of the general council of the Church that had recently met at Lyons.[39] But there was still domestic opposition to be overcome, and once again it's Matthew Paris who tells the story of the king shaming his knights into taking the cross by having cloth crosses sewn into the robes that they were given at

6 King Louis IX of France takes the cross in 1244 (top right).

court, probably at Christmas 1245.[40] It took well over a year for Louis to 'sell' his vow to his subjects, but his patience paid dividends. It enabled him to set about organizing his crusade with confidence, mustering all the authority and prestige of the king of France. Repeatedly in this book we'll view the remarkable advantages that this brought. Its antithesis was the attitude of Henry III, who wouldn't allow Louis' crusade to be preached in England at all because, he said, he was surrounded by enemies, couldn't trust the pope, and couldn't afford to lose soldiers and money to the crusading cause.[41] They were hard arguments to counter.

Short-circuiting the process – the French pastoureaux *of 1251*

So the Seventh Crusade shows the positive benefits that flowed from a synergy between strong government and individual piety, always provided that the piety was the king's. In striking contrast, a sequence of events that occurred towards the end of Louis' crusade reveals a divergence between group enthusiasm and effectiveness. This was the *pastoureaux*, or Crusade of the Shepherds, of 1251. The magnificent army that St Louis recruited met with defeat in the East in 1250, and in the spring and summer of 1251 a man

called Master Jacob, or 'the master of Hungary', recruited a host of some
thousands of shepherds and herdsmen in north-western France with the goal
of leading them eastwards to help their king. These people made their
way to Paris where they were well received by the king's mother, Blanche of
Castile, who was acting as Louis' regent. But when they moved southwards,
apparently in several groups, they caused a riot at Orleans, attacked the
Dominicans at Tours, and assaulted Jewish synagogues at Bourges. The
inevitable backlash set in and by the end of the summer the *pastoureaux* had
been dispersed. Many of them had been *crucesignati*, fired by a genuine desire
to assist their king, and it's more than likely that this explains Blanche's initial
goodwill towards them. But the apparent absence of any forward planning
or direction made it virtually certain that the movement wouldn't be able to
achieve anything. Besides which, the large numbers involved made it very
hard for the *pastoureaux* to avoid getting entangled in disturbances that
provoked their condemnation and suppression. Matthew Paris spotted that
the pattern was that of the crusade of the *pueri* of 1212. On that occasion, too,
what began in great enthusiasm had ended in violence and bitterness.[42]

Both in 1244–5 and in 1251 it's the Church's weaknesses that are most
apparent. The fall of Jerusalem demanded a strong response, but if Louis IX
hadn't taken the cross in 1244 it's likely that Pope Innocent IV would have had
to rest content with sending financial assistance; at best he might have scraped
together a small expedition similar to the 'Barons' Crusade' of 1239–41. In 1251
many thousands of ordinary people were eager to take the cross, but they
ignored the procedures for doing so that by this point, as we'll see, had been fully
set in place by the Church. Master Jacob claimed that he acted on the direct
orders of the Virgin Mary, thus bypassing the Church's authority, and according
to Matthew Paris Jacob had a low opinion of every religious order of the day.[43]
The surviving sources for the *pastoureaux* are mainly clerical ones, so the view
they give of the movement is patchy and selective. None the less, the movement's anti-clericalism was one of its most striking characteristics, and it was a
hatred that clerical commentators paid back in full. They even asserted, without
any real evidence, that the *pastoureaux* were in league with the Muslims.[44]

All in all, not much could be further from the truth than the idea that crusade
preaching exemplified the power that was wielded by the medieval Church.
On the contrary, it was one of the Church's most challenging responsibilities,
because it brought together a cluster of sensitive issues that included the
Church's pastoral role, its relationship with Europe's great rulers, the extent of
the pope's authority over the Church, and the ever-present danger of spawning
unorthodox religious practices and unleashing social disorder. Declaring a
crusade was like opening Pandora's box.

Spreading the word – preaching tours

We can assume that issues like these were in the mind of every pope when he considered the key question: how was the call to crusade to reach the ears of the faithful? By definition there were only two ways in which churchmen could preach; either those already on the spot could be ordered to do so, or individuals or groups could carry out preaching tours. The most famous of all these tours was Archbishop Baldwin of Canterbury's journey through Wales in 1188, preaching the Third Crusade. Baldwin took with him the archdeacon of Brecon, Gerald of Wales, who immortalized the journey in his travel-diary, *The Tour of Wales* (*Itinerarium Kambriae*) of 1191. The tour lasted seven weeks and, as Gerald himself put it, it was nothing if not thorough:[45] starting at Hereford, Baldwin's party made their way first through the Anglo-Norman south, then entered the lands of the Welsh princes before returning to England via Chester. Part of Baldwin's plan was to celebrate mass in all four of the cathedral churches that were subject to him, at Llandaff, St David's, Bangor and St Asaph. There was a language problem but it was overcome through the use of interpreters.[46] On the other hand Gerald, who didn't suffer from modesty, claimed that he was struck by the number of people who took the cross when he himself preached at Haverfordwest, even though he'd spoken in Latin and French; he compared himself to St Bernard, who had moved the Germans to tears when he preached the Second Crusade in his native French. With all due allowance for Gerald's boasting, we can infer that delivery mattered at least as much as content.[47]

The Welsh tour proved a great success, with people surging forward to take the cross at town after town.[48] The recruits reached a total that Gerald estimated as 3,000 men, 'all of them highly skilled in the use of the spear and the arrow, most experienced in military affairs and only too keen to attack the enemies of our faith at the first opportunity'.[49] This wasn't surprising given the impact on sensibilities of the disasters recently suffered at Hattin and Jerusalem; as Peter of Blois put it, 'the whole of Jeremiah isn't enough to express our misery'.[50] It's likely that the rationale behind the Welsh tour was King Henry II's hope to recruit large numbers of Welsh archers for the crusade. But few of the recruits seem to have taken part in the crusade, probably because they were deterred by the two-year delay that followed before Richard I and the English army set out.[51]

Gerald's *Tour of Wales* is an engaging source and it acts as a snapshot of how a well-organized preaching campaign could function at that time. After almost a century of crusading, everybody engaged in its preaching had a pretty good idea of what they wanted to achieve and how best to do it. The king wanted his archers, and Archbishop Baldwin and Gerald seem to have known how best to recruit them. All this was in striking contrast to the preaching of the First Crusade in 1095–6. When Urban II preached his famous sermon outside Clermont's city walls in November 1095, he designated the Feast of the Assumption, 15 August 1096, as the departure date. The pope thus allowed less than nine months for the preaching of the expeditions and all the preparations that were needed. This compact timetable is remarkable; it was challenging but perhaps also astute, showing that Urban understood the need to keep the momentum going. What remains perplexing is the fact that the pope made no provision for having the crusade systematically preached. He himself carried out a gruelling preaching tour that took him as far as Le Mans in the north, and many crusaders came from the regions which he passed through. Outside this area, however, the process by which his crusade was preached is lost in mystery. At this point bishops alone would have possessed the learning and authority to preach in the pope's name and there's evidence for no more than a handful of them doing so. Given the warmth with which many religious houses greeted the crusade it's likely that some monks persuaded their lay patrons to take the cross.[52] Other than this, the news of the pope's proclamation at Clermont appears to have spread like the proverbial prairie fire.

Tools of the trade – manuals and metaphors

Contemporaries called crusade preaching 'the business of the cross' (*negotium crucis*), and for the most part the development of preaching revolved around procedures for making sure that 'the business' was properly carried out. In a country like medieval England, where the Church was used to working closely with royal government, this had largely been achieved when Baldwin and Gerald set out in 1188. Elsewhere the key changes happened more gradually, many of them as a result of the reforms of Pope Innocent III (r. 1198–1216). His contributions towards crusading were so fundamental and wide-ranging that he's considered second only to Urban II in significance. From Innocent's reign onwards the declaration of every crusade was accompanied by specific instructions relating to how it was to be preached. There was no hard and fast formula. Sometimes the resident clergy were given the task, at other times legates were sent out, as Odo of Châteauroux was in 1245. Increasingly though the bulk of the preaching was entrusted to the new orders of the friars, Franciscans and Dominicans.[53]

It was in this context that men like James of Vitry, Odo of Châteauroux and Gilbert of Tournai composed their 'model' sermons, while two more substantial manuals were written as guides for preachers. One of these originated in England in the early thirteenth century, while the other, much more ambitious in scope, was written by the general of the Dominicans, Humbert of Romans, in the late 1260s. This text, *On the Preaching of the Holy Cross* (*De predicatione sanctae crucis*), is our most revealing source about how sermons were put together and delivered. It rivals Gerald of Wales's *Tour of Wales* as a window into how the call to crusade was managed by the Church when it was at its most organized and purposeful.

The authors of model sermons and manuals knew that they had to maximize the appeal of their message, and a key way to do this was by making full use of metaphors. One of the most popular was promoting the crusader's cross as a bargain. Preachers could take it for granted that their audiences were deeply aware of their own sinfulness, anxious about what would happen after they died, and looking for a solution. The cross as an escape route from the consequences of sin was a theme that few preachers could resist from its introduction during the preaching of the Second Crusade by St Bernard. For Bernard the crusade was best viewed as a 'jubilee', a period of time when God allowed sinners unusually easy access to forgiveness. 'I call blessed the generation that can seize an opportunity of such rich indulgence as this, blessed to be alive in this year of jubilee, this year of God's choice.' Bernard compared the jubilee to a buyer's market: 'But to those of you who are merchants, men quick to seize a bargain, let me point out the advantages of this great opportunity. Do not miss them. Take up the sign of the Cross and you will find indulgence for all the sins which you humbly confess. The cost is small, the reward is great.'[54] Bernard's commercial metaphor caught the mood of an age in which trading of all kinds was gathering pace throughout western Europe. Poems that date from the time of the Second and Third Crusade made much use of it. 'I have heard it said proverbially / A sensible merchant spends money from his purse / And he has a very fickle heart / Who sees what is good and chooses what is evil. / Do you know what God has promised / To those who wish to take the cross? / God help me, a very fair wage: / Paradise, by firm promise.'[55]

These lines form one of the first examples of the genre of homely metaphor, derived from the Gospel parables. The technique must have worked because preachers drew on it incessantly. James of Vitry wrote, 'In vernacular French we say: "if someone shouts: Have a halfpenny!, many come running"; [but] when someone shouts: "Have paradise!", or "Hurry up to paradise!", few come . . . As if drunk, the Lord now makes a good bargain and gives his kingdom for just about nothing. There is nothing cheaper to buy than the kingdom of God and nothing dearer to possess.'[56] A rather more elevated image of the balance between work and reward was evoked by James earlier in the same sermon, when he compared the crusader to Jacob, whose seven years of work for Rachel 'seemed to him like a few days because of the greatness of his love'.[57] And in an affecting metaphor of the Church as a

7 A fourteenth-century illustration of crusade preaching.

generous and welcoming mother, Humbert of Romans wrote in one of his
model sermons that 'during the time when the cross is preached the flood-
gates of heaven stand open for an abundance of indulgences, mother church
opens her arms and extends her hands to the poor'.[58]

Sales resistance

Given that the alternative was many years of indescribable suffering in
Purgatory, it was logical enough to emphasize the bargain that crusading
constituted. But contemporaries could hardly be blamed for failing to focus
on the longer term, dwelling instead on the more immediate effect that taking
the cross would have on their lives. They knew that crusading entailed heavy

expense, a long absence from loved ones, a lot of suffering and quite possibly capture or death. So listeners became aware of the danger of giving way to spontaneous enthusiasm. We know this because crusade preachers sometimes described the ingenious defences that their listeners created to avoid being seduced by the honeyed words thrown at them. In one anecdote (*exemplum*) a friar comes to preach the crusade in a town where all the inhabitants have promised to each other that they won't take the cross. The friar faces a conspiracy of rejection. At the start of his sermon he asks his audience to make the sign of the cross to keep the devil away. Then he accuses them all of perjury, on the ground that they've mutually undertaken not to cross them-selves yet have done precisely that. In the *exemplum* at least, the crowd is so entertained by the trick that they take the cross.[59] Others were held back by force. Gerald of Wales told of men at Hay-on-Wye who came running to take the cross, 'leaving their cloaks behind in the hands of wives and friends who had tried to hold them back'.[60]

Thibald of Champagne portrayed those 'who love neither God, love, nor honour' asking ' "My wife, what will she do? Nor would I leave my friends at any cost." '[61] Sources like these underscore the implications of individuals taking the cross for all whose well-being, spiritual or material, depended on them. When Gwion the bishop of Bangor took the cross in 1188 both men and women in his congregation 'wept and wailed'.[62] Above all it was spouses who objected. In contrast to the exuberance of some of the chroniclers ('brides urged their husbands and mothers incited their sons to go'),[63] the wife who tries to restrain her husband's desire to take the cross forms a recurrent motif or *topos* in these sources; it's Gerald again who provides the story of one such woman being punished for her negative attitude by inadvertently smothering her child while asleep.[64] But as is often the case with *topoi*, to a degree this surely reflected reality. Pope Innocent III, who was usually a stickler for upholding the obligations of the marriage vow, went so far as to decree that in the case of a crusade vow a man was entitled to overrule his wife's opposition and go.[65]

So while nobody openly disputed that the crusader's cross was a golden opportunity and a wonderful bargain, contemporaries were wary of seizing it. During his tour of Wales in 1188 Baldwin of Canterbury encountered apathy at Haverfordwest and on Anglesey. 'God, what a hard-hearted nation is this!' he exclaimed at Haverfordwest.[66] As Gerald of Wales put it, sometimes it was like getting blood from a stone.[67]

Breaking down resistance – the imperilled holy places

Gerald noted that the occasional miracle proved handy,[68] but there were more reliable ways to break down resistance. It helped powerfully that crusading was preached in terms of the Holy Land's significance and plight, as well as the individual listener's search for salvation. Devotion towards Jerusalem set up a whole range of emotional resonances and in the hands of skilled preachers these could be cleverly interwoven with their audience's personal anxieties. St Bernard set out a brilliantly modulated argument for the Second Crusade. 'That blessed land, that land of promise' was threatened by the Muslims, and if they were not driven back they would take Jerusalem itself, 'and defile the holy places which have been adorned by the blood of the immaculate lamb'. Of course God could save his land with a single word, but instead he was providing a chance for his people to prove their allegiance to him. In particular, it was a chance for fighting men to turn from shedding Christian blood towards a worthier cause. 'O men of war, you have a cause for which you can fight without danger to your souls; a cause in which to conquer is glorious and for which to die is gain.'[69]

When Bernard wrote this, Jerusalem faced no immediate threat. But after the city was taken by Saladin in 1187 its loss provoked grief throughout Europe that can be viewed time and again in the preaching of the Third, Fourth and Fifth Crusades. The preachers knew well that grief was closely related to shame and fear, and this generated rhetoric that was furious and at times odd. Peter of Blois was ready to take issue with his maker: granted that Christians had sinned greatly, he wrote after Saladin's victories, surely it was shameful to God as well that his enemies had occupied his lands? Wasn't this an example of cutting off your nose to spite your face?[70] When he proclaimed the Fourth Crusade in 1198 Innocent III cannily placed Christian shame within a national setting. The pope drew a humiliating verbal sketch of the Muslims taunting the Christians for their failure. The French, English, Germans and Spanish were each abused in turn, and the stream of insults concluded with the threat that, once the few remaining Christians in the Holy Land had been annihilated, the Muslims would 'launch an attack on your lands, for the purpose of effacing your name and memory'.[71] So neither in spiritual nor in strategic terms could any Catholic afford to shrug their shoulders about the Muslim occupation of Jerusalem. Almost as deep as grief for the Holy Land was sorrow about the capture at Hattin of its greatest relic, the True Cross. This was considered to be a worse loss than that of the Ark of the Covenant by the Jews.[72] During the Children's Crusade of 1212 one of the chants attributed to the *pueri* when they were on the march was 'Lord God, give us back the True Cross!'[73]

Holy Land and holy war

We might suppose that any expedition raised to put this right would be overtly preached as a holy war. But the reality was somewhat different. Crusading was preached as a redemptive process, a jubilee, and a trial set by God to test the faith of the new Israel that was Christendom. Only to a much lesser degree was it preached as a war, and when it was it happened in a revealingly round-about way. It took almost a century for a distinctive vocabulary to emerge for the practice of crusading, and it's likely that the main reason for this was the Church's reluctance overtly to accept that it was preaching a holy war. By hiding behind a vocabulary that was mainly adapted from pilgrimage it managed to evade this difficult issue. When military matters made their appearance in preaching it was largely in an abstract and generalized form. The military situation in the East was rarely given much specific description even in the crusade bulls issued by the popes, which we can assume were used if not quoted extensively by preachers.[74]

This wasn't just due to clerical sensibilities. Audiences wanted to hear about shrines, not castles; their frame of reference for what they heard was scriptural rather than contemporary. The Muslim historian Baha' al-Din claimed that after Saladin's capture of Jerusalem Conrad of Montferrat toured Europe with a large picture designed to stir his audiences into action:

> He produced a picture of Jerusalem on a large sheet of paper, depicting the Sepulchre to which they come on pilgrimage and which they revere . . . He pictured the tomb and added a Muslim cavalryman on horseback tram-pling on the Messiah's tomb, upon which the horse had staled [urinated]. This picture he publicised overseas in the markets and assemblies, as the priests, bareheaded and dressed in sackcloth, paraded it, crying doom and destruction.

It's a fascinating story and, although it's unsupported by any Christian source, its combination of shame and grief rings true. Baha' al-Din added a telling observation: 'Images affect their hearts, for they are essential to their reli-gion.'[75] The identity of the Muslim cavalryman was much less important than what he was doing.

It was as imagery that warfare forced its way into preaching. Urban II and his successors knew that their paramount need was for fighting men and from the start 'Christ's knights' (*milites Christi*) was one of the most common terms applied to crusaders. This made good sense. It was the tempers of fighting men that were most likely to be aroused by Pope Innocent's taunting Muslims and Conrad of Montferrat's insulting picture. Christianity was well used to spreading religious ideas by assimilating them to familiar social relation-ships, and a Church that was uncomfortable with preaching holy war located in this approach a more congenial way to target the emotions and instincts of the fighting elite. Most of them were vassals or fief-holders with military obligations to their lords, as well as being members of families that owned patrimonial lands which constantly made demands on their fighting skills. So the Holy Land was depicted as Christ's patrimony. The Muslims threatened his lands and he needed the help of his vassals.

In a society that accepted warfare as the normal condition of existence, and violence as the natural response to insult, no images could be more resonant than these. They were almost certainly used in 1095, and for the following two centuries they constantly recurred in crusade preaching. James of Vitry compared the salvation won by crusaders with a fief, and the cross itself with the token, typically a glove, with which lords customarily invested their vassals with their fiefs.[76] The earliest surviving crusading songs referred to Palestine as God's fief or inherited lands, the shame involved in its loss, and the vengeance that would be exacted. One song compared the conflict for the Holy Land to a tournament arranged by God between Hell and Paradise.[77] Barred from the theological front door, holy war slipped in through the tradesmen's entrance of metaphor.

The mise en scène *of preaching the cross*

There was another way to break down resistance to the message of the cross, and this was more calculated: the attention given to the staging and delivery of preaching.[78] From the reign of Innocent III onwards there existed a high-profile liturgical framework of processions, prayers, vigils and fasts for the Holy Land's recovery. Chests were placed in all important churches into which alms (mainly money but also merchandise that could later be sold) might be deposited for the good of the crusade. The faithful were urged at confession to make provision for the Holy Land in their wills. Crusade preaching was more selective, and it's clear that certain days and periods were regarded as especially appropriate and promising. The key ones were the feast-days of the Invention (that is, discovery) and Exaltation of the Cross (3 May and 14 September). The first of these days commemorated Helena's excavation of the True Cross underneath what later became the Church of the Holy Sepulchre, and the second its recovery from the Persians by the Emperor Heraclius. In 1291 Archbishop Romeyne of York mobilized thirty-five friars to preach the cross at designated locations throughout his diocese on 14 September. Archbishop Baldwin of Canterbury in 1188 was typical of many in favouring Lent for his preaching tour of Wales: the timing fitted well with a spring embarkation for the Holy Land.

Stage business was commonplace at sermons. Crosses were deployed as props, relics were displayed during preaching, and members of a preaching group might themselves take the cross with a great show of eagerness so as to get the ball rolling. Like a lot of medieval preaching, it was extrovert and theatrical. Experience taught that it was more effective to punctuate sermons with a number of invitations to take the cross, rather than waiting until the end and then throwing out a single invitation. The experts gave careful thought to the best modes of delivery. Humbert of Romans suggested that talking to small groups might prove to be more successful than addressing large audiences. In general anecdotes, metaphors and word-play were preferred to theological explanations.

The author of the *Ordinance on Preaching the Holy Cross* (*Ordinacio de predicacione sanctae crucis*), a manual intended for the use of crusade preachers in England, recommended telling stories about pious heroics not just to inspire the audience but also 'to hold the attention of your listeners and keep boredom at bay'. One of these incorporated a dire pun, with the English crusader Hugh Beauchamp uttering the dying words 'never was I in a fair field [*beau champ*] until today'.[79] But this unknown author also recommended a series of instructive contrasts between Adam and Eve on the one hand, and Christ and Mary on the other. These included the hand movements of Eve as she seized the apple in Genesis 3 compared with those of Christ as he suffered on the cross; hands stood for deeds, because it was through them that deeds were done.[80] This was sound pastoral theology, but it's not hard to see why stories were thought to be more effective. At the same time in Flanders the crusader's indulgence was being compared to the short poles that were in common use to leap across the canals. In exactly the same way the crusader would leap across Purgatory to get to Heaven.[81]

Superstars and stars of the preaching circuit

Analogies like these sprang from local knowledge, and in some cases local priests proved more successful than visitors because they knew their flocks.[82] But nothing could beat a visiting celebrity for whipping up enthusiasm. This was demonstrated in 1095–6 during Urban II's own tour. The pope's status, the size of his entourage and the unprecedented message that he brought with him undoubtedly made his visit an unforgettable experience.[83] When he entered Limoges just before Christmas he was accompanied by two cardinals, four archbishops and five bishops. Much church building and rebuilding had recently been completed and Urban spent a good deal of his time dedicating altars. He began doing this even before his preaching tour, when he consecrated the high altar of the new abbey church at Cluny while *en route* for Clermont. Once he had proclaimed the crusade he must have been in constant receipt of news and envoys relating the progress of his great project, though on this we remain woefully ill informed.[84]

Urban was a successful recruiter for his crusade but he was outclassed by Peter the Hermit. We know little about Peter except that he was born at or near Amiens and that before the First Crusade he toured the towns of northern France preaching repentance and helping out destitute people and prostitutes who wanted to reform their lives. It was a career pattern that would frequently recur with crusade preachers. The chronicler Guibert of Nogent wrote that even the hairs from Peter's mule were treated by his audiences as holy relics. It's a comment that nicely captures the disdain of the educated monk for charismatic popular preachers like Peter.[85] But Peter's persuasiveness is beyond doubt. It enabled him to recruit an entire army, which he himself led east in the spring of 1096; he wasn't the only example of a preacher leading an army that he himself had created, but there weren't many others. Peter's preaching incorporated themes that Urban would almost certainly have frowned on, including that of vengeance for Christ's sufferings on the cross. In chapter four we'll see how grim the consequences were for the Jews of the Rhineland. We've very few details of just why Peter was so impressive a preacher, but his impact on his audiences was clearly a lasting one. Even though his own record on the crusade turned out to be mediocre, he left such strong memories in the region where he'd preached that the belief took root there that it was Peter, not Urban II, who had initiated the crusade.[86]

Peter's equivalent for the Second Crusade was Bernard of Clairvaux.[87] In Bernard's case it's much easier to see how he proved so effective as a recruiter.

8 Vézelay in Burgundy, the scene of St Bernard's spectacular preaching of the Second Crusade in 1146.

The power of Bernard's rhetoric radiates out both in his surviving writings and in various contemporary descriptions of his preaching style. Odo of Deuil, the principal French historian of the crusade, left a vivid account of Bernard's preaching at Vézelay in March 1146. The numbers that assembled forced Bernard to speak in the open air from a wooden platform, and 'when heaven's instrument poured forth the dew of the divine word . . . with loud outcry people on every side began to demand crosses'. Bernard had brought along a parcel of cloth crosses but these ran out, and he had to make them in *ad hoc* fashion from his own clothes.[88] This was terrific theatre. It's the first detailed passage that we possess testifying to mass enthusiasm for crusading.

Like Gerald of Wales later, Bernard provided his own testimony to his success, boasting that he'd all but emptied towns and villages of their menfolk. 'Everywhere there were widows whose husbands were still alive.'[89] But it was in Germany that he enjoyed his most remarkable success, and not with a crowd but with one man. Bernard was determined to enlist Conrad III for the crusade and at the king's Christmas court in 1146 he acted the part of Christ, rebuking Conrad for his gross ingratitude. The king, who'd refused to respond to Bernard's sermon on the same subject on Christmas Day, caved in and agreed to take the cross.[90] It's not going too far to see the Second Crusade as Bernard's personal project, which helps to explain the depth of misery and guilt he experienced when it failed.

The last in this remarkable trilogy of preachers was Fulk of Neuilly. In the eyes of many contemporaries Fulk made the Fourth Crusade possible almost to the same extent that St Bernard had created the Second and (at least according to some) Peter the Hermit the First. The Fourth Crusade resembled the Second in its problematic start. When Innocent III came to the papal throne in 1198 the situation in the Holy Land remained precarious. The Third Crusade had staved off the threat of total expulsion but Jerusalem hadn't been regained. So the new pope proclaimed another crusade, which was scheduled to assemble in March 1199. Political conditions were far from favourable. In particular, the title to the Holy Roman Empire was in dispute, with England and France backing rival candidates. The papal deadline passed without much happening. But one man who was commissioned to preach by Innocent was Fulk, priest of the little church of Neuilly near Paris. Like Peter the Hermit a century previously, Fulk had acquired a reputation as a powerful preacher of repentance, particularly in terms of money-lending and prostitution, two sins that dominated the imagination of the age as Europe's economy became increasingly commercial and its towns mushroomed in size.

Geoffrey of Villehardouin began his great narrative of the Fourth Crusade with a reference to Fulk's work, commenting that Innocent had commissioned Fulk to preach after hearing about his extraordinary powers. These included the performance of miracles of healing.[91] Ralph of Coggeshall recorded the impact that Fulk exerted on his listeners when he preached outside Cîteaux in September 1198: 'And when the people saw that the man of God himself would be signed with the cross, and when they heard that he would be the leader and commander of this sacred march, they eagerly rushed to him on all sides; from everywhere he was mobbed by rich and poor, by the noble and lowly, by the old and the young, by a vast multitude of people of both sexes who eagerly accepted the sign of the cross from him.'[92] Fulk signed thousands with the cross before dying in May 1202, as the crusaders were assembling at Venice to embark for the East.[93]

Although there were to be no more superstars, the generation that followed Fulk's didn't lack effective crusade preachers. The Fifth Crusade in particular benefited from the input of some extraordinary men. Master Oliver of Paderborn and John of Xanten both preached in the Low Countries. Oliver's preaching career was notable for the appearance of supernatural signs in the sky. As Oliver himself put it, 'the province of Cologne was stirred up to the service of the Saviour of the world through signs which appeared in heaven'.[94] John of Xanten was a master of the use of pithy exempla. James of Vitry was a figure of greater stature. A graduate of the University of Paris, where he had heard and been deeply impressed by Fulk of Neuilly, James was exceptionally skilled in expounding the devotional and talismanic associations of the cross. Like St Bernard, he had a gift for making the abstruse come alive, as in his explanation of how penance operated: 'in contrition sin dies, in confession it is removed from the house, in satisfaction, it is buried'.[95] He also had a dry and appealing sense of humour. When he went to Genoa to preach in 1216 the city's government requisitioned his party's horses for a campaign in the vicinity. During the absence of the fighting men James preached to the poor and the women, and he managed to recruit many of the better-off women. As he wryly remarked, there was a *quid pro quo*: 'the citizens made off with my horses and I signed their wives with the cross'. The benefit for the crusade was that on their return from campaigning the citizens too were shamed into taking the cross in order to protect their spouses.[96] James's appeal was clearly universal, since he even persuaded residents of some of the towns in the crusader states, including Tyre and Beirut, to take the cross – men, women and children alike.[97]

Setbacks and response

After the failure of the Fifth Crusade in 1221, preaching the cross became an increasingly uphill task. In the spring of 1251 Odo of Châteauroux preached a sermon about the French crusaders who had died a year earlier at Mansurah in Egypt. It was a *tour de force* of exegesis in which Odo seized the bull of defeat by the horns.[98] And both in his preaching manual *On the Preaching of the Holy Cross* and in his treatise *Opus tripartitum*, written in the early 1270s, Humbert of Romans devoted a good deal of space to outlining the objections that contemporaries were raising to the idea of taking the cross. Humbert was frank. People were ensnared by sin, they were worried about the physical suffering involved, they were too attached to their homeland, over-fond of their families, and they made excuses based on gossip or what had happened in the past. Past defeats were a burden. It's revealing that in the prayer *Deus qui admirabili*, a remarkably concise encapsulation of crusading theology first issued by Innocent III in 1213, an addition of no more than a dozen words was later inserted making the point that the Muslims had been successful not because of their own virtue but owing to Christian wickedness.[99]

There had always been good reasons for not taking the cross, but by the mid-thirteenth century they were being pressed with alarming vigour. The authors of model sermons felt compelled to insert passages 'against those who put off being signed and are slow in coming to the aid of the Holy Land'.[100] In a truly bizarre image, Gilbert of Tournai described such people as 'old logs full of mud and water', insusceptible to the fire of charity blowing on them from the bellows that Christ constructed from his own skin, and the wood and nails of his cross.[101] The French poet Rutebeuf put the whole development into dialogue form, with various arguments for taking the cross being advanced by a crusader and countered with eloquence by a knight who refuses to follow his example. God is everywhere, he says, not just in the Holy Land, and salvation can be won at home without all the suffering involved in going on crusade, which is 'paying homage to folly'. As for the Muslim threat, let the sultan come to France and that will be the right time to fight him. Even the bargain metaphor beloved by the preachers was turned upside down: taking the cross was like selling for 40 *solidi* something that had cost 100.[102]

Rutebeuf may well have copied these arguments from crusade preachers who in turn had heard them from hecklers.[103] Hecklers there certainly were, 'who distract crusaders and those who are ready to take the cross and like dogs they bite the stick of the cross'.[104] Answers to their objections were provided both by Humbert of Romans and by Rutebeuf's imaginary enthusiast, whose clinching argument – the call to salvation – wins over his adversary. But there could be no doubt that times had changed.

Reluctant preachers?

It's apparent that the circumstances were no longer suited to the barnstorming techniques practised by Peter the Hermit, Bernard of Clairvaux and Fulk of Neuilly. But it's more difficult to form a reliable picture of the calibre of crusade preaching as the thirteenth century wore on. In common with most aspects of crusading we've a lot more evidence than for earlier generations, and this tends to reveal tensions and deficiencies which it's possible to exaggerate. The creation of stable institutions and structures always opens the door to laxity and fraud, and crusade preaching was no exception. At the time of the Fifth Crusade Oliver of Paderborn complained about the apathy of some people who were charged with crusade preaching, the bad practices of unauthorized preachers and the use of fake letters and privileges. The issues highlighted by Oliver proved to be persistent headaches, and there was no effective remedy against them.[105] We have the accounts of forty-five men who made up a group that toured northern France in 1265 preaching the crusade, and it's obvious that they didn't go hungry. Their diet included bread, wine, eggs, meat, poultry, fish, vegetables, salads, beans, oil, spices, garlic, fruits and nuts. Many a crusader in the field would have envied such meals, a comparison that may seem trivial but is actually perfectly valid given that by this point preachers got the full crusader's indulgence for their work.[106]

'Instinctively', one historian has commented, 'one supposes that these men had neither the time nor the taste for the barefoot procession of a Baldwin of Canterbury, or for performing the miracles of a St Bernard or Oliver of Paderborn ... Were [contemporaries] moved to tears by these well-fed preachers?'[107] It's a fair if unanswerable question, and it's true that Humbert of Romans might have been advised to add to his list of issues anti-clerical feeling, which he was aware of but had good reasons not to address openly. We've already seen that antagonism towards the clergy was strongly felt by the *pastoureaux* of 1251, arguably this period's most impressive example of crusading zeal. Crusading always reflected the society that produced it, and this was an age in which attitudes towards the Church were becoming deeply ambivalent. Rutebeuf's stay-at-home knight included rich prelates among his targets, and Rutebeuf himself not only had an axe to grind about the mendicant friars but also considered it equitable that clerics should contribute more towards the cause by paying taxes and subsidizing less well-off nobles to go to the Holy Land.[108] On the other hand, criticism of abuses associated with the preaching of the crusades went back at least as far as the Third Crusade.[109] And it's only fair to add that the sweeping and undiscriminating recruitment of Peter the Hermit, Bernard of Clairvaux and Fulk of Neuilly had created as many problems as it had opportunities.[110]

Saints and sinners

Whether or not there was a major shift in attitude in the mid-thirteenth century, the fact is that most people were no different from their ancestors in

9 A bishop gives the cross to a man who already has the purse and staff of the pilgrim.

deciding *against* going on crusade. The figures given for people taking the cross often seem vast – for example Fulk of Neuilly's claim that he recruited 200,000 for the Fourth Crusade, or the assertion by Raymond Foulque, the provost of Arles, and the prior of St-Pierre de Mayne that they had signed 30,000 at Marseilles alone for the Fifth.[111] But in the context of Europe's total population at the time such figures, which are usually not much more than guesses anyway, lose much of their impact. We have to set to one side the rhetorical exaggerations of sources like the *Itinerarium peregrinorum*, a leading narrative of the Third Crusade, that 'it was not a question of who had received the cross but of who had not yet done so'.[112] Enthusiasts like Conon of Béthune might claim that nobody who was 'healthy, young and well-off' could stay at home without incurring shame,[113] but the reality was that most did. Taking the cross was always a minority activity, which means that we have to ask why some contemporaries responded positively and others didn't.

A handy group to start with is those who were exceptional, either for the exemplary nature of their devotion or for past behaviour that was reckoned to be so appalling that they desperately needed all the spiritual gain that crusading had to offer. One of the best examples of the first type was Raymond of St Gilles, count of Toulouse and a prominent leader of the First Crusade. In 1095 Raymond was a successful and well-respected man in his mid-fifties. He was renowned as a strong supporter of the reforming programme that the papacy had pursued in the years that led up to the First Crusade, belonging to a network of 'the faithful of St Peter' (*fideles Sancti Petri*) on whom the papal court had come to depend. It's more than likely that Urban II sought out Raymond's advice on the crusade before the council of Clermont. There are signs that Raymond regarded himself as the crusade's natural leader, though this status was never publicly ratified by the pope.[114]

Profoundly pious men like Raymond recur throughout the history of crusading, but given the nature of the exercise it's unsurprising that they were equalled by those who'd taken the cross in severe remorse for individual crimes or whole catalogues of misdeeds. The First Crusade produced two extraordinary examples in Emich of Flonheim and Thomas of Marle. They were violent and cruel men who fascinated and appalled their contemporaries.[115] In some ways the archetype for such figures was Fulk Nerra, the ferocious count of Anjou who made several pilgrimages to Jerusalem and on one of them bit off a piece of stone from the Holy Sepulchre to bring back home.[116] Observers were astonished by the number of 'robbers, highwaymen and murderers' who took the cross at Usk in 1188.[117] John of Joinville, the narrator of Louis IX's Egyptian crusade, tells a dramatic and moving story about his kinsman Josserand of Brancion. Josserand was struck with remorse following a skirmish in a church. Falling on his knees before the altar, he begged Christ to release him from the endless cycle of conflicts against fellow Christians, and to allow him to spend his remaining years 'in thy service, and so come to enjoy thy kingdom in paradise'.[118]

Joinville's anecdote is welcome because it confirms lots of similar stories that we encounter among the charters and chronicles of the First Crusade. Many of these stem from monastic authors. They were strongly attracted by the idea of a sudden 'Damascene conversion', especially when it happened to men who had habitually attacked and exploited the dependants and lands of their religious house. In recounting these instances there's an element of satisfaction, almost of glee, in the narrators' tone, so they have to be treated with caution. Given the fact that we find similar stories in non-monastic sources like Joinville there's less reason to doubt that some people who took the cross did experience a blinding revelation that they must change their ways. And it's likely that such a revelation was triggered most frequently by particularly powerful preaching, and at large gatherings of the kind associated with Peter the Hermit and the other great preachers described earlier. In other words, the emotional impact of the call to take the cross was at its height when the personal appeal was experienced in a collective atmosphere of excitement and anticipation.

'The ties that bind' – family traditions and social pressure

Yet while it's true that the decision to take the cross could come like a bolt from the blue, it's also the case that certain families of nobles were predisposed to respond positively to the crusade call. Crusaders from these families were often keen pilgrims in the decades before 1095. They and their relatives were also generous donors to religious houses, which eagerly supported their decision to embark on crusade and, as we'll see in the next chapter, played a key role in providing the finance that they needed. In fact in many cases taking the cross fitted patterns of devotion that were rooted in the cross-taker's family background as well as his own past.[119] These patterns fertilized the practice of crusading itself, so that some aristocratic lineages produced enthusiastic crusaders generation after generation. It was the 'friends and relatives' of the Templars massacred after Hattin who were expected to come to avenge them.[120] The marriage between Joinville's own son Geoffrey and Mabille of Villehardouin, the great-granddaughter of the historian of the Fourth Crusade, brought together two crusading lineages and may have planted in Joinville's mind the idea of writing up his own experiences in the East.[121]

There was a freight of feeling attaching individual crusaders not just to their living relatives but also to their dead ones. It was believed that the entire lineage past and present would benefit from one individual's taking the cross. This is clear from charters for the First and Second Crusades.[122] By the early thirteenth century James of Vitry was urging crusade preachers to emphasize that whole kinship groups, 'the spouses, children and parents of those signed, those alive and those dead', stood to gain from the indulgence.[123] Some believed that families would be judged together at the Last Judgement.[124]

What I've termed a predisposition to respond to crusade preaching was far from being determinism. But it's useful as a reminder that any individual's response to a crusade sermon was shaped by more than just the manner in which the preacher's message worked on their personal anxieties about what would happen to them after death. There was a whole spectrum of other circumstances that jostled for attention in the minds of contemporaries, including their responsibilities to families and other dependants, and their consciousness of how hard it would be actually to manage their participation in the expedition that was in gestation. The impact of feudal relations mattered a lot. Vassals of a great lord who took the cross were aware not just that his decision would make it significantly easier to fulfil any vow that they made, but also that failing to accompany him on crusade might well be construed as disloyalty. Joinville put it neatly in describing the quandary facing Louis IX's knights in 1267 when the king took the cross for the second time. 'If we don't take the cross ourselves, we shall lose the king's favour; and if we do, we shall be out of favour with God, because we shall not be taking it for his sake, but for fear of displeasing the king.'[125] On balance it was best to go.

In 1096 the entire ruling class of Chartres took the cross for the First Crusade alongside its count, Stephen of Blois.[126] This tendency applied the more strongly in the case of household knights and other skilled personnel. For people like this, crusading arguably meant little more than business as usual, admittedly in a much more exotic and dangerous arena. There's at least one case of a huntsman who accompanied his lord on the First Crusade, and in 1266–7 Hugh of Neville's retinue at Acre included not just his marshal Reimund but also his page Jakke, clerk Colin, cook Lucel and groom Thomas.[127] There was surely no question of a 'Damascene conversion' for men like Jakke, Lucel and Thomas. For those who did take the cross the crucial point was that it was voluntary. So in a sense every individual decision was *sui generis*, resulting from a combination of impulses that was unique. But as in the case of other voluntary religious commitments in the Middle Ages, such as becoming a pilgrim or entering a religious order, it would be foolish to deny that patterns and trends existed and that they sprang from social conditioning, constraints and expectations of many kinds. This of course takes us into the contentious sphere of motivations. These were as varied as responses, though like responses they are susceptible to analysis provided that due care is used. Motivation, however, is a question best looked at in the context of activities while on crusade, because these have most to tell us about the overall state of mind of those who had taken the cross, and it's only by investigating mental states that we can hope to get close to motivational drives.

The elusive vow

The creation of a commitment to crusade was both a private and a public matter, a duality expressed in the fact that an intending crusader (*crucesignandus*) made a vow and assumed the cross. Since the cross was public it's hardly surprising that we know much more about it than about the vow. But it's still surprising how little we know about the vow. There are scarcely any recorded instances of vows. One, written in September 1290 a few months before the final fall of Acre, committed Hugo of Fonte, a notary of Marseilles, to setting out 'with the next general passage' (that is, the next major expedition) to assist the Holy Land, or making a financial payment in lieu of service.[128] Another, undated though probably also originating in the thirteenth century, similarly showed a crusader vowing to set out with the next general passage or send a substitute.[129] It's likely that vows made before Saladin's capture of the city in 1187 focused on the intention of worshipping at the Church of the Holy Sepulchre. For example, in a passage in the _Gesta Francorum_, the most important of our eyewitness First Crusade narratives, the author wrote that 'our leaders then decided to attack the city with engines, so that we might enter it and worship at our Saviour's Sepulchre'.[130] It could hardly be more succinctly put.

The reason for the paucity of evidence about vows seems to have been the Church's recognition that the vow was intensely personal, a matter for the crusader and God. Both parties knew what the vow was and the crusader would have to answer for it at the Day of Judgement if he or she reneged on it. So even the canon lawyers, for whom it was second nature to impose precision, proved remarkably reluctant to address the issue in much detail. Not until the 1150s was the idea of a ceremony even mentioned, let alone a ceremony that had to involve a cleric. It was only at the end of the twelfth century, when problems involving release from vows began to escalate, that the lawyers began commenting on them in earnest. And it's no coincidence that the two vows mentioned above specified money or the sending of a substitute, detailed provisions that called for written testimony.

The ubiquitous cross

One factor that enabled the Church to maintain a non-interventionist stance on vows was the fact that every person who made a crusade vow also took the cross, which they normally wore on their right shoulders until the vow had been fulfilled.[131] This meant that there was a glaring reminder of the individual's vow that family, neighbours and lords could scarcely ignore. If the vow is all but invisible in the written and visual evidence, the cross, normally worn stitched on to clothing, is everywhere. In the _Gesta Francorum_, which has claims to be considered a kind of seedbed for crusading ideas, the novelty and centrality of the cross are affirmed in a famous and detailed passage narrating how Bohemund of Taranto first heard about the crusaders who were on their way to the East in 1096.

As for Bohemond, that great warrior, he was besieging Amalfi when he heard that an immense army . . . had arrived, going to the Holy Sepulchre and ready to fight the pagans. So he began to make careful inquiries as to the arms they carried, the badge which they wore in Christ's pilgrimage and the war-cry which they shouted in battle. He was told, 'They are well armed, they wear the badge of Christ's cross on their right arm or between their shoulders, and as a war-cry they shout all together "God's will, God's will, God's will!" ' Then Bohemond, inspired by the Holy Ghost, ordered the most valuable cloak which he had to be cut up forthwith and made into crosses, and most of the knights who were at the siege began to join him at once, for they were full of enthusiasm.[132]

Since the *Gesta Francorum* was written immediately after the capture of Jerusalem in 1099 (and parts of it perhaps even beforehand), this passage is a remarkable example of the precocious formation of an entire cluster of iconic references and images. They include the impromptu preparation of crosses that was adopted by St Bernard when he preached the cross at Vézelay fifty years later. The cross was the equivalent of the wooden staff (*baculum*) and 'scrip' (satchel, *pera*) traditionally carried by the pilgrim. Many early crusaders had all three. Writing shortly after the First Crusade, Ekkehard of Aura described 'a priestly blessing [that] bestowed, according to a new rite, swords with staffs and wallets'.[133] A sculpture of a returning crusader from the mid-twelfth century (probably Count Hugh of Vaudémont) shows him wearing his cross and carrying both staff and scrip.[134] As with the latter insignia, it was normal practice to receive the cross from the hands of a cleric, and in the earliest rites setting out the language to be used on these occasions the cross is simply added to the staff and scrip.[135]

10 A highly unusual picture of crusaders carrying rather than wearing their crosses.

The many meanings of the cross

In the Coventry pontifical of *c.* 1200 the significance of the cross for the person who received it was described thus: 'an especial means of assistance, a support of faith, the consummation of his works, the redemption of his soul and a protection and safeguard against the fierce darts of all his enemies'.[136] Clearly the devotional and talismanic associations of the cross were being emphasized, just as they were in the *Ordinance on Preaching the Holy Cross*, and in the sermons given by contemporaries like James of Vitry. Indeed, only this broad frame of reference can explain James's tantalizing comment that Oliver of Paderborn 'had signed with the cross many cogs [sailing ships] and countless men'.[137] How could a ship be given the cross? The cross didn't possess the practical uses of the pilgrim's insignia; instead it linked its wearer, the *crucesignatus*, to the redemptive act of suffering undergone by their Saviour. In so doing it set up a tension, even a rivalry, between two sacred sites, Calvary and Christ's Tomb. The development of a cult of Calvary during the crusades was shown in the proliferation of relics that were associated with the crucifixion, in particular portions of the True Cross, and the lance that was supposedly used to pierce Christ's side.

Fulcher of Chartres, a historian and veteran of the First Crusade who attended the council of Clermont, rhapsodized over the crusader's cross. 'Oh how fitting, and how pleasing it was to us all to see those crosses made of silk, cloth-of-gold, or other beautiful material which these pilgrims . . . sewed on the shoulders of their cloaks. They did this by command of Pope Urban once they had taken the oath to go.'[138] There's no reason to doubt Fulcher's assertion that the idea of wearing the cross was the personal invention of Pope Urban II, and it was a stroke of genius. To begin with, cloth crosses were cheap, easy to make and to transport. They were conspicuous, though somewhat less so than the yellow crosses that confessed heretics were later sentenced to wear on both chest and shoulder.[139] As a symbol the crusader's cross was a gift for skilled preachers like Gilbert of Tournai, who interpreted it in terms of 'direction, distinction, recollection [and] reward'.[140] It lent itself equally well to imagery. For James of Vitry people who refused to take the cross were like old cloth, too weak and rotten to hold the thread; by contrast its recipients were susceptible to the piercing thrust of God's fear in the needle and the binding force of his love in the thread.[141]

Once it had been taken, the cross brought the sacred sites of Jerusalem and the events that had occurred there into the everyday life of crusaders right up to the point at which they fulfilled their vows. It could function as a new type of stigmata, as in the case of the six or seven poor crusaders who were captured and killed by the Muslims on the First Crusade, and were later found to have crosses imprinted on their right shoulders.[142] There was an apocalyptic dimension as well. In its shape the cross resembled the tau, the nineteenth letter in the Greek alphabet, which in the Middle Ages was considered to be the mark placed on the forehead of those who were saved from death in Ezekiel 9.[143] During the First Crusade Patriarch Simeon of Jerusalem claimed to experience a vision in which Christ promised that all the crusaders would accompany him crowned at the Last Judgement,[144] and for Gilbert of Tournai the 'elect crusaders' were those who would stand before the Lamb in Revelation 7:9.[145]

The symbol's religious significance was therefore immense. But so too were its legal implications. It was possible to take the cross privately but this was frowned on, and as we saw in the case of the French *pastoureaux* of 1251, by the mid-thirteenth century it had come to be regarded as illicit. The reason was partly organizational, and the fate of the *pastoureaux* showed that to be sound enough, but it was also juridical. The assumption of the cross and its prominence on the shoulder of the *crucesignatus* was proof that a vow to go on crusade had been made, and could therefore be enforced. This made it desirable that it should occur at a ceremony that people would note and remember; it was a precaution against backsliding under pressure from spouses, relatives and friends.[146]

'Prisoners of the cross'

We've seen that in the course of time procedures did evolve for escaping from personal participation, such as sending a substitute or providing a sum of money. But the votive commitment in itself was a lot harder to shake off. One of the most poignant documents bequeathed by the 'Children's Crusade' of 1212 is a papal dispensation granted in 1220 to a man called Otto who had enlisted in the ranks of the *pueri*. Getting such a dispensation was an expensive business, and it has been suggested that Otto had no choice if his vow, taken with rash enthusiasm eight years earlier, wasn't to blight the rest of his life.[147] Some decades later the canon lawyer Hostiensis (Henry of Susa) paid close attention to the circumstances in which crusaders ought to be allowed dispensation from their vows. He conceded that they could be allowed to 'redeem' (buy back) their vows if they could make no useful military contribution. But this didn't apply to those who would be accompanied by fighting men or who could 'do battle with their tongue' (give useful advice); nor should it apply to artisans and farmers whose skills might meet the Holy Land's needs; nor, most strikingly, did it apply to those whose main intention it was to go as a pilgrim rather than as a combatant.[148]

It's possible that Hostiensis was trying to tighten up a system that had recently become too lax, with redemptions being handed out willy-nilly, as

Matthew Paris and others claimed.[149] But a crusade vow was never something to be made lightly. The author of the *Itinerarium peregrinorum* believed that 'a person who is bound by a voluntary vow should be absolutely condemned if it remains unfulfilled through negligence, because there was no obligation to vow'.[150] It was a strong argument and one considered effective in emergencies, as when Frederick of Swabia encouraged his fleeing troops to hold fast in May 1190 by reminding them of the day when they had taken the cross.[151] Canon law even established that the vow was inherited by a legatee, who could be disinherited if he failed to discharge it.[152] But it's unlikely that any argument based on law could match the force of religious fear as an incentive. In a vision experienced in 1196, just a year after the crusade call with which this chapter opened, an Eynsham monk called Edmund witnessed the sufferings in Purgatory of a young knight who'd thrown his cross away. Every day he was tormented by demons and every night made to undergo the pains of the pilgrimage that he'd evaded when alive; it was the standard punishment, Edmund was told, for such sinners.[153] There was a grim irony to this: the same horrors that drove people to take the cross were being mobilized to hold them to it.

For the most part, men and women who took the cross were held fast by the ties of law, social expectation and religious anxiety; they'd made themselves 'prisoners of the cross', as one thirteenth-century sceptic put it.[154] Their vow pushed their normal concerns into the background, and making preparations for their journey to the East became their daily preoccupation. In the next chapter we'll see that for most of them this was far from being a straightforward matter.

❖

3

SIGNED WITH THE CROSS

Preparing for crusade – the challenge and its repercussions

People who took the cross were under no illusions about the massive effort of will that crusading demanded. King Louis VII of France wrote in 1149 that the eastern Church was subjected to daily attacks by the Saracens and appealed to 'us westerners' for help; but providing that help was both laborious and costly.[1] Forty years later Peter of Blois fleshed out Louis' generalization. He exhorted the Third Crusade's leaders to send ahead reliable agents who would assemble food supplies, assess the perils in store, prepare for the sea crossing and evaluate the enemy's strength.[2] Fifty years on and English crusaders outlined the agenda in yet more detail: supplies and equipment had to be gathered; lands, properties and their contents had to be mortgaged or sold to raise cash; money had to be forwarded to the Holy Land so that it would be on hand when needed; the Christian authorities in the East had to be placed on a state of alert in order that joint military efforts could be co-ordinated; farewells had to be said; and finally, ports had to be accessed.[3]

Such preparations called for enormous effort, and the 1239 list didn't include the urgent need to ensure that the crusaders' family and dependants wouldn't suffer during their absence in the East. Nor did that list even touch on crusading's religious prerequisites, the creation of a devotional framework that would help in achieving the crusade's religious goals. Though this activity was often focused on the needs of one man or woman, it all happened within a setting that was overwhelmingly social. Each person's preparations reflected their rank and responsibilities; moreover, most crusades were a collective rather than an individual activity. As crusading developed, the Church started helping crusaders to cope with the twin processes of raising resources and providing security for dependants, and from the late twelfth century onwards the West's leading governments initiated similar measures. When kings had taken the cross these measures were pursued with especial force and persistence. So even before the armies converged at their designated points of departure or embarkation, the myriad processes of individual preparation that crusaders engaged in had formed a collective whole. It was a vast mosaic of activity. Christendom's efforts were being mobilized for the 'Lord's war', with most of the important figures and groups in society making some contribution towards the success of an enterprise that hinged on a host of individual vows, yet shaped the spiritual well-being of all Catholic believers. The ripple effects of crusade preparations were extraordinary and in the case of the biggest expeditions they left almost nobody unaffected.

11 William of Normandy's preparations for his invasion of England in 1066. This was the only recent military venture that approached the First Crusade in the logistical challenges that it posed.

The lessons of experience

Even for the first crusaders, what was in prospect was rarely a leap into the dark. Guibert of Nogent tells of children who accompanied their lower-class parents on crusade constantly asking if each town they passed was Jerusalem, but the anecdote tells us more about his snobbery than anything else and shouldn't be taken at face value.[4] Many first crusaders had a fairly sound idea of what they faced and what they needed to do by way of preparation for it. Some westerners had been to Constantinople as mercenaries entering service with the Emperor Alexios Komnenos. Italy's trading cities, especially Pisa, Genoa and Venice, already had links with Constantinople, Alexandria and to lesser degree the ports of Palestine and Syria. There were even some trading links with Jerusalem itself. The Order of St John of Jerusalem had its origins in a monastery that was founded in Jerusalem during the eleventh century by the merchants of Amalfi to meet their needs there.[5] More important was Urban II's preaching of the crusade as an armed pilgrimage. Many of those who took the cross had been pilgrims to Jerusalem or knew people who had visited its shrines. We've already seen that Urban's summons had a particular appeal to people who preferred devotional practices like pilgrimage. Moreover, pilgrimages to Jerusalem had often been conducted in large groups; in fact one German pilgrimage in 1064–5 led by the bishop of Bamberg numbered several thousand people.[6]

In terms of the demands posed by preparation there was relatively little difference between such pilgrimages and the First Crusade, given that most pilgrims had preferred the overland route through the Balkans and Asia Minor to the hazards of travel by sea. The biggest difference was uncertainty about the length of time that crusaders would be away. Pilgrimages to Jerusalem had varied a lot in the time they lasted, but usually a year proved to be enough. In 1095–6 it would have been very hard to place an estimate on how long it would take the crusaders to fight their way through to Jerusalem. Fulcher of Chartres provided an estimate of up to three years, which turned out to be remarkably accurate and for that very reason smacks of hindsight.[7] This uncertainty would apply to most later crusading. People who set out on the Third Crusade for example didn't know how long they would have to stay in the East to recover Jerusalem, or for that matter how much of the Holy Land would still be in Christian hands when they got there. The only thing that could be said with certainty was that the more thorough your preparations, the better.

After the disasters of the Second Crusade the issue of preparations became a highly charged subject for many promoters of crusading. Odo of Deuil, who wrote up the history of the French host, saw one of his goals as 'cautioning

those who follow after' by pointing out the errors that had been made. 'For
people will never fail to make their way to the Holy Sepulchre, and they will,
I hope, be more cautious because of our experiences.'[8] For example, he thought
it a serious mistake to take heavy carts, some of which needed four horses to
pull them; when they broke down they created a logjam on the roads.[9]

More problematic was the issue of the non-combatant pilgrim. Odo was
convinced that many of the difficulties that overwhelmed the French army
happened because its progress was held up by the defenceless mob. In Odo's
eyes Pope Eugenius III was right when he tried to ensure that knights should
be properly equipped for the expedition, but he hadn't paid the same attention to the military preparations of the infantry. 'Would that he had instructed
the infantry in the same way and, keeping the weak at home, had equipped
all the strong with the sword instead of the wallet and the bow instead of
the staff; for the weak and helpless are always a burden to their comrades
and a source of prey to their enemies.'[10] In other words, Odo thought that
Urban II's innovative brainwave of 1095 had entailed a workable balance
between warfare and pilgrimage and that this had been lost.

The experience of the German crusading host seems to have been similar,
for Conrad III commented on the fact that the 'mob on foot' couldn't keep
up with the army and fell prey to incessant Turkish attacks.[11] Like Odo,
Frederick Barbarossa was scarred by his experiences on the Second Crusade,
and though he never referred to them when preparing for the Third, he tried
to apply the lessons he'd learnt. Barbarossa shared Odo's concern about the
preparations of the poor, 'the weak and feeble mob' whose presence was a
hindrance rather than a help, and the emperor decreed that anybody who
intended to set out with the German host had to be able to show that he
could fund himself for at least two years.[12] This was good thinking but it
didn't meet Odo's central criticism, which was directed at the mob's military
incapacity. Its vulnerability remained a paradox with serious consequences for
crusading as a military venture.

The Church's input – crusader privileges

What did the Church do to assist people who responded to its crusading
appeals? There were times when it was distinctly unhelpful. By 1239 the Latin
empire set up at Constantinople after the Fourth Crusade was in dire straits,
and Pope Gregory IX made a determined attempt to persuade French and
English barons who had taken the cross to assist the Holy Land to 'commute',
or exchange, their vows to fighting against the Greeks instead. The crusaders
resisted resolutely. English *crucesignati*, gathered at Northampton to make their
preparations, affirmed their oaths on the high altar of All Saints Church.[13] It

was paradoxical that they were mobilizing and publicizing their devotion in order to defy the pope's intentions.

Usually, though, there was a convergence of goals that led crusaders to rely on all the support they could get from churchmen. From the start the Church extended to crusaders the rights that for generations had been granted to pilgrims. It did its best to build a wall of protection around both the person of the crusader and his dependants and possessions. Anybody who attacked them was liable to be excommunicated. Second only to protection against physical assault was a range of legal privileges. The crusader enjoyed the right to be tried in an ecclesiastical court (*privilegium fori*); in French royal courts in the thirteenth century he laid claim to this by the simple statement 'I will not reply because I am a crusader'. Cases that pertained to a crusader could be either speeded up or put on hold (*essoin*) depending on the state of his preparations.[14]

More contentious than any of this were the financial privileges that accreted around the crusader's status. It seems that from the start the Church was aware of crusading's heavy costs; it would have been surprising if it hadn't been. It's possible that Urban II made a point in 1095–6 of visiting towns that possessed mints in order to alert them to the demands that they'd face.[15] From the Second Crusade onwards an active policy of assistance was developed. *Quantum praedecessores*, Pope Eugenius III's ground-breaking encyclical of 1145, contained two highly significant clauses. Eugenius exempted crusaders from paying interest on past loans; and if the relatives and lords of crusaders refused to lend them money, they were permitted to raise capital from a third party, using family and feudal lands as backing for the loan. In the early thirteenth century clerics holding Church offices (*benefices*) who took the cross were given similar rights: in particular, they were allowed to borrow money on the strength of future income from their benefice. The essential proviso for this was that they had the right to draw the income from the benefice despite the fact that they'd be away on crusade. A general ruling that originated not long after the First Crusade exempted crusaders from paying taxes and tolls; in 1189 the German crusaders burnt the town of Mauthausen to the ground for daring to demand passage money.[16] Late in 1215 these measures, which had been steadily accumulating over the course of a century, were consolidated in the crusade decree issued at the Fourth Lateran Council. After that they could easily be referred to and were usually taken for granted.[17]

Violations and abuses

This clutch of privileges looked impressive, but enforcing them in such a way as to benefit the cause of the Holy Land was another matter. In the autumn of

1216 James of Vitry complained about the wholesale violation of crusader privileges that had been reported to him in France. Individuals who had taken the cross were harassed with taxes and other financial burdens, and were even locked up, in open defiance of the bishops whose job it was to protect them. In circumstances like these anybody who tried to preach the crusade would simply be spat on by his audience.[18] The strenuous efforts that were made by crusaders to find powerful lay guardians for their wives, families and possessions imply that the Church's ability to provide protection was limited. To a large extent it depended on the support that could be got from the secular powers, such as the decrees of King Philip II Augustus of France relating to crusaders in 1188 and 1214, or the stream of mandates ordering compliance in thirteenth-century England.[19] Immediately after taking the cross in 1188 Henry II sent out ordinances that were intended to allow crusaders access to mortgaged revenues, and to facilitate the raising of fresh loans.[20]

It was easy to abuse the crusader's legal and financial privileges: men took the cross when in prison to escape punishment, or when heavily in debt to evade their creditors. The generosity of the rulings on debt was probably self-defeating, since potential lenders would refuse to give credit unless their contract included a clause setting aside the privilege of claiming the suspension of interest.[21] Crusaders desperately needed cash and in a free market there was no compulsion on anybody to lend it; Jews didn't even stand to benefit from the grants of partial indulgences made available to people who furthered the crusading cause. Jews were also excluded from Eugenius III's ruling in *Quantum praedecessores* on crusaders raising credit from a third party. It's hard to see how the Church's rulings on crusader credit did anything to help actual crusaders.[22]

Overall it seems likely that the most effective assistance that the Church as an institution could provide lay in the numerous grants of financial aid that the papal court placed at the disposal of barons and magnates, largely in the mid- to late thirteenth century. Such crusaders could usually rely on sums that were to be collected from chests placed in churches for the alms of the faithful, or on money gathered together from vows that had been redeemed, legacies for the Holy Land, fines and other miscellaneous income. Often this was channelled through men of high social rank because they could use it to support themselves and the fighting men whom they hired to serve them on crusade. In the lead-up to Louis IX's first crusade Pope Innocent IV told his legate in France to give 500 marks raised from redeemed vows to the lord of Château-Chinon.[23] Much bigger sums of money were available to the pope from taxing the Church, but these were usually held in reserve for the needs of monarchs who took the cross; for obvious reasons their preparations were different in scale from those of humbler crusaders and we'll come to them later.

'They sell the pasture now to buy the horse' – the search for support

As a first step, most people who took the cross looked to local sources for protection, support and encouragement. In practice this was a combination of family, lordship and religious houses. Many individuals who took the cross had hardly anything that needed protecting and nobody whom they could approach for material backing. They went as servants, or they simply trusted to providence and their own skills or trades for their well-being.[24] A lot of crusaders were under-funded, and some of the baneful results that flowed from this will become apparent later. Others, and certainly many knights, could rely on their own sword-arm and they enlisted in the company of the better-off.[25] Either way little sign of preparations has come down to us. There's Gerald of Wales's charming story about the Welsh prince Maredudd compassionately giving his cloak to one of his associates who was taking the cross in 1188, because the man's own cloak was so threadbare.[26] The story is unusual, which is a pity because this sort of 'trickle down' support must have been commonplace. Mainly we know about the social elite, particularly people who approached religious houses, because these kept good records for their own future use.

That said, the importance of family ties for a good many crusaders is crystal clear. Until recently it was thought that family groups, above all in France, were shrinking in this period and that they were becoming obsessed with keeping their shared property ('patrimony') intact. Virtually the only way to square this development with the unquestionable popularity enjoyed by early crusading was to argue that crusade was seen as a way to get rid of surplus mouths. But settlement was never uppermost in the minds of the first crusaders, who none the less received the backing of their relatives.[27] There's a contradiction here, and the explanation for it is that the noble family doesn't seem to have been shrinking after all.[28] The aristocracy both in France and elsewhere could respond generously to the demands that crusading posed because it was still broad-based as a social unit. And its 'strategy', if that's not too grand a term, was primarily spiritual rather than economic. For as we saw in the previous chapter, contemporaries believed that the activity of a son on crusade would bring a harvest of spiritual benefits to all his relatives, alive and dead.

So it usually proved possible to persuade relatives to give their permission to the pledging and if necessary the sale of lands or other rights that formed part of the family patrimony. This isn't to say that their support was always willingly given, or that they didn't later renege on their agreement. Perceptions of property ownership in this period were so familial that any recourse to patrimonial possessions to fund crusading would have been inconceivable without a measure of family agreement. The usual approach was to cushion the blow. So when Maurice of Glons, preparing to set out on the Second Crusade in 1146, resigned a fief that he held from the abbey of St James at Liège, the agreement included provision for payment to his mother of half the revenues from the fief for the remainder of her lifetime.[29]

Religious houses and the hunt for cash

Monasteries came into the equation mainly by dint of their possession of supplies of cash, gained from rents or the sale of surplus produce, that they could make available to crusaders. But they also provided pack animals, which were much sought after, and precious metals or fabrics that could be carried fairly easily and used for bartering. The resulting transactions could be complicated. One charter drawn up at the abbey of St Jean d'Angély narrated that in 1101 'when Berard [Silvain] wanted to go to Jerusalem he asked the lord abbot to give him, over and above the forty and twenty *solidi* [shillings] he owed, twelve silver marks and a mule and fox pelts . . . This the lord abbot did. For he gave him twelve silver marks, each of which was then worth fifty *solidi*, and a mule worth 200 *solidi* and pelts costing forty-five *solidi*.'[30] Even the monetary system referred to here is complex, the mark being a weight and the *solidus* a unit of account, each of them comprising twelve silver *denarii* (pennies) that varied considerably in quality.

In return for cash and items, abbeys like St Jean d'Angély normally gained either property or the immediate or prospective abandonment of rights of lordship. Many of these rights had been gained by force, which was gratifying for the monks because they saw violence against their own communities as one of the worst of the sins calling for penance. But whatever form the transfer took, the economic backcloth to both the First and the Second Crusades was a buyer's market for land, lasting for well over a year. 'Each seemed to be offering whatever he had, not at the seller's, but at the buyer's price, lest he be late in setting out on the path of God.'[31] What may well be the earliest extant crusading song, 'Jerusalem mirabilis', comments that those intending 'to win the temple of God and destroy the Saracens' must 'sell their fiefs'.[32] It seems that from the start contemporaries were fully aware of the horrific cost of crusading; precision on this score is impossible but one estimate is that a knight would have needed to raise four or five times his annual income.[33]

This frantic activity didn't fully meet the needs of those preparing to set out. Europe was 'scoured' for coin and plate in the 1090s,[34] and the unceasing search for liquid cash, denigrated as 'greed' by many contemporaries, was a major cause of the attacks that took place on Jewish communities in the

Rhineland. But the achievement should be acknowledged. The simple fact that expeditions up to 100,000 strong could be equipped and furnished with at least some cash reserves was a testimony to the existence of a reasonably buoyant exchange economy. Since the West at this time had no coin of higher value than the penny, the volume of metal involved was remarkable: Godfrey of Bouillon may have assembled as many as a third of a million pennies.[35]

In addition to the hundreds of small-scale transactions between noble families and religious houses revealed in the charters, there are a handful of more conspicuous cases relating to the men who emerged as the leaders of the early crusades. Godfrey of Bouillon is again a case in point. He sold a cluster of lands and rights, but his biggest sale was that of the castle and estate of Bouillon itself. These he agreed to hand over to Obert, the bishop of Liège, for the sum of 1,300 marks of silver and three marks of gold. Almost certainly Obert was getting a bargain, but he didn't have these large amounts of precious metal to hand. Gold was particularly scarce, and Obert resorted to stripping the reliquary of St Lambert, the patron saint of Liège, of its gold plates. The monks of St Hubert-en-Ardenne were shocked by these methods and accused Obert of being 'concerned with his own glory', but the bishop's answer to such criticism was that he was acquiring castles that had been used as centres of brigandage.[36] It was a powerful argument. A similar high-profile example from the Second Crusade is that of King Louis VII of France. The king wasn't prepared to sell or mortgage parts of his limited lands (the royal domain), and he seems to have demanded straightforward subsidies from French churches and monasteries, proceeding on an individual basis. Robert of Torigny took a dark view of this, complaining that the crusade 'was for the most part undertaken out of plunder from the poor and despoiling of churches'.[37] It wasn't a good start to Louis' crusade.

Gains and losses

Preparations for the Third Crusade brought greater sophistication. Towns were becoming the driving force in the market system, with more cash regularly changing hands and a growing reliance on credit. At the root of these changes lay the circulation of vast amounts of silver that had recently been mined in central Europe. The result was dramatic – 'a total transformation took place of practically every facet of the economy and of society in which money was involved'.[38] This relegated to the past the acute shortage of precious metals that had been the constant bane of early crusading. In 1201 the dean of Magdeburg was able to contribute 550 marks of silver, a very substantial sum, to Bishop Conrad of Halberstadt's expenses on the Fourth Crusade.[39] No longer were religious houses able to make fat profits. In 1152 the archbishop of Salzburg remarked that at the time 'when the expedition to Jerusalem inspired almost the entire West with a marvellous and hitherto unheard-of fervour, people began to sell their property as if they were never going to return, which the churches, looking out for their own interests, bought according to their means'.[40]

No doubt some ecclesiastics had acted in the canny way ascribed to Obert of Liège, seizing the chance to store up wealth for their churches or religious houses and even driving a hard bargain. But there were usually other motives as well. Some tried to deepen existing ties with prominent aristocratic line-ages and others made use of this opportunity to redress grievances that were of long standing and especially vexing. Often these themes were intertwined. Three brothers from the Toucy family all took the cross at the time of the First Crusade and were supported by the monastery of Molesme with funding and two mules, in exchange for the establishment of a priory. The case involved litigation and called for the intervention of two papal legates because one brother granted away some property twice. All three brothers died while crusading or *en route* to Jerusalem.[41]

Most revealing though was the case of Nivelo, the castellan of Fréteval. In *c.* 1096 Nivelo agreed to surrender his custom of exacting food from the inhabitants of Emprainville in exchange for ten pounds in *denarii* towards his crusading expenses, accompanied by lesser sums given, presumably as sweeteners, to his brother and sister. What's remarkable about this charter, from St Père de Chartres, is the frank way in which the writer described the custom that Nivelo was abandoning, which to his eyes seems to have amounted to little more than daylight robbery. 'Whenever the onset of knightly ferocity stirred me up, I used to descend on the aforesaid village, taking with me a troop of my knights and a crowd of my attendants, and against nature I would make over the goods of the men of St Père for food for my knights.'[42] Together with the snide reference to Nivelo's noble birth ('raised in a nobility of birth which produces in many people an ignobility of mind'), these words betray a hostility that was seldom allowed to become so overt. Normally what's on show in these sources is a relationship that was turbulent and rough-edged, but (at least over the long term) of mutual benefit for all parties.

'I would sell London if I could find a buyer' [43]

With Richard I's preparations for the Third Crusade the scale of activity expanded. Like earlier crusaders, the king knew that he'd need as much liquid cash as he could possibly find, but in locating it he displayed an energy that was unprecedented and also contentious.[44] Of all the crusades that were organized by crowned heads, Richard I's seems to have evoked the most resentment, in part because his quest for money was accompanied by a thorough purge of Henry II's advisers. In a famous passage one critic wrote that:

> The king removed from office Ranulf Glanville, the justiciar of England, and almost all the sheriffs and their officers; the closer they had been to his father, the more he oppressed them. Anyone who did not have as much as he demanded was immediately arrested and sent to jail where there was weeping and gnashing of teeth; then he appointed other sheriffs in their place. And everything was put up for sale, offices, lordships, earldoms, sheriffdoms, castles, towns, lands, the lot.[45]

This aspect of Richard's campaign is a long way from the romanticized portrait of 'the Lionheart'. And it's true that, given the horrified reaction that swept Christendom after Hattin and the fall of Jerusalem, contemporaries may have been prepared to turn a blind eye to questionable practices if action resulted. The fact remains, though, that the king's deep-cutting search for money was indicative of the rising costs of crusading, to which the expenses of sea travel were making a substantial contribution. Ordinary English crusaders, getting their private preparations under way at the same time that Richard's agents were on the prowl, must have found their efforts hindered. Resentment of royal policy might help to explain the attacks on the Jews in England in 1190, at their worst in the massacre of the Jews of York: the Jews were associated with the government, and they could be attacked without too much fear of offending the king.[46]

Like monarchs who took the cross before and after him, Richard didn't undertake to shoulder the costs of all those who were going with him, or agree to pay them wages, though in many cases circumstances drove him to do both. But his assumption of the cross did make it clear that the expedition would have an authoritative organization and structure. 'The king of England was first and foremost in the whole Christian army, surpassing everybody else in his resources.'[47] This is why the popes were by this time placing such emphasis on persuading Richard and his fellow monarchs to take the cross. They knew that many others would follow suit. After Henry II and Philip II took the cross near Gisors in January 1188, 'an immense number of people of both sides also took it, partly from love of God and for the remission of their sins, and partly out of respect for the kings'.[48] Richard I laid in shiploads of equipment intended for general use in the English army, including thousands of horseshoes made in the Forest of Dean. Substantial amounts of food were bought up by royal agents, among other things 14,000 cured pigs' carcasses.[49] Such equipment and food might be charged for, but at least they

12 The fortifications of Aigues-Mortes, the port constructed by Louis IX for the embarkation of his crusade in 1248.

were available, which they might well not have been without the king's attention to detail.

The provision of shipping

The greatest benefit of Richard's vigorous interventionism was the removal of the individual crusader's need to arrange transportation to the East. The king provided a fleet of more than a hundred ships. He paid two-thirds of the cost of the vessels and the wages of their crews, 2d a day for sailors and 4d for steersmen.[50] The extent of the gain is most readily grasped when the position of the English crusaders berthed on Richard's ships is compared with the radical mismanagement of the Fourth Crusade's transportation needs twelve years later. When the troops assembled at Venice in 1202 there were too few of them to pay the fee that their leaders had agreed on for the ships scheduled to take them east. This placed the whole expedition in jeopardy and precipitated the course of action that led to diversion, scandal and ultimate failure. The débâcle didn't occur because the Venetians overcharged for their vessels: it was simply human error on the part of the crusade's leaders.[51]

The English situation was unusual if not unique. Certainly French crusading kings didn't undertake the provision of shipping to the same degree. Philip Augustus hired his vessels from Genoa but the size of the anticipated force, just 650 knights, 1,300 squires and their horses, reflects the fact that a lot of French contingents made their own way to the East.[52] At this point the extent of centralized management provided by Richard was an inconceivable prospect in the case of the French kingdom. In 1246 Louis IX made arrangements for a total of thirty-six ships with Genoa and Marseilles. Since Marseilles was situated outside the kingdom, in the county of Provence, none of those who provided ships for these crusades were subjects of the king; even the admirals of Louis' fleet were Genoese. Like Philip Augustus before him, Louis didn't undertake to transport all the French crusaders on the ships that he hired, let alone those who came from outside France. Joinville tells us that he joined forces with a cousin to hire a ship for their entourages; inexplicably, the count of St Pol commissioned a ship to be built in far-off Inverness. But things had moved on since Philip Augustus's day, and in other respects the French monarchy could and did match the efforts of the English. Louis poured substantial sums of money into the purchase of equipment and supplies for his fleet, and he paid the wages of the sailors. In one major respect Louis' naval planning exceeded Richard I's in scope. This was his construction of port facilities at Aigues-Mortes, a fishing village lying between Montpellier and Marseilles. It was a massive project, which had been started before Louis took the cross but was pushed ahead with vigour in the years leading up to the army's embarkation in 1248. Given that Aigues-Mortes had access to no fresh water and was subject to severe silting, it was hardly a wise choice.[53]

With the exception of these expeditions led by monarchs, where contracts and mandates have largely survived, the provision of ships for crusading remains an annoyingly obscure topic. We've little idea where the ships came from that transported the Anglo-Flemish contingent on the Second Crusade in 1147, or the thirty-seven vessels that carried crusaders from Dartmouth ahead of the royal armies in 1189, or even the ships used by Rhenish and Frisian crusaders on the Fifth Crusade. From the Fourth Lateran Council (1215) onwards, 'partial' indulgences (promises of release from a specified period of time in purgatory) were offered to shipowners who placed their vessels at the disposal of crusaders, and there was no ban on their charging for them.[54] We've few examples of this being acted on, though there is an intriguing reference in one of James of Vitry's letters to Oliver of Paderborn 'signing with the cross many cogs and countless men'.[55] It's possible that the dispersed nature of recruitment for the Fifth Crusade meant that the demand for naval resources was spread around and didn't pose much of a problem.[56]

Homeland security

At the end of December 1189 Richard I met Philip II near Nonancourt to settle various issues relating to their co-operation on the Third Crusade. Among other things they swore to help each other defend their lands against hostile third parties. Their barons too swore to keep the peace while their lords were abroad.[57] The conflict between the two kings was western Europe's most wide-ranging and destructive dispute, but, with the sole exception of funding, the issue addressed at Nonancourt was the biggest problem facing any nobleman signed with the cross, whatever the size of his estates. This was 'homeland security', guaranteeing the basic safety of his dependants and possessions while he was in the East. For those who weren't already aware of the dangers, Richard's long absence (1190–4) provided a test case for how seriously things could go wrong, with his brother John attempting to seize power in England and Philip overrunning Richard's lands in France. In a precarious world, the crusade was virtually Richard's undoing. The ecclesiastical immunity due to a crusader protected him neither from Philip's attacks nor from his own year-long imprisonment at the hands of Leopold of Austria in 1192–4.[58]

There's no doubt that by this point hundreds of returned crusaders could have told similar stories. First crusaders resorted to every imaginable device to protect their lands and families; they knew that their daughters would be particularly vulnerable to being coerced into marriages by land-hungry neighbours. Although no crowned head went on the expedition there was widespread fear in 1095–6 that disorder would break out with so many great lords away. When monarchs did start to go, two major issues had to be dealt with, the regency and the succession. Clearly Richard I's regency went badly wrong. Regencies for French royal crusaders had a much better track record, especially those of Abbot Suger of St Denis for Louis VII in 1147–9 and the queen-mother Blanche for Louis IX in 1248–54. That said, both Suger and Louis expressed anxiety about the safety of the realm during the king's absence; Louis was worried about 'the machinations of wicked men' and Suger was alarmed when Louis remained 'in the midst of the barbarians' after his leading barons, 'disturbers of the realm', had made their way home; this was like handing the sheep over to the wolf. Louis was eagerly awaited 'like an angel of God'.[59] Such language was rhetorical but it communicates a strong sense of the fragility of royal power in France.

Apprehensions about their death overseas unleashing a succession crisis and civil war led crusading kings to ensure that adequate preparations were made for their heir to succeed. In the case of the key fatalities, the deaths of Barbarossa in Armenia in 1190 and Louis IX in Tunisia in 1270, there was no hindrance to the succession of either Henry VI or Philip III. Barbarossa's preparations were exceptionally thorough. Henry had been left to act as regent in Germany and Barbarossa's most dangerous rival, Henry the Lion, agreed under pressure to go into exile for three years.[60] As for Philip III, the position of the dynasty was so secure that his succession went unchallenged in spite of the fact that he accompanied Louis on crusade and took several months to get back to France with his father's corpse. But the two men who were left behind as regents, Matthew of Vendôme and Simon of Nesle, still pleaded with Philip to return as soon as possible. Delay was dangerous even for a kingdom which at this time faced no powerful threats, either external or internal.[61]

The Saladin tithe

Yet for kings, as for all others, it was always funding that loomed largest. This was because the twelfth and thirteenth centuries saw an inexorable growth in the costs of waging war. In England, a warhorse that cost between £2 and £4 in the early thirteenth century could cost £8 by its close.[62] A song composed to celebrate Louis IX's taking the cross in December 1244 represented his mother Blanche of Castile joyfully promising to give him forty horses loaded with pennies with which to pay his soldiers: it's unlikely that Blanche made any such offer, but the image reflects the funding challenge that Louis faced.[63] So it's not surprising that the late twelfth and thirteenth centuries gave rise to significant initiatives by the Catholic world's authorities to tap its resources in a public and systematic fashion, as opposed to a private and piecemeal one.

The most famous such initiative was the Saladin tithe, the tenth imposed on income and movable property throughout England and France in 1188 as part of the forward planning by Henry II and Philip II for the Third Crusade. The tax's origins go back as far as a plan for a levy in 1166, but the circumstances in 1188 were crucial; it is a strong indication both of the devastating impact of Jerusalem's loss and of the realization of how expensive it was going to be to get the city back. The crusading cause was woven into the collection procedure set up in England, where members of the two great military orders, a Hospitaller and a Templar, were to form part of the eclectic collecting team that was supposed to be set up in every parish. People who took the cross were exempt from payment, and according to one contemporary this caused quite a few of the 'better-off' to enlist when the edict was proclaimed.[64]

But in both England and France the tithe proved only patchily successful. Although collection was brutal (you could be imprisoned for evasion), it was also *ad hoc*, and contemporaries recognized the danger of the precedent: they were perfectly capable of making the distinction between zeal for the recovery of Jerusalem and willingness to pay taxes. For at least some people the tithe was as destructive as warfare,[65] and in France Conon of Béthune claimed that barons were taking the cross in order to get their hands on money that had been squeezed out of clerics, townspeople and sergeants.[66] Neither the partial indulgences offered to people who paid in full nor the threat of excommunication for non-payment was considered fair.

In England Henry II's reputation for prevarication in carrying out his crusade projects can't have helped, and when the Saladin tithe was collected under Richard it was regarded as falling disproportionately on the poor. Nonetheless, Richard did benefit from it, especially from his lands in England, where it's likely that the tithe was one of the most conspicuous ways in which crusading affected the lives of the population at large. In France Philip was persuaded to abandon the tax in 1189–90, and there was never any question of its being levied in the lands of the Holy Roman Empire. So it remains mysterious how two of the Third Crusade's leaders managed to finance their ventures,[67] especially in the case of Philip, who lacked the miscellaneous range of revenues, above all judicial fines, that Barbarossa was able to tap into. The French army's under-funding condemned its king to playing a satellite role in the East; Richard of Devizes gloated that 'it became a perpetual torment to [Philip's] conscience that a camp-follower of the king of the English lived more splendidly than the butler of the king of the French'.[68] Together with Barbarossa's premature death, Philip's relative poverty allowed Richard I to hold sway over the operations of the Third Crusade.

Levies on the Church and the Jews

Clearly, taxing the laity for crusading threw up all sorts of problems. The only later attempt to do so, a poll tax decreed at the general council of the Church held at Lyons in 1274, seems never to have been implemented for lack of support from the secular authorities.[69] It was an embarrassingly stark demonstration of the limits that governments were placing on the exercise of papal power by the late thirteenth century. But if the pope couldn't reach into the pockets of the laity, he could tax churchmen, and from the early thirteenth century the imposing of an income tax on the revenues that they enjoyed from their benefices became standard practice whenever a big crusade was in prospect. In financial terms this saved the day. Louis IX's two crusades seem to have been heavily dependent on money dragged out of the French Church, to the extent that about two-thirds of his known expenditure in the East between 1248 and 1254 was met from its contributions.[70] There were levers that worked in the case of clerics, in the last resort stripping them of their benefices, and their complaints inflicted a lot less political damage. Reasonably enough, clerical crusaders and members of the military orders were exempt from these levies.

13 Frederick Barbarossa, *crucesignatus* for the Third Crusade, the second time that he took the cross.

For most of the thirteenth century this meant that when a pope proclaimed a crusade he usually also imposed an income tax on the Church in selected dioceses, if not throughout the Catholic world. The collection of the tax was just as important as the preaching of the cross, and it was certainly organized with as much attention to detail. This wouldn't have been possible without the creation of a papal financial bureaucracy that worked hand in glove with the big Italian banking companies.[71] Clerics made numerous and ingenious excuses to avoid paying but they couldn't defy the pope for long if the king was backing the tax. Haggling over what would be done with the money that was raised played a big part in the planning process, until a settlement was hammered out which persuaded the pope that an expedition would set out that was worthy of the support granted to it. Crusading had become big business, and a highly politicized one.

The other group that was often singled out for crusading levies, this time by the secular rather than the ecclesiastical authorities, was the Jews. This was again in part because their complaints didn't matter much. In the mid-twelfth century Peter the Venerable, the abbot of Cluny, argued that the Jews should have all their property stripped from them for the benefit of the crusade.[72] The Church edged its way in this direction at the Fourth Lateran Council in 1215 when princes were urged to make Jews 'remit' (hand over) the profits of their usury. The decree was a licence to pillage, and following its reissue at the general council that convened at Lyons in 1245, Louis IX used it to raise sums towards the expenses of the Seventh Crusade.[73] So the Church, Christ's revered bride, and the Jews, the hated descendants of Christ's killers, came to be yoked in a bizarre fiscal union.

Public and private in thirteenth-century England

Crusading preparations in thirteenth-century England are especially interesting.[74] This was a 'mixed economy' in which the private and the public, the secular and the spiritual, constantly interwove, sometimes facilitating the labour of preparation and at other times impeding it. English crusaders didn't resort to levies on their tenants to finance their expenses because this hadn't become a custom in English law, nor for the most part did they resort to borrowing from Jews. As in the early days of crusading, they raised cash mainly by selling or pledging property, the purchasers and lenders being family members, ecclesiastical corporations, magnates, local knights and merchants. Sales of woods were prominent because timber was always in demand; thus Simon of Montfort sold most of the forest of Leicester to meet his crusading expenses in 1240. Crusaders made full use of their ecclesiastical status and appointed attorneys (normally a trained lawyer coupled with a close friend or relative) to represent them during their absence. Crusading magnates like Richard of Cornwall, William Longespee, Walter Cantilupe bishop of Worcester, William of Valence and Simon of Montfort were subsidized generously with money collected by clerics in England, on the assumption that they would assist others of lesser rank.

Around such high-ranking figures, above all the Lord Edward, the future Edward I, in 1270, there clustered other English crusaders, and they were increasingly bound to serve them through the precocious use of written contracts that supplemented their crusade vows. Commoners of the type that had been lambasted by Odo of Deuil were largely elbowed out of English crusading, unless they managed to attach themselves to such retinues. Thus William of Weston, wishing to prove his status as a crusader before royal justices in Northamptonshire in 1203, produced in court an open letter of William of Hommet 'in which it is contained that he has retained him in his company to take him to Jerusalem'.[75] England escaped the popular turbulence that generated the crusades of the *pueri* and *pastoureaux* in France and the Low Countries. In other respects, though, there were many points of contact with the scenario in France. In both countries the royal or national interest was acknowledged to be paramount, and nobody could leave on crusade if it was reckoned that their services would be needed at home. Overall, English crusading was mature and comparatively professional, characteristic of a highly commercialized and legally advanced society. The situation in, say, Scandinavia or Hungary, was a lot less sophisticated.

Religious preparations

Although there were more than enough practical matters to sort out, crusaders gave just as much thought to the religious nature of the enterprise that they were about to embark on. They were responding to unending exhortations from the Church to bear it in mind. Humbert of Romans counselled crusade preachers to spend a lot of time expounding the varied meanings of the cross as a symbol. Even its display on the right shoulder had various messages to convey: it led the wearer to God's right hand; it was a reminder that Constantine, the first Christian emperor, wore his cross on the right arm; and the word 'right' signified a true state of penitence.[76] Pastimes and expenditure that were associated with sinful activity should be avoided. Eugenius III instructed people preparing for the Second Crusade that 'precious clothes or elegant appearance or dogs or hawks or other things that are signs of lasciviousness' should be set aside. Crusaders should rather focus on 'arms, horses and the rest with which they may the more ardently overcome the infidels'.[77] It was in this spirit that Henry II in 1188 tried to ban games of chance, attractive women and colourful clothes from his crusading army.[78]

This was asking a lot given the contemporary association of aristocratic status with display and generosity (*largesse*). Richard I's long-awaited arrival at Acre in September 1190 took place amid a blaze of colour and noise that was calculated to generate astonishment and admiration. It achieved this aim: 'We had heard of his great reputation, but the reality that we see is far greater.'[79] John of Joinville, Louis IX's biographer, was a remarkably religious man, but he described without any sense of unease the week of feasting and dancing that he hosted for his vassals at Easter 1248, shortly before his departure for the East with Louis IX. He did this just three years after the council of Lyons had specifically instructed the faithful not to waste their money on feasting; instead they should spend it on subsidizing the crusading cause.[80] It's true that the occasion was exceptional. Joinville's wife had just borne him a son, and presumably he felt that it would be wrong not to celebrate the event in due style despite the circumstances; besides, there was a cluster of men of standing, including his brother, who expected to provide banquets to mark the birth and who would have felt slighted if they weren't allowed to do so.[81]

Making amends

Crusaders of all ranks believed that leaving for a crusade without first undergoing a range of devotional exercises would undermine what they were doing. Like the need for material preparations, this spiritual dedication flowed directly from the pilgrimage tradition and was therefore both familiar and congenial to them. Essentially there were three phases to it. The first was the perceived need to ensure that the crusader had done as much as he reasonably could to make amends for sinful deeds against others. 'Repent your sins and pay your debts' was the simple message they received from the preachers, and in general they were receptive to it.[82] We've seen that to some extent this dovetailed with fund-raising, through the reciprocal character of the deals that they struck with religious houses. It's not surprising that in these circumstances the scribes who drew up the charters of donation used lurid language to describe their donors' misdeeds, such as Stephen of Villars' 'hands stained with blood and rapine' in 1139.[83]

But it wasn't just monastic houses that had suffered: many crusaders repented having offended against relatives, feudal dependants and neighbours. At the end of his week of feasting in 1248 Joinville addressed his presumably replete vassals thus:

> 'My friends, I'm soon going oversea, and I don't know whether I shall ever return. So will any of you who have a claim to make against me come forward. If I have done you any wrong I will make it good, to each of you in turn, as I have been used to do in the case of those who had any demand to make of me, or my people.' I dealt with each claim in the way the men on my lands considered right; and in order not to influence their decision I withdrew from the discussion, and afterwards agreed without demur to whatever they recommended.[84]

The process mirrors what King Louis himself had already undertaken, in spectacular fashion, in 1247 when he appointed teams of 'investigators' (*enquêteurs*) to carry out a survey of royal administration and report on the abuses they uncovered. This was an unprecedented procedure, and the strongest sign of its link to Louis' crusader status was the personnel involved, for they were nearly all Franciscan and Dominican friars, men whose drafting into royal service could only be justified in terms of the investigation's association with the king's planned crusade.[85]

Intercession – targeted prayer

Both Joinville and King Louis clearly felt that to set out on crusade when people nursed justified grievances against them would impair or even wreck the prospects of the whole exercise. The second aspect of religious preparation was in a sense the complement to this fear: the conviction that intercession on behalf of the crusade by those who stayed at home would benefit the crusaders. Above all this meant consolidating existing ties with religious houses. It may seem odd that, at a time when crusaders were already selling or pledging substantial amounts of landed property and rights so as to raise the cash and equipment needed for their venture, they would also make gifts purely in exchange for prayers. But such a distinction is artificial. For contemporaries the material and devotional features of their preparation were intermingled. They sprang from a holistic view of the world in which the spiritual armour of intercessional support at home was just as important as the provision of good weapons and mounts. In the case of the First Crusade, we've evidence for at least seventy-eight endowments made in exchange for such support, quite apart from new foundations.[86]

The anxiety that lay behind the gifts was typified by the phrasing used when Stephen count of Blois gave a wood to Marmoutier before he left on the First Crusade: 'So that God, at the intercession of St Martin and his monks, might pardon me for whatever I have done wrong and lead me on the journey out of my homeland and bring me back healthy and safe, and watch over my wife Adela and our children.'[87] Some of the grants made were, in any case, part of more complex arrangements in which a number of future scenarios were catered to. When the cleric Raymond Eic gave half of a church to the abbey of Lézat before leaving on the First Crusade, he attached the condition that if he returned safe he'd get the gift back as a fief to be held of the abbey; he could also enter the abbey if he wanted to do so, while should he die there was provision for him and his relatives to be commemorated by Lézat's monks.[88]

'The shout for the Holy Land'

Over time these individual processes of intercession came to form part of an impressive tapestry of support that was offered up by the whole Church, what one historian has described as 'the complete mobilization of liturgy in the service of the crusading movement'.[89] At its heart lay a remarkable liturgy called 'the shout for the Holy Land' (*clamor pro Terra Sancta*) that was introduced almost immediately after the fall of Jerusalem in 1187, probably in London. The *clamor* was modelled on the practice that had taken root during the worst upheavals of tenth-century Europe, when religious houses and cathedrals that had suffered attacks on their lands resorted to a liturgical appeal or 'shout' to their saintly patrons for assistance against their assailants. In some cases it had been accompanied by the humiliation of the saints involved, whose relics would be taken out of their reliquaries and placed on the floor of the church. The point of this had been to shock those lay nobles present, coercing them into amending their own behaviour or supporting the monks against malefactors.[90]

Nothing so dramatic was done during 'the shout for the Holy Land' but it still represented a collective cry of pain. At its most elaborate the *clamor* comprised a full week of daily masses but its core was a sequence that could be inserted into any mass.[91] Roger of Howden wrote nothing less than the truth when he commented on the crusading army besieging Acre in 1189–90 that 'prayer was offered to the Lord on their behalf without ceasing by the Church' (Acts 12:5).[92] James of Vitry in 1218 begged the pope to 'pray constantly on our behalf', appending a list of his dead companions for whom intercession was requested.[93] His requests fell into a pattern that went back to the participants in the First and Second Crusades, but Roger and James could be more confident than their predecessors that the intercession they longed for was actually being organized and that among other things it would generate reinforcements to assist them in their struggle.

Innocent III took the process even further in 1213. In *Quia maior*, the bull in which he proclaimed the Fifth Crusade, he gave 'the shout for the Holy Land' the stamp of papal authority and lodged it within the framework of a far-reaching spiritual strategy. There should be a monthly procession carried out by each of the sexes, whose participants would pray to God for the liberation of Jerusalem. These processions should be accompanied by crusade preaching, and fasting and almsgiving were also encouraged. Most important, however, were two other provisions set out in *Quia maior*. First, Innocent issued a short prayer that eloquently encapsulated the essence of crusading theology, bringing together God's providential power, Christ's sacrifice, the sanctity of Palestine and the role and reward of the crusader in fewer than fifty words.[94] And secondly, the pope decreed that Ps. 79 ('Oh God, the heathen are come into thine inheritance') should be sung every day, at every mass that was celebrated, following the kiss of peace, while the whole congregation lay prostrate on the ground.[95]

This liturgical focus on Ps. 79 originated in the period immediately after Hattin: indeed in *Audita tremendi*, the bull in which he declared the Third Crusade, Pope Gregory VIII commented that resort to Ps. 79 was the only possible response to the devastating news that had arrived from the Holy Land.[96] No other psalm or indeed passage in the whole of scripture could so encapsulate the sensation of hollow misery created by the fall of Jerusalem, conjoined with the earnest hope that God would show mercy to his people, 'so we thy people and sheep of thy pasture will give thee thanks for ever'. As a result Ps. 79 became so familiar that when he renewed the preaching campaign for a new crusade in 1224 Pope Honorius III referred to its daily chanting 'in the usual way'. For the next few decades its message of despair, tempered by the expectation of divine forgiveness, resonated through the churches and chapels of Europe. During the lead-up to Louis IX's first crusade in the 1240s it was said every day in Franciscan houses. In such circumstances anybody who took the cross could hardly fail to be aware that the spiritual resources of the whole of Christendom were being mobilized on his behalf.[97]

Rites of departure

As the time for setting out drew near, the thoughts of crusaders naturally came to focus on their own status and needs as penitents. This third phase in their spiritual preparations was characterized by rituals of personal dedication that signalled the placing to one side of their normal preoccupations and way of life. Typically, they paid visits to the shrines of their favourite saints, at which the staff and satchel of the pilgrim were often given to them in token of their imminent departure. At this point the more devout also changed, sometimes in a dramatic way, into pilgrim dress. In 1248 Joinville sent for the abbot of Cheminon, who had a reputation for saintliness, and received his pilgrim insignia from his hands. Then he left his castle, 'on foot, with my legs bare, and in my shirt', and made his way to local shrines where relics were held.[98]

In this, as in so much else, Joinville's piety mirrored that of his king. Louis went to St Denis, the shrine church that by this point had the closest of links with the monarchy, to receive his pilgrim tokens from the papal legate Odo of Châteauroux. He was also handed the oriflamme, the war banner of the French monarchy which legend said had been given to Charlemagne by the pope. Louis returned to Paris and heard mass in Notre-Dame, then walked barefoot to the abbey of St Antoine, which had been founded in 1198 by Fulk of Neuilly, the preacher of the Fourth Crusade. The first stage of the king's journey to the south was painfully slow thanks to his inability to resist stopping off at hermitages en route.

Jacques Le Goff, one of Louis' modern biographers, has laid much emphasis on the king's assumption of pilgrim costume on 12 June 1248. Le Goff has depicted it as a turning point in Louis' life, after which he remained a perpetual penitent.[99] This may be true, but the fact remains that Louis was following in the footsteps of his grandfather Philip Augustus and more significantly of Louis VII, the first French king to lead a crusade and one for whom the pilgrimage element had been dominant. Odo of Deuil gives a detailed description of the king's assumption of the pilgrim insignia at St Denis on 11 June 1147. The pope was present when Louis arrived at the abbey church, which had only recently been rebuilt by Abbot Suger. The atmosphere was highly charged. It was hot and there were dense crowds because the famous Lendit Fair was meeting. Pope and abbot opened the golden door of the reliquary that held the remains of St Denis. Tentatively, perhaps teasingly, they drew out the silver casing 'a little way' so that the king could venerate and kiss the saint's relics. Then Louis received the oriflamme, and Eugenius III handed him his pilgrim's satchel and blessed him. The king retired to the dormitory and the day concluded with dinner in the monks' refectory, after which Louis exchanged the kiss of peace with the brethren and left.[100]

Family and grief

'We say good-bye to you: Pray to the Lord to lead you and, if he pleases, bring you back healthy and without injury, and to guide us and you to everlasting joys.'[101] Departure brought to a head the contrast between what lay ahead and what was being left behind, 'the sweetness of the flesh, the abundance of things [and] the company of relatives'.[102] It might indeed be possible for those who stayed to follow those setting out 'in their hearts, in their prayers, and with financial help', as Odo of Châteauroux put it in a sermon,[103] but there would still be an unprecedented distance between them. Fulcher of Chartres, writing soon after the First Crusade, painted a picture of tears being shed by those remaining, contrasted with high-minded determination on the part of those setting out. Thus the crusader's wife fainted while the crusader 'departed with firm resolution'. 'Sadness was the lot of those who remained, elation of those who departed.'[104]

This became the picture of leave-taking that churchmen came to view as appropriate. The crusader was following Christ's injunction in Matthew 11:37 by setting his sight on higher things.[105] Bishop Peter of Oporto painted a lyrical picture. 'The alluring affection of wives, the tender kisses of sucking infants at the breast, the even more delightful pledges of grown-up children, the much desired consolation of relatives and friends – all these they have left behind to follow Christ, retaining only the sweet but torturing memory of their native land. Oh, marvellous are the works of the Saviour!'[106] Tears, grief and wailing (*lacrimae, luctus, planctus*) punctuate Odo of Deuil's account of the events at St Denis in 1146; but it's the king's wife and mother, the crowd and the monks who are weeping, not the king.[107] The illustrator of one thirteenth-century bible made this point by showing departing crusaders attached to God by thin lines. They are striding in his direction, undistracted by the wailing and gesticulating relatives that they've left behind them.[108]

Affection for homeland, belongings, family, wife and children were regarded by the preachers as chains that were dissolved by love for Christ.[109] But Fulcher, Peter, Odo and others who took the same line were celibate clerics, and the more likely situation is that described with pathos on a number of occasions by lay crusaders. The author of the *Itinerarium peregrinorum* included not just one but two scenes of departure in which tears were shed on all sides.[110] One crusader poet thought he would lose his mind when he said farewell to his beloved.[111] Villehardouin wrote that 'many a tear was shed for

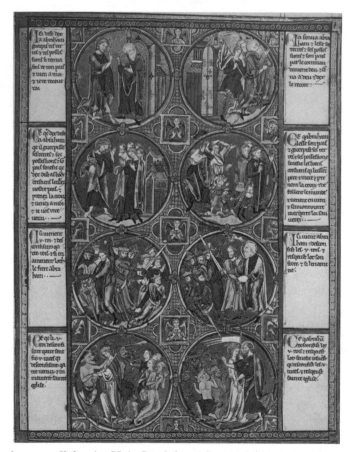

14 Crusaders set off for the Holy Land (second on right), ignoring their distraught relatives behind them.

sorrow at parting from their lands, their own people, and their friends',[112] while Joinville narrated that 'all the way to Blécourt and Saint-Urbain I never once let my eyes turn back towards Joinville, for fear my heart might be filled with longing at the thought of my lovely castle and the two children I had left behind'.[113] It's true that all were handling a literary commonplace or *topos*, but that's insufficient reason to dismiss such scenes. The pain of leaving behind young children may explain the image introduced into sermons of the Virgin holding out her infant son to those who took the cross: the baby Christ became a surrogate for what was being left behind.[114]

Fighting the attractions of home

The appeal of home and loved ones was dangerous and some of the themes that we encounter most frequently in songs and poems about crusading were designed to counter it. The most straightforward motif was the contempt shown for those who failed to rise to the challenge of crusade, which was held up as a test of virility as well as religious fervour. When the Third Crusade was preached in England men who were slow to take the cross were handed wool and distaff, signifying that they were only fit for women's work.[115] In Wales one man who was about to take the cross dismissed the argument that he was legally bound to consult his wife first with the words 'this is man's work . . . there is no point in asking the advice of a woman' (thereby entirely misconstruing the issue).[116] The troubadour Marcabru wrote that 'the lecherous wine-swillers, dinner-gobblers, fire-huggers, roadside-squatters will stay within the place of cowards; it is the bold and the healthy whom God wishes to test in his washing-place'.[117] Another theme, found in the songs of Marcabru and Guiot of Dijon, was that the crusader's love for God was akin to the knight's for his lady.

As for the woman who was left behind, she would show herself worthy of being loved by making the most of her situation. This needn't be entirely stoic: 'And when the sweet wind blows which comes from that sweet country where the man is whom I desire, then I turn my face towards it gladly, and it seems to me then that I can feel him beneath my mantle of fur.'[118] This looks like an attempt to give a more human, even erotic, face to the astringent tone of self-sacrifice that clerics regarded as the ideal. It's unlikely that the clerics would have found it palatable, any more than they would have agreed with the sentiment expressed by Conon of Béthune, around 1200, that although his body would be serving his Lord his heart would remain in the West with his loved one.[119] In fact Conon went even further, portraying his lady's love as one of the crusader's rewards: 'there you win Paradise and honour and reputation and praise and the love of your lady'.[120] Another poet hoped that 'good sir God' would reward his crusading efforts with salvation for his lady as well as himself, so that both would enjoy 'bliss for evermore'.[121]

'When I lose a lady, by a lady may I be helped!'

There are a number of dissonant themes jostling here, and they're encapsulated in the three crusade poems that were composed by Thibald of Champagne. It's possible that they were written precisely at this point in Thibald's crusading, while he waited to embark at Marseilles in August 1239.[122] Whether this was the case or not, the texts bring together admirably the thoughts of a man who enjoyed the delights of love, friendship and material prosperity but was leaving them behind in favour of the perils and deprivations of warfare in the East. 'God!' he exclaims, 'why does the Holy Land exist which will separate so many lovers?'[123] Why then go on crusade? Typically, the answers given by Thibald are a mixture of the religious and the social. Human life is short, Paradise can only be won through suffering, and the needs of the Holy Land are acute: 'the kingdom of Syria cries out to us in a loud voice that we repent, for God's sake, for not going there'.[124] This was service worthy of a knight: 'I am ready and armed to serve you; I render myself to you, good father of Jesus Christ! Such a good lord I could never find on earth.'[125] Daringly, the Virgin is portrayed as substitute lover: 'Lady of the heavens, great, powerful queen, greatly am I in need of succour! May I be inflamed with love for you! When I lose a lady, by a lady may I be helped!'[126]

Wife, children, lover, lordship, land and locality (*patria*) had an attraction that crusade preachers, and enthusiastic crusaders like Thibald, couldn't simply duck. They had to be contended with, either by tackling them head on ('think of the crusade's leaders, who are leaving behind more than you are'),[127] or by somehow drawing them into the way crusading was depicted ('act courageously, think of what you've left behind to be here today').[128] So not only was the sacrifice of crusading worth it in spiritual terms, it was demanded by social status, while worldly loves, like knightly prowess and glory, were imported into the ideology of crusading. In the process the idea of individual conversion that lay at the heart of crusading was somewhat softened. Clever as this was, it was inevitable that on the point of leaving rhetoric and images counted for precious little, compared with the human appeal of the domestic, familiar and cherished. It was just as well for the cause of crusading that those who left soon had to give their attention to more pressing matters.

4

❖

EASTWARD BOUND

When thinking about the issues that faced crusaders making their way to the East it's hard not to focus on the great expeditions. But it's important to bear in mind that many men and women took the cross outside the context of the numbered crusades. This was particularly the case between 1099 and 1187, though it applied also to the thirteenth century. In 1244 it was estimated that there were about 100 pilgrim knights or footsoldiers in the Holy Land.[1] For some decades after 1099 the difference between pilgrimage and crusade was slender; writing about the year 1113, Fulcher of Chartres noted that 'in that season the pilgrims from overseas were arriving as was customary, and our army grew from day to day'.[2] It was around this time that a former castellan of Radnor castle came east. God had deprived him of his sight for what seems to us a minor act of sacrilege (spending a night in a church with his hunting dogs) and he 'ended his life with honour' by charging into the Muslim ranks on horseback.[3] People like these planned their journey eastwards not in the company of thousands of others, but as members of much smaller groups and in some cases as individuals.

It was an approach that brought both losses and gains. The principal loss was the devotional charge that flowed from being part of a great host that was simultaneously an army with military objectives and a penitential community carrying out a religious exercise. Such crusaders were also less well placed to make use of the sources of finance and support that were created with such effort by both Church and state to make possible the great crusades. On the other hand they benefited from the absence of competition by fellow crusaders for scarce specie, provisions, berths on ships and travelling ameni-ties. And they avoided getting caught up in the violent disputes with host communities that made the journey to the East such a stressful episode for several of the bigger expeditions. The problems and choices that individual crusaders and small groups had to address and make in travelling to the East would have been familiar to their ancestors who had made pilgrimages to

Jerusalem for many generations: difficulties over shipping and lodgings, sickness, losses at the hands of thieves and fraudsters, and bruising encounters with local officials.[4] There was a lot to be said for being in charge of your own crusade. You could focus on the twin goals of the exercise: getting to the East as quickly as possible and by the easiest and cheapest means; then worshipping at the Holy Land's shrines, above all those at Jerusalem. If circumstances brought combat on to the agenda, that was considered to be a bonus.

Assembly points and dates

By contrast, both the organization of the journey and the character of the destination were more problematic for people who took the cross to participate in one of the great 'passages' as they came to be called. From the council of Clermont onwards these crusaders received some basic instructions about when and/or where to assemble for the journey, and these directions tended to come with an assumption about the routes they would be following. Urban II almost certainly established the Feast of the Assumption of the Virgin (15 August 1096) as the departure date for the First Crusade, intending it to benefit from the summer harvest.[5] Innocent III set March 1199 as the departure date for the Fourth Crusade, and 1 June 1217 as that for the Fifth.[6] Innocent was typically prescriptive about the issue of departure points. He insisted that crusaders who intended to go by sea on the Fifth Crusade should make their way to Brindisi in Apulia or Messina in Sicily. These ports weren't just geographically well suited to act as rendezvous, they were also located in territory that was subject, notionally at least, to Innocent's political control. And the pope wanted crusaders who were proposing to march by land to make sure that they co-ordinated their departures with people who were sailing.[7]

Directives from lay commanders followed similar lines. Official departure dates were set and reset for the Third Crusade, leading a substantial number of informed contemporaries to criticize the delays with angry eloquence.[8] Peter of Blois exclaimed that those Christians holding the fort in the Holy Land were starting to get desperate, like the British awaiting the arrival of Arthur or the Jews their Messiah.[9] Some of the English and French crusaders went on ahead, in contrast to their German counterparts, nearly all of whom seem to have obeyed Barbarossa's order that the host should assemble at Regensburg for St George's Day (23 April) 1189.[10] Irrespective of announced delays, some fluidity in departure schedules was inevitable. A whole group of the armies that set out on the First Crusade jumped the gun by leaving in the spring of 1096. Even on a tightly controlled expedition like Louis IX's crusade of 1248, some left before or after the king himself embarked at

Aigues-Mortes on 25 August. But simple logistics dictated that hosts proceeding by land should assemble at designated points in the West, even if in the case of the First Crusade few of these points can now be located with any certainty.

Shipping contracts of course necessitated embarkation ports. This was the case even when, as on the Third Crusade, the armies assembled elsewhere (Vézelay, July 1190) and marched to their designated ports (Marseilles and Genoa). The Fourth Crusade's commanders felt a growing sense of anxiety as they gradually realized that too few of their comrades, whose money was needed to pay the Venetians, were making their way to Venice. Their alarm is captured well in the pages of Villehardouin's account. 'What immeasurable harm was caused by those who had gone off to other ports when they should have come to Venice! Had they only done so, Christendom would have been exalted, and the land of the Turks brought low.'[11] Even if the marshal of Champagne was over-simplifying things, the lesson was painful and it was clearly learnt, by Innocent III among others. Crusading had to become more effective, and this meant that crusaders must be more disciplined, not just on the field of battle but also while getting there.

Destinations

The ultimate destination of all crusaders was the heavenly Jerusalem and most of them hoped to reach it via the earthly one. The First Crusade's objective was to capture the city and the Third Crusade's to recover it: in both cases the expedition's religious and military goals were in complete harmony, a balance that was reflected in contemporary judgements on the outcomes. Success generated extravagant joy in 1099, while contemporaries expressed disappointment and the sense of a task left incomplete after 1192. It's likely that during the last weeks of the Third Crusade the eagerness of many crusaders to undertake peaceful visits to Jerusalem sprang in part from anxiety that unless they did so their vows would be regarded as unfulfilled. Hence Saladin's willingness to encourage the visits, so as to deter their returning, 'leaving the Muslims safe from their wickedness'.[12] No other crusade enjoyed such a clear focus. In strategic terms the Second Crusade was the oddest of all. Recovering Edessa from Zengi had been the rationale behind the crusade's launch, but it had always been a highly problematic goal and was made more so by the terrible losses that the crusaders suffered during their crossing of Anatolia. The course of action they adopted, in conjunction with the settlers, was a siege of Damascus that failed. In recent years an attempt has been made to justify this in military terms,[13] but even if the reassessment is accepted it doesn't alter the intractable strategic dilemma that the crusade's leaders faced: given that there was no immediate threat to Jerusalem, what was the military point of their being there?

Following the partial success of the Third Crusade every major venture either headed or intended to head for the Nile delta, with the goal of destroying the concentration of Muslim power that was correctly perceived as most perilous for the Latin states; as James of Vitry put it in 1218, 'once that land has been conquered, we would easily be able to recover the whole kingdom of Jerusalem'.[14] By that time the inherent difficulty of harmonizing religious and military goals had been solved by the drastic expedient of uncoupling them. The consequences for the general outlook and devotional lives of crusaders of this significant change of approach have proved singularly tricky to pin down. Many if not most of the participants in the Fourth and Fifth Crusades, and possibly later ones too, continued to consider themselves to be primarily pilgrims. As Richard I had put it in relation to his plan to invade Egypt in 1191, the crusaders would be fighting there 'for the advantage of the holy land of Jerusalem'.[15] It's likely that some of them nurtured the hope that they'd be able to capitalize on the recovery of the holy city by going to worship there.[16] But there can be no doubt that something of importance had happened when people took the cross without having their eyes set all the way through on Jerusalem's sacred shrines. It was one of the features of crusading in the thirteenth century that gradually accentuated the differences between it and pilgrimage.

Decision-making – land or sea?

The decision to travel to the East overland or by sea was reached largely on practical grounds. A possible exception was the Second Crusade, whose commanders were heavily influenced by the memory of the First Crusade and attempted to imitate it as fully as possible.[17] Most of the first crusaders didn't even consider travelling by sea, but it's unlikely that this was because they placed any particular value on making their way overland: in the summer of 1096 Urban II was in contact with Genoa,[18] and ships were used to ferry the crusaders across the Adriatic and Bosphorus. Fleets supplied by all the emerging Italian sea-powers made their appearance during or shortly after the crusade's campaigning in the Middle East. Very soon large forces began travelling by sea, such as the Norwegians who sailed from Bergen in 1107. It's likely that providing enough vessels to transport the First Crusade's massive armies would have exceeded the capacity of the seaports, but this is hard to prove and in any case nobody at the time could have predicted that such substantial numbers would assemble. It has proved possible to draw up an ideal strategy for the First Crusade that would have comprised a seaborne passage from Constantinople to Jaffa, followed by the rapid seizure of

Jerusalem and the entire littoral from Tripoli to Ascalon.[19] But such proposals belong more to the world of game play than history. In reality, the sheer novelty of crusading and the many uncertainties that it generated during the crucial winter and spring months of 1095–6 ruled out the sort of detailed negotiations that would have been necessary to arrange sufficient shipping.

The decision to march to the East that's hardest to explain is Barbarossa's in 1189–90. By this point the huge problems that came with such travel were well known – indeed the emperor had suffered them at first hand during the Second Crusade. It wouldn't have been hard for Barbarossa to arrange sea transport with Venice. The greatest headache facing earlier seaborne crusaders, the safe transport of their chargers, had been solved by the increasing use of round-hulled sailing vessels (*naves*) and of galleys that were equipped with hull ports at the stern.[20] The author of the *Itinerarium peregrinorum* says that the land route was chosen because of the numbers that assembled,[21] but it's likely that they only turned up because they'd been told that this was scheduled as another old-style overland crusade. It's been suggested that Barbarossa was pessimistic about the likelihood of any ports still being in Christian hands when he arrived in the East. But it's quite possible that the choice was made mainly on personal grounds. Maybe the emperor agreed with the idiosyncratic view expressed by one of the expedition's historians that a penitential pilgrimage must include the labour of the overland march.[22] One source claimed that Barbarossa avoided the sea route because a soothsayer had correctly predicted that he would die in water.[23] Whether this was true or just a good story, it wouldn't be surprising if Barbarossa had an exceptional fear of dying in a shipwreck because in such cases the corpse could rarely be recovered and given a proper burial.[24]

15 Blessed by the Church, Louis IX and his companions begin their journey to Aigues-Mortes in 1248.

The hazards of travel by sea

Travelling by sea entailed numerous dangers from unfamiliar coastlines, stormy weather, human error and hostile strangers. This catalogue of potential disasters is nowhere more vividly illustrated than in Joinville's lengthy account of Louis IX's return journey from Palestine in 1254.[25] First the king's sailing vessel nearly came to grief on rocks off Cyprus, because heavy mist caused the sailors to miscalculate their approach. The vessel narrowly escaped the rocks but it did get stuck on a sandbank, and none of the galleys accompanying it could approach to rescue the king because they feared being swamped by a rush on the part of the 800 passengers. The sandbank tore off a large portion of the ship's keel, but Louis refused to abandon the vessel because he knew that everybody else would follow his example. There were too many of them to find alternative berths, and they'd be confined to Cyprus; some would find it impossible ever to get home again. This traumatic sequence of events was closely followed by a storm that again placed the passengers in fear for their lives. At Joinville's suggestion, the queen vowed to St Nicholas, the patron saint of travellers, that if she survived she would commission a miniature silver ship for the saint's shrine at Varangeville, which she later did.[26]

Off Pantelleria, an island south of Sicily, the disappearance of three galleys led the sailors to conjecture that local Arabs had captured the ships and their crews (as it turned out, they'd simply been delayed). Later in the voyage negligence on the part of a maid caused a fire in the queen's cabin. Joinville was evidently responsible for making sure that all flames were put out before going to bed, and he was rebuked by the king. The rebuke was a fairly good-natured one, but the nightmare of fire breaking out on a vessel far from land was clearly reflected in Louis' resolution that for the rest of the voyage he wouldn't retire for the night until Joinville had reported to him that all the fires were out.[27] In addition to these group dangers, there was always the prospect of individuals falling overboard. This happened to a squire from Provence who was travelling in a smaller vessel in the French fleet and was working on the hull's exterior. Like the queen earlier, he sought refuge in the intercession of a saint, Our Lady of Vauvert, who supported him in the sea until he could be rescued. Joinville was very impressed by this, so much so that he had it commemorated both in a fresco and in a stained-glass window.

Storms at sea terrified crusaders and not without good cause. A stroke of lightning that hit an English galley off Messina in December 1190 sent it to the bottom.[28] Another storm that occurred near Messina, this time during the Fifth Crusade, was accompanied by thunder so powerful that it scared some crusaders to death and by lightning strikes that left others permanently scarred.[29] The only refuge was supernatural, such as the visions of St Thomas of Canterbury that were experienced by several of his fellow Londoners in 1190; the saint assured them that he, St Edmund and St Nicholas had been designated to look after the vessel and that its passengers would come to no harm provided they behaved properly.[30] When James of Vitry was voyaging from Genoa to Acre in the autumn of 1216, to take up his duties as bishop of Acre, he experienced a storm that lasted for two days and nights. His vessel was in harbour, but even fifteen anchors could scarcely hold it steady, and the merchants travelling with him were so alarmed that they clamoured to confess their sins and receive the cross from him.[31]

Even if the sea was calm and the winds favourable, for most crusaders travelling by sea entailed confinement and discomfort. James of Vitry's berth in 1216 was remarkably spacious: he had a room in which to read and eat, another to sleep in, a third where he stored his belongings and food, and a fourth where his meals were prepared and his servants lived.[32] But James was a high-ranking ecclesiastic. By contrast, the preacher Humbert of Romans depicted a crusader who travelled by sea complaining to Christ that he was unable even to stretch his legs.[33] Given that the commune of Marseilles in 1233 was prepared to allow up to 1,500 pilgrims to be carried on each vessel that made use of its harbour,[34] Humbert wasn't exaggerating; indeed, since medieval galleys and cogs rarely offered more than about 140 sq metres (1,500 sq ft) of deck space the congestion is almost unimaginable.[35] Jean Sarrasin compared the experience to being in prison, and he marvelled at the energy with which the French engaged the Turks immediately after disembarking at Damietta.[36]

Inevitably food at sea was poor and in short supply, especially when following winds turned out to be weaker than anticipated. Frisians who intended to join Louis IX's second crusade in 1269 were instructed to bring with them not just a specified sum of cash, but six jars of butter, a leg of pork, a side of beef and half a measure of flour.[37] Even if this food could have been assembled at a time of famine,[38] most of it would surely have become inedible in the heat of a Mediterranean sea voyage. Galleys were less dependent on following winds to make progress than sailing vessels were, but they needed to make landfall with greater frequency because of their rowers' enormous requirements for fresh water; and since most fleets that carried crusaders were mixed, the accompanying sailing ships had to stop just as often. Despite this, drinking water became putrid and swarmed with worms.[39] As James of Vitry noted, this was less of a problem if you travelled in the autumn[40] – though, as he found out, that was also the season when storms were most likely to happen.

The numerous factors that caused travellers by sea to fall ill were summed up by an author called 'Pseudo-Brocard', who wanted to advise the king of France on his planned crusade in the early 1330s: 'sudden change of air, the stink of the

sea, tasteless and rough food, fetid and polluted water, crowded people, limited
space, hard beds and the rest, causing all sorts of sickness'.[41] According to this
writer even those crusaders whose constitutions resisted illness at sea were likely
to succumb when they disembarked because of the sudden change of climate
that they experienced, like the 250 companions of Louis IX who supposedly died
in Cyprus in 1248–9.[42] We've just seen Jean Sarrasin recording the alacrity with
which the French disembarked at Damietta, and there's no doubt that Pseudo-
Brocard's fierce hostility towards sea travel led him to play up its perils for all they
were worth. But he was certainly right to emphasize the problems that horses
faced, and it's likely that the shipping of crusaders to the East was the first occasion that contemporaries had to address this problem. For horses sea travel
necessitated a prolonged period of standing: they could be supported with straps
but there wasn't enough space for them to lie down. In such circumstances the
buffetings of stormy weather could maim or kill them, and unless landfalls were
frequent enough to enable them to be exercised on shore, their recovery on
arrival was a lengthy business.[43]

In truth almost all the evidence specifically relating to crusaders travelling by
sea makes grim reading.[44] Baldric of Bourgueil, a historian of the First Crusade,
claimed that he became terrified just looking at a map of the Mediterranean,[45]
but even those made of sterner stuff had good cause to anticipate the crossing
with a dread that it takes a big leap of the imagination for us to comprehend
today. Indeed, it's likely that the only thing worse than travel by sea was the
unpredictable delays that sometimes entailed putting off the horrors themselves
for many months. German crusaders setting out from Vienna in August 1190
found that rough weather caused a cancellation of the autumn passage, forcing
them to sit out the whole autumn and winter at Zadar.[46]

Logistical problems of sea travel

These micro issues were significant deterrents for many, above all the poor, for
whom the cost of a berth alone was sometimes enough to make the journey
impracticable. At Marseilles in 1239 'many poor people were prevented from
crossing by lack of money, and others by illness and physical troubles'.[47] But
there were macro issues associated with sea travel that nobody, rich or poor,
could avoid. The first was logistical. Transporting such large armies as these to
the East by sea called for the assembly of imposing numbers of vessels. For the
most part they were heavily booked for commercial ventures; and of course their
services would be lost to commerce for the entire duration of the crusade.
Moreover, the requirements of their human and animal passengers, in terms of
provisions and fresh water, called for an infrastructure of berthing facilities,
coupled with a hinterland of suitable markets, that was greater than seems to

have existed anywhere in the Mediterranean Sea before the mid-thirteenth century. How requirements were met before that point begs many questions, and it's ironic that the technical demands of large-scale seaborne transportation, above all the switch from galleys to sailing vessels, were addressed just at the point when crusading as a mass movement started to falter.[48]

Still greater problems were faced by the several fleets of sailing vessels that crossed 'the endless swathes of the sea'[49] from northern Europe, beginning with Sigurd's in 1107–10. They were particularly vulnerable to Mediterranean shipworm (*teredo navalis*), and it was only in the late thirteenth century that improvements in design enabled them to navigate westwards through the straits of Gibraltar. Astonishingly, up until that point all the ships had to be either sold or abandoned in the Mediterranean and the return trip made overland. Naturally this adds to the northerners' achievement in mobilizing the shipping that they needed, such as the vessels (between 164 and 200 in number) that sailed from Dartmouth in May 1147. Identical or similar questions about logistics and infrastructure pose themselves in the northern seas as in the Mediterranean. It remains puzzling, for example, how at least 164 vessels could have sailed out of the Dart river during a single outgoing tide, or how the horses that they transported could have received the approximately thirty-two litres of water that each required on a daily basis during a voyage to Oporto that lasted twenty-four days.[50]

Diversionary drift

The second macro issue was diversion. From almost the first point at which armies made their way east by sea the possibility arose of the fleet travelling to the scene of combat via one or more other destinations. Some distinctions are called for. When Louis IX wintered in 1248–9 on Cyprus he wasn't engaging in a diversion but resting his army in preparation for an assault on the Nile delta, and giving other groups time to join him. Like the construction work that he'd organized at Aigues-Mortes, this was part of a considered strategic approach towards crusading that placed an emphasis on planning for maximum military effect. Cyprus lent itself readily to the role of a winter resting point and Louis had built up supplies there ahead of his arrival.[51] What the king couldn't foresee was that a dispute between the sea-powers of Pisa and Genoa, which supplied many of his ships, would further delay his departure from Cyprus in 1249. This caused problems with provisioning and funding, and it curtailed the campaigning season in Egypt, which Louis only reached in May.

But the Cypriot phase of Louis' crusade was inherently different from the diversions that occurred during Richard I's journey to the East in 1190–1. The English and French armies set out from Vézelay on 4 July 1190, already three years (to the day) after the disaster at Hattin. There were difficulties in effecting a link-up between the army and the fleet that was making its way from England, and while a section of the army went on ahead to assist in besieging Acre, the rest accompanied Richard to Messina in Sicily, which he reached in September. Here dynastic complications relating to Richard's sister Joan held him up until April 1191. He made his way east but then became embroiled in a dispute with the Byzantine ruler of Cyprus. In a lightning campaign in May 1191 Richard conquered the island, and he finally arrived with his troops outside Acre on 8 June, eleven months after leaving Vézelay.

It was mainly due to good luck that Richard's two diversions inflicted little damage on the crusading cause. Given that sailing in the Mediterranean was usually avoided between the start of November and the end of February, the king arrived at Acre only a few months later than he would otherwise have done. It can be argued that Richard planned his conquest of Cyprus because of the benefits that it would bring to the defence of the Holy Land; it was certainly rationalized in these terms at the time. 'For it seemed very much in the general interest to subjugate the island of Cyprus because it is so indispensable for the land of Jerusalem.'[52] It's also true that the First Crusade shows that diversions and delays could afflict expeditions that made their way to the East almost entirely by land: Baldwin of Boulogne led a significant diversion to Edessa in 1098, though as with Cyprus in 1191 it's proved possible to see this as the last stage in a planned strategic design.[53] There were almost always plausible reasons to justify straying from the most obvious approach route to the military objective, be it Jerusalem, Acre or Egypt. Even the bizarre decision of one group of the 1101 crusaders to march in entirely the wrong direction began as an attempt to enforce the release of Bohemund of Taranto from a Turkish prison.[54] In the 1250s William of Rubruck advocated an overland march so that crusaders could conquer not just Anatolia but Hungary as well.[55]

Sea travel did much to worsen this diversionary drift. This was because of the relative speed with which deflections could be accomplished, and the large number of tempting targets that were scattered around the shores of the Mediterranean Sea. It required surprisingly little effort to forge links between crusading in the East and attacks on one or more of these targets while on the way there. In many cases it was possible to fall back on the catch-all objective of weakening Islam. This played a part in persuading the commanders of forces sailing from north-western Europe to lend their assistance to attacks on Arab strongholds in Iberia, a tendency that started during the Second Crusade and thereafter recurred frequently, especially in 1189 and 1217; one chronicler even took issue with the 'accursed haste' that prevented crusaders in 1189 from conquering most of the Algarve for Christendom.[56] A more precise argument was that financial and other resources would be brought together that would make the job of the crusaders easier once they reached the East; again, this was deployed during the campaigns in Iberia.[57] And the case was made that diversions were actually consolidating the position of the Latin East and so directly benefiting the crusading cause. As we've seen, this argument was used to justify Richard's conquest of Cyprus and Baldwin's capture of Edessa, but its most dramatic and desperate deployment was by Pope Innocent III when he attempted to make the most of the capture of Constantinople by the Fourth Crusade in 1204. The pope took his cue from Baldwin of Flanders, the first Latin emperor of the city, who in a letter to Innocent asserted again and again that Constantinople's capture would be of immediate benefit to the Holy Land.[58]

Sea travel and the diversion of the Fourth Crusade

The Fourth Crusade is not just the most notorious example of diversion but also the one that most clearly reveals the importance of sea travel in making it possible. In purely causal terms, the deflection of the crusaders, first to attack the Christian port of Zadar and then to seize Constantinople, occurred as a direct result of the financial quandary that was created by the decision to travel to the East by sea. But, in addition to this, a powerful argument in 'selling' the journey to Constantinople to the crusading rank and file was that the diversion wouldn't take long and could be beneficial to the crusade. Once the pretender Alexios was installed on the throne, the crusaders would have paid off their debts to the Venetians and they could set sail for the south with the additional support that he guaranteed for the defence of the Holy Land. Even after Alexios had turned against his former allies, it was still possible to argue that the crusaders would resume their journey southwards once the impasse was broken through the capture of the city and the systematic pillaging of its massive resources.

The key point was that the presence of the Venetian galley fleet, including its formidable array of horse transport galleys (*huissiers*),[59] simply removed from the equation the huge obstacle that had been posed in the past by Turkish Anatolia. The Holy Land and Egypt were only a few weeks' sail away, and for all the discomforts and perils of sea travel, unquestioned Christian control over the seaways meant that the journey carried no risk of large-scale enemy attack. In the circumstances of 1203–4 these arguments turned out to be wishful thinking, but from a broader perspective the Fifth Crusade was to prove them correct. For between 1218 and 1221 wave after wave of seaborne 'passages' (*passagia*) brought fresh and well-equipped crusaders from the West to join the front line in the Nile delta. In terms of getting western fighters and their *matériel* out to the East quickly and with fewest difficulties *en route*, there are grounds for viewing the Fifth Crusade as the most efficient.

16 Peter the Hermit leads his followers, cavalry and infantry, men, women and children, eastwards in 1096.

Travel by land

By contrast, there was little positive to be said on behalf of the land route other than the fact that it avoided the need to find large sums of specie for the hire of shipping. An overview of what was in prospect for all who set out along it, whether in 1096, 1100–1, 1147 or 1189, makes this apparent. First, the crusaders had to negotiate the crossing of fellow-Christian lands in the Balkans as far as Constantinople. Some of these lands, notably the kingdom of Hungary and the European provinces of the Byzantine empire, were reasonably well governed and it was usually possible to negotiate terms that guaranteed safe passage and regulated markets. The first groups to cross Hungary, in 1096, were badly behaved and violence broke out at several places, but thereafter this early phase usually went well enough.[60] It's come to be recognized that given the enormous demands that the crusaders posed in terms of food, forage and water, the Balkan phase of their journey to the East was remarkably free of trouble.[61] 'Here we had such marketing privileges as we wished' was Odo of Deuil's comment on the experience of the French in 1147.[62]

The Roman roads in the southern Balkans, above all the Via Egnatia which ran from Durazzo (Dyracchium) via Thessalonica to Constantinople, were kept in generally good condition. In other areas, such as Dalmatia (Sclavonia to contemporaries), in the mountainous territories adjoining the Adriatic, not only was the terrain treacherous, but the reception the crusaders enjoyed from the indigenous was far from warm. The only army that followed this route was that of Count Raymond of Toulouse in the winter of 1096–7. It's hard to explain this decision; possibly Raymond thought that if he kept close to the coast provisioning would be easier, and he was ill informed about the difficulty of the terrain. The count's chaplain, the chronicler Raymond of Aguilers, described the journey southwards to Scutari as forty days of suffering (the biblical resonance of the figure is unmistakable), and it's significant that Count Raymond resorted to atrocities to try to keep local brigands at bay.[63] This initial phase of the journey to the East ended at Constantinople where the leaders of all the early crusades faced the wearisome and time-consuming task of establishing a working relationship with the Byzantine emperor. Until this was achieved there was no prospect of crossing into Anatolia, and their stationary armies rapidly fell short of food.

Anatolian ordeals

All of this was taxing enough but it was overshadowed by the crossing of central Anatolia. Much of this terrain was as difficult and sparsely inhabited as Dalmatia, while the Turks of Iconium (Konya) posed the first serious military obstacle to the crusaders. Those early bands of crusaders that made it as far as Constantinople all came to grief in encounters with the Turks north of Nicaea. The author of the *Gesta Francorum* included two vivid passages detailing the immense difficulties the members of the main army faced in getting from Nicaea to Antioch. First he described the region north of Iconium, which the army crossed in July 1097, as 'a land which was deserted, waterless and uninhabitable, from which we barely emerged or escaped alive, for we suffered greatly from hunger and thirst, and found nothing at all to eat except prickly plants which we gathered and rubbed between our hands'.[64] This was and still is desert plateau, 'a majestic, rather frightening landscape'.[65] A few weeks later the crusaders had to cross the Anti-Taurus mountain range in northern Syria, a 'damnable mountain, which was so high and steep that none of our men dared to overtake another on the mountain path. Horses fell over the precipice, and one beast of burden dragged another down.'[66]

These were terrifying experiences, but the fact remains that, because they had managed to inflict a crushing defeat on the Turks at Dorylaeum on 1 July, the first crusaders didn't face the additional challenge of armed resistance to their southward march. Their successors were less fortunate. The crusaders who arrived in 1101, in the follow-up expedition to the First Crusade, were massacred by the Turks in a series of engagements in June and July.[67] More significantly, the German army on the Second Crusade was largely destroyed in a one-sided battle fought near the old battlefield of Dorylaeum on 25 October 1147,[68] while Louis VII's French host suffered heavy casualties in 'daily encounters with the Turks' during its trying march along the Anatolian coastline towards Adalia a few weeks later. By the time it reached Adalia the French army was in such bad shape that the decision was made to proceed onwards by ship.[69] But Louis couldn't find enough ships for the whole force and had to leave most of the army behind at Adalia, where it just disintegrated. So both in 1101 and in 1147 the Seljuq Turks of Anatolia acted as a shield, saving their co-religionists further south from the impact of the massive crusading forces that had reached as far as the Bosphorus.

The events of 1101 and 1147 were full of tragedy. A large proportion of those who had taken the cross died or were captured and enslaved while they were still hundreds of miles from the shrines that they longed to see. Louis VII's frustration at the loss of most of his army is evident in his hollow boast at Antioch that 'either we'll never return, or we'll come back with the glory of God and of the kingdom of the Franks'.[70] Odo of Deuil commented that 'The flowers of France withered before they could bear fruit in Damascus. In saying this I am overcome by tears, and I groan from the bottom of my heart.'[71] Rhetoric this may have been but it wasn't hyperbole. For some of the survivors the memories proved so depressing that they left no full account of what had happened, seriously impairing our ability to piece events together in detail. As for the first crusaders, who made the journey from their homes to northern Syria successfully, recollections of these preliminary months were probably overlaid by the epic events that occurred at Antioch and Jerusalem. At the time normal life for the ordinary participant must have been composed largely of exhaustion caused by the long marches (between twenty and thirty kilometres – twelve and eighteen miles – a day seems to have been the norm),[72] anxiety about where each day's food and drink would come from, and friction-filled encounters with local communities whose language and customs alike were incomprehensible.

The weeks spent waiting outside the walls of Constantinople, while the crusading leaders negotiated in secret with the Byzantine court, were surely filled with rumour and suspicion; it was all too easy for ordinary fighting men like the author of the *Gesta Francorum* to conclude that his leaders had been hoodwinked by Alexios.[73] The marches across Anatolia were accompanied by the daily fear of attack and harassment, and weren't helped by the fact that at the start the armies had to pass the battlefields where the first wave of crusaders had been slaughtered and their bodies lay unburied.[74] It's possible that following their successes at Nicaea and Dorylaeum the crusaders became buoyed up by a general sense of pride at what was already being achieved, not just on the battlefield but also in terms of conquest. In a letter which he wrote to his lord Manasses, the archbishop of Reims, towards the end of 1097, Anselm of Ribemont boasted that the crusaders had already won 'two hundred cities and fortresses for the Lord'.[75] Anselm was a middle-ranking crusader and the detail in his two letters to Manasses reveals an awareness of strategic issues that enabled him to rise above the quotidian ordeal of survival, including perhaps the idea that what had been done in Anatolia, above all in Cilicia, was of benefit to the Holy Land. Others may not have shared this insight.

Regulating the march east

Crusading leaders made attempts to render the land route workable, benefiting from painful experience. This is evident in the various measures that Louis VII took during his march through western Anatolia. The virtual destruction of Conrad III's army was a warning of the perils in store. To maximize their access to food supplies the French decided to avoid the Anatolian plateau altogether and to hug the Aegean coast. Since they were marching in the late autumn this brought its own problems in the form of heavy rain and swollen rivers, and it didn't save them from Turkish attacks. In the event finding enough food proved to be an additional problem because the walled Greek cities that they passed on the way showed an understandable wariness of the crusaders. 'Already hunger was assailing the horses, which for many days had eaten little grass and no grain; already there was no food for the men, who still had to march for twelve days; and, like a beast which becomes more savage after tasting blood, the enemy harassed us the more boldly after learning of our weakness and the more greedily after profiting thereby.'[76] None the less, the march to Adalia was a comparative success. The Turks were defeated in a battle at the Maeander river, and a confused and bruising encounter near Mount Cadmos didn't become a rout. With the Templars playing a major role, the army was organized into disciplined units that withstood a series of Turkish attacks and managed to reach Adalia enfeebled but intact.

The debate that took place at Adalia was reported in detail by Odo of Deuil and it epitomized the arguments for and against the land and sea routes. Louis was in favour of pressing on to Antioch by land because there was insufficient fodder available for the horses at Adalia. The barons reported a general desire in the army to take ship: 'From the natives they have learned that the journey to Antioch by sea takes three short, well-provisioned, safe days from one port to another and that by land the journey takes forty days in territory blocked by torrents, beset by enemies, and consistent in barrenness.' It was hard to argue with this, though Louis initially responded by proposing that 'the defenceless mob' go by sea while the knights 'follow the route of our fathers' on the First Crusade. But the condition of the surviving horses ruled out such an approach. The decision that was made, that all the crusaders should proceed to Antioch by ship, was in essence a sensible one; the drawback was that since it hadn't been made earlier it placed too great a strain on local resources.[77] It was a curious reversal of the situation that would arise at Venice in 1202, when there were too few passengers and too many ships. It would be unfair to blame the resulting débâcle on Louis. Throughout the winter of 1147–8 the king did his best to hold together a large and very mixed host. He had to contend with his own misguided obsession with replicating the events of the First Crusade and with unhelpful and possibly duplicitous behaviour by the Byzantine authorities. Above all, he was hindered by the fact that the leadership expected from him as king of the French outstripped the authority he could exert in practice over the barons who had come along on the expedition.

Regulation at its height – Barbarossa and the Third Crusade

None of these problems beset Barbarossa when he planned and exercised his leadership of the German army on the Third Crusade. The emperor enjoyed unparalleled experience, prestige and *ex officio* authority;[78] and he was personally familiar with the difficulties that he could expect to encounter. He addressed virtually every major issue that was likely to occur on the march to the East. Provisioning occupied his thoughts as much as military and political planning. He attempted to secure agreements on market procedures and prices with the Hungarians, Byzantines and Seljuqs of Iconium, with whom he hoped to remain at peace. He punished crusaders who plundered the inhabitants of regions which the expedition passed through.[79] The Germans' passage through Hungary in the spring of 1189 was probably the least difficult of all the crusades; the crusaders had nothing to complain about except the exchange rates offered.[80] The situation deteriorated somewhat in Byzantine Bulgaria and Thrace, but this wasn't due to deficient planning on the part of the crusaders. The Byzantine emperor Isaac Angelos was allied to Saladin and did all he could to put obstacles in Barbarossa's path. But Barbarossa refused to allow himself to be diverted from the recovery of Jerusalem,[81] and he adroitly used threats to compel Isaac to allow his troops to cross into Anatolia at Gallipoli. At this point casualties had been relatively light though the army had sustained heavy losses of horses;[82] for all the irritation caused by the Greeks, this stage of the march was characterized as a period of 'great prosperity'.[83]

When compared with what followed it certainly was. Relations with the Seljuqs of Iconium broke down, and in April–May 1190 the army carried out a fighting march on Iconium via Philadelphia. At this point its provisioning system collapsed and the death rate rose as both men and animals suffered as badly from thirst and hunger as earlier armies had done.[84] By mid-May it was largely Barbarossa's willpower that was holding the army together. When the Germans had almost reached Iconium some of the emperor's advisers argued that the city couldn't be taken by these starving and exhausted men; the crusaders should instead make a dash southwards to friendly Armenia. This astounding and suicidal proposal was vetoed by Barbarossa.[85] His judgement was confirmed when the Turks were defeated and their city fell. Barbarossa's good sense and control over his troops were nowhere more evident than in his insistence that they pay fair rates for the animals and provisions that they purchased from Turkish merchants at Iconium. From here the march southwards into Armenian territory went smoothly. According to a letter that the Catholicos of the Armenians sent to Saladin, discipline and an ascetic lifestyle were rigorously maintained. 'They have forbidden themselves pleasures even to the extent that, if they hear that anyone has allowed himself any pleasure, they treat him as an outcast and chastise him. All this is because of grief for Jerusalem.'[86]

Then came Barbarossa's death by drowning in the Saleph river, an event so destructive to German morale that according to Pseudo-Ansbert some crusaders responded by committing suicide while others apostatized.[87] The emperor's death is an insuperable obstacle to our making a fair evaluation of his crusade up to that point. In the year that followed Barbarossa's demise the German army withered away from desertion, plague, shipwreck and deaths in action. This disappointing performance owed something to a loss of direction and morale, but there's every reason to believe that the thousands who perished of disease at Antioch and Acre were weakened by the severe trials of the year that it took them to get from Regensburg to Armenia.[88] In addition, while crusading numbers always pose insuperable problems, it's been estimated that by the time Barbarossa died his force had already shrunk to 40 per cent of its original strength.[89] His soldiers had lost many of their horses and had used much of their wooden equipment and arms for firewood.[90] Muslim contemporaries reckoned that the Germans were no more than 5,000 strong by the time they reached Syria.[91] Overall, it's hard to resist the conclusion that this

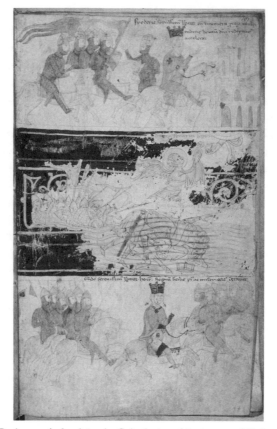

17 Following Barbarossa's death in the Saleph river, his tiny, swaddled soul is carried heaven-enwards by an angel to a waiting God.

extremely well-planned and well-executed venture demonstrated that even in the most favourable circumstances the land route to the Holy Land exacted too severe a toll on the physiques of both people and animals to be viable. What's remarkable is not the terrible ordeals and casualties suffered by all those crusaders who attempted it from 1100 onwards, but the fact that the first crusaders had survived something similar. It's among the most admirable features of their achievement.

'The sons of the crucifiers' – the anti-Jewish pogroms of 1096

Whether they took the decision to reach the East by land or sea, the crusaders left their normal lives behind and entered a world of new experiences; in particular, they encountered ethnic groups whose cultural and religious ways were unfamiliar to them. But the experience of crusading often included an encounter with a radically different religious community whose members lived within the heartlands of Catholic Europe. From the very start crusading was a powerful force in promoting anti-Jewish attitudes and behaviour, and the first crusaders carried out devastating attacks on the settled Jewish communities of the Rhineland towns. The attacks were launched by the initial waves of crusaders, which set out for the Holy Land in the spring of 1096 in advance of the armies led by the princes; but there's every reason to think that the visceral feelings of antagonism that fuelled these assaults were shared by most crusaders. It's misleading to dismiss the attacks either as the product of fanaticism or as a misunderstanding of the 'genuine' crusading message.

The worst violence occurred at Worms, Mainz and Cologne. In May 1096 crusaders led by Emich of Flonheim killed many Jews at Worms, and almost wiped out the Jewish community at Mainz. In June–July the Jews of Cologne, who had dispersed on hearing the news from Worms and Mainz, were hunted down and killed. The assailants didn't explain their behaviour but their motives can be pieced together from other sources. They were trying to augment cash reserves for their journey to the East, and from this point of view their seizure of Jewish belongings can be viewed as a more brutal version of the forced levies that were practised by leaders like Godfrey of Bouillon. But the attacks sprang also from the infection of crusading ideas with the theme of vendetta. This became associated with the concept of Jewish guilt for the crime of their ancestors in calling for Christ's crucifixion. Any emphasis on the cross in Christian thinking was likely to rebound against the Jews.[92] To some crusaders it simply seemed anomalous that they should set out on a long journey to the Holy Land while leaving behind in their home-lands such large numbers of guilty non-believers. As one author had the crusaders proclaim, 'you are the descendants of those who killed our deity and crucified him. Indeed he said: "A day will surely arrive when my children will come and avenge my blood." '[93]

Those who attacked the Jews often gave their victims the choice of baptism or death. This was in plain defiance of the Church's rejection of enforced conversions, which helps explain why some Christian chroniclers of the First Crusade were ambivalent about the 1096 pogroms. Ekkehard of Aura commended them, but Albert of Aachen criticized Emich's crusaders because they 'punished the exiled Jews . . . with a great massacre, rather from greed for their money than for divine justice, since God is a just judge and commands no one to come to the yoke of the Catholic faith against his will or under compulsion'.[94] But most Christian authors ignored the persecutions entirely,

and the fullest and most evocative evidence for them derives from Jewish
sources, especially those often attributed to 'the Mainz Anonymous' and
Solomon ben Simson. They write with astonishing immediacy about the
sudden and unexpected nature of the attacks, and the willingness of the Jews to
embrace martyrdom rather than undergo the hated conversion. The German
Jews were primarily Ashkenazim, and an ironic feature of the pogroms is that
they had assimilated well with the host communities. They even showed some
understanding of the religious goals that lay behind the First Crusade, more
so than the Orthodox Greeks for example, though they naturally had no
sympathy with them.

The zeal with which the Jews died for their faith in 1096 reveals a devotional pattern and a view of the workings of providence that weren't that
different from those of the people who were attacking and killing them. A
remarkable interaction of faiths was at work here; in much the same way, the
arrival of the crusaders in the East stimulated a resurgence of jihad ideology
among the Muslims. In turn the deep veneration with which later Jewish
commentators wrote about their martyrs shows that for Jews the events of
1096 were an affirmation of their people's unique status in God's eyes, a theological vantage point that mirrored what some chroniclers said about the
crusaders who perished. The assimilation that the Jews had achieved meant
that the human losses and accompanying trauma in 1096 didn't constitute a
watershed in the development of German or European Jewry. The attacks
didn't signify rejection of the Jews by the Rhineland's Christians. Some of
their leaders, including the bishop of Speyer and archbishops of Mainz and
Cologne, did all that they could to protect the Jews from the crusaders. As a
result the Jewish communities seem to have revived fairly quickly.[95]

Later crusading violence against the Jews

Yet the massacres of 1096 proved to be far from unique, and all too often the
preaching of fresh crusades brought with it more attacks on the Jews. Some of
the most successful preaching of the Second Crusade in 1146 in the Rhineland
was carried out by a Cistercian monk called Rudolf or Ralph. He was not
authorized to preach and seems to have called for the expedition to be preceded
by the killing of the Jews.[96] St Bernard had to intervene in person to put a stop
to Rudolf's preaching. During the preaching of the Third Crusade there were
attacks on the Jews in England, at Norwich, Stamford, Lincoln, Bury, King's
Lynn and above all York. Some of the motives and ways of thinking that lay
behind the 1096 attacks recurred. Rudolf, for example, was quoted as preaching,
'Avenge the crucified upon his enemies who dwell among you, and subsequently
you shall go forth to battle against the Muslims.'[97] William of Newburgh

18 Knights massacring Jews: for many Jews the best they could expect from crusaders was harassment and robbery, and the worst violent death.

commented on the murder of several Jews at Stamford that 'a multitude of young men from different areas, who had accepted the sign of the Lord and were about to set out for Jerusalem arrived there. They were indignant that the enemies of the cross of Christ who lived there should possess so much, while they themselves had so little for the expenses of so great a journey.'[98]

By this point there were further elements at work. One was a growing tide of resentment of the Jews, reflected in William's remark that none of the inhabitants of Stamford or the people attending the town's fair opposed the attacks, and some joined in.[99] This was countered by the readiness of the authorities to prevent assaults becoming threats to public order, coupled with a determination on the Church's part to prevent both killings and forcible conversions. As St Bernard put it in 1146, 'Is it not a far better triumph for the Church to convince and convert the Jews than to put them all to the sword?'[100] In general this prevented the recurrence of full-scale persecutions like those of 1096. The main reason why the massacre at York happened in 1190 was that the situation was mishandled by the sheriff of Yorkshire and the royal castellan of Clifford's Tower.[101] Less welcome for the Jews was the stream of papal and royal pronouncements shielding indebted crusaders from the demands of their creditors. It was sometimes specifically stated that the latter included Jews, for whom the religious goals that justified such detrimental pronouncements were distasteful or worse. At times, moreover, forced loans or 'gifts' were exacted from the Jews.[102]

It may be argued that the financial needs associated with crusading proved to be advantageous to individual Jews, who managed to circumvent the legal constraints imposed on their profits, but as a group they undoubtedly found it one of the most stressful developments with which they had to live. If the greatest medieval pope could refer to the Jews as 'the sons of the crucifiers, against whom the blood cries to the Father's ears',[103] it was hardly likely that ordinary crusaders would view them benignly. In the mid-thirteenth century crusade preachers were still demonizing the Jews – Gilbert of Tournai drew a particularly vicious comparison in one of his model sermons between the Jews who crucified Christ and archers practising at a target range.[104] In 1251, more than a century and a half after Emich of Flonheim's crusaders appeared outside the walls of Mainz like the angel of death, the Jews of Bourges suffered attacks at the hands of the French *pastoureaux*.[105]

Keeping control during the journey east

Any idea that the 1096 pogroms were outbreaks of hysterical mob violence is dispelled by a reading of Solomon ben Simson. In his account the dominant role of Emich of Flonheim, 'the persecutor of all the Jews', becomes apparent. Emich's fierce animosity was the more dangerous because of the control that he exercised over the crusaders whom he led. It's clear that from the beginning, and this in an army where power rested not on status but on charisma, the medieval genius for improvising methods of control was present. It would be hard to exaggerate the importance of this. Without the imposition and maintenance of order and discipline during the movement of crusading armies eastwards the entire venture would have collapsed, even if all the equipment, supplies, mounts, food, money and shipping required had been successfully put in place. Methods of control were of various kinds, the most overt being the assumption on the part of secular rulers who'd taken the cross that they bore the responsibility to impose order on the armies that they led.

The Geddington ordinances set out by Henry II of England in February 1188, and the measures later drawn up for the fleet, are among the best examples of this approach. The 1188 ordinances tried to give royal backing to the attempts which the papal court had been making since the Second Crusade to bar unruly and licentious behaviour. They weren't just out of place on a pilgrimage, they also encouraged general indiscipline. Swearing, gambling and whoring were key targets. The regulations for the fleet also dealt with swearing, but they included more specific provisions about thieving, murder and other crimes of violence, which the cramped conditions of sea travel both encouraged and made more repercussive. When the French and English armies were at Messina important provisions were also made for the disposition of the goods of those who died. The intention was to assist the impoverished from the possessions of the deceased better-off.

Concern for decent behaviour, restraint of criminal behaviour, basic social security: these were characteristic goals of royal government at the time and their extension to crusading was natural and uncontentious. They represented the importing into crusading's early stages of the close attention to detail that had been so evident during planning and organization.[106] Most crusaders undoubtedly welcomed them. What such measures couldn't do was diminish the mutual suspicion that plagued the English and French armies: the English were shocked when the French stood by during the riots at Messina that led to twenty-five English deaths, 'although they were brothers [*confratres*] in that pilgrimage'.[107]

There is a similar pattern in the measures taken by Barbarossa at much the same time. He attempted to enforce papal injunctions on Christian behaviour, though like Richard I he was prepared to ignore them when it suited him: the English king took his wife on crusade with him and the emperor enjoyed himself hunting and presiding over jousts.[108] At Vienna 500 people judged to be simple hangers-on were sent packing.[109] Criminal behaviour was punished with death, mutilation and public humiliation.[110] But the emperor paid rather more attention than his English and French counterparts to holding his army together, no doubt anticipating the problems that would be caused by his use of the land route. When the army entered Hungary an oath of obedience to the emperor was exacted from everybody. At Nish in Bulgaria the host was divided into four divisions in order to carry out the march more effectively, and at Philippopolis a fifth division was added.[111] As one contemporary commented, 'it was wisely arranged. They did not all march together, nor spread out, but in troops; and although there were many commanding the parts, one governed the whole.'[112] It was also at Philippopolis that Barbarossa took the ambitious step of dividing the entire host into units of fifty, each of which was placed under the jurisdiction of a man whom he appointed. Not surprisingly, this doesn't seem to have worked, and before the army made the crossing into Anatolia a new and highly interesting oath was exacted to the effect that the host would stay together until at least six weeks after it reached Antioch.[113] The disintegration of the German host that occurred after Barbarossa's death demonstrated both the wisdom of this series of measures and the ineluctable fact that they were worthless unless backed up with strong authority of a personal nature.

At other times provisions were put in place as a form of crisis management. The finest example is the French response to the difficulties that threatened to overwhelm Louis VII's army while it was marching southwards through Anatolia in 1147. In the encounter that took place near Mount Cadmos in January 1148 the army's defeat was largely caused by its over-extended lines, and by the vulnerability of the knights to Turkish hit-and-run tactics. The exception was the contingent of Templars led by Evrard of Barres, who were familiar with Turkish ways of fighting. Odo of Deuil wrote that they 'saved their own possessions wisely and alertly and protected those of other people as courageously as possible'. Louis VII was impressed and decreed that 'during this dangerous period all should establish fraternity with the Templars, rich and poor taking an oath that they would not flee the field and that they would obey in every respect the officers assigned them by the Templars'. Each Templar was put in command of fifty knights, and each unit was taught to hold its ground when subjected to Turkish tactics of harassment. The infantry were to be consolidated at the rear of each of the new units and had the job of repelling the Turks with arrows. Only the king himself was exempted from subjection to Templar guidance on the grounds of his status. The new approach was described as a 'pact of mutual aid' between infantry and cavalry, and it succeeded. Faced with a situation not far short of disaster, those nobles who were still mounted took commands from men who were often their social inferiors, while their peers who had lost their mounts accepted the need to fight as infantry.[114]

The Dartmouth ordinances of 1147

Some of the most interesting provisions for the maintenance of order were invented when royal leadership was absent. An excellent example is the set of ordinances instituted by those participants in the Second Crusade who assembled at Dartmouth in 1147. Their geographical origins were diverse, for they comprised men from England, the Low Countries and northern Germany. A priest called Raol, who composed a text celebrating their exploits, opened his account with a description of the 'very strict laws' that they adopted for the maintenance of order during their voyage to the Holy

Land. Once again religious behaviour loomed large. Costly clothing was to be avoided and, in what seems to be a veiled reference to prostitution, women were forbidden to appear in public. While they were at sea each ship should function as a parish, with a priest who was designated to hear weekly confessions and celebrate mass on Sunday. Punishments for crimes were to be severe: 'a life for a life and a tooth for a tooth'. Each infringement of the peace should be investigated by a judge, of whom there should be two chosen for each 1,000 members of the expedition. There was provision for a common chest, the contents of which would be distributed by the judges, and for weekly meetings that would normally be separate for the laity and clergy, though they could assemble as a single group if the situation called for it. And nobody was to hire a seaman or servant who was already in somebody else's service.[115]

The Dartmouth crusaders were relatively egalitarian; indeed it's been suggested that the reason why their remarkable success in helping to capture Lisbon wasn't celebrated more was the fact that the army contained few people of high social standing.[116] When the king of Portugal asked who was in charge they replied that 'such and such were our chief men and that their acts and counsels carried especial weight, but that we had not yet decided on anyone on whom authority should be conferred to make answer for all'.[117] Some of the rulings by which they operated seem to have derived from Eugenius III's bull *Quantum praedecessores*. Consciously or otherwise, others like the common chest followed approaches that had been implemented in the course of the First Crusade. When crusaders from Frisia and Germany again gathered at Dartmouth, exactly seventy years later, they had an easier time of it: they simply chose William count of Holland as their leader, 'under whom laws and new rules were established for keeping the peace'.[118]

Flight from the cross – desertion

Oaths, fraternity, harsh punishments for criminal offences, the regulation of religious and social behaviour, attempts to make basic military and dietary provision for the needs of the most vulnerable: mechanisms like these were all very well, but arguably more important was each crusader's determination to reach the East, and this in turn hinged on his vow.

In some cases votive commitment couldn't stand up to the journey's multiple strains. From the start some people lost heart and fled home. Fulcher of Chartres, who accompanied Baldwin of Boulogne on the First Crusade, recorded desertions occurring remarkably early. When his group was still in Apulia waiting to cross the Adriatic in the winter of 1096–7, 'many of the common people who were left [to their own resources] and who feared privation in the future sold their weapons and again took up their pilgrims' staves, and returned home as cowards'.[119] It looks as if a combination of enforced idleness and second thoughts about the whole venture was operating in this case. When others in the group did manage to cross from Brindisi, in April 1097, one vessel sank with the loss of 400 lives, and this proved too much for some crusaders. 'At the sight of this disaster we were much afraid; so much so that many faint-hearted who had not yet embarked returned to their homes, giving up the pilgrimage and saying that never again would they entrust themselves to the treacherous sea.'[120] The disaster was presumably the last straw for people who'd already become very uneasy about their participation.

After this the First Crusade suffered a constant leaking of its strength through desertions. They grew especially serious once it became engaged in the lengthy operations around Antioch. Remarkably some crusaders deserted during the siege of Jerusalem, though since they carefully carried out the rites of pilgrims who'd discharged their vows it's likely that they regarded the mere sight of the holy city as sufficient to claim fulfilment.[121] Some of these losses were made good by new arrivals, but given the difficulties the crusaders faced it's not surprising that desertion, alongside the failure on the part of some who had taken the cross to set out at all, became something of an obsession among them. In a letter written in October 1097 leading clerics referred to the stay-at-homes as apostates and excommunicates. They must be compelled to come eastwards so that they could join the army by Easter 1098.[122] More or less the same point was made in a letter written the following January;[123] and in a letter to the pope in September 1098 the leaders of the army expressed their astonishment that Urban had given some dispensations to individuals who had taken the cross. 'Those who put off that journey ought to receive neither counsel nor anything good from you until they have fulfilled the journey which they began.'[124]

The treatment of deserters from the First Crusade

It's possible that the dispensations referred to by the princes in this letter may have been the ones that Urban II had given to Spanish crusaders, whom he advised to stay at home to fight the Moors.[125] The Church's usual approach was that the crusading vow must be enforced. Towards the end of 1099 Archbishop Manasses of Reims ordered his bishops 'that you constrain by threat all who vowed to go on the expedition and took the sign of the cross upon themselves to set out for Jerusalem, if they are vigorous of body and have the means to accomplish the journey'.[126] Pope Paschal II was as strict as Manasses, referring specifically to those who had deserted at Antioch: 'We decree that those be held in disgrace who left the siege of Antioch through weak or questionable faith; let them remain in excommunication, unless they affirm with certain pledges that they will return.'[127] Given the severity of the penalties attached to desertion it's hardly surprising that some who fled to the West tried to camouflage their guilt. We have a text that purports to be a letter written home from the leaders of the First Crusade and it's likely that it was actually concocted as a cover story by one deserter.[128] Then there's the curious case of Bruno of Lucca. His exploits at Antioch were trumpeted by the people of Lucca even though Bruno, who went east by sea, spent no more than a few weeks at the siege. This is more than hinted at by the hyperbolic language used – 'he shared in their travail and danger, their triumph and rejoicing, fighting with the fighters, starved with the starving, and conquered with the conquering'.[129] In actual fact he hadn't.

Ecclesiastical sanctions were bolstered by social ones. Unquestionably many knights who deserted were driven to do so by shame at their loss of status because their mounts died and couldn't be replaced. The *Gesta Francorum* memorably describes how during the crossing of the Anti-Taurus range in 1097, the knights 'stood about in a great state of gloom, wringing their hands because they were so frightened and miserable, not knowing what to do with themselves and their armour'.[130] We've already seen shame being used to persuade people to take the cross and set out, and it was often the most effective means of persuading deserters to return to the East, because extended ignominy lay in store for those who were notorious for having fled home. The crusade of 1100–1 included a large number of repentant deserters, including Stephen of Blois, Hugh of Vermandois, Hugh and Norgeot of Toucy and Simon and William Sansavoir of Poissy.[131] Guibert of Nogent regarded the subsequent deaths of Stephen of Blois and Hugh of Vermandois as martyrdoms, though he also leant over backwards to exculpate them from the charge of desertion; indeed Guibert, ever adroit at twisting arguments to suit his purpose, went so far as to assert that their overall behaviour on the First Crusade was superior to that of many who boasted of reaching Jerusalem.[132] Others who took the cross in 1100, such as Miles of Bray and Guy of Rochefort, may have set out on the expedition to expunge from the family name the dishonour caused by the earlier desertion of a kinsman.[133]

Sources like the crusaders' letters home, the decrees of Pope Paschal II and Guibert of Nogent's rather strained apologia for his fellow (and well-connected) Frenchmen indicate that desertion was a significant factor on the First Crusade. Evidence for its impact on later expeditions is scantier. This could simply be because our sources are never again as abundant as they are for the First Crusade. But it's also possible that vows were enforced more rigorously, or that the measures gradually put in place to secure cohesion, order and welfare did their job in checking the hopelessness and loss of face that so often proved to be triggers in making people flee. In all probability the general movement towards travel by sea reduced the opportunities for flight, at least on the part of the majority; individuals with enough cash could usually locate a suitable ship.

Desertion and seaborne crusades

But sea travel also helped to make the whole question of desertion more complex. For those who took part in the Fourth and Fifth Crusades in particular, the issue of desertion became tangled up with the nature of the actual enterprise. Geoffrey of Villehardouin was frank in stating his opinion that those groups that declined to go along with the series of diversions that moulded the fate of the Fourth Crusade were defectors. The problem began with the failure of some to embark at Venice. When the crusade's future was being debated at Zadar, Villehardouin's party argued that those who had adopted this approach had 'deserted us'.[134] The same applied to Simon of Montfort and others who seceded at Zadar. 'Such defections were a great misfortune for the army,' Villehardouin commented, 'and a great disgrace to those who left it.'[135] In the marshal's eyes keeping the army at full strength was the supreme good, the only means of achieving the crusade's goal of saving the Holy Land and hence of discharging their vows. So the delegation charged with convincing more would-be seceders to change their mind on Corfu was directed to plead that they 'not disgrace themselves nor deprive us of the chance of delivering the land oversea'.[136] Concepts of honour; fear of shame; the use of oaths and compacts: these crucial values and mechanisms played the same role on the Fourth Crusade that they had on earlier expeditions, but their effect in this instance was not to sustain the crusade on the intended course of action but to steer it in a fundamentally different direction.

On the Fifth Crusade the major problem wasn't desertion but premature departure. It may seem that the two were synonymous but there was actually a difference, because strategic change brought with it the fundamental problem of judging whether or not a crusader's vow had been fulfilled. *Quia maior*, the bull of 1213 in which Innocent III proclaimed the crusade, was incomparably rich in both theology and rhetoric, but it contained no military objective aside from the recapture of Mount Tabor. Although attempted in December 1217, this was abandoned as impracticable, and most of those who took the cross instead fought in the Nile delta, where operations stretched from May 1218 to August 1221. The experience of the first crusaders, of constant desertions made good by fresh arrivals, thus became institutionalized in a pattern dictated by the Mediterranean sailing seasons, above all their spring and autumn passages. Oliver of Paderborn described eight such passages.[137] The crusade's leaders fought for an average of fifteen months each,[138] but some participants stayed at the front for no longer than the few months that separated the spring and autumn passages.

Oliver of Paderborn commented of one departure for the West that 'the sailors, who were betrayers of Christianity, and with them very many pilgrims whose love of themselves was greater than their compassion for their brethren, before the time of the accustomed passage, left the soldiers of Christ in the greatest danger; hoisting their sails and leaving port, they afforded dejection to us and courage to the Babylonians'.[139] James of Vitry, an eyewitness with strong views about the nature of crusading, expressed his opinion about how much service was required in letters that he wrote during the campaign. In September 1218 he complained bitterly about 'the many weak and fickle people who left the Lord's army with their vow unfulfilled'. Like deserters from the First Crusade, they tried to disguise their guilt by spreading lies about the progress of the campaign in Egypt.[140] But a year later James referred to crusaders leaving once their year's service was done. He implied that this was their right but commented that it caused anxiety and ill-will among their comrades-in-arms who were sticking it out.[141]

Even if a year's service was adhered to by the majority, the discontinuity that it entailed proved to be one of the crusade's biggest problems. The gravity of the situation was reflected in the promise made by the legate Pelagius in April 1219 that the crusade indulgence would be enjoyed by the close kin of anybody who stayed until the autumn passage rather than returning with the imminent spring one.[142] This was truly splitting hairs. It's noteworthy that if a crusader stayed for the whole duration of the Egyptian campaign he would still have served for no longer than a first crusader, and without the gruelling overland march that the first crusaders went through at the start. Innocent III pragmatically halved the period of service that he expected of crusaders from two years to one because his initial proclamation of the Fourth Crusade in 1198 met with little response.[143] It seems that once crusaders started going east by ship they expected their overall period of service to be reasonably short; most of Louis IX's crusaders left France in the summer of 1248 and returned home two years later.

Mobilizing Christendom – the military defects of crusading

Desertion is a military concept, so any reflection on the subject draws attention to the inherently clumsy character of Urban II's synthesis of holy war and pilgrimage. Starting with the simple fact that nobody could be made to take the cross, crusading contained a number of idiosyncratic features that presented Christendom's authorities, ecclesiastical and lay, with daunting problems of management and control. Some they succeeded in solving or containing, but others proved intractable. A crusading appeal that worked could raise many thousands of willing recruits, but in almost every other respect it was a remarkably inefficient way of providing for the defence of the Holy Land. The permanent service of the military orders was much better suited to the situation, as was the provision of groups of paid troops who represented an ongoing commitment by the West. The second approach was advocated by a number of commentators in the thirteenth century and it was implemented to some an extent in the shape of the paid troops who were kept at Acre from 1254 onwards by the French crown.[144]

Payment was a reasonably secure guarantee of service. The appeal for military assistance that Alexios Komnenos sent to Urban II in 1094, which may have acted as the catalyst for the First Crusade, was almost certainly couched in terms of such paid service. Two centuries later crusading strategists like the Venetian Marino Sanudo Torsello argued that mercenaries ought to form the cutting edge of a new crusade. The wheel had come full circle. In the meantime countless thousands had saved their souls, or so the apologists for crusading argued, through the practice of armed pilgrimage.[145] But the Holy Land had been lost. And the root cause of its loss was encapsulated in the series of telling arguments that Baha' al-Din put into the mouth of his lord Saladin during the sultan's negotiations with Richard I's messenger early in August 1191:

> [The king's] wintering in these lands cannot be avoided, because he has become master of them. [But] he knows that when he goes away, they will necessarily be seized, and the same if he stays, God willing. If it is easy for him to winter here and to be far from his family and homeland, two months' travelling time away, when he is a young man in the flower of his youth and at a time when he seeks his pleasures, how easy is it for me to spend a winter, a summer, then a winter and another summer in the middle of my own lands, surrounded by my sons and my family, when whatever and whoever I want can come to me?[146]

It's hard to imagine a more realistic appraisal of the shortcomings of crusading as a military device.[147]

❖

5

CRUSADING WARFARE

Turkish conquests in the Middle East

'A grave report has come from the lands around Jerusalem and from the city of Constantinople . . . that a people from the kingdom of the Persians, a foreign race, a race absolutely alien to God . . . has invaded the land of those Christians, has reduced the people with sword, rapine and flame and has carried off some as captives to its own land.'[1] The 'foreign race' that Robert of Reims was referring to in his version of Urban II's Clermont sermon was the Turks. They were a nomadic people who actually originated in Central Asia, not Persia, though in 1095 the centre of power of the dominant Turkish clan, the Seljuqs, did indeed lie in Iran. The arrival of the Turks in the Middle East in the early eleventh century transformed the region's balance of power. For several generations there had been three contenders for control over the lands of the Fertile Crescent. Only one of them was Christian: this was the Byzantine empire, which held Anatolia and northern Syria. The other two contenders, Buyid Persia and Fatimid Egypt, were Islamic, both of them Shi'a, though the former maintained the Abbasid caliphate, which claimed to be the seat of Sunni authority. Coming from the East, the Turks' initial impact was on the Buyids, from whom they seized Baghdad in 1055. But they quickly moved against both the Byzantines and the Fatimids. At Manzikert in 1071 the Turks destroyed a Byzantine army, opening the way for their occupation of much of the Anatolian plateau. The Turks were Sunni so they were welcomed by the caliph at Baghdad, who bestowed on Tughrul Beg the title of sultan and sanctioned attacks on the Fatimid lands on the grounds that the regime there was heretical. Turkish forces seized Jerusalem from the Fatimids in 1073 and Damascus in 1076.

Within just forty years of their defeat of the Buyids, the Turks had come to be seen as a threat to both Constantinople and the Nile delta. This was a remarkable geographical stretch and it's not hard to appreciate the sense of crisis that pervades passages like the one quoted above. But to some extent Turkish victories were illusory. Many of their advances were handled not by organized armies but by war bands that were subject in only a nominal sense to the control of the sultan at far-off Baghdad. For the most part they acted independently of the sultan or hired out their services to third parties. This would be the case as late as 1244, when Jerusalem fell to the Khorezmian Turks. It was war bands like these that were making life difficult for the Byzantines in the 1060s. For reasons of internal politics at Constantinople Romanos IV Diogenes misman-aged his response. By fielding a massive army he pushed the sultan Alp Arslan into campaigning against him, and Romanos's defeat at Manzikert turned a war of attrition into one of conquest. Even 'conquest' is an inappropriate term since the Turks were pastoralists and their occupation of Anatolia in the years between Manzikert and the arrival of the crusaders was a superficial one.

When individual Turks established control over cities, whether in Syria, Lebanon or Palestine, they were in practice acting independently. It took the threat of conquest by the first crusaders to make them appeal to the sultan in Baghdad, and even then the mobilization of an armed response took a long time. So while the upheaval caused by the Turks acted as the catalyst for the unleashing of a holy war in 1095, their *modus operandi* played a crucial role in enabling the First Crusade to succeed. For the crusaders arrived in a region where power was intensely fragmented and localized. The Turks based in Anatolia had broken away from Baghdad, while from Antioch southwards it was possible to play one emir off against another, as well as making use of the fundamental antagonism between Sunni Seljuqs and Shi'a Fatimids. In addi-tion to this, the crusaders enjoyed a specific though coincidental advantage: in the years just before their arrival there was a wipe-out of almost the entire upper echelon of the Middle East's Islamic hierarchy. The Seljuq vizier Nizam al-Mulk and the sultan Malikshah both died in 1092, and the Fatimid caliph al-Mustansir, his vizier Badr al-Jamali and the Abbasid Sunni caliph, al-Muqtadi, followed in 1094. Add to this the fact that the Byzantine emperor Alexios I was at the height of his power when the First Crusade was preached, and circumstances could hardly have been more favourable for the expedition. No later crusade would enjoy such advantages.[2]

Turkish tactics

But when all the caveats are registered, the fact remains that in the decades before 1095 the Turks had managed to defeat every enemy they encountered, and the first crusaders knew it. They also had a fair idea of how it had been done. 'What man, however experienced and learned, would dare to write of the skill and prowess and courage of the Turks, who thought that they would strike terror into the Franks, as they had done into the Arabs and Saracens, Armenians, Syrians and Greeks, by the menace of their arrows?'[3] The Turks were renowned for their mastery of horseback archery. A Turk would charge an opponent, wheel his horse around when virtually at the point of impact, and fire with accuracy at his disoriented opponent from the saddle while retreating. At the origins of the Turkish rise to power in the ninth century al-Jahiz commented that 'if a thousand Turkish horsemen charge and discharge a thousand arrows all at once, they prostrate a thousand men; and there is no other army that can charge as well . . . Their arrows hit the mark as much when they are retreating as when they are advancing.'[4]

Tactically, this skill was best harnessed in small units that worked in rotas to confuse and demoralize the enemy, maddening him into pursuing the retreating archers. In doing so he'd lose formation and make himself vulnerable to piece-meal annihilation. The mobility that these tactics bestowed on the Turks made it very difficult to engage them *en masse* and inflict a defeat on them.[5] The contemporary description of Manzikert given by Nikephoros Bryennios is almost a textbook example of such tactics at work.[6] They remained essentially the same two centuries later, when Fidenzio of Padua wrote that 'the Saracens retreat and scatter; they rush, some here, others there. Afterwards, at the sound of a trumpet . . . they are reunited and they attack the Christians, striking the men and their horses with many arrows and killing them.'[7] A more lyrical depiction was given by the poet Ambroise in relation to the Third Crusade (in particular, note the analogies with swallows and gadflies) –

When to pursue them one essays
Their steeds unrivalled like a swallow
Seem to take flight, and none can follow.
The Turks are so skilled to elude
Their foemen when they are pursued
That they are like a venomous
And irksome gadfly unto us.
Pursue him, he will take to flight
Return, and he renews his spite.[8]

Muslim and Christian sources alike show that the Turks were aware of the advantage to be gained from positioning their army in such a way that the sun shone and the wind blew into the enemy's eyes. They also used shouting and loud musical instruments to alarm and demoralize him. As Ambroise put it, 'So loud their tabors did discord, / They had drowned the thunder of the Lord.'[9] It's not hard to see how easily confusion could lead to panic, and panic to miscalculation and defeat.

The crusaders were unfamiliar with this way of fighting, but it was never entirely unexpected. At the crusaders' first big encounter with the Turks,

Dorylaeum in July 1097, they owed their victory largely to good fortune. The bulk of the army was marching some five kilometres (three miles) behind its vanguard and was able to relieve its comrades when they were attacked. The Turks were taken by surprise by the arrival of the relief force and lost a lot of men during the flight that ensued. But the response to the Turkish attack on the part of those in the vanguard shows that they had a fair idea of what to expect, because they managed to defend themselves reasonably well during several hours of hard fighting. Their knowledge came partly from the Byzantines, and partly from an armed clash that they'd had with the Turks during the siege of Nicaea a few weeks previously. None the less, Dorylaeum was an invaluable schooling in what they had to face, and it's possible to observe Bohemund of Taranto in particular applying what he'd learnt during a series of battles around Antioch.[10]

On later expeditions crusading commanders had the experience of their predecessors to draw on, to which they added advice from the settlers and the officers of the military orders. One chronicler of the Fifth Crusade believed that only the presence of John of Brienne and the brethren of the military orders saved the army from total destruction when it fell victim to a Turkish ambush in 1219.[11] Another author gave a precise description of the way Peter of Brittany's crusaders in 1239 penned the opposing Turks 'into a narrow place where they could not ride to and fro to shoot or fight. They had to give up their usual spurring technique and fight with swords and maces, which was not nearly so easy for them.'[12] It's hardly likely that such tactics were impro- vised by Peter, given that he'd only been in the East for a few weeks. So the crusaders were never acting in the dark tactically.

But however familiar the crusaders became with Turkish mobility, it never ceased to pose extraordinary challenges to them. The Christians' preferred method of combat was man-to-man exchanges, initiated by cavalry charges that for best effect had to be delivered against a static defensive formation.[13] The military techniques used by the Fatimids were rather closer to the Frankish model, but the renown enjoyed by Turkish military prowess was so great that Turks were increasingly hired by the Fatimids during the twelfth century; and they naturally became the cutting edge of Egypt's army after Nur ed-Din conquered Egypt in 1171. The Ayyubids, like the Fatimids and Seljuqs before them, made some use of infantry, but the role that they played is hard to reconstruct, such were the élan, reputation and cultural hegemony of the Turkish cavalry.[14]

Non-combatant roles in crusading armies

The need to put into place an effective response to Turkish tactics was one of two features of crusading warfare that marked it out as different from what

19 Women help to besiege a medieval tower. It was unusual for female crusaders to take part in military action in this way.

the Christians were used to in the West. The other one was the heterogeneous character of most crusading forces. So far in this book the word 'army' has been used interchangeably with its medieval equivalent, 'host', to designate the groups that made their way to the East. The rationale for using such words is the fact that a goal of every crusade was the military recovery or defence of land. But, as we've already seen, the armies always contained large numbers of individuals who went as pilgrims. The closest contemporary parallel would be refugees who are shielded during their flight from danger by professional soldiers (for example, UN peacekeepers), the radical difference being that in the case of crusading these people were moving into a danger zone rather than escaping from one.

Such people fell into several different groups. To begin with, there were able-bodied women. There are instances of women who took up arms on crusades but they're comparatively few, and the sources testifying to some of them are Muslim ones, in which an element of fantasy and/or of vituperation can't be discounted.[15] More significant were women whose wealth enabled them to lead fighters to the East; interestingly, their contribution was welcomed by the Church.[16]

Secondly, there were churchmen. Medieval bishops were militarized, above all German ones. In November 1189 Barbarossa left the Greek town of Philippopolis in the custody of five of his bishops,[17] and no fewer than twelve German bishops and archbishops enlisted in Henry VI's crusade in 1195–6.[18]

Out of habit or a sense of duty some of these crusading clerics couldn't refrain from commanding their vassals in battle. Far from being frowned on, this was sometimes singled out for praise. During the Third Crusade, for example, 'The clergy claimed no small share of military glory. Fighting faithfully for the Faith, abbots and bishops led out their cohorts and joyfully contended for God's Law.'[19] Writing to the pope in 1204 to report the capture of Constantinople, Baldwin of Flanders emphasized the role that had been played by the bishops of Soissons and Troyes: 'The banners of the bishops are the first to gain the walls, and the first victory is granted by heaven to ministers of the heavenly mysteries.'[20] We know that this letter was composed with exceptional care because of the need to win the pope over, yet there's no sense of incongruity in the passage quoted.

Bishops were expected to be versatile. At the siege of Acre in 1190 the archbishop of Besançon 'prayed for the faithful with the heart of a dove but fought the wicked with the cunning of a serpent'.[21] But even the medieval Church recognized that there were limits. Clerical leadership in battle had to stop short of shedding blood, which was forbidden by canon law. The line was drawn by rule of thumb. The bishop of Acre incurred censure for carrying the True Cross at Hattin, which led to his death, but this could well have been because all the commentators on Hattin were on the lookout for individuals and groups who could be blamed for the disaster.[22] When the archbishop of Rouen deserted the Third Crusade on the ground that 'the shepherds of the Church should preach rather than fight', Richard of Devizes dismissed it as a flimsy excuse for cowardice.[23]

Women and clerics alike played highly regarded non-combatant roles on the battlefield and in its vicinity. Female crusaders exercised an important auxiliary job in caring for the wounded, bringing water and food to combat personnel, and encouraging those who were engaged in the fighting.[24] Clerics could play similar parts, notably at the siege of Acre during the Third Crusade. 'There was a stonethrower which had been constructed at general expense, which they called "God's Stonethrower". A priest, a man of great probity, always stood next to it preaching and collecting money for its continual repair and for hiring people to gather the stones for its ammunition.'[25] More importantly, clerics were regarded as a 'spiritual army' (*militia spiritualis*) whose support for the combatants through strenuous intercession was just as significant in bringing victory as the fighters' physical efforts. In his description of one encounter during the Fifth Crusade, Oliver of Paderborn linked the two groups: 'The women fearlessly brought water and stones, wine and bread to the warriors; the priests persisted in prayer, binding up and blessing the wounds of the injured.'[26]

The real headache was the third group of non-combatants, which was much more miscellaneous in character. It was made up of children, the old and the infirm, to whom we should add those individuals who became so demoralized and worn down by hunger and stress that in practice they couldn't be relied on in combat. Fulcher of Chartres described the majority of the crusaders at the battle of Dorylaeum in 1097 as 'huddled together like sheep in a fold, trembling and frightened'.[27] It was a good analogy. Two of the anecdotes told by Baha' al-Din to illustrate Saladin's generous nature refer to members of this eclectic group who were captured in the Holy Land in 1191. In one story the sultan returned to its mother a child just three months old who'd been captured in a raid on the Christian tents outside Acre.[28] In the second Saladin freed 'an old man, very advanced in years, without a tooth left in his head and with only just enough strength to move'. Obviously this was no potential combatant, and when the puzzled Saladin asked why he had journeyed so far from home he claimed (though of course it was in his interests to do so) that he'd only come east as a pilgrim to the Holy Sepulchre.[29] Given the circumstances it would have been better for all concerned if he'd stayed at home, like the elderly Welshman Cador who bartered cannily for the full indulgence with Archbishop Baldwin of Canterbury in 1188.[30]

It wasn't always possible to defend people like this from the enemy. During his encounter with the Turks on 14 May 1190 Barbarossa did his best to shield 'the non-belligerent masses' with crossbowmen and archers,[31] but in the crucial battle fought outside Iconium four days later the emperor's shortage of able-bodied fighters meant that he could offer no protection to the clerics, incapacitated combatants, non-combatants and baggage train.[32]

The Church and non-combatants

Because it was no secret that the aged, sick and desperate, the 'lower sort' or 'poor' of the *Gesta Francorum*,[33] were a hindrance in any combat situation, a variety of attempts were made to bar them from going at all. These ranged from Pope Paschal II's willingness to dispense the vows of poor crusaders in 1099[34] to Odo of Deuil's condemnation of the 'weak and helpless' on the Second Crusade, who should have been left at home.[35] But for some the situation wasn't so straightforward. Even the snobbish Guibert of Nogent thought that 'in our time God invented holy wars' as a way of earning salvation for the 'wandering mob' as well as 'the order of knights'.[36] The papal legate on the First Crusade, Adhemar of Le Puy, did his best to expound a way of looking at the crusade's operations that gave Guibert's 'wandering mob' a role as a 'third estate' alongside the knights (who fought) and the clergy (who preached): 'he used to keep the clergy in order and preach to the knights, warning them and saying, "none of you can be saved if he does not respect the poor and succour them; you cannot be saved without them, and they cannot survive without you" '.[37] During the Fifth Crusade there was an echo of Adhemar's outlook in the special provision that was made for 'the common people, unarmed', to accompany the army when it set out to fight the Muslims, even though they could easily have been left behind at Damietta.[38] On the other hand, when a large contingent of crusaders turned up from Acre in the autumn passage of 1220, the leaders siphoned off those who were obviously poor and allowed them to go home.[39]

Clearly there were different views about the value of such people, and the clash of opinions was irresolvable because its roots lay in the dual nature of crusade as both pilgrimage and war. A rational reformer like Ralph Niger might argue for selectivity,[40] but his contemporary Peter of Blois believed that the inexcusable delays of the well-off in setting out on the Third Crusade showed that the job of recovering Jerusalem belonged to the poor. Practical issues Peter airily dismissed, 'who embraces Christ lacks for nothing'.[41] Odo of Châteauroux was an active crusader who knew from personal experience the problems that were caused by poor crusaders both in the East and, in the form of the *pastoureaux*, at home in France. But this didn't cause him to adopt Odo of Deuil's dismissive stance; instead he advanced an Adhemar-like argument that the poor served the crusade by encouraging the better-off to take action. In what looks like a reference to the leverage that had been exerted by the poor crusaders in 1099, Odo of Châteauroux called to mind the go-it-alone attack on the Philistines by Saul's son Jonathan in 1 Kings ch. 14.[42]

Odo of Châteauroux argued that while nobles were indispensable in the provision of leadership, the help of all the faithful was needed if the Holy Land was to be saved from its attackers.[43] In this he echoed the approach of the canon lawyers, who maintained that a distinction should be made between those who took the cross in order to defend the Holy Land and those who went as pilgrims. It wasn't a question of excluding the second group completely, but of deciding whether they possessed the physical capacity and resources to carry out their devotional exercise without becoming a burden to the combatants. But what the lawyers couldn't legislate for was those pilgrims who started off both physically healthy and well resourced, only to be afflicted in the course of the crusade by the twin spectres of *debilitas* (weakness) and *inopia* (poverty).[44] For this reason it's wrong to deduce that crusading armies became 'leaner and fitter' as they progressed, because the weak were culled by privation and disease: the ranks of the enfeebled were all too easily replenished.

Combat roles of the knights

Combatant crusaders fell into one of two categories according to their military function. The first were the elite fighting men, the knights. It's significant that, for all his strength of feeling about the poor, Odo of Châteauroux still placed

20 A crusader at Damietta fells his opponent with couched lance.

emphasis on recruiting knights.[45] It would have been odd if he hadn't. This was the group whose participation every pope hoped for when launching a crusade from Clermont onwards, which was why so much of the crusading message was tailored to the mental world that knights inhabited. From the late twelfth century onwards knights fought alongside mounted sergeants, who possessed most of the equipment and skills of knights but lacked their social status. Knights were trained for combat, on foot or on horse. They brought their armour with them as well as their chargers; so when observers compared the forces arriving at Acre for the Fifth Crusade in 1217 with those that had besieged the port twenty-seven years previously, the yardsticks were arms, horses and fighting men.[46] Knights were disciplined and used to fighting either as individuals or as members of units. In the latter mode, using the lance, they could deliver a shock charge which impressed the Muslims as much as the horseback archery of the Turks impressed the Franks. They were used to exertion, danger and injury, so it's testimony to the stress involved in crusading that at times even the knights' nerves snapped. One revealing example occurred early in 1098 when the Provençal knights started refusing to act as escorts to foraging expeditions at Antioch;[47] and a second exactly fifty years later when the French barons on the Second Crusade, undoubtedly speaking for the knights generally, defied their own king by refusing to continue marching towards Antioch.[48]

Common to both occasions was the crippling loss of horses. This demoralized the knights because it reduced them to the status of common soldiers, not just for a specific military operation like a siege but on a long-term basis. It also put limits on their ability to gather booty and make prisoners, and it threatened their capacity to retain their armour, because for this they needed pack animals during the long marches. One of the most extraordinary military features of the First Crusade is the steadily declining number of cavalry that were available. The sources give us specific and convincing figures, and they're astonishingly low: fewer than 1,000 mounts by late 1097 (shortly before the foraging incident mentioned above), and 100–200 by the following June. Knights were reduced to riding on donkeys or mules and the chance of securing a horse was not to be missed under any circumstances.[49]

Naturally it was the overland trek that was chiefly responsible for such a situation. So it recurred on the Second Crusade and during Barbarossa's march on the Third: an eyewitness in Barbarossa's army claimed that when the Germans beat the Turks at Iconium they had no more than 500 mounted troops.[50] But all campaigns took their toll. Equine casualties were reported as heavy during the siege of Acre in 1190, and during the Fifth Crusade losses of mounts sustained during the early stage of the fighting couldn't be made good.[51] Armour could be patched up and munitions replaced from local sources, but heavy chargers had to be reared and trained. The Turks wore armour so their horses were hardly ponies, but they were lighter animals than the crusaders were used to riding. It was in this respect that fighting so far from the homeland had its most damaging effect on the crusaders' military capability. Their opponents became well aware of their Achilles' heel. Following the battle of Arsuf in 1191 the Bedouin did a count of the crusaders' dead horses and reached a total of over 100.[52]

Knights were first and foremost a vocational group, and there were big differences of wealth and social status within their ranks. This is exemplified by the accounts of the Fourth Crusade written by Geoffrey of Villehardouin and Robert of Clari. Geoffrey was the marshal of Champagne and one of the expedition's leaders, whereas Robert was an ordinary knight from Picardy. So whereas Geoffrey gives his readers a clear impression of the cut and thrust of debate about what the crusaders should do, Robert's version is vaguer and less well informed. But Robert compensates by providing many insights into the resentment which 'poor knights' felt about the way their social betters feathered their own nests. After the crusaders had conquered Constantinople 'the high men, the rich men, came together and agreed among themselves to take the best houses of the city, without the common people or the poor knights of the host knowing anything about it. And from that time on they began to betray the common people and to keep bad faith and bad comradeship with them, for which they paid very dearly later, as we shall tell you.'[53] It's a passage full of social envy.

The quest for glory – chivalry and crusading

On the other hand, knights did share a group code, that of chivalry. On crusade this expressed itself above all in the value that they placed on individual prowess and achievement. In terms of military efficiency it had both strengths and weaknesses. On the plus side, it created an atmosphere not unlike that of the modern Olympics, generating camaraderie but making the knights compete one with another in the quest to excel. Crusading was a test of chivalric prowess as well as faith: as Thibald of Champagne put it in 1239, 'Now the valiant knights will go forth, those who love God and the honour of this world, and who rightly wish to go to God; and the snivelling, the cowardly, will remain behind.'[54] Commanders were expected to set an example, so when Frederick of Swabia was wounded by the Turks in 1190 his father Barbarossa told him that the scar would be lasting proof that he had fought for God; Frederick would reap God's reward and men's praise.[55]

The downside of chivalry was that the incessant and implicitly competitive search for glory could produce acts of astonishing rashness. Richard I was obsessed with glory. He speeded up his departure from Famagusta for Acre in 1191 when he heard that the port was on the verge of falling: 'God forbid that Acre should be won in my absence, for it has been besieged for so long, and the triumph – God willing – will be so glorious.'[56] Commanders like Richard were capable of putting reputation before good sense. He couldn't be dissuaded from placing his life in danger near Jaffa in November 1191 when some of his troops were ambushed: 'When I have requested my beloved companions to go ahead to battle on the solemn promise that aid would follow, if I fail to do as I said . . . so that they meet their deaths . . . then may I never again usurp the name of king.'[57] Richard got away with it, but the most notorious example of such boldness was disastrous. In 1250 Louis IX's brother, Robert of Artois, was commanding the French vanguard during the crossing of the Nile tributary called the Bahr as-Saghir. Exultant at his success over the enemy, Robert ignored the warning of the master of the Templars and pursued the fleeing Muslims into the narrow streets of the fortified town of Mansurah. Here he and his troops were easily cut down by troops from the elite Bahriyah regiment.

The trouble was that Robert's miscalculation at Mansurah was far from exceptional. When Gautier of Autrèche embarked on a single-handed charge into the Turkish ranks outside Damietta, which cost him his life, Louis IX ruefully commented that he couldn't afford a thousand Gautiers.[58] Much more serious in its consequences than Gautier's suicidal charge was an encounter that occurred ten years previously when Henry count of Bar was fighting in Palestine. Jealous of the booty won by Peter of Dreux, the count of Brittany, Henry and a cluster of other baronial leaders carried out a raid south of Jaffa that had no strategic purpose. This involved ignoring not just the advice of the masters of all the military orders, but the orders of the crusade's designated commander, Thibald of Champagne. Surprised by the Muslims while dining, the crusaders were then lured to death and captivity by a feigned retreat.[59] The whole disaster was a textbook example of knightly folly and one contemporary couldn't contain his scorn: 'Such was their pride and their arrogance that they felt little or no concern about their enemies, into whose land they had thrust so far forward and who were very near them. Then they learned indeed that Our Lord will not be served in this way.'[60]

'So eager in your arrogance / to show off all your strength / pig-headed, stupid, brave, you rode / outstripping all support. / Now Turkish masters hold you fast / and Mary's son must mourn. / Great will the grief and sorrow be / if God loose not your bonds.'[61] This popular song coined in the aftermath of the Jaffa raid indicates that the public reaction to it may have been particularly vehement. It's tempting to interpret the behaviour of Robert of Artois in 1250 and Henry of Bar in 1239 as examples of the intrusion into thirteenth-century crusading of chivalric pride, a familiar and recurrent *topos* in the period's literature. It's certainly ironic that Robert's proposal to take part in his brother's crusade had been singled out for praise in a song written to celebrate Louis' assumption of the cross.[62] The fact remains, however, that similar examples can be found without difficulty almost at the very start of crusading, in the 1101 expedition. No great effort of the imagination is needed to conceive of Duke William of Aquitaine, one of the leaders in 1101, initiating a raid just like Henry of Bar's. Commentators on William's expedition rebuked its participants for their pride, levity and lax behaviour. It became fashionable to contrast behaviour in 1096–9 with that in 1101, but in reality it's unlikely that the differences were that great.[63]

Attempts to tame chivalry

At least as early as the Second Crusade the Church began to regard piety not just as appropriate to penitential pilgrims, but also as conducive towards military efficiency. It tried to exclude from crusading many of the more extrovert features of knightly behaviour. In this it was unsuccessful. Like the rest of the laity, knights were perfectly capable of creating their own interpretation of what crusading entailed. If they confessed before battle, they also bolstered their morale by 'joyously' singing their own war songs (*cantus militares*).[64] To some extent the Church implicitly accepted this; it had after all dressed its own call to crusade in a rhetoric of honour and shame that was familiar to the nobility. It could hardly expect such values not to resonate throughout their crusading activity in the East. For example, a song that aimed to persuade the French

21 Christian chivalry in the eyes of the Church, combining military and religious strengths.

nobility to remain with Louis IX in the Holy Land in 1250 dwelt not on military matters but on shame, vengeance and the recovery of honour.[65] It was the fear of 'disgrace, shame and eternal reproach' that drove Henry of Bar to try to emulate Peter of Brittany's successful raid eleven years earlier.[66] And when the commander of the Temple attempted to dissuade Robert of Artois from rashly continuing his advance in 1250, he used the argument that the count had *already* 'achieved one of the finest acts of courage and chivalry seen for a long time in the Holy Land' – in other words, that when the situation was viewed from the right perspective, the demands of honour and prudence weren't at odds.[67]

There's no denying that at times there was a lack of realism in the Church's stance, an apparent conviction that instead of consistently working with the grain of aristocratic values and instincts, it could try to separate out wheat from what it regarded as chaff. This was a translation into the sphere of military behaviour of the famous distinction that St Bernard made between *militia* (being knightly) and *malitia* (being wicked). It was misguided; the exceptional courage, resilience and initiative that were displayed on numerous occasions by knights while on crusade couldn't be dissociated from their desire to exhibit their skills and win the praise of their peers and renown in posterity. Richard I was a great commander, yet at the battle of Jaffa in August 1191 he rode the entire length of the Christian line, in effect daring the Muslims to attack him.[68] Such behaviour was on a par with that of Robert of Artois at Mansurah, and if the king had been killed history would judge him as harshly as it has Robert. As it turned out, however, Richard's bravado helped to demoralize the enemy and he imposed a humiliating setback on Saladin. Rashness was audacity's unlucky brother. This was Richard's way of fighting: 'in every engagement he ... rejoiced to be first to attack and last to retire after it was over. For who can completely renounce their own nature, even under pressure?'[69] Who indeed?

Combat roles of the infantry

The second group of combatants comprised the footsoldiers. These were men who habitually fought on foot as opposed to doing so only when the occasion called for it. Medieval infantry used to be viewed as little more than pre-cannon fodder for the knights, but in recent years they've come to be seen as a vital element in warfare.[70] And it's likely that in the East their importance was greater than in Europe, because the most effective response to Turkish tactics was to integrate the battlefield activity of infantry and cavalry. The infantry, especially archers and crossbowmen, were expected to form a protective shield for the knights until the best moment had come for the cavalry to engage with the enemy.[71] The basic technique was noted by the observant eyewitness Baha' al-Din at the battle of Arsuf in 1191: 'their cavalry massed together and agreed on a charge, as they feared for their people and thought that only a charge would save them. I saw them grouped together in the middle of the footsoldiers. They took their lances and gave a shout as one man. The infantry opened gaps for them and they charged in unison along their whole line.'[72] Baha' al-Din also commented on the battle fought on 14 November 1190 when the crusaders 'formed their infantry into a wall, loosing a hail of bolts and arrows'; the cavalry was kept safe inside this human wall and 'on that day not one of them was seen'.[73]

By contrast, the author of the key text describing the disaster at Hattin, the *Libellus de expugnatione Terrae Sanctae*, laid much emphasis on the separation of infantry and cavalry among the factors bringing about Christian defeat, both at Hattin and at the costly encounter that preceded the battle on 1 May.

'The Saracens' tricks split the knights and infantry into two parts, so that knights couldn't support infantry or infantry knights.'[74] Resisting such 'tricks' called for discipline and steadiness under fire – at times, as Baha' al-Din observed, for the knights to accept that they wouldn't fight at all. In the case of the first crusaders these qualities were acquired through experience, by two years (1097–9) of constant campaigning side by side. But what about the shorter expeditions of the thirteenth century? It's likely that much of the value of the infantry on these occasions derived from supplementing the service of crusaders with that of mercenaries who were hired, either in the West or in the Holy Land itself. Oliver of Paderborn reckoned that out of 4,000 archers who took part in the march up the Nile, 2,500 were mercenaries.[75] Joinville narrated that some of the sergeants who were wintering with the French army on Cyprus in 1248–9 got to hear about the impending conflict between the Armenians and the Turks of Iconium, and headed off to take part in it, 'attracted by the chance of a fight and in the hope of gaining booty'.[76]

Our clearest view of footsoldiers usually involves archers and crossbowmen. The English archers acquired a fine reputation for their accuracy on the Third Crusade, while Louis IX made very effective use of crossbowmen in Egypt. John Sarrasin was Louis IX's chamberlain, situated at the heart of the royal bureaucracy, and he reckoned that the king had no fewer than 5,000 crossbowmen when he sailed for Damietta, twice the number of knights.[77] The Muslims evidently feared these crossbowmen because they killed them on capture.[78] Oliver of Paderborn described how some crusaders and Teutonic Knights rode out to meet a party of Templars that was returning from a raid in 1220, and were cut off by the Turks. They were vulnerable because 'our men went out, not for battle, but to meet the Templars, and *therefore* were without crossbowmen and archers'.[79] A number of the anecdotes about the siege of Acre in the *Itinerarium peregrinorum* testify to the skill of these two groups when acting in sniper mode, including the tale of the Turk who unwisely exposed his genitals on the walls of the city in order to urinate on a cross, and was shot through the groin.[80] In another story a Welsh archer is praised for his wit as well as his marksmanship.[81]

Other types of infantry are less conspicuous. We've already seen that many were infantry by default, that's to say knights who had lost their mounts. We know a fair amount about the Frisians, who generally fought on foot. They won high praise from Oliver of Paderborn as 'that obedient and energetic nation, who from the beginning attacked Damietta with great courage, and considered no position either humble or lowly'.[82] The leaders of the Fifth Crusade took the decision to copy the Lombard practice of providing their infantry with a rallying point, a wagon (*carroccio*) equipped with a banner that would be visible from a distance. The Muslims were terrified of it, thinking that it was something akin to the Israelite ark of the covenant.[83] We know of two crusading confraternities (brotherhoods) that were most likely formed to assist the efforts of footsoldiers; both were important enough to have their statutes confirmed by the pope and one of them survived until the fall of Acre.[84] These were surely exceptional.

It's safe to assume that any able-bodied adult male on crusade was both expected and able to fight. This can be inferred from Fulcher of Chartres' account of Urban II's Clermont sermon, in which the military aim of driving off the Turks is allotted to 'knight or footsoldier, rich or poor'.[85] But there are issues about training, weapons and body-protection (at the very least, a helmet and padded jerkin were essential) that remain difficult to address in any detail.[86] Reviewing the troops available to Richard I in 1191, Richard of Devizes made a distinction between a mass of 'infantry' (*pedites*), 'who were useless', and a force of 2,000 shield-bearers (*scutarii*).[87] On the other hand, when the German crusading army was marching through the Balkans in 1189 Barbarossa established a battle formation made up of 'infantry and the strongest of the youths [*pueri*]'.[88] And in the course of praising the outstanding quality of both the forces that faced each other at Acre, one Third Crusade author specifically included the Christian footsoldiers: 'I don't believe that anybody at any time has seen such a large and effective army of Christians as could be seen there. In the wake of the battle there arrived 500 of the best knights and 10,000 fighting men, trained in the use of arms.'[89] It looks like things had changed radically since Odo of Deuil's laments about the Second Crusade.

Naval personnel and combat

The combatant role of naval personnel shouldn't be left out though it's less clear-cut in character than that of cavalry or infantry. Above all these people were oarsmen, rowing the galleys that carried the crusading armies to the East or came to their assistance at a later stage in their operations. As in the case of the footsoldiers, the importance of naval warfare in crusading is now being accorded its proper place. Not all the crewmen had taken the cross, though there's certainly a lot of evidence that those in the fleets that sailed for the East to help the first crusaders had done so. Their devotional practices as crusaders are described in rich detail.[90] When James of Vitry preached the Fifth Crusade at Genoa in September 1216 he found his audience highly responsive; James claimed that he signed thousands with the cross, and considered the city an important target. 'I don't believe that there's any other city which could provide more assistance for the Holy Land.'[91] James had a very high opinion of the combat value of the Genoese, Pisans and Venetians, when they could be persuaded to fight the Muslims rather than each other.[92]

Rowers commonly doubled up as fighters in this period. There was little call for combat on the open sea because in the twelfth and thirteenth centuries none of the Islamic powers had a naval capacity that could challenge that of the crusaders. The Fatimid fleet had once been powerful but it had gone into decline when the first crusaders arrived. The rapid Frankish conquest of the Palestinian ports in the years following the First Crusade robbed the Egyptians of anchorages where their ships could pick up supplies and fresh water.[93] The Seljuq Turks never developed a naval arm, and although Saladin put a lot of effort into doing so, he largely abandoned the attempt after his fleet performed wretchedly in 1187. After Saladin's death the situation became even more one-sided; the fall of Beirut to German crusaders in 1197 placed the Ayyubids in the same logistical impasse that the Fatimids had faced. A fleet of thirty-three Egyptian galleys managed to maul a merchant convoy that was reinforcing and supplying the crusaders at Damietta in August 1220, but this was highly unusual.[94]

By this time traditional Arab disdain for naval service reached such heights that it became an insult in Egypt to call somebody a sailor.[95] Nor did the situation change with the arrival of the Mamluk sultanate in the later thirteenth century. They considered that only combat on land was worth investing in, and continued to denigrate naval operations.[96] Part of this neglect surely stemmed from a recognition of how hard it would be to stage a convincing challenge to the Christians' dominance of the seaways. It was better not to lose face by trying. Ibn Khaldun commented of the mobilization of shipping for the Third Crusade that 'one fleet of unbelievers after another came to the relief of the ports, from all the regions near Jerusalem which they controlled. They supported them with equipment and food. The fleet of Alexandria could not stand up against them.'[97]

So participation in combat by naval personnel occurred much less at sea than in the support they could provide to coastal or inland operations. The main advantage that the crusaders gained from their control of the Mediterranean lay in the relative ease with which they could transport people, horses, *matériel* and food. But they gained a further advantage from the fact that so much of the warfare that they waged in the East took the form of sieges of fortified ports or of towns situated within easy reach of the sea. Naval support played a central role in the reduction of Acre in 1191, Constantinople in 1204 and Damietta in 1219, with the last two providing the best examples of a combination of operations on land and water. Antioch lies twenty-five kilometres (fifteen-and-a-half miles) from the coast, but Genoese sailors came to contribute to its siege in 1097–8. Even at Jerusalem in 1099, the crews of a flotilla of ships that had been abandoned at Jaffa under Egyptian attack brought valuable timber and supplies to help with the siege. Both at Jerusalem and at Antioch the sailors' practical skills with wood and cordage made them highly competent siege engineers. It's hard to believe that some didn't also take part in the fighting, perhaps above all during the assault on Constantinople where about half of the army was made up of the Venetian galley crews.

The heart of crusading warfare – sieges

Such assistance was all the more important because sieges dominated the military history of crusading, perhaps even more than they did medieval warfare generally. Every big expedition to the East included at least one substantial siege: Nicaea, Antioch and Jerusalem stand out on the First Crusade, Damascus on the Second and Acre on the Third, Constantinople on the Fourth and Damietta on the Fifth. Damietta would once again have overshadowed Louis IX's Egyptian campaign if it hadn't fallen to the crusaders so easily, while the siege of Tunis would have occupied the attention of the French in 1270 if it hadn't been for the king's death. The crusaders expected siege warfare and were perfectly at home with it. The construction and conquest of stone castles were integral to the control of territory at every level from locality to kingdom in Europe.

It was the scale of the fortifications in the East, and their use to enclose large towns and ports, that posed a novel challenge. It couldn't be evaded. In some cases conquest of the town in question had become the crusade's objective – Jerusalem in 1099, Damascus in 1148, Constantinople in 1204 – while in others the town had to be secured in order to make further advance possible – Nicaea and Antioch in 1097, Damietta in 1218. The techniques that the crusaders used were ones that they brought from the West. Walls might be stormed by troops on ladders, demolished by stones released from mangonels and petraries or hurled from trebuchets,[98] hacked away by men with picks protected by wooden structures (mantlets or cats),[99] or brought down by mining. These were the classic techniques for capture by assault, which were listed by Oliver of Paderborn when he explained why they couldn't work in the case of the chain-tower at Damietta.[100] Alternatively the commanders within besieged towns could be persuaded to surrender through threats or pressure brought to bear by non-combatants, while ambitious individuals within the defending garrison might be bribed to betray the defences. As in the West, the greatest threats were that the besieging army might suffer crippling losses through drought, famine or disease, and that a substantial relief force might show up. The biggest difference was the fierce climate and harsh terrain that characterized some of the sieges, though even these factors weren't entirely new to those crusaders who came from the Mediterranean lands.[101]

22 The magnificent citadel at Aleppo is a UNESCO World Heritage Site.

Landmark sieges of the First Crusade – Antioch and Jerusalem

The pivotal event of the First Crusade was the siege of Antioch, which occupied more than seven months, from late October 1097 to 3 June 1098. There were several reasons why Antioch posed a massive obstacle. One was the sheer strength of its walls, a circuit of twelve kilometres (seven miles) which dated back to the sixth century and included a double-wall along its northern flank. A second was Antioch's highly unusual location, for to the east it rose sharply to 500 metres (1,640 feet), and the walls here incorporated a rugged landscape that ruled out an assault from this direction.[102] A further reason was the courage and size of Antioch's garrison, several thousand men including many cavalry, and the initiative that was shown by their commander, Yaghisiyan. They proved capable of mounting sorties that made life highly uncomfortable for the besiegers. One took place in December 1097 when many of the crusaders were away on a foraging expedition and another happened in February 1098 when a strong force was again away fighting off a relief force led by Ridwan, the lord of Aleppo. On these occasions Turkish mobility was particularly vexing. Raymond of Aguilers noted that 'the Turks, not prepared to fight with lances or swords, but with arrows at a distance, were to be feared while they fled, as well as when they pursued'.[103]

The crusade's leaders weren't able to surround the whole city, which would have dispersed their strength too much, and any attempt to focus on one section of the walls wouldn't have presented much difficulty to such a powerful and well-led garrison. So the Christians pursued a strategy of containment, building a series of forts that shared the task of controlling the approaches to the city's main gates on its western side. The first, Malregard, was constructed in November 1097 near the gate of St Paul. La Mahomerie followed, near the Bridge Gate (where the walls converged with the Orontes river) in March 1098. Tancred's Tower, named after its commander, was built in the following month near St George's Gate in the south. By the end of this arduous process Yaghisiyan's options for attacking the crusaders in force were heavily reduced.[104]

With hindsight we can see that during these months the first crusaders achieved a lot more than just the building of the forts. They were learning to work together as a single force, overcoming their regional antagonisms. In particular, the operations at Antioch forced into being a pattern of decision-making by the princes, supported by some pooling of resources: Tancred was paid 300 marks for his command of his tower. In February 1098 Bohemund of Taranto won the crusaders' first victory since Dorylaeum when he defeated Ridwan of Aleppo's relief force to the north-east of the city, at what's usually called the 'Lake Battle'. But there's no doubt that for the rank and file this was one of the grimmest periods of the whole crusade. Because the army was stationary it ran out of food and endured famine conditions during the winter months. There was heavy rain. The military operations that were being conducted were uninspiring and the attacks organized by Yaghisiyan cost many lives and induced a constant state of anxiety. The spring of 1098 ended the provisioning crisis but news arrived of a relief force that was much more dangerous than Ridwan's. The Seljuq governor (*atabeg*) of Mosul, Kerbogha, had been ordered by the sultan to break the siege.

There was no hope of taking the city by storm before Kerbogha arrived, but Bohemund had been approached by a Turkish captain called Firuz, who offered to surrender the towers that he commanded in exchange for a reward. Provided Firuz could deliver his side of the bargain this was promising, but as in all such cases the issue of who would become lord of Antioch immediately arose. For

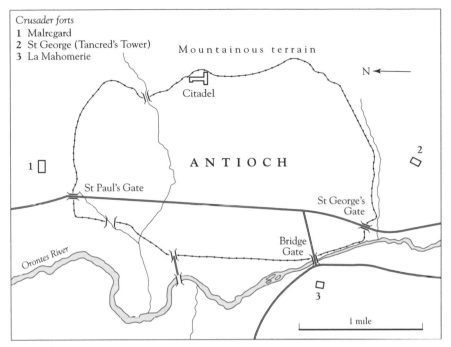

Crusader forts
1 Malregard
2 St George (Tancred's Tower)
3 La Mahomerie

Map 4 Siege of Antioch, 1097–8

this reason Bohemund made no headway with the deal until the threat of Kerbogha's imminent arrival forced the issue. There was no alternative but to accept Bohemund's terms, though the proviso was that if Alexios came to the assistance of the crusaders the city would be handed over to him. During the night of 2–3 June an assault party was admitted into Antioch by Firuz and the city fell. The events were described with great panache by the anonymous author of the *Gesta Francorum*, who was clearly a member of Bohemund's assault group.[105] Just a day later the vanguard of Kerbogha's great army arrived: it was the biggest stroke of luck that the first crusaders enjoyed.

So the siege of Antioch was in essence a protracted blockade brought to a successful conclusion by treachery. It had proved to be an exceptionally wearing experience for the crusaders but it opened the route southwards to Jerusalem. In one crucial respect the siege that the crusaders conducted here in June and July 1099 replicated that at Antioch. The Fatimids had recovered Jerusalem from the Turks the previous summer and a powerful attempt to relieve the garrison had to be expected: Ascalon, a stronghold of Fatimid power, was only about eighty kilometres (fifty miles) to the south-west. No local renegade

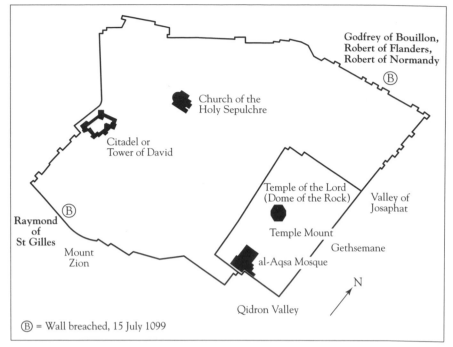

Map 5 Siege of Jerusalem, 1099

offered to betray the city, but it was feasible to take it by storm. Jerusalem was smaller than Antioch, its walls and defenders presented less of an obstacle, and there were some topographical features that worked to the besiegers' advantage. In the south-east the Qidron Valley and the Valley of Josaphat allowed the walls to loom over the surrounding terrain; it was pointless trying to attack here. But in the south-west, adjoining Mount Zion, and along the whole northern and north-western stretch of the walls as far as the citadel (the Tower of David), the ground began to rise just outside the walls, and this placed the attackers at an advantage. It was here that the crusaders attempted to storm the walls. There were difficulties. Much of the northern wall was double and/or moated, and a first attempt on it on 13 June ended in failure. The heat was exhausting and water as well as wood was in short supply on the Judaean plateau. It's a sign of how grim conditions were that even at this late stage in the campaign some crusaders deserted.

Early in July news reached the camp that an Egyptian army was on its way, and the crusaders were galvanized into building enough siege machines to try another attack. Even when the equipment was ready and a second assault was mounted, on 13–15 July, the chief impression one gets is of the sheer difficulty

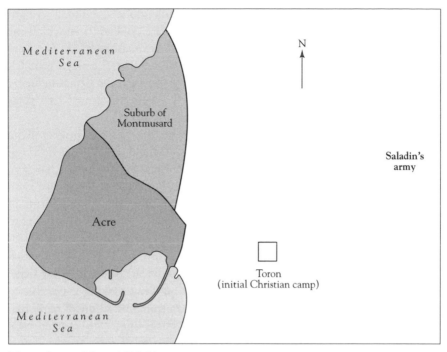

Map 6 Siege of Acre, 1189–91

of storming a city that was strongly walled and, like Antioch, tenaciously defended. The crusaders gained an element of surprise by secretly moving a giant ram, tower and several mangonels from their construction point around to the north-eastern section of the city wall. The demolition of the outer wall by the ram took all of 13 July and much of the 14th. The ram had then to be disposed of by fire so that the tower could be pushed into place. This tower was very tall and it loomed over the inner wall, forcing its defenders to flee to safety. After several attempts by the Muslims to destroy the tower, the crusaders finally succeeded in climbing down from it on to the wall, so effecting their entry into Jerusalem.[106]

The key to Christian recovery – the siege of Acre 1189–1191

The long siege of Acre (August 1189 to July 1191) lay at the heart of the Third Crusade and it shared some of the epic qualities of the siege of Antioch by the first crusaders. As one contemporary put it, 'if the ten-year war made Troy famous, and the Christian triumph made Antioch more illustrious, then

Acre will certainly win eternal fame, for the whole globe assembled to fight
for her'.[107] The siege was seen as the fulfilment of Isaiah 43:5–6, in which the
prophet had foretold just such a gathering of the nations.[108] These were
pardonable exaggerations. The sheer length of time that the siege lasted is
indicative of the way Frankish sea-power had transformed the situation facing
the besiegers: no army could have maintained a siege of almost two years
without reinforcement and replenishment from the sea.[109]

The siege of Acre had two distinct phases. The first was begun when King
Guy of Lusignan, in an act that was as much a clever and desperate assertion of
his royal authority against his rival Conrad of Montferrat as a military stratagem,
marched south from Tyre to lay siege to Acre in the wake of his release from
captivity by Saladin. Nobody questioned the assumption that the recapture of
the port city was essential if the rest of the kingdom of Jerusalem was going to
be recovered. Almost immediately Guy received seaborne help from the West,
but just a few days later Saladin brought troops southwards from Belfort, which
he'd been besieging. A pattern had been set that would last throughout the siege.
Crusaders steadily arrived by sea to reinforce King Guy, making it possible to
establish a full blockade of Acre; and they were mirrored by a flow of reinforcements to Saladin, enabling him to blockade Guy's siege lines. The besiegers were
themselves besieged. The arrival of such a Muslim relief force would almost
certainly have spelled disaster for the first crusaders at Antioch and Jerusalem. It
could be coped with at Acre thanks to strong links with the West, complemented by some provisions and arms that were grudgingly despatched by
Conrad from Tyre. The nature of the situation was clear to Saladin, whom Baha'
al-Din depicted saying in mid-October 1189 that 'if this enemy survives and
lasts until the sea is open, he will receive vast reinforcements'.[110]

That said, the winter of 1189–90 brought conditions for the crusaders at
Acre that would have seemed all too familiar to the first crusaders besieging
Antioch in 1097–8. They included hunger, for Saladin's ships established a
short-lived control over the western approaches to Acre which for several
weeks made provisioning hazardous.[111] The whole of 1190 passed in a series
of attempts by the crusaders to storm Acre's walls while Saladin tried to break
the crusader lines. For many crusaders it proved unbearably frustrating. There
was much desertion.[112] 'Time passed, and the army grew listless from long
inaction. The common people, greedy for excitement, began to accuse the
princes of being cowards and started agitating for a fight.'[113] The outcome
was an ill-considered and costly attack that the rank and file launched on
25 July, on their own initiative, against the camp of Takieddin, Saladin's
nephew, 'without advice from the princes and in defiance of the patriarch's
veto . . . without a leader, commander or proper banners, in search of booty
rather than battle'.[114] But neither side possessed enough strength to break the

back of the other, even after the arrival of high-ranking leaders like Frederick of Swabia and Baldwin archbishop of Canterbury.

In the siege's second winter, 1190–1, hunger and disease again took a heavy toll of the crusaders. The difficulties that they faced can be gauged from the care that Saladin took to ship out of besieged Acre 'the emirs who had been there because of their many complaints about their long spell of duty, their endurance of fatigue and broken nights, and their constant fighting night and day'.[115] For the Christian opponents of these exhausted Muslims there was no equivalent opportunity to move out of the line. Their spirits lifted when Philip Augustus joined them in April 1191, but it was Richard I's arrival two months later that transformed the situation. The king was greeted 'as if he had been Christ himself',[116] and 'tongue cannot tell, pen cannot do justice to the people's joy at his arrival'.[117] The siege now entered its second phase, in which the twin tasks of destroying the city's walls and probing the garrison's weaknesses were pressed with much greater vigour. Philip managed the French contribution with diligence and Richard's experience of siege warfare was unmatched, but their best efforts were constrained by the limitations of the technology available. Both Acre's garrison and the two armies stationed outside its walls had become severely debilitated, and the English and French crusaders were divided by the dispute over the throne between Guy and Conrad, with Richard supporting Guy and Philip Conrad. But it was the will of the city's garrison commanders that snapped, mainly because Saladin had now lost control of the sea and wasn't able to get supplies to them. In July 1191 they negotiated the city's surrender.

Land and sea operations at Constantinople

At Acre Christian control of the sea eventually proved important, arguably even decisive, in tilting the balance in favour of the crusaders. Two sieges that occurred outside the Holy Land demonstrate a more proactive use of sea-power in the form of combined land and sea operations. At Constantinople in 1203–4 the crusaders and Venetians faced land walls that for the most part had triple lines, effectively rendering them unassailable. Their only weak point lay at the north-eastern tip of the great Theodosian wall, where the wall reached the magnificent harbour called the Golden Horn. Here the sprawling complex of the imperial Blachernae Palace was protected by a single wall which presented a viable military target, though hardly an easy one given that it was seventeen metres (eighteen-and-a-half yards) thick and fourteen to seventeen metres (fifteen to eighteen-and-a-half yards) high. On 17 July 1203 the crusaders attacked this wall with scaling ladders, while the Venetians launched a seaborne assault on the less imposing wall that stretched along the harbour in the Golden Horn's northern reaches. Central to their tactics were wooden platforms that

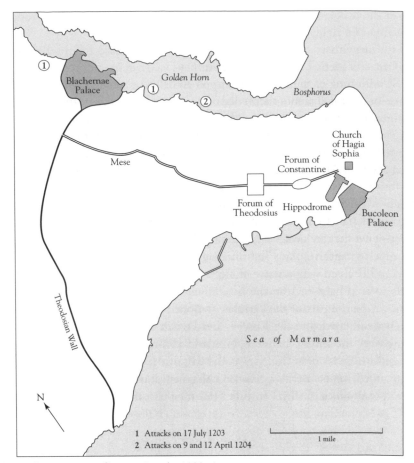

Map 7 Operations at Constantinople, 1203–4

they hung from their ships' masts and swung around on to the walls to act as
catwalks for their soldiers to charge across. The land attack was a failure but the
Venetians managed to get some troops on to the walls. The Emperor Alexios
III successfully foiled this by appearing to offer battle outside the city, which
compelled the Venetians to recall their soldiers from the harbour walls. But,
although all the day's operations eventually came to nothing, Alexios lost
control within the city and fled during the following night. The Emperor
Alexios's political weakness had tipped the scales in favour of the westerners and
they were able to install the pretender Alexios in power.

The crusaders and Venetians learnt a valuable lesson from these events, and
when circumstances drove them to organize a second assault on Constantinople

in April 1204, they again focused their energies on the harbour wall overlooking the Golden Horn. The catwalks were pressed into service for a second time, in conjunction with landing parties that had the task of undermining the walls from below. The first assault on 9 April failed, leading to demoralization and some questioning of the leadership's approach, but a second attempt three days later using modified tactics succeeded. One contributor towards this success was the chronicler Robert of Clari. His assault group, led by Peter of Amiens, worked at the foot of the harbour wall, where they managed to hack their way through a sealed-up postern gate. Robert described the event in a wonderful passage that is strongly reminiscent of the author of the *Gesta Francorum* narrating his group's role in the capture of Antioch in 1098. Robert's brother, a cleric called Aleaumes, was first through the hole in the door that they created, foiling Robert's attempt to grab his foot and hold him back from what must have seemed certain death.[118] The tactics applied with such persistence had succeeded in capturing, not just once but twice, one of the best-fortified cities in the world. Even with a powerful fleet behind them, such extraordinary feats of arms would have been inconceivable without political disunity and military ineptitude on the part of the Greeks.

Ingenuity and perseverance at Damietta

The imaginative use that was made of ships at Constantinople in 1203–4 was replicated at the siege of Damietta during the Fifth Crusade in 1218–19. Damietta, lying on the eastern bank of the Nile, was a formidably well-fortified city with a triple set of walls, and a successful siege called for attacks by land and water. The first obstacle to this was an immense chain that stretched across the Nile from the city to a tower situated close to the river's western bank. The chain-tower had a garrison of about 300 men. The crusaders landed in May 1218 and immediately concentrated their efforts on taking the tower. It was Oliver of Paderborn, the cathedral schoolmaster from Cologne, who demonstrated his versatility by devising a siege machine supported by four masts erected on two ships that were lashed together with beams and strong ropes; with admirable modesty Oliver refrained from naming the contraption's architect in his own written account of the crusade.[119] Due to the crusade's remarkably decentralized way of doing things the purchase of the two ships had to be funded from charitable donations.[120] Oliver's construction was both more rigid and more complicated than the platforms that had been used a few years earlier at Constantinople. In addition to a ladder that would reach on to the top of the tower, it held a bridge that could communicate with its lower section. Both ladder and bridge worked well and the chain-tower was seized after a bitter struggle on

23 The great circuit of walls built by Emperor Theodosius II in the early fifth century made Constantinople virtually impregnable by land.

25 August. Oliver's invention must have been well constructed because it was later recycled for use as a bridge over the Nile.[121]

At this point the difficulties of investing the city became fully apparent, because the situation at Acre recurred: Sultan al-Kamil had based himself not far south of the city on the Nile's eastern bank. A bridge of boats constructed across the Nile prevented the crusaders' ships sailing up it and the Muslims sank other vessels to present further obstacles. Moreover, this crusade seems to have faced more difficulties in creating an effective decision-making procedure than any of its predecessors. By the time winter set in little progress had been made and the crusaders suffered heavily from storms. In February 1219 it looked as if a breakthrough had been achieved when al-Kamil left his camp to deal with a plot against him; when his troops found out about this there was intense confusion and the crusaders were able to cross the Nile unmolested. At last they could set about the task of reducing Damietta's walls. But al-Kamil returned and on 31 March launched a serious attack on the crusaders who were based south of Damietta. Although it was beaten off, the situation that the Christians faced in the summer and autumn of 1219 was bleak. The crusaders fell victim to a Turkish feigned retreat on 29 August, suffering heavy losses.

By this time the ebb and flow of crusaders that was characteristic of the Fifth Crusade had set in. To those who resisted the temptation to take ship for the West it seemed that their prospects were hopeless, for they believed that the Muslims outnumbered them by fifty to one.[122] But as at Acre in 1191 it was the garrison, also worn down by starvation and disease, which cracked first. In the first days of November 1219 a military code of exceptional severity was drawn up preparatory to an all-out assault on the walls.[123] It proved unnecessary, for on 5 November 1219 a group of Italian crusaders noticed that one of the city's towers was undefended. They secured the tower and Damietta was captured. It had taken the crusaders twenty months to wear down the besiegers. On neither side had the leadership displayed during these months been particularly impressive. The crusading sources reveal a level of frustration and despair among the rank and file about the lack of progress that was high even when compared with that experienced at Antioch in 1097–8 and Acre in 1189–91. It was the loud complaints of the infantry about the unwillingness of their knights to engage with the enemy that propelled them into the disastrous action on 29 August.[124] What remains inexplicable is why the same people tolerated the long period of stagnation that followed Damietta's fall, rather than lobbying for action as their predecessors had done in similar circumstances in 1098–9.

Battles and fighting marches – the great commanders

The Venetian catwalks at Constantinople and Oliver of Paderborn's tower at Damietta show the crusaders improvising during their practice of siege warfare, but that improvisation was minor compared with the adaptability that Turkish tactics, plus the heterogeneous character of their own armies, forced them to resort to during combat on land. During the First and Third Crusades they were fortunate enough to be led by two commanders who would be viewed as outstanding in any context, Bohemund of Taranto and Richard Coeur de Lion. Bohemund's appreciation of what he faced was already on display at the battle of Dorylaeum, when he appears to have formed his column into something like a defensive enclosure, and to have restrained most of his knights from chasing after the Turks while the latter discharged their arrows. The problem that Bohemund and all later commanders faced was two-fold. First, coping with Turkish tactics was less a matter of learning a lesson than repeatedly curbing the temptation for energetic and hot-blooded young men, obsessed with honour and personal ambition, to pursue what seemed to be a retreating enemy. Secondly, the enemy had to be persuaded or compelled to engage in close-quarter combat where the fighting skills, courage and religious enthusiasm of the knights and infantry could be used to best advantage. In many cases there was the added complication that provision had to be made for the protection of the army's non-combatants.

Bohemund of Taranto and the battle of Antioch

In a muddled encounter with Duqaq of Damascus at the very end of 1097 the first crusaders showed that they were still perplexed by Turkish tactics, but a few weeks later, at the Lake Battle fought against Ridwan of Aleppo, Bohemund first clearly showed his quality of leadership. He engaged with Ridwan's army while it was still compact, and won the encounter through a well-timed cavalry charge. This was probably the first time that the crusaders were able to deliver such a charge against a Turkish army. But Bohemund's masterpiece was the battle of Antioch, fought against Kerbogha's army on 28 June 1098. He was placed in overall charge of the army and the plan adopted was certainly his. For some weeks the crusaders had themselves been besieged within Antioch, suffering enormous privations as well as a near-complete collapse of morale. The decision to fight came none too soon and in part it was a result of a religious revival stimulated by the discovery of a great relic, the Holy Lance. But no number of holy artefacts could replace dead chargers or enable the crusaders to defeat Kerbogha's huge force without blunders on his part coupled with tactics of a high order. Luckily Kerbogha did make a disastrous mistake, dispersing his army along the whole length of Antioch's long western perimeter. By emerging to give battle at a single point, the Bridge Gate in the south, the crusaders were able to take on and defeat the Muslims piecemeal.

The crusaders had no more than 200 chargers left so they fought very largely on foot, but they enjoyed a number of advantages that made up for this. They were able to leave all their non-combatants within Antioch. This was crucial because starvation, injury and disease had created a very large number of people who would have been worse than useless in the battle; it was precisely the difficulty that plagued the French during their march through Anatolia in 1147. The crusaders mobilized almost all their fighting men and arranged them in four 'divisions' organized largely along national lines so that they fought alongside people they knew. Many of their combatants had by now fought several battles and numerous skirmishes against the Turks and knew what to expect. Each division protected its neighbour from encirclement. Morale was high thanks to the discovery of the Holy Lance and there was a general perception that this was the crisis of the crusade, 'a gambler's throw of all or nothing' as one historian has put it.[125] Defeat would mean either annihilation or captivity, while victory would, it was hoped, clear the way for the final march southwards to Jerusalem.

Richard I and the battle of Arsuf

The quality of Richard I's command was well demonstrated on the journey east at Messina and on Cyprus. Already famed for his lightning movements, he took Messina 'at the first assault more swiftly than any priest could sing mass', and then conquered Cyprus in less than a month (abbreviated by one source to fifteen days).[126] His greatest encounter in the Holy Land itself was the battle of Arsuf, fought against Saladin in September 1191. The battle was the culmination of a march of some 112 kilometres (seventy miles) southwards from Acre that would bring the army of the Third Crusade to Jaffa. From here an attempt to recover Jerusalem could be staged. For his part, Saladin had to prevent the march occurring and if possible defeat Richard's army. His tactics were essentially the tried and trusted Turkish methods of harassment, encirclement and annihilation, but they were applied with a skill and resolve that had been singularly lacking at Antioch in 1098. Richard didn't have many non-combatants: the English and French armies had fewer in any case than previous crusades, and the sick and wounded from the siege of Acre were left behind in that city.

Richard knew that his march would be opposed and he planned it with care. The crusaders marched in three divisions, which as at Antioch had national or regional profiles. Their western flank was protected by the Mediterranean and the English ships, and their vulnerable baggage train proceeded alongside the sea. It was sheltered from attack by the main army, whose divisions were in turn shielded by a force of infantry marching on the army's eastern flank. This force suffered most from enemy harassment, so Richard alternated periods of service in this unit with breaks that were spent marching with the baggage train. The system worked. Despite constant attacks Saladin couldn't break through the infantry shield. Baha' al-Din paid the rank and file, whose body armour was not chainmail but simple padded jerkins, a notable tribute: 'I saw various individuals among the Franks with ten arrows fixed in their backs, pressing on in this fashion quite unconcerned ... Those resting [from the fighting] were carrying the baggage and tents because they were short of beasts of burden. Consider the endurance of these people, bearing exhausting tasks without any pay or material gain.'[127] One advantage that Richard had over Bohemund was the assistance of the military orders. After a Turkish breakthrough in the rearguard on the first day of the march had got as far as threatening the baggage train, the king placed the Hospitallers and Templars in

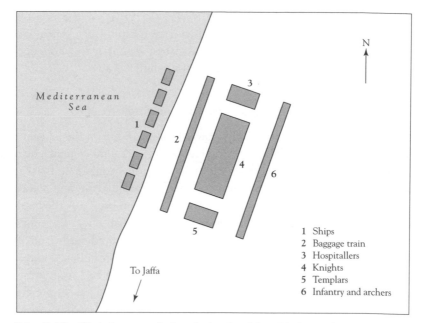

Map 8 The Christian army during the battle of Arsuf, 7 September 1191

24 The shock of combat at close quarters is well caught in this fourteenth-century illustration of a crusading encounter.

charge of the rearguard. It was a move reminiscent of Louis VII's reliance on the Templars during the French march southwards to Adalia in 1147. When the army of the Fifth Crusade advanced up the Nile from Fareskur in July 1221 the formation adopted was remarkably similar to that used in 1191.[128]

On 7 September 1191 Saladin committed his army to a full-scale engagement. Customary Turkish tactics were deployed on a massive scale and they impacted on both the infantry shield and the cavalry. As usual they included the use of loud music to encourage their own troops and terrify the enemy: one source speaks of trumpets, clarions, horns, flutes, tambourines, rattles and cymbals. 'Even a thunder crash would not have been heard above the great uproar of trumpets and sounding horns.'[129] Richard did his best to hold his ground until the Turks showed signs of tiring, which would be the optimal point to order a general charge. His wishes were frustrated by the Hospitallers, who held the rearguard and came under exceptional pressure. When two Hospitallers, including the order's marshal, could no longer resist the temptation to charge the Muslims a general attack began to take shape. Richard realized that not supporting this attack to the hilt could prove disastrous. He therefore joined in with his own knights, though by retaining the English and Normans in reserve he forestalled the tendency for the crusader battle line to lose all shape.

This combination of careful planning and flexibility in response to the unexpected was the true sign of genius. With pardonable exaggeration Richard claimed in a letter to the abbot of Clairvaux that 'so great was the slaughter among Saladin's more noble Saracens that he lost more that day near Arsuf . . . than on any day in the previous forty years'.[130] Baha' al-Din wrote that the battle 'wounded Muslim hearts'.[131] Saladin's attempt to break up the Christian army had failed, and on the same day its southwards march was resumed. Jaffa was reached three days later. Of equal importance was the fact that Saladin's reputation, built up by years of success and crowned with triumph at Hattin, was dealt a substantial blow. From this point onwards it was impossible for Saladin to challenge Richard, whose failure to recover Jerusalem resulted from strategic factors rather than military inadequacy.

Hand-to-hand combat at Mansurah

In the battles of Antioch and Arsuf we can see exceptional qualities of command at work. Contemporaries, including many of the crusaders, shared this perception. But few commanders on either side possessed the abilities of Bohemund, Richard or Saladin. Similarly, most battles were more confused and their outcomes less clear-cut. Mansurah, fought on 8 February 1250, was one such. Unlike his predecessors on the Fifth Crusade, Louis IX took Damietta relatively easily on 6 June 1249. The contrast was one of which the

25 Intense combat between crusaders and Muslims.

king and his comrades-in-arms were well aware, and it would have been reinforced by their encounter with the fifty-three Christian slaves whom they liberated in the city, and whose captivity dated back to the earlier expedition.[132] The French knew too that the rising of the Nile had played the key role in bringing about the downfall of their predecessors.[133] Despite this, the pattern of the earlier expedition was replicated. The king delayed for many months before beginning an advance up the Nile valley towards Cairo. It was only in mid-December that he reached the strategically crucial fortress of Mansurah, and here further progress was blocked by the Bahr as-Saghir river. Futile attempts to cross the river occupied several weeks before, at the start of February, the French learnt of a ford that would enable them to cross the river and assault Mansurah. The battle on 8 February grew out of the river crossing, which was handled by a vanguard led by Robert of Artois, the master of the Temple and a prominent English crusader, William Longespee.

We've already seen that initial success was thrown away by the rash folly of Robert of Artois in charging into Mansurah, and when the main army crossed it found that the Muslims had successfully regrouped. For some time the French cavalry had no support from their infantry, but when the crossbowmen appeared the crusaders gained the upper hand and the Muslims gave up the field. It looked as if the French had won the day since they had crossed the Bahr as-Saghir and captured the enemy camp north of Mansurah. But losses in the battle had been heavy, and they weren't able to mount a siege of Mansurah. The Muslims seized the initiative, cutting the crusaders' supply route down the Nile to Damietta. The army was afflicted by disease and famine, and four months after the battle it began its doleful and ultimately disastrous attempt to retreat northwards along the Nile. 'Thus by land and water and in various ways were lost all the Christians who had assembled there against the enemies of our faith.'[134]

Our best description of the battle of Mansurah is given, typically, by Joinville who fought in it. His account is full of vivid detail and anecdote, and one has to make some allowance for Joinville's pointillist technique of scene-painting. But there's good reason to believe that on this occasion, and maybe even in the case of such encounters as Antioch and Arsuf, the noisy, volatile and frightening ebb and flow of combat that he depicts comes close to how things seemed to people at the time. According to Joinville French ill-fortune started because a deaf knight called Foucaud of Merle held the bridle of Robert of Artois' horse. Foucaud couldn't hear the sensible arguments made by Robert's Templar comrades in favour of delay, and he initiated the mad rush towards Mansurah.[135] It's a comic incident, true enough to life to believe, as is most of what follows. Joinville emphasizes the French use of loud music, a procedure that directly paralleled the Turkish one: 'as the royal army began to move there was once again a great sound of trumpets, kettledrums and Saracen horns'.[136] Urgent and brusque orders alternate with encouraging cries and jocular comments like that of the count of Soissons, ' "Seneschal, let these dogs howl as they will. By God's bonnet" – that was his favourite oath – "we shall talk of this day yet, you and I, sitting at home with our ladies." '[137]

Amid all the muddle two things emerge clearly from Joinville's packed pages. One is the extraordinary peril that the French were placed in by Turkish methods of combat combined with Robert of Artois' foolish behaviour, whether or not it was aggravated by Foucaud's deafness. The other is the importance of the crossbowmen in rescuing the knights and saving the day. 'That evening, as the sun was setting, the constable came up with a company of the king's unmounted crossbowmen, who drew up in rank in front of us. As soon as the Saracens saw them setting foot to the stirrup of their crossbows, they left us and

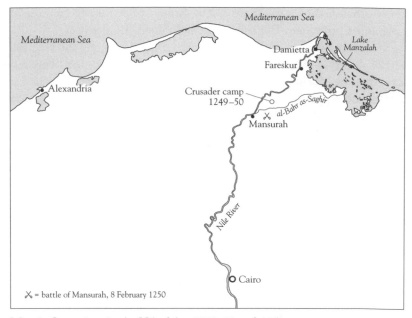

Map 9 Operations in the Nile delta, 1218–19 and 1250

26 Louix IX's army arrives at Damietta, June 1249.

fled.'[138] This fine tribute on the part of both Joinville and the Muslims to the effectiveness of the crossbowmen is echoed by an equally vivid passage later in his account. Louis IX has just been released from captivity and makes his way under strong Muslim escort towards a galley that appears to contain a single man. But he whistles, and immediately eighty crossbowmen rush from the hold on to the deck, crossbows already wound and bolts at the ready. 'On seeing these men emerge the Saracens took to flight like so many sheep.'[139]

The balance sheet

Neither the deadly accuracy of the crossbowmen nor the courage and panache of a Joinville or a count of Soissons could save Louis IX's Egyptian expedition from crushing defeat. This was typical of the military balance sheet of the crusaders in the East. Nobody can question that the crusaders and their commanders achieved some remarkable successes. In particular, they showed ingenuity when laying siege to fortified cities and a strong measure of tactical adaptability when engaging with enemy forces in battle or on the march. Much of their military activity was underpinned by reserves of determination and resilience that seemed boundless. But these positive qualities were balanced by human errors, and by the capacity to make the same or similar mistakes time and again, mainly as a result of misplaced values of honour or ambition.

It's not difficult to single out crucial strategic failures; following 1187 the key ones were the crusaders' inability to restore the kingdom of Jerusalem's defensive infrastructure,[140] and to achieve the conquest of Egypt. But it's possible to place undue emphasis on strategic shortcomings like these at the cost of considerations that were broader in scope. Above all there was the demographic inadequacy of Frankish settlement in the East,[141] the inability of the Catholic West to co-operate over the long term with Byzantium, and the essential bluntness of crusading as a mechanism for defending the Latin East against surges of Islamic power that were dangerous but also relatively short lived. There were factors working in favour of the crusaders, notably their control over the seaways and the disunity that so frequently plagued the Muslim world. But they could only postpone defeat, not stop it occurring.

For individual crusaders, combat in the East brought much that was novel. This was especially the case for mounted troops and for those members of the infantry who weren't professional combatants. Both groups had to learn how to fight in an unaccustomed way, and many of the infantry had to learn to fight from scratch. Yet fighting, like any other human activity, can't be treated in isolation. For all the crusaders their engagement in combat was heavily influenced by experiences that shaped their physical capacities, behaviour and mental worlds. It's these experiences that will form the subject matter of the next four chapters.

❖

6

THE NEEDS OF THE FLESH

Time on the cross

In the treatise about crusade preaching that he wrote in the mid-1260s, Humbert of Romans included an eccentric passage depicting a crusader defending himself before Christ on Judgement Day. 'Lord, you were on the cross one day for my sake, and I have been on it for your sake for many days and have suffered many torments.'[1] Humbert's point was not to play down crucifixion but to play up crusading. He was saying that crusading was such an extended ordeal that the crusader who had fulfilled his vow would have nothing to fear from a just God. As we saw in Chapter 2, after many generations of crusading the problem faced by preachers like Humbert was that their audiences were all too well aware of what an ordeal the experience would be. Highlighting the spiritual value that arose from this was an astute and appropriate response, but it's beyond question that many in the audience would see the trees rather than the wood. They would have sympathized with the chronicler of the Fifth Crusade who wrote that 'no human tongue could describe the misery, impoverishment, torment, exhaustion and sickness that the Christians suffered at the siege of Damietta for the love of Jesus Christ and on behalf of the Christian faith'.[2]

As a synthesis of warfare and pilgrimage, crusading brought together the privations and dangers that were involved in both. Death, wounds and capture were in grim alliance with exhaustion, hunger and disease. The second group of tribulations, moreover, were likely to be aggravated by the size of crusading armies. Big numbers were bound to place a strain on local amenities like shelter; they heightened the competition for supplies of food and water; and they increased the risk of contagion. The logistics of any medieval army were primitive, but crusading hosts were unusually large, and they operated in terrain that for the most part was unfamiliar and often inhospitable. Furthermore, they reached those areas only after long journeys which had already sapped their physical strength. They were at an inherent disadvantage compared with their enemies, who had usually travelled much shorter distances to fight and were used to the climate.[3]

Food and drink

The single most nagging concern was finding enough food and water for people and animals. This was such a prerequisite that it can't be exaggerated.[4] Crusading accentuated what a leading historian of Barbarossa's crusade described as the 'deeply rooted preoccupation of medieval people with their daily bread'.[5] In the mid-thirteenth century the Franciscan missionary William of Rubruck maintained that the crusaders could 'conquer the whole world' if they would be content with the sort of food that Mongol armies ate, but medieval Europeans drew the line at carrion, lice and the afterbirth of mares.[6] Their standard diet was bread, supplemented by meat and legumes. As in all aspects of medieval life there were social differences. Those in the hierarchy's upper reaches advertised that fact by consuming large quantities of wine, wheaten bread, red meat, game and fish, and disdaining vegetables. Their inferiors relied heavily on ale (rich in carbohydrates) and dairy products, while the poor made do with the ubiquitous 'pottage' made from coarser grains. There were seasonal and regional variations but no substantial dietary divide in the areas where crusading proved popular.[7]

It's clear that as far as possible the crusaders stuck to this diet while in the East. In a will drawn up in 'the holy army of the Christians at Damietta' at the end of 1219 the food bequeathed consisted of biscuit, flour, meat and wine.[8] One of the most famous of Joinville's anecdotes relates to Louis IX's prudence in shipping ahead to Cyprus vast supplies of wine, wheat and barley to await the French crusaders' arrival there: because of the rain the mounds of stored grain sprouted grass, but when this was sliced away dry and usable grain lay underneath.[9] At the height of the Egyptian campaign Joinville was storing sacks of barley in his chapel, and when he was residing continuously in the Holy Land, between 1250 and 1254, he carefully laid up supplies of wine and flour and kept his own sheep and pigs. He and his household may have followed 'the custom of the country' by eating while seated on mats on the ground 'facing each other', but what they ate doesn't seem to have been much different from what they would have lived on back in France.[10] The aspect of the Mongol diet that seems to have surprised Joinville the most (and there was much that he found strange) was the fact that they ate no bread: he illustrated this with a story about a horse-load of flour that had been laboriously carried for three months to the Great Khan's court, only to be treated as worthless.[11]

Joinville's regime at Acre and Caesarea seems to have been well upholstered. He enjoyed a relatively stable lifestyle coupled with access to markets that most crusaders could only dream of. On the march things were very different. Indeed, historians who have attempted to work out the basic nutritional requirements of men and animals, not just mounts but beasts of burden too, during the early expeditions have expressed astonishment that they could be met. In the days between 26 June and 1 July 1097, for example, it's been reckoned that the first crusaders would have required 600 tonnes (661 tons) of grain.[12] The same astonishment was expressed by a contemporary who asserted with wonderful hyperbole that if God hadn't provided for the army's requirements then its 300,000 combatants would have drunk all of Anatolia's rivers dry and consumed all of its pasturage in just twenty-four hours.[13] However it's judged, the achievement remains remarkable, because it's been plausibly suggested that in normal circumstances an army 15,000 strong needed 288,400 kilograms (636,813 pounds) of provisions for each three weeks of its operation.[14] When armies of this size or larger were stationary, their ability to survive becomes a deep mystery that the sources don't allow us to solve.

Famines of the First Crusade

Starvation was a real possibility. During their operations in northern Syria, autumn 1097 to early 1099, the first crusaders endured a series of periods when food reached such short supply that famine conditions prevailed. The first of these periods was the winter of 1097–8 when the army was slowly establishing its blockade of Antioch. It had exhausted the food in the city's vicinity, and even bringing in supplies from as far afield as Edessa and Cyprus couldn't keep hunger at bay; the cold and wet conditions in the camp only made things worse. Looking back on things in July 1098 Anselm of Ribemont summed up the situation grimly: 'from lack of horses, or food, or through excessive cold, almost all were dying'.[15]

The spring of 1098 brought some relief, but the arrival of Kerbogha's army immediately after the capture of Antioch in early June reduced the crusaders to reliance on such food as was available in the city: and of course its Muslim garrison and inhabitants had already eaten most of that. During the preparations for the battle with Kerbogha whatever food remained was reserved for the army's few surviving chargers; in a bizarre nutritional exchange, some horsemen drew blood from their chargers so as to sustain themselves.[16] The fact that these debilitated men were still able to defeat Kerbogha's troops is testimony both to the way that the discovery of the Holy Lance had lifted their spirits and to the desperate situation that they knew they were in. We have to remember that they fought largely on foot and with weapons that demanded substantial and sustained physical effort. That in circumstances like these the fighting men consented to fast before they went into battle becomes, as one historian has put it, 'quite incredible'.[17]

The rout of Kerbogha's army didn't end the crusaders' supply problems. Fighting moved about 100 kilometres (62 miles) south, but the countryside here had already been stripped clean of stored food by long-range foraging. So the winter of 1098–9 brought a third famine, which only ended when the march south began in January 1099. The hunger of the poor was a key factor in persuading Raymond of Toulouse to resume the march despite his unwillingness to accept Bohemund's possession of Antioch. During the siege of Jerusalem food supplies again proved insufficient but a more serious problem was finding enough water. There was none in the immediate vicinity with the exception of the inadequate pool of Siloa, and thanks to harassment by partisans trips to water sources lying some way off had to be organized in convoys. One consequence was that the garrison's use of fire to destroy the crusaders' siege machines couldn't be countered by extinguishing the flames with water.[18]

Because their authors were keen to emphasize the miracle of survival in such dire conditions, the First Crusade's keystone narratives are generous with circumstantial detail about these periods of acute hunger and thirst. Their commentaries focus on two things, the high prices demanded for such food as there was, and the unusual things that people resorted to eating in their desperation. The author of the *Gesta Francorum* remarked on the situation in the New Year of 1098 that an ass's load of food fetched 120s, a sum which was way beyond the means of the poor; while during the June 1098 famine a small loaf cost a bezant, a hen 15s, an egg 2s and a walnut 1d. 'So terrible was the famine that men boiled and ate the leaves of figs, vines, thistles and all kinds of trees. Others stewed the dried skins of horses, camels, asses, oxen or buffaloes, which they ate.'[19] Early in 1098 fodder became so expensive that 7 or 8s scarcely bought a single night's food for a horse.[20] It was ironic that at this time a group of the expedition's higher clerics wrote to invite their co-religionists in the West to come to 'the land flowing with milk and honey and abounding in all good things'.[21] Following the capture of Antioch, 'a horse's head without the tongue was sold for two or three solidi, the intestines of goats for five, a cock for eight or ten'.[22] The situation was certainly critical, though it's hard to credit Albert of Aachen's hyperbolic claim that the poor were reduced to eating their own shoes.[23] The winter of 1098–9 gave rise to the most dramatic visual image, conjured up by Raymond of Aguilers' remark that 'you could see ten thousand men going about the fields like cattle, digging and looking to see if by chance they might find grains of wheat, or barley, or beans'.[24]

27 The siege of Antioch in 1097–8, including an anachronistic trebuchet. The long siege of the city placed an almost intolerable strain on the first crusaders' physical capabilities.

What passages like these can't provide us with is a reliable index of the relative severity of the various bouts of famine that occurred. It's highly likely that a cumulative weakening of the system took place. There was cannibalism during the shortages in the winter of 1098–9.[25] This caused alarm. Some crusaders were so shocked that they construed it as a sign of the crusade's imminent collapse and fled for home.[26] It's true that there was normally a taboo on eating human flesh,[27] but we shouldn't assume that its breaking proves that people were more desperate than they had previously been. We're on safer ground with increasing social tensions, as in one complaint that at the siege of Jerusalem the poor suffered from thirst while the rich had grapes and wine.[28]

Periods of hunger during the Third and Fourth Crusades

An immobile crusading army operating at a distance from its sources of supply, or cut off from those sources by the enemy, faced starvation. It's true that armies on the move could also suffer if their supplies ran out and the terrain couldn't support them. The Germans discovered this in Anatolia in 1190. By the second week of May shortages were causing prices to soar just as they had in 1098, 'flour was guarded and concealed like gold', and the situation only improved some two weeks later when Iconium fell into German hands. Before the crusaders reached this point hunger had been joined by a shortage of drinking water that seems to have been more acute than that experienced by any other expedition.[29] But stationary forces were especially vulnerable, and in the previous chapter we saw that crusaders were all too often forced to be stationary thanks to the number of sieges that they had to engage in.

During both winters of the siege of Acre by the forces of the Third Crusade (1189–90 and 1190–1) the army suffered from food shortages. Not many ships would sail during these months from the West and the condition of virtual civil war in the Holy Land meant that little could be expected from Conrad of Montferrat at Tyre. In 1189–90 the situation was aggravated by a shortage of timber with which to cook and build shelters against the weather.[30] The situation in the summer and autumn months of 1190 remained difficult,[31] but it was the second winter that bit hardest.[32] One eyewitness reckoned that it was unprecedented in its severity.[33] Food prices soared, the staples quoted being much the same as a century earlier – bread, hens and eggs. The starving resorted to offal, grass and bones that had already been gnawed by the camp dogs.[34] Horseflesh was considered a luxury, and as at Antioch in 1098 knights killed their own mounts for food: 'Those who used to carry them, vice versa, they now carried in their stomachs.'[35]

This isn't the only comment in the *Itinerarium peregrinorum* that shows the author using the famine at Acre to indulge his penchant for social and moral reflections. He regarded it as instructive that the severity of the food shortage meant that even nobles starved: 'Wherever they happened to see grass growing, noblemen and potentates' sons, those who were once delicately nourished, devoured it.'[36] Nor did the situation bring out the best in everybody, 'for many unworthy deeds were committed under the pressure of necessity'.[37] Nobles stole because they were ashamed to beg, and people who had food ate it in secret so that they wouldn't have to share it.[38] The overall losses suffered at Acre were estimated by this author as 300,000, to which he added another 100,000 who allegedly died as a result of a misguided celibacy, 'reckoning that it was wicked to gain bodily health by sacrificing their purity'.[39]

Grotesque though such estimates are, the actual losses were evidently high, and the wide-ranging consequences included a dynastic scandal. The death of Queen Sibylla of Jerusalem in the late summer of 1190 left her sister Isabella with the right of succession to the crown. The fact that Isabella was married to Humphrey of Toron didn't stop the ambitious Conrad of Montferrat making a pitch for her hand, and the need to secure supplies from Tyre was cited to justify separating Isabella from Humphrey by force and marrying her off to Conrad in November. Isabella's divorce on trumped-up grounds was distasteful in the extreme, so it's not surprising that twenty-three years later witnesses to it had clear memories of the discord that it generated.[40] There were religious repercussions too. Some individuals deserted to the Turks and apostatized to save their lives, and others ate meat during Lent because it was more readily available than bread. A Pisan merchant stored grain in the hope that prices would continue to rise; God burnt down his storehouse as punishment.[41] It's striking that when Richard I took Count Henry of Champagne into his service soon after his arrival at Acre, the count's 'pay' comprised food supplies – 4,000 measures of wheat and 4,000 cured pig carcasses – as well as 4,000 pounds of silver.[42]

For the Fourth Crusade too the supply situation gave rise to problems that were close to critical. The demands of provisioning played their part during the debate about the crusade's future in the summer of 1203.[43] In late August 1203 the crusade's leaders claimed to Pope Innocent III that the unexpected rejection of the pretender Alexios by the Greeks presented the crusaders with the alternatives of 'either perishing or conquering'.[44] Their plight grew worse during the winter of 1203–4, when Alexios IV reneged on his promise that he would supply his former allies. Robert of Clari reported that although there was biscuit in abundance, wine soared in price while hens cost 20s and eggs 2d (compared, respectively, with 12s and 6d at Acre in 1190).[45] Once again knights killed their horses for food, a visible draining away of the army's military capability.[46] The threat of famine, a direct result of Alexios IV's treachery, propelled the crusaders and Venetians into initiating action against the emperor, the only alternative being their ignominious return home.[47] The crusaders argued that the Greeks had presented them with no choice and deserved what they got: the pope was informed that one of the providential aspects of Constantinople's capture was that 'those who totally denied us small things . . . relinquished everything to us'.[48]

Food shortages in the Nile delta

The Nile delta was famed for its agricultural surpluses but, in the case of both of the major crusades that campaigned there, food shortages played an important though not exclusive part in bringing about disaster. They formed part of a pattern of strategic outmanoeuvring by the Muslims that was the more painful because the crusaders were caught out twice. Volunteers for the Fifth Crusade became familiar with famine conditions from the start, because they arrived at Acre in the autumn of 1217 at a time of dearth. They were advised to go home, and some did so.[49] Ironically, when they laid siege to Damietta they were in a stronger position, because the spring and autumn 'passages' brought fresh supplies. They also enjoyed a windfall of captured provisions when they overran the Muslim camp south of the city in February 1219.[50] But there were disparities too. Biscuit, lard and cheese were abundant but bread, wine and freshly slaughtered meat were in short supply; chickens cost 30s and eggs 2d.[51]

It was when the crusaders finally marched southwards from Fareskur in July 1221 that their supply problems became serious. They became trapped in the triangle of land between the Nile and the Bahr as-Saghir because the sultan won control over the Nile behind them. Supplies of food dwindled, though not to the point of famine. Unable to retreat due to the rising waters of the Nile and the Muslim tactic of cutting the dykes and flooding the low-lying land east of the river, the crusaders surrendered to the sultan after negotiating a deal which allowed the army to leave Egypt after handing over Damietta. Oliver of Paderborn put a brave face on it: 'the flood of waters and the lack of food, not the bow or the sword, humbled us in the land of our enemies'.[52] Events took a remarkably similar course when the French crusaders advanced southwards from Damietta in 1250. After the failure of the French to capture Mansurah the Muslims regained control over the Nile to the crusaders' rear, this time by dragging galleys overland and launching them behind the French lines. They thus cut the crusaders off from Damietta and their supplies. Once again it's the catalogue of inflated prices that tells the story best. Joinville reported that an ox cost eighty pounds, a sheep or pig thirty pounds, an egg 12d and a barrel of wine ten pounds.[53] The religious demands of Lent posed a problem, not because the crusaders were driven to eat meat like their predecessors at Acre, but because the only fish available were eels that carried disease from feeding on corpses in the rivers.[54] Other factors, including sickness and the overall strategic impasse, combined with this shortage of provisions to induce the king to order a general retreat in April 1250. It ended with the capture of the whole army, and on this occasion there was no disguising the severity of the disaster.

Responses to shortage

Sometimes famine or the threat of famine compelled crusading leaders to take vigorous action. Most emphatically this happened in January 1099 when the desperate poor started to tear down the walls of Raymond of Toulouse's power-base at Maarat al-Numan. Raymond had no choice but to place himself at the head of a resumed march southwards. Something similar had occurred earlier in the First Crusade during the first period of shortage at Antioch. Collectively the princes had to maintain a military presence along Antioch's western walls, but individually they absented themselves for long periods of time to go off and look for food supplies with which to feed their followers, and more generally to search for the booty and money they'd need to pay the high prices demanded. The entire region around Antioch was carved up into informal zones of control with Godfrey of Bouillon and Robert of Flanders holding the north-east, Bohemund the west and north-west and Raymond of Toulouse the lands south of the city, known as the Ruj.[55] Most remarkably Robert of Normandy secured the port of Latakiah, which placed him in a strong position logistically but exposed him to the accusation that he preferred the soft beds of Latakiah to the tough conditions outside Antioch.[56]

Such land-grabbing was second nature to the princes and it was probably the only way in which the long period of time that the army spent in northern Syria could have been managed. But it has been pointed out how far afield ordinary crusaders also foraged, driven by the gnawing fear of starvation. We know an unusual amount about the movements of a poor servant called Peter Bartholomew who came to prominence in 1098 through the contentious visions that he enjoyed, and it's been calculated that between the end of 1097 and June 1098 Peter travelled at least 540 kilometres (340 miles) in search of food.[57] This was possible because the crusaders had fairly firm control over much of the territory as far north as Cilicia and as far south as the Ruj.

A similar pattern came into being during the winter of 1203–4 when the crusaders and Venetians reacted to Alexios IV's betrayal by pillaging the densely populated and prosperous region around Constantinople. They weren't trying to blockade the city so most of their forces were freed up, and with 20,000 mouths to feed there was no alternative to this despoliation.[58] The crusaders who besieged Acre in 1189–91 didn't have such an option: they were boxed in by Saladin's lines and this may explain why the famine conditions in the camp in 1190–1 proved to be so harsh. As for the crusaders campaigning in the Nile delta, they were caught out by famine in conjunction with well-managed enemy operations against them, so it was impracticable to disperse in search of food, either singly or in foraging groups.

Welfare support

Aside from providing protective shields for foraging parties, the only thing the leaders could do to try to curtail famine was to set up a rudimentary provision for the poor. This made sense in terms of containing demoralization and curbing desertion, both of which were highly contagious. It was also a Christian duty and it harmonized with crusading ideology, which placed strong emphasis on the expression of love for one's neighbour. One might expect to find this way of thinking leading to extensive welfare support for fellow crusaders. After all, one of its most enduring creations was the order of St John of Jerusalem (the Knights Hospitaller), established soon after the First Crusade to care for the welfare of poor pilgrims.[59] But circumstances during the campaigns simply told against organized welfare provision. Price control for example wasn't a realistic option, as the leaders of the Christian army found out at Acre in the winter of 1190–1.[60] Many of those who brought food to crusader camps, by land or sea, did so because they expected to find a seller's market. If they were denied free-market rates they'd just go elsewhere. The *Gesta Francorum* addressed this point explicitly when it noted that the Armenians and Syrians observed the failure of a foraging expedition despatched from Antioch at the end of 1097 and proceeded to bring in corn and other supplies from sources that they had researched beforehand.[61] When an army was immobile the free market was bound to prevail.

In such circumstances the only option was to establish a common treasury from which the poor's most basic needs might be met. The first crusaders were slow to address this; they operated a common fund from an early stage but its proceeds were directed towards military uses, such as subsidizing Tancred's command of the tower that received his name at the siege of Antioch,[62] and paying skilled artisans for their work at the siege of Jerusalem.[63] It was only in the spring of 1099, at Arqa, that they resolved to tithe all spoils and divide the proceeds between the clergy and the poor.[64] This was too late, for the worst periods of famine were past. It seems that earlier the only recourse of the indigent had been individual alms, so that Stephen of Blois claimed that only 'God's mercy and our money' had saved the poor from starving to death in the winter of 1097–8.[65]

Such charity was encouraged by Adhemar of Le Puy, and his example was followed on later crusades. During the siege of Acre a group of high-ranking clerics, led by Hubert Walter the bishop of Salisbury and the bishops of Verona and Fano, were horrified by the starvation and they managed to enlist the support of some influential nobles. Astutely, the clerics argued that the famished should be assisted on grounds not just of charity, but also of canon law, which stated that anybody who stood by while another person died of starvation carried guilt for their death. They could have added that in looking after the poor they were following the wishes of Henry II, who had decreed in 1188 that a share of the money of deceased crusaders should be reserved 'for the support of the poor'.[66] Hubert Walter and his group organized a collection on behalf of the poor and according to the author of the *Itinerarium peregrinorum* it helped a good deal.[67] Not long afterwards this policy was

somewhat curiously turned on its head by Richard I. During the march south
from Acre the king was alarmed by the disorder that broke out whenever a
horse died and the 'common people' fought to buy its flesh; he undertook to
provide a live horse to the owner of each one that perished, and reserved the
horsemeat for the army's knights.[68]

Disease

Starvation and disease were usually found together, and we can assume that
many of the poor crusaders who are described as perishing of hunger actually
died of illnesses contracted while severely weakened, or of conditions like heart
failure. The Muslims thought that between 100 and 200 crusaders were dying
each day at Acre in the winter of 1190–1, through a combination of disease
and famine.[69] Disease could afflict the able-bodied too. Diphtheria, typhoid
and dysentery were major killers in medieval armies; at Henry V's siege of
Harfleur in 1415 far more people would die of dysentery than of battle
wounds.[70] The army at Antioch in 1097 camped near marshes, which were
breeding grounds for mosquitoes, while the French crusaders at Mansurah in
1250 drank water that had been contaminated by corpses.[71] It's been pointed
out that when Anselm of Ribemont asked the archbishop of Reims to pray for
the souls of thirteen men who had died on the First Crusade, seven of them
had died in battle and six of disease. The number of deaths from disease is
significant given that Anselm was writing shortly after the crusaders arrived at
Antioch. Food was still plentiful; indeed he claimed that 'we are abundantly
supplied with grain, wine, oil, and all goods beyond belief'.[72]

When Richard I arrived at Acre in 1191 he immediately fell ill with a debilitating condition that caused his hair and fingernails to fall out: and Richard
was a well-fed man, who was never happier than when he was campaigning.[73]
But a mixture of famine, exhaustion, stress and miserable weather wore down
the constitution of even the fittest. At Acre in 1190–1 heavy rain caused
swelling in the limbs of the starving and their teeth fell out.[74] The sufferings
of the Muslims at the siege were hardly less severe.[75] Both the crusading army
at Damietta in the autumn/winter of 1218–19 and Louis IX's crusaders in
1250 suffered from a disease that sounds like scurvy, caused by a severe defi-
ciency of vitamin C.[76] At Damietta, where it was aggravated by the floods and
cold, the chroniclers described it as an affliction that attacked the nails on
hands and feet, and gums and teeth.[77] James of Vitry left a particularly telling
description of what happened, describing the condition as a wasting disease
whose victims fell into a coma 'like those falling asleep'.[78]

Joinville itemized much the same symptoms, adding that the army's barber
surgeons had to cut away the gangrenous flesh around the gums, and 'it was

pitiful to hear around the camp the cries of those whose dead flesh was being cut away; it was just like the cry of a women in labour'.[79] The French army was decimated by the disease. Joinville caught it, together with fever and a severe cold, while the king's scurvy was accompanied by a bad attack of dysentery, and he became so ill that his death was expected.[80] Irregular diet and unfamiliar food could cause problems. One chronicler of the Fifth Crusade linked dysentery to disorderly food intake and heat.[81] English crusaders who were taking part in a raid outside Acre in 1271 'died on the road, from heat and from exhaustion and from the hot food which they had eaten'.[82]

Medical provision

Medical facilities weren't negligible, but their provision was governed by chance. After he was captured by the Muslims Joinville had a blocked throat which stopped him swallowing, and he attributed it to a tumour. He took it for granted that he was doomed, but his captivity saved him, because a Muslim provided him with a liquid that reduced the swelling and cured him in two days. At this point the Muslims believed Joinville to be the king's cousin, hence a valuable captive worth taking trouble over.[83] Other sick captives were subjected to a simple test: if they could walk off the ship they lived, if they couldn't they were killed and their bodies dumped in the Nile.[84] The availability of medically trained personnel in a crusading army depended largely on how many nobles and groups brought along their household physicans or hired one on the spot. When he was in Egypt and Palestine Louis IX had a female physician called Hersende, and the Bologna contingent on the Fifth Crusade contracted the services of a medic called Hugo of Lucca. Hugo was a figure of note; his pupil Theodorich Borgognoni wrote a book on surgery, *Chirurgia*, based on his teachings.[85]

The ability of such individuals to cater to the hundreds of wounded needing urgent attention after a major engagement was obviously limited. The author of one preaching manual depicted a wounded crusader being attended to by a doctor, but it's likely that this was wishful thinking.[86] Trauma surgery on the battlefield was impracticable, and for the vast majority a lost limb or a deep cut to the head or chest cavity meant death. Gautier of Autrèche benefited from the immediate attention of several surgeons and physicians after receiving a pummelling from the Turks outside Damietta in 1249, but they couldn't save him.[87] On the other hand, a strange story about Godfrey of Bouillon inadvertently severing an artery in his own leg while fighting a wild bear indicates, if true, that such wounds could be cauterized.[88]

Medical practice in the Latin East generally was advanced for its time, a remarkable hybrid that had learnt and adapted from western, Islamic and

Byzantine techniques. In particular, the hospital that was maintained by the order of St John at Jerusalem excited the admiration of those westerners who encountered it.[89] But these were mainly pilgrims: very few crusaders were in a position to make use of the hospital's large capacity and excellent regime, given that the Second Crusade didn't conduct operations inside Palestine and the hospital fell into Muslim hands in 1187. In the field catering for the sick was one of the tasks customarily allocated to women crusaders, and it's hard to imagine that their skills extended to much more than washing wounds, applying and changing dressings, and providing food and drink. Even talk of 'dressings' was surely unrealistic in such a context, in which keeping wounds free from infection was difficult enough.[90]

Networks of financial support

We can assume that one advantage of belonging to the household of a king or magnate on crusade was access to the expertise of their physician. Another was the cushion of their financial support. By 1200 the Church was making a distinction between crusaders who went east at the expense of others and those who funded themselves; people who did pay all their own expenses were promised not just forgiveness of sins but something called 'a greater share of eternal salvation'.[91] We might conjecture that it was worth exchanging such an imprecise spiritual gain for the security of going east in the company of a powerful lord, but of course the ability to do so was subject to social and economic circumstances that varied considerably.

Beyond lordship itself, regional solidarities played an important role. When the crusaders geared themselves up for their make-or-break encounter with Kerbogha's army in 1098, for example, trumpeters went around Antioch 'shouting that each man should stay with the princes of his people'.[92] In the case of some groups this solidarity extended beyond simply combat. The Provençals on the First Crusade had a 'brotherhood' (*fraternitas*) which replaced dead horses, its core funding being 500 silver marks that were donated by Count Raymond.[93] Similarly, *ad hoc* confraternities and bands, in which crusaders collaborated under oath to achieve a shared goal, were commonplace and largely based on regional identities. Albert of Aachen has a tantalizing reference to such groups being formed to facilitate foraging around Antioch.[94] But there's no reason to suppose that regional cohesion was more than patchy. The support of kinsmen and neighbours was more significant. We know of many instances of crusaders who enjoyed the company of their own relatives and neighbours, and presumably they could rely on their support *in extremis*; these people certainly became conspicuous when wills were made, though perhaps that's unsurprising.

Leaders as paymasters

Even when crusaders were campaigning alongside their lords we can't assume that they were getting fixed and regular wages from them.[95] True, we have glimpses of some who were: in July 1191 for instance, Richard I gave forty marks of silver to each of the hundred knights whom he was despatching northwards to Antioch, to cover their service from Michaelmas to Easter.[96] These men could have been mercenaries rather than crusaders; or the king might have been compensating them for the fact that they were, in effect, taking time out from their pilgrimage to Jerusalem. Either way they probably stood for no more than a small percentage of crusaders, because even the greatest lords were themselves financially hard pressed. The leaders of the First Crusade left home with substantial reserves of specie and they received generous presents from the emperor Alexios at Constantinople, but few of them remained well off. Possible exceptions were Stephen of Blois, who claimed in a letter home written in March 1098 that he was twice as rich as when he had left,[97] and Raymond of Toulouse, who for unexplained reasons never seems to have been hard up.[98] Louis VII lavished praise on both the Hospitallers and the Templars for helping him sustain his activities in the Holy Land with loans.[99] On the Third Crusade Richard I was exceptionally well funded and it's likely that the soldiers he took with him benefited accordingly. As early as his stop at Marseilles, in August 1190, Richard took into his service pilgrims who came to him in a destitute condition.[100]

To a large extent, however, leaders offered temporary rather than long-term support. In 1191 Richard I 'cheerfully distributed great quantities of gold and silver to the French and foreigners of any nation so that they could more than recover their means and redeem the securities they had given for their debts'.[101] In 1221 in Egypt the papal legate Pelagius 'distributed wages with a generous hand to the knights and their attendants'.[102] This money presumably came from the 'common store' from which Pelagius had already funded costly operations.[103] A song complaining about the behaviour of the leaders of the crusade of 1239 criticized the 'great lords' for failing to provide financial support for the expedition's lesser nobles, *bacheliers* and *vavassours*, whose resources were exhausted.[104] And when Joinville discovered, on arriving in Cyprus in 1248, that he couldn't afford to pay the eleven knights whom he had brought with him on crusade, he was taken into royal service.[105] Louis IX's inability to maintain payments to those whom he'd taken into his service in this way was one of the problems that faced the French when they were cut off from Damietta in the spring of 1250.[106]

These and similar instances look like 'bail out' measures rather than a planned system of support; in any case, in the central Middle Ages military wages were usually regarded as core funding that would be supplemented by other means.[107] That said, when there was nobody able to provide even a minimal infrastructure of funding, a crusade's viability was at risk. At Corfu in May 1203 this led the leaders of the Fourth Crusade to argue in favour of accepting the tempting offer that had been made by the pretender Alexios; it's likely that their unspoken hope was that Alexios would become the expedition's milch-cow, another Richard I.[108]

Dependence on plunder

Hence many crusaders were thrown back on their own resources. Some benefited from the high rate of attrition in the form of legacies,[109] but for most

28 The most famous crusading booty: the four bronze horses carried back to Venice after the sack of Constantinople in 1204.

survival entailed an incessant search for plunder. It's clear that much pillaging, both on land and at sea, was driven by need.[110] The point was made with force in a description of the events of the Fourth Crusade up to 1203 that Hugh, count of St Pol, set out in a letter. 'You should know that, after I quit my lands, I had nothing from any source, except what I was able to acquire and win. Indeed, on the night preceding the day on which the city surrendered itself to us, I had fallen into such poverty that it was necessary for me to exchange my surcoat for bread, although I kept my horses and weapons.'[111] This is remarkable testimony and it's reliable, for Hugh was writing to a vassal and close friend. And there were worse plights than Hugh's. At Antioch in 1098 Count Hartmann of Dillingen-Kybourg, one of the richest lords in Swabia who'd distinguished himself at the capture of Nicaea, was reduced to begging and to handouts from Godfrey's table, 'one loaf with a portion of meat or fish'. He rode into action against Kerbogha on a donkey and with captured Turkish armour; this was humiliating, but at least it gave him the chance to salvage his financial situation with booty.[112]

In the interpretation of booty's function on crusades a single short passage in the *Gesta Francorum* has caused a lot of misunderstanding. This passage narrates how, before the crusaders joined battle with the Turks at Dorylaeum in 1097, a morale-boosting message was passed between the combatants: 'Stand fast all together, trusting in Christ and in the victory of the Holy Cross. Today, please God, you will all become rich [*divites*].'[113] This seems to be such a frank appeal to acquisitiveness that it's often been cited with reference to what motivated crusaders. But the passage needs close attention. Even assuming that its words refer to material rather than spiritual wealth,[114] when we bear in mind the obsession which each man had with meeting his essential bodily requirements, the condition of being *dives* (rich) surely refers to short-term needs rather than any hopes to set aside a store of gains that could later be taken home. We have to remember that this was a very early stage in the crusade. A crusader who seized anything at Dorylaeum would have had carry it all the way to Jerusalem before then taking it back home to the West.

The *Gesta Francorum* passage is illuminated by a similar but fuller one in an account of Barbarossa's host in 1190. The emperor exhorted his troops not to be distracted by the prospect of booty during their imminent encounter with the Turks outside Iconium. After all, on the day after the battle everybody would be wealthy (*ditabimur*): if they died they would enjoy heaven's riches, and if they survived they would have access to the enemy's food supplies and spoils.[115] In its simultaneous addressing of transcendental hopes and short-term needs this rings true in terms of crusading psychology; and nobody could seriously argue that Barbarossa's starving crusaders, who still faced a march of some hundreds of miles to regain Jerusalem, were mapping out future investments back home any more than their predecessors in 1097.

It's undeniable that much of the booty that was acquired by the first crusaders took the form of livestock that was either consumed or replaced pack animals that had perished. After Dorylaeum itself 'gold, silver, horses, asses, camels, oxen, sheep and many other things' are specified,[116] and following the defeat of Kerbogha 'gold and silver and many furnishings, as well as sheep, oxen, horses, mules, camels and asses, corn, wine, flour and many other things of which we were badly in need'.[117] Even the gold and silver that are referred to in both these passages seem to have entered the daily economy of expenditure rather than forming a long-term gain. When Richard I conquered Cyprus in 1191 'he plundered everything necessary for his expedition as if it had been collected for him'.[118] Much of the insatiable greed for which the crusaders were criticized by Greeks, Muslims and their own clerical companions was rooted in desperation. From that point of view it's hardly surprising that plundering became wearily predictable. So when the commoners at Acre launched a misguided attack on al-Adil's lines on 25 July 1190 they were easily lured into pillaging among his tents, where they were dispersed and formed easy prey for a Muslim counter-attack.[119]

Times of plenty

Typically there were two occasions when significant amounts of plunder were available. These were major victories in the field, which were normally crowned by the capture of the enemy's camp, and the capture of cities. After their victory over Saladin at Arsuf in September 1191 'those who were greedy for gain and wished to gather the enemy's booty returned to the battlefield and returned well laden, carrying off whatever they wanted'.[120] A successful attack on a Muslim caravan in June 1192 yielded a treasure trove of gold and silver, spices, textiles, armour, tents, foodstuffs, medicine and money. A sizeable yield had been expected: Richard had had to forbid all looting until victory was certain.[121]

After the storming of Jerusalem in 1099 'our men rushed round the whole city, seizing gold and silver, horses and mules, and houses full of all sorts of goods'.[122] But the sack of Jerusalem was small fry compared with that of Constantinople by the Fourth Crusade on 13–15 April 1204. This became notorious because of the volume of the plunder, quite possibly the greatest since the sack of Rome in 455, allied to the fact that it was extorted by Christians from the inhabitants of a Christian city. Comparatively few people were killed but rape was commonplace. The most shocking aspect of the pillaging was that the crusaders treated churches and monasteries no differently from imperial palaces and the estates of the nobility, stripping them of any movables of value that they managed to detach from their settings.

For obvious reasons, crusading commentators tended to be fairly reticent in their comments on what occurred. Geoffrey of Villehardouin noted only the unusual diversity of the goods seized, adding that 'so much booty had never been gained in any city since the creation of the world'.[123] Robert of Clari remarked that the city held more wealth than the next richest forty cities combined.[124] It was left to others to fill in the detail and to pass judgements. The most outraged Greek commentator was Niketas Choniates, who like many other members of the city's nobility was rough-handled by the pillagers. Pope Innocent III was offended by the killing of Christians, the sexual misbehaviour, and the robbing of churches, 'even ripping away silver tablets from altars and breaking them into pieces among themselves, violating sacristies and crosses, and carrying away relics'.[125]

The regulation of plundering

Plundering was never a complete free-for-all. It was invariably subject to rules, not just in the way it was carried out but also in arrangements for the division of the spoils that were taken. But because of the nature of the exercise the various approaches adopted were rarely trouble-free. In the case of both movable and immovable property the first crusaders operated on the basis of 'free seizure' (in effect, he who grabs keeps). This is puzzling given that some system of formally dividing booty was already established practice in European warfare; it had been shaped in part by market forces and in part by the power wielded by political and social elites.[126] Free seizure was a notorious recipe for indiscipline. So when the army prepared for battle with the Fatimid army after the Christian capture of Jerusalem 'the patriarch [of Jerusalem, Arnulf of Choques] had it announced throughout all the host that . . . anyone who turned aside for plunder before the battle was finished should be excommunicated, but that thereafter they might return with great joy to take whatever the Lord should grant'.[127]

It's likely that what drove the first crusaders to adopt such an unusual and problematic approach was their lack of a unified command structure. Immovable property was claimed by the first-comer, as Raymond of Aguilers testified 'it was a custom among us that if any one came to a castle or a villa first and placed his standard there with a guard, it was touched by no one else afterward'.[128] Fulcher of Chartres noted that at Jerusalem this applied to houses, so poor people could become rich on the spot. It was a veritable lottery.[129] The lordship of cities posed particular difficulties. The dispute over who should have Antioch came close to breaking up the crusade; Raymond of Toulouse dug his heels in and wouldn't cede to Bohemund the various towers that he controlled. The situation recurred at Jerusalem, where Raymond took possession of the Tower of David, and, piqued at his failure to be elected as the city's first ruler, he declined to surrender it into Godfrey's hands.[130]

As late as the 1170s the practice of free seizure by the first crusaders exercised an influence on the way captured property was handled in the kingdom of Jerusalem: the chronicler William of Tyre remarked that 'even to this day a custom stands among us for a law that, in cities violently stormed, anyone entering shall possess for himself and his heirs by perpetual right whatever he seizes'.[131] But by this point crusaders fighting in the East had moved towards division of plunder. This usually caused its own difficulties, not least because suspicion was fuelled by the confusion that invariably accompanied plundering: nobody really had a clear idea of what was going on.

This was well demonstrated by events at Lisbon, which crusaders travelling by sea helped the Portuguese to capture en route for the Second Crusade. It had been agreed that all booty would be divided between the participants in the city's capture, but it proved impossible to control the Flemings and the men of Cologne. 'They rushed about hither and thither; they pillaged; they broke open doors; they tore open the innermost parts of every house . . . [and] they secretly snatched away all those things which ought to have been made the common property of all the forces.' By contrast, at least according to the Anglo-Norman priest Raol, his fellow countrymen were models of sobriety and order, 'preferring to keep their hands from all rapine rather than violate their engagements and the ordinances of the oath-bound association'. Order was gradually restored and a fair distribution of spoils took place.[132] This passage has such an obvious patriotic message to convey that it has to be taken with a pinch of salt, but its essence rings true: bickering and resentment were inseparable from the practice of dividing booty.

Similar problems cropped up when Silves was captured by crusaders on their way to the East in 1189. Their original agreement with the Portuguese was that the crusaders could have all of the city's gold, silver and food supplies. But this was amended in King Sancho's favour to stop the Portuguese withdrawing, and the surrender agreement reached with the Muslims allowed them to leave with their belongings intact. Confusion and quarrelling followed and there was some pillaging by the crusaders, but King Sancho held the trump card: he was staying and the crusaders needed to move on. Reliance on royal generosity gained the crusaders little, and the tenth part of all conquests which the king had grandly promised to dedicate to the Holy Sepulchre remained a pipe dream.[133] As at Lisbon, part of the problem was bickering among the groups that made up this composite expedition, which stopped the crusaders presenting Sancho with a united front. When Alcacer do Sol fell in October 1217 to men from Germany who were on their way to the Fifth Crusade, the threat of excommunication was required to make some place what they had seized in the common pool. It's clear that for some of these northerners the sheer beauty of the artefacts they grabbed in Alcacer, quite apart from their value, proved hard to resist; one man was 'seduced by the beauty of the object he had taken' and illicitly kept it hidden until he nearly choked to death at a meal, a divine warning that he heeded by handing it over.[134]

Dividing the spoils during the Third Crusade

Even among kings the division of booty caused quarrels, notably during the notorious incident in 1191 when Philip Augustus lodged a claim to a half of Cyprus on the basis that he and Richard had previously agreed to a fifty–fifty split of all their conquests while they were on crusade. The French claim spawned some arcane legalistic bickering; it's possible that it even caused Richard to play down the strategic thinking that lay behind his conquest, so as to detach his actions on Cyprus from the crusade and hence from his prior agreement with Philip.[135] The spoils of recaptured Acre on the other hand, including Muslim prisoners, were divided between Philip and Richard, the immovable property being handed back to the Christians who'd been driven out in 1187.[136] Crusaders who'd spent almost two years of their lives besieging the city were understandably shocked to receive nothing. They called a special meeting outside Acre's walls and informed the two kings that they would withdraw their support 'unless they were allowed to share in the profit just as they had in the labour'. Philip and Richard promised to comply but delays in doing so forced many crusaders to sell their weapons and withdraw.[137]

Gradually Richard did pump what he gained into the sustenance of the crusade, in particular hiring the services of every archer in the army.[138] But when he tried to resume operations in mid-August 1191 considerable resistance remained on the grounds of inadequate resources: 'This speech is hard to bear. We're poor people, we've got nothing to eat or drink, no clothes to wear or horses to ride on. So how can we follow him? He doesn't give us anything.' Richard responded by making fresh hand-outs.[139] His problem was that he was faced with supporting the French contingent as well, advancing a loan of 5,000 marks to Hugh duke of Burgundy.[140] When the English and French planned a joint attack on a caravan in June 1192, Hugh demanded a third of the booty.[141] The whole sequence of events highlighted the inherent clumsiness of the way in which the crusade operated.

The plundering of Constantinople

It's not surprising that the crusade whose participants paid the closest attention to the division of plunder was the Fourth. In the agreement reached at Venice in 1201 it was specified that all booty should be divided fifty–fifty between the crusaders and Venetians.[142] This basic approach was greatly expanded during the preparations for a second assault on Constantinople in 1203–4. The allies clearly debated the future ownership of both city and booty in detail. It's tempting but unfair to argue that this shows that the expedition had degenerated into a squalid affair of conquest: the westerners knew that if they were successful they'd have unprecedented amounts of spoils and immovable property to dispose of. It made good sense to have a thorough and workable ground plan. In March 1204 the crusade's leaders and the Venetians concluded an overall agreement for the partition of Constantinople and its plunder. First they made provision for the settling of the debts still owed to them by Alexios IV; they then agreed that any booty remaining should be divided fifty–fifty between crusaders and Venetians. They also arranged for the election of an emperor and for the division of the city. Crucially, each individual then swore to bring his booty to a common hoard. They also undertook to respect the sanctity of religious houses and not to attack women.[143]

As we've already seen, this attempt to shield religious houses and women went by the board during the sack, though Niketas Choniates' account of his experiences at the hands of the westerners demonstrates that it was possible to appeal to the crusaders' better nature.[144] The division of both movable and immovable booty proceeded in a reasonably orderly way, but it generated much resentment among the rank and file. Robert of Clari gives an excellent eyewitness view of their grievances. First the leaders took possession of the best properties, leaving the poor to make do with what was left. Then the common hoard was pillaged both by the rich and by the very people who were supposed to be guarding it, 'so that nothing was shared with the common people of the host or the poor knights or the sergeants who had helped to win the treasure, save the plain silver, like the silver pitchers which the ladies of the city used to carry to the baths'.[145] The unknown author of one description of the sack, the *Devastatio Constantinopolitana*, went a lot further: he regarded the unfair division of the Constantinople booty as typical of the way the rich and powerful had misled and short-changed the poor throughout the crusade. The ordinary crusaders had been fleeced by the Venetians when they were awaiting transport,[146] and after the capture of Zadar 'the barons kept the city's goods for themselves, giving nothing to the poor'.[147]

The riches of Egypt

As at Constantinople, attempts to implement the strategy of conquering Egypt held out the prospect of rich conquests. Like their predecessors on the Third Crusade, crusaders in Egypt consented to take their cue from their leaders, partly because they feared to challenge their authority openly but probably also because they realized that these individuals bore a heavy burden of expenses. They grumbled about the procedures followed but they didn't rebel.[148] When Damietta fell to the army of the Fifth Crusade in 1219 both the divisions of spoils and the ownership of the city became points of heated dispute between the papal legate Pelagius, King John of Jerusalem and the crusaders generally. There was confusion over the fate of the spoils. James of Vitry claimed that the booty was disappointing because many crusaders, 'pilgrims in name only', concealed their gains, while the Muslims had buried much of their money and thrown some of it into the Nile. Only 400,000 besants were available for distribution, and this caused unrest, which struck James (adopting a somewhat condescending attitude) as both foolish and undisciplined.[149] Oliver of Paderborn's account of events was rather different. He wrote that Damietta's movable wealth was divided up proportionally 'not only among clerics and knights, but also among attendants, women and children'.[150] But in a curious passage he commented that 'not an old woman nor a boy of ten years and over was excluded; to Christ alone, the bestower of the goods, was a share denied, not even a tenth being paid to him'.[151]

The lordship of Damietta itself caused the biggest uproar, and to this day its outcome remains unclear. Both James and Oliver stated categorically that the city was incorporated by Pelagius into the kingdom of Jerusalem,[152] but other evidence points towards the city's future being unsettled. This was largely because of hopes that the Emperor Frederick II would arrive and take over the leadership of the crusade, in which case he'd expect to make the decision.[153] The eyewitness John of Tulbia claimed that Damietta was temporarily placed under the rule of John of Brienne,[154] while Oliver of Paderborn wrote of its partitioning, 'the towers of the city with its homes were distributed among the kingdoms whose warriors had assembled for its capture'.[155] The confusion reflected disagreement over who was in charge of the crusade. By way of contrast, Louis IX's approach in 1249 was nothing if not forthright: as a lawfully acquired conquest Damietta belonged exclusively to the French crown. But, as in 1219, the disposal of its movable plunder caused friction. John of Valery referred to a 'good custom of the Holy Land, by which,

29 In 1219–21 coins were minted by John of Brienne, the king of Jerusalem, to proclaim his lordship over Damietta. The port's name circles the king's head.

whenever a city belonging to the enemy is captured the king takes a third of all the goods found in it, and the other crusaders two-thirds'. John claimed that this custom had been implemented in 1219, and he urged that it should apply not just to non-perishable goods but also to the huge supplies of food-stuffs that had been captured, which the king wanted to retain under his own control. Louis refused to budge on the issue.[156]

The devil's work?

Given the crucial role that plunder played in their survival, it's understandable that the members of crusading armies were obsessed about its equitable division. But for clerics such concerns were overshadowed by the moral issue of intention. Niketas Choniates accused the Fourth Crusade's participants of being driven by greed. 'In truth, they were exposed as frauds. Seeking to avenge the Holy Sepulchre, they raged openly against Christ and sinned by overturning the Cross with the cross they bore on their backs, not even shuddering to trample on it for the sake of a little gold and silver.'[157] His scepticism about what truly motivated crusaders was typically Greek, and it more than likely went back all the way to the First Crusade. It was certainly deeply ingrained by the 1140s, when the Byzantine princess Anna Komnena assessed the motivations of the first crusaders in *The Alexiad*, her life of her father Alexios I. 'The simpler folk were in very truth led on by a desire to worship at Our Lord's tomb and visit the holy places, but the more villainous characters (in particular Bohemund and his like) had an ulterior purpose, for they hoped on their journey to seize the capital itself, looking upon its capture as a natural consequence of the expedition.'[158]

It's not surprising that the Greeks, and a lot of Muslim commentators too, dismissed crusading as hypocritical. The religion and culture of neither group equipped its commentators to understand penitential warfare. But Catholic churchmen weren't naive in their assessment of their crusading contemporaries. They believed that the devil was constantly at work luring people into behaviour that would condemn their souls to Hell; and nothing would please the devil more than persuading Christians to sin 'more gravely and wantonly under the cover of religion and the banner of the Cross'.[159] From personal experience they knew how acquisitive their contemporaries were. Social and vocational stereotyping was irresistible; for clerical moralists like Alan of Lille knights were addicted to plundering (*rapina*) in the same way that townsfolk couldn't avoid usury.[160] This determinism was reinforced by national or regional stereotypes. Some of the combatants at Lisbon in 1147 regarded the Flemings as 'covetous of the goods of others, although at the moment under the guise of pilgrimage and religion'.[161]

Most of the time this didn't matter, given that crusading entailed a bleak diet of hunger, disease and suffering. But, as we've seen, military success could generate a sudden shower of material prosperity and this, it was thought, straightway closed men's hearts to Christ and let the devil in. It's notable that the author of the *Gesta Francorum* could recall the exact value of the belt and scabbard that were pillaged from the dead body of Antioch's commander, Yaghisiyan, presumably because he saw them fetch this price when sold.[162]

So the fact that hostile commentators like Niketas Choniates had axes to grind didn't mean that the conclusions they reached about crusading weren't shared by some Catholics. The letters that Innocent III wrote to the leaders of the Fourth Crusade showed this all too well. Writing to Doge Dandolo in

January 1205, the pope expressed his opinion that 'since you have thus far served the world and have gained not a little glory from it, in the future you should serve the Lord faithfully'.[163] This was as close as Innocent could come in writing to questioning the Venetian's underlying intentions. As for the French, Innocent treated them throughout the Fourth Crusade like boisterous children who had to be controlled. The danger lay in the convergence of large quantities of transferable booty, ready access to Venetian shipping and the presence of a pliable legate, Peter Capuano. He was too willing to dispense the crusaders from their vows to assist the Holy Land. A year after the fall of Constantinople the pope wrote furiously to Peter that the crusaders' premature return, 'stuffed with spoils', leaving not just the Holy Land but the conquered city of Constantinople itself without defenders, imperilled all future recruitment for crusades.[164]

'For devotion alone' – the foregrounding of intention

This last point was vital: it was never just the souls of individual crusaders that were at stake. It was always crucial to hold in balance the Church's duty to assist Christians to reach salvation and meet the military requirements of the Holy Land.[165] Innocent and his successors needed crusades. They knew that while successful crusading called for discipline, which had to be enforced through the vow, the constant need for support in the field meant that it also hinged on plunder and conquest. Sometimes the compromises imposed were both legalistic and impracticable. In 1203, when the Fourth Crusade was bogged down in Greek territory, Innocent III ruled that if the Greeks denied the crusaders food then they could requisition it, but 'without hurting people and with fear of the Lord and the intention of making reparation'; there were biblical precedents which the pope cited at length.[166] Churchmen didn't dissent from the popular viewpoint that God rewarded his faithful servants with material benefits, though they rarely dwelt on it because it sat awkwardly with the penitential asceticism that they much preferred to promote. The attitude they followed throughout was that a crusading army could plunder in order to fight, and conquer in order to win, but it shouldn't fight in order to plunder, nor should it allow its conquests to distract it from its ultimate goal. 'The sin is not in waging war, but in waging war for the sake of plunder.'[167]

At the individual level the mechanism for securing this was the vow that each crusader had taken; for God would know if a person was serving Him rather than aiming to enrich himself, and His vengeance on the deceiver was certain.[168] Such a person would lose his soul, not save it.[169] The distinction was set in place at the very start of crusading. The council of Clermont's surviving decree about the First Crusade stated that 'Whoever for devotion alone, not to gain honour or money, goes to Jerusalem to liberate the Church of God can substitute this journey for all penance.'[170] The point was forcefully reiterated almost a year later when Urban II wrote to the Bolognese about the crusade.[171] For the annalist of Würzburg the disastrous outcome of the Second Crusade was only explicable in terms of the corrupt intentionality of its participants. The majority of the crusaders, 'simulating a holy zeal', set out 'for the sake of learning about strange lands', to escape from poverty, debts or obligations, and to evade punishment.[172] It's a remarkable passage, so much at odds with what we know about the burdens shouldered by those who had undertaken the crusade that it's best viewed as testimony to the depth of shock felt at its failure.

'Greed and her daughter envy' – condemning collective behaviour

But a crusading army was more than just a collection of individuals; it demonstrated a group behaviour that shifted markedly according to the level of material prosperity. Contemporaries were on the lookout for certain tell-tale signs that resolution and decency alike were slipping, construed as proof that the devil was indeed managing to wreck the holy enterprise in both the military and the religious senses. These signs weren't uniformly associated with good times. We've seen the author of the *Itinerarium peregrinorum* noting that famine made people selfish and criminal during the siege of Acre. But the idea that luxury, idleness and wicked activity were bedfellows crops up time and again in the main narratives. Raymond of Aguilers wrote of the first crusaders spending their time after their capture of Antioch in 'counting and identifying their spoils . . . listening to the pagan dancing girls . . . [and feasting] in splendour and magnificence'.[173] The image conjured up is like a Victorian painting (one by Alma-Tadema?) of Roman high society at play.

Luxury allegedly bred conflict. So after the crusaders' successful battle against Kerbogha in 1098, the division of spoils generated disputes among companions and between lords and their servants.[174] Among Barbarossa's crusaders in 1190 the accumulation of Greek booty caused 'faith and unity' to be subverted by 'greed and her daughter envy'.[175] This censorious language recurs in the way the author of the *Itinerarium peregrinorum* describes the crusaders reluctantly forming up to march southwards after they had taken Acre in 1191. 'The people came out of the city in a trickle, because they were too addicted to idleness and easy living, and the city had too many pleasures, i.e. excellent wine and the most beautiful girls. Most of them led a dissolute life, resorting to women and wine, so that the city was polluted by their foolish pleasure-seeking and the gluttony of its inhabitants.'[176] Even when the march south began, 'no small part' of the army succeeded in slipping back to Acre's taverns.[177] The conspicuously well-tailored clothes of the French deserters particularly caught the attention of this author. 'Their behaviour proved that they did not take their pilgrimage seriously.'[178]

Nor was the situation any different at Damietta during the Fifth Crusade. In the course of the long siege of the city 'our army was so given over to dissipation that the knights devoted themselves to leisure, neglecting the work of God, while the common people turned to the taverns and to fraudulent dealings'.[179] There was no change for the better once Damietta had been won. 'No one can describe the corruption of our army after Damietta was given us by God . . . Lazy and effeminate, the people were contaminated with chamberings and drunkenness, fornications and adulteries, thefts and wicked gains.'[180] An ill-fated advance on Tanis late in 1219 was conducted 'not with tears and devotion but with pomp and jubilation, for the sake of plunder and worldly gain'.[181] Even sentences of excommunication had no effect on such people.[182] Needless to say, all these commentators were clerics. According to one commentator the moral degeneration of the army besieging Acre depressed Baldwin of Canterbury so much that it contributed to his death.[183] And in 1198 Innocent III went so far as to claim that the things crusaders got up to were worse than anything they would have tried at home, where bad behaviour was subject to closer scrutiny and censure.[184]

The reality of day-to-day life on crusade

The recurrent banes of crusading armies were held to be swearing, gambling and illicit sex. On this point at least there's no need to fear that we're being misled by the prejudices of the chroniclers, for it was precisely this behaviour that Louis IX tried to ban in his army in Egypt. The king was only partially successful. On one occasion during the crossing to Acre he heard that his own brother Charles was playing dice on the deck of his ship with Gautier of Nemours, and Louis indignantly threw board and dice into the sea, though Gautier had managed to grab the stakes first.[185] As for prostitutes, they accompanied Louis' army despite the king's best intentions; they found that the trick was to keep out of his sight.[186]

It's hard to judge how far prostitutes accompanied earlier crusades because clerical commentators were so generalized in the way they described sexual activity. Albert of Aachen maintained that sexual misdemeanours on the First Crusade were harshly punished. This could take the form of public humiliation, as in the case of the man and woman found guilty of adultery. They were stripped and 'forced to walk around the whole army, while being roughly beaten with sticks', so as to form an example to others. Punishment could also come from God, as when an archdeacon and his mistress were cut down by Turks while playing dice in an orchard. The bizarre *mise en scène* makes

bruno. eodem die inipso monas/
terio uibente papa tria uitrib'
pmis cancellis sacrauit alta
ria. Tunc papa ur̄ sac̄ndo mis
sasq; agendo. p̄ alia salutis hor
tamta. cor̄l ep̄is ₹ cardinalibus
multoꝛq; p̄sonis. huicemodi
[...] habuit ad ipp̄m.

tutelamq; commendauit. nisi
deo et beato Petro eiusq; uica/
rius. romanis scilicet pontificib'
Quoꝛ numero uel ordini diuina
me dignatio licet indignum as
sociauit. me olim monachum
prioremq; monasterii huius. sub
domno ac uenerabili hugone

1 Pope Urban II consecrates the high altar of the new church at his former abbey, Cluny, in
October 1095. Three weeks later the pope would summon the faithful to the First Crusade at
Clermont.

2 The gaping mouth of Hell, future abode of all who failed to do penance for their sins while they were alive. Their sentence is terrible but just: an angel turns the key to lock them in for eternity.

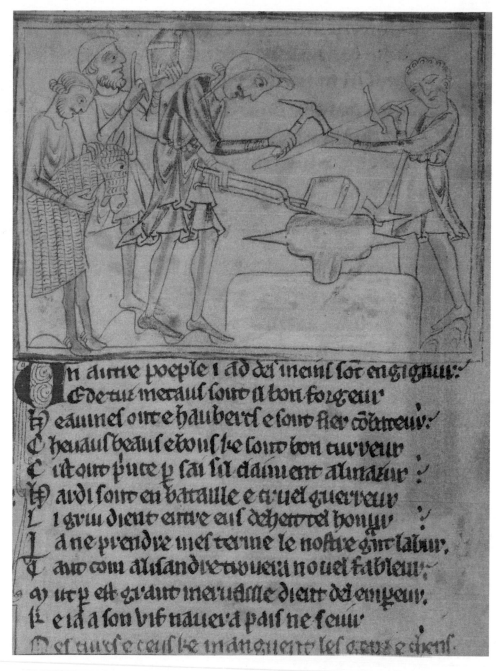

C n ainie poeple i ad dei incuil for engignur.
E de tut meraus foiw il bon forgeur
H eaumes oirre haubertf e foiw fier courreur.
C heuaus beaus e bonf fe coiro bon curveur
C ift oiro puire p fai fil daincirt alinatur.
H aidi foiro en bataille e tr uel guerreur
L i gruu dicur arrive eif dehetorel honur.
I a ne prendre mef terine le noftre gui labur.
E auro cou alifandre trouera nouel fableur.
O y urp eft graure incruaille dicur del empur.
L e id a fon vif nauera paif ne feur
O el cuefe ceuf fe in du gueiro lef geus e chenf.

3 The manufacture of armour and weapons. Appropriately the depiction comes from an English manuscript: sources for Richard I's crusade of 1189–92 are particularly rich on preparations like these.

4 The belongings of crusaders are loaded onto galleys and sailing vessels, prior to the much-feared sea voyage to the East.

pergam ab eo: neque notcou in
te mea.

5 The almost incredible congestion aboard medieval ships is well caught in this illustration from the Luttrell Psalter of *c.* 1320–40.

6 Barbarossa's crusaders clear a path through the Hungarian woods in 1189. The emperor's march eastwards was the best organized and controlled of them all.

7 In the Holkham Bible Picture Book, *c.* 1325–30, combat involving knights (above) and infantry (below) is sharply differentiated. The illustration reflects social difference rather than military reality: in practice their contributions were usually much more integrated.

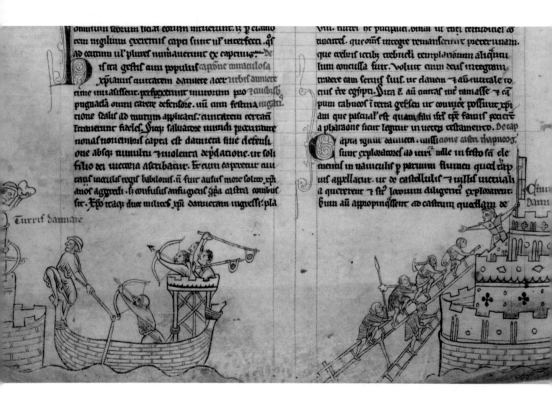

onimum scorum ligat eorum miserunt. 13 p clamo
rem uigilum exercitus capti sunt ul interfecti. qs
ad eorum ul plures numauerunt ex captiuis. De
is ra gestis cum populus capone miraculosa
xpianus ciuitatem damiere acer urbis damiere
sime mirasseint. prospexerunt murorum pro auibsb
pugnaclu omni carere defensore. uii cum festina nugati
cione scalis ad murum applicant: ciuitatem certam
tramserunt fideles. Iuq; saluatore mundi procurante
nonas nouembris capta est damieta siue defensi
one absq; tumultu uiolenta expilatione. ut soli
filio dei uictoria ascribatur. Et cum caperetur ciui
tas inclitus regis babilonis. ii fuit ausus more solito xpi
anos aggredi. s; confusus aufugeret ipsa castra comibuss
sit. Ego itaq; dux melious ipsi damietam ingressi. pla

uiii. turres ut principatuel.omiu ut turel cerudinel es
quarrel. que oms integre remanserint preter unam.
que acerbis ictibs trebucti complanorum aliquan
tum concussa fuit. Voluit eam deus integram
tradere eam seruis suis. ur clauem tantumale to
cius ire egypti. Item e. au ciuitas ie ramasse ca
pum tabucos i terra gessen ut couicte possiunt xpi
ani que pascual'est quam filii isrl tpe famis pocere
a pharaone sicut legitur in uecep testamento. De cap
apta igitur damieta . uissaone autem daphnieos
sunt exploratores ad turri uele in festo sa cle
menis in nauiculis p paruum flumen quoc cap
us appellatur. ut de castellulis uisllis uictualia
a quererentur sic locorum diligenti exploratore
bium au appropinguissent ad castrum quidam de

Turris damiate

8 Amphibious operations during the siege of Damietta in 1218–19. Matthew Paris provides a narrative, moving from the strategically crucial storming of the chain-tower on the left to the capture of the city on the right.

9 Women are gathered together for expulsion from a crusader camp. Separating the sexes was a theatrical way of proving to a vengeful God that the crusaders had resolved to mend their ways.

10 Probably the most famous portrayal of a crusader, and certainly the most beautiful one. The knight is anonymous, though he could be King Henry III of England, who took the cross at the time Matthew Paris drew the picture. He is shown fully prepared for hard combat, but deeply reverential.

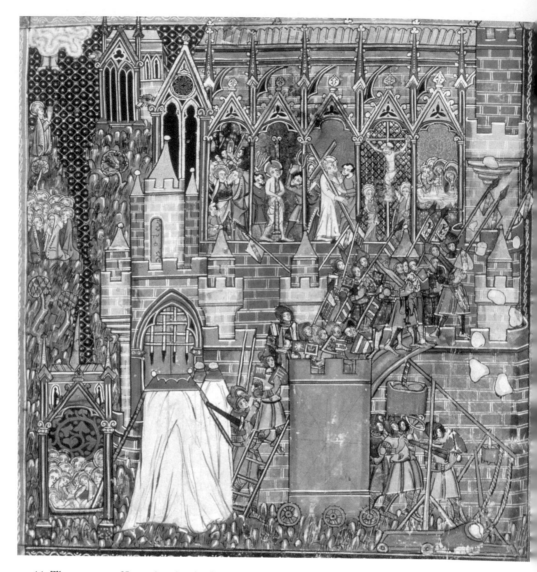

11 The capture of Jerusalem by the first crusaders in 1099: as the Christians storm the city below, their Saviour's passion is enacted above. It's a brilliant interweaving of scriptural and historical events, encapsulating medieval views of what crusading meant as a devotional act.

12 Christian captives are beheaded by Muslims. On both sides, capture often brought with it a choice between conversion and execution.

13 This illustration from the Luttrell Psalter shows Richard I in single combat against Saladin. This time the victor of Hattin loses, dramatically run through by the English king's lance.

14 This fourteenth-century depiction of Saladin makes a fascinating contrast with plate 13. The Muslim commander has stature and dignity. Neutrally described as 'king of Egypt', he is accorded his rightful place among the great men of history.

15 The mythical Queen Camilla and her Amazon warriors. The idea of Amazons fascinated medieval Europeans and they frequently crop up in crusading histories and romances.

16 Matthew Paris's grisly portrayal of the Mongols as cannibals. On the left they are killing, spit-roasting and eating their victims. On the right a bound captive anxiously awaits his fate while a Mongol horse nonchalantly munches fruit from the tree.

Illustris Rex anglie a ierosolimis rediens capi psentaur augusto

Rex anglie d'morte vracluois accusat quod abnegas se ensina marin exculsaurii pmittit

tande ueniā peteg lit absolut

17 Ineffectually disguised as a pilgrim, the returning Richard I is captured by the Austrians (above) and pleads for his release before Henry VI (below).

18 The Sainte-Chapelle in Paris. Masterpiece of Gothic art, repository of Louis IX's relics from the East, and for the French kings an inescapable reminder of their glorious crusading past.

one wonder whether 'playing dice' was a euphemism, or was it a genuine activity that Albert regarded as aggravating their sexual relations?[187] Painful public humiliation was also the punishment handed out to those caught having illicit sex in Barbarossa's army in 1189–90.[188] It's clear that such shaming cut deep, for a knight who was caught in a brothel during Louis IX's crusade in the East was offered a choice between public humiliation and dismissal from the army, and he chose the latter.[189] 'Purges' of prostitutes formed a recurrent pattern on crusades, the procedure followed being their removal to a separate camp that was actually not far away. According to James of Vitry those sex workers who defied the expulsion were whipped through the camp and branded with hot irons.[190] Fulcher of Chartres even claimed that during the siege of Antioch by the first crusaders all women, including wives, were compelled to move away from the main army.[191]

It doesn't seem likely that crusading armies oscillated between the poles of quasi-monastic asceticism and bacchanalian debauchery that are described by the clerical chroniclers. There seem to be two distorting forces at work here, one arising from expectations and the other from circumstances. Notwithstanding Innocent III's view that crusaders thought they were on the medieval equivalent of a Club 18–30 holiday, clerical commentators expected better behaviour than back at home and they over-reacted when their expectations weren't met. Recognizing that everything is relative, the perceptive James of Vitry commented that 'the Lord's army looked like a monastic cloister *compared with how it had been*'.[192] On the other hand, there's no reason to doubt that crusaders did experience collective mood swings that were dictated by the outcome of engagements, the availability of provisions and a perception of how well things were going. Almost certainly these swings were more violent than would have been the case in ordinary armies thanks to the nature of the enterprise, and above all their belief in God's shaping will. Both individually and collectively, crusaders experienced unusually emphatic 'highs' and 'lows'.

That said, this volatility of response was stopped from becoming excessive by a regular current of day-to-day activity that was much more mundane and invariable: clothes were mended, weapons sharpened, armour repaired and goods exchanged, conversations took place, friendships blossomed and antagonisms formed. Gossip about the weaknesses of prominent individuals did the rounds. Usually it took the form of anecdotes and ditties, for example 'the vulgar songs' written during the First Crusade about Robert of Normandy's allegedly 'incontinent' chaplain Arnulf of Chocques.[193] Sometimes the gossip acquired a polemical or political edge, as in the songs that were composed by both the French and the English in the later stage of the Third Crusade, and in 1239–40 in response to the disappointing calibre of the baronial leadership.[194] These exchanges were contentious enough to be noted, but the vast majority of the social intercourse that occurred on crusade has been lost, simply because, like celebration of the liturgy, it was taken for granted.

Occasionally it can be glimpsed, particularly in some of the letters written home during the First Crusade, in the rag-bag of stories about the siege of Acre that were included in the *Itinerarium peregrinorum*, above all in the crowded pages of Joinville. Two of Joinville's stories can stand for many. In one Joinville told how meal-times in his quarters were disrupted by the count of Eu, who was his neighbour; the count used a miniature ballistic device that he'd built to fire stones on to the dining table, smashing plates and dishes.[195] It's reminiscent of antics in the trenches of Flanders during quiet spells in the First World War. Another time Joinville reprimanded six of his knights, 'lolling against some sacks full of barley', who were talking while a mass was being said for a deceased comrade, a knight-banneret called Hugh of Landricourt. 'They began to laugh and told me, with a chuckle, that they were arranging the remarriage of the dead man's wife.' This was the eve of the battle of Mansurah, in which all the knights were killed or mortally wounded, 'so that the wives of all six were in a position to marry again'.[196] Joinville told the story for its moral message, but we catch in it a fascinating glimpse of crusaders being neither heroic nor depraved, engaging in relaxed and cynical banter that reflected their camaraderie, social status and economic concerns.

'The sweet but torturing memory of the native land'

Irrespective of the impact of mood swings, crusaders, like all men fighting far from home, felt acutely homesick. This is apparent in the letters of the first crusaders, in which their incessant requests for prayers, and their injunctions to loved ones to look after their affairs properly, reflected the fact that their thoughts were constantly reaching back to what they'd left behind. The grief that they had felt at departure subsided into a constant ache of longing. One chronicler of the Fifth Crusade commented that by the end of the winter of 1218–19 the crusaders besieging Damietta were so sick of sand that they longed to see green grass 'like a sick man yearns for health'.[197] Relationships were naturally most missed. In the mid-thirteenth century Count Thibald IV of Champagne wrote lyrically of the crusader's longing for his mistress: 'Lady, my most desired one, / I greet you from across the salty sea, / As the one I think of night and day, / So that no other thought gives me joy.'[198] Tactics already used at the time of departure, such as focusing on love for the Virgin, were most likely pressed into service to cope.[199]

Anxiety about home is best reflected in the taunts that were placed in the mouths of the Moors of Lisbon by the priest Raol, in his account of the city's capture in 1147. 'And they taunted us with numerous children about to be born at home in our absence, and said that on this account our wives would not be concerned about our deaths, since they would have bastard progeny enough.'[200] This was the nagging anxiety of soldiers through the ages, a *topos* as old as Homer's *Odyssey*, though no less realistic for that. It cropped up in the lord of Couci's crusade song, 'A vous, amant, plus qu'a nule autre gent', composed at the time of the Third Crusade.[201] It was probably not much consolation to argue, as Conon of Béthune did in a song written around 1200, that if a crusader's lover did betray him then her partner would have to be a wicked coward, given that all the decent men had left for the East. His suggestion that those women who remained faithful would share in the spiritual rewards earned by their crusading lovers has rather an air of desperation about it.[202] No matter how many precautions a crusader had taken before departure to safeguard his family and possessions, the signs are that concerns like these stayed with him throughout the expedition. So 'the sweet but torturing memory of their native land' was one more source of stress to add to all the others.[203]

7

❖

STORMING HEAVEN

Crusading as penitential theatre

'We shall seize heaven by violence, because "since the days of John the Baptist the kingdom of heaven has suffered violence" [Matthew 11:12]. And what could be more violent than using penitence to win something that's barred to us by human nature and God's justice?'[1] Peter of Blois wrote this extraordinary comment at the time of the Third Crusade. It's an emphatic reminder that crusading was a penitential activity, and that medieval penance was extrovert in character. No way of showing devotion was regarded as too extreme by men and women who were desperate to prove to God that they were truly contrite. So each crusade became a theatre in which God and his saints, lobbyists on behalf of the sinners, made up the audience. One preaching manual includes the story of a knight captured by the Muslims, who is suspended on the exterior of a wall which his Christian comrades are busily pounding with stones. 'Don't stop on my account,' he cries, and the stones which are then thrown miraculously break the ropes holding him in place.[2] At the siege of Acre a woman dies while helping to fill in the city's moat. 'Don't take my body away,' she implores her husband, 'just leave it here to help fill up the ditch.'[3] A knight about to set out on crusade proves his religious commitment by setting up a painful farewell scene with his young sons, the point being to demonstrate to God the depth of his anguish.[4]

Such stories were homiletic, that is, they aimed to instruct through example. A long line of sceptics from Edward Gibbon to the Monty Python team have taught us to smile at their naivety. Even when we manage to set aside this scepticism they tend to sound implausibly extravagant. Contemporaries valued irony and it's just possible that some of them would have shared our questioning response,[5] but it's much more likely that most of them would have viewed behaviour like this as exemplary. This was why such anecdotes cropped up so frequently both in crusade sermons and in accounts of the expeditions by authors who were setting out to praise what had been done. 'O zeal of woman worthy of imitation!', as the author of the *Itinerarium peregrinorum* remarked about the dying woman at Acre.[6] And on occasion such heroes and heroines of the Christian faith *were* imitated. A Muslim eyewitness of the siege of Acre confirmed that the corpses of crusaders were indeed used to fill the city's moat, adding the bizarre detail that members of the garrison later extracted them and threw them into the sea.[7]

The fact remains, though, that the evidence about the religious practices of crusaders puts the historian in a tricky position. Devotion is inherently different from the sorts of issues looked at in the previous two chapters. The scale of victories and famines might be exaggerated, but it's unlikely that either would have been invented; extravagant displays of contrition were another matter, the recording of visions and miracles even more so. They were wonderful events in both senses, and few contemporaries would question them. Both the creators of our sources and their audiences had a vested interest in clothing the subject in an exquisite aura of piety. It can't be written off but neither can it be taken at face value. When so much of the evidence is tendentious in character, can any recreation of the spiritual lives of the crusaders hope to be accurate?

The answer is yes, because in many of our sources the tendency to emphasize the devout is balanced by rich detail. Because the authors weren't setting out to deceive, their accounts are permeated by reality, disclosing aspects of human nature that were 'unworthy of imitation' but bear the hallmarks of social realism. It's possible that the source of the wholesome anecdote about the knight suspended on the wall was the unfortunate Hainault knight Gerard of Avesnes. Gerard was sent as a hostage to the Muslims of Arsuf towards the end of 1099. Hung over the town's walls to deter Godfrey of Bouillon's assault on the port, Gerard unheroically begged Godfrey not to allow him to be killed, but Godfrey turned down his request. Realizing that he was doomed anyway, Gerard made the best of a bad job with a last-minute display of piety, requesting that his horse and arms be presented to the Church of the Holy Sepulchre.[8]

There were crusaders who behaved a lot worse than Gerard, including some who were guilty of apostasy and treachery. Both during the First Crusade and in Egypt in 1250 crusaders who were captured were offered the choice between conversion and death and many opted for the former.[9] In 1190 a few German crusaders resorted to apostasy to escape the gruelling march across Anatolia,[10] as did their starving comrades at Acre, who fled to the Turkish siege-lines and embraced Islam.[11] Baha' al-Din even tells the story of one group of deserters who persuaded Saladin to give them a vessel with which they could attack Christian merchant ships, on the understanding that they'd share their profits with the Muslims.[12] Shortly before Damietta fell in the autumn of 1219 nine of the Christians, 'led on by the devil and touched by a malign spirit . . . whose hearts had been blinded by the sultan's gold and silver', attempted to let a Muslim relief force into the city. A Genoese man tried to destroy the Christian bridge over the Nile for 6,000 besants while a Spaniard was found guilty of selling provisions to Damietta's starving Muslim garrison.[13] Famished French crusaders fled to the Turkish lines at Mansurah in 1250.[14]

More telling than these examples of malign betrayal are those that demonstrate human weakness. As so often we find plenty of these in Joinville's memoir of St Louis. One is Joinville's story of the presumably non-noble cellarer in his household who argued that the French should prefer death and martyrdom to captivity by the Muslims. Joinville laconically recorded that 'we none of us heeded his advice'.[15] These were men who'd fought with irreproachable courage at the battle of Mansurah, but like Gerard of Avesnes they saw no reason to die if it could be avoided. Unlike James of Vitry, who would probably have agreed with Joinville's high-minded cellarer and who complained because the crown of martyrdom was denied him on the Fifth Crusade,[16] these laymen didn't yearn to achieve the ultimate imitation of Christ by dying for him. They were too deeply rooted in the world for that, as a group of their fellows had shown just a few days previously when they'd laughingly discussed what would happen to the widow of one of their fallen comrades.[17] We've seen that they constantly thought about their homes and families, and most of them planned to return to the social networks and concerns that they'd left behind them. The crusade was an episode in their lives. One day it would end, and while it lasted they didn't metamorphose into kamikaze warriors.

Pilgrims and Israelites as prototypes for crusaders

When we look at it in the round, crusading confronts us with a religious profile that was characterized by fewer extremes of devotion than some of its admirers would admit. But it retains its unique status as a military conflict that simultaneously functioned as a penitential exercise. Its participants believed that its religious value derived not just from its achievement of an objective like the capture or recovery of Jerusalem, but also from the way the combatants behaved while fighting to bring this about. Religious behaviour of a particular kind wasn't something to be imposed on crusading just because it was considered appropriate, like being quiet in church. It was inseparable from the nature of the war that was being fought. Crusading surpassed all other pilgrimages as an enterprise, so it followed that the behaviour of its participants must surpass that of all other pilgrims.[18]

30 In this illustration of crusading combat from the early fourteenth century, the crusaders still wear the purses of pilgrims.

In 1189 it didn't seem inappropriate to German crusaders travelling to the Holy Land by sea to drop anchor off Galicia so that they could pay a visit to the shrine of St James at Compostella.[19] The episode was characteristic, for as a form of pilgrimage crusading largely fed off existing pilgrim traditions and terminology.[20] There was little need to add anything. By contrast, as a holy war its religious profile was both more novel and more eclectic. The crusaders and their apologists assembled and synthesized a bewildering range of scriptural, patristic and geographical reference points for the violence that they were carrying out in God's name. Commentators freely ransacked the Old Testament. Much use was made of the rich rhetoric of holy war that permeates so many of the Psalms, and of the well-known events that demonstrated God's covenant with the Jews, at a time when they were his chosen people. For the crusaders formed 'God's army' (*exercitus Dei*), and as such it was inevitable that they would view their activities as being closely foreshadowed by the Israelites.

It was a tendency that set in early: just months after the fall of Jerusalem Pope Paschal II wrote about the need to 'effectively aid our brethren who have remained in those districts which were once the lands of the Palestinians or Canaanites'.[21] When the German crusaders were stalled in Byzantine territory in 1189, Pseudo-Ansbert saw them as the Israelites 'exiled' in Egypt, 'the people of God, that is those wearing Christ's sign'. The Emperor Isaac II was Pharaoh, his troops the Egyptians intent on stopping the crusaders from escaping.[22] Reviewing the Third Crusade's partial success in January 1193, Pope Celestine III called on Christians to look at the history of the Israelites. God had warned them to maintain their purity of life if they wanted to win victories but they'd failed to do so. In the same way, the Christian cause in the Holy Land had been set back by quarrelling and other poor behaviour.[23] The Egyptian parallel recurred in 1203, when Innocent III drew a rather odd analogy between the Fourth Crusade and the Israelites; the doge Enrico Dandolo was now cast as Pharaoh, attempting to lure the crusaders back into the servitude of sin with his false promises.[24] And when the Fifth Crusade was making no progress outside Damietta, 'following the example of the Israelites, the Christian army complained about the legate and the princes and lamented "why did you lead us into the land of Egypt, to die in this wilderness?" [Exodus 14:11–12]'.[25] Exodus was a natural text to turn to for an army that was fighting in Egypt with the goal of liberating the Holy Land: James of Vitry hoped for a replay of all the miracles with which God had assisted the Israelites.[26] James and other crusade preachers found a treasure trove of exemplary material for their sermons in Exodus and Maccabees.[27]

Medieval Christianity had a troubled relationship with the Jewish faith and this meant that Old Testament precedents for crusading couldn't be wholly straightforward. The chronicler Guibert of Nogent had no love for the Jews and was severe in his comments on the wars of the Old Testament. Guibert thought that the crusaders' achievements far surpassed 'the fleshly wars of Israel, which were waged merely to fill the belly' by 'inconsequential people of . . . little faith'. From this derogatory verdict Guibert had to make an exception for those Old Testament figures that the Church had 'christianized', 'the blessed Joshua, David, Samuel', 'whose radiance is now celebrated by the church of God'.[28] But even commentators who were less ferociously anti-Jewish than Guibert accepted that, while the Israelites had foreshadowed the crusaders, they hadn't been their equals. On grounds of simple arithmetic, Raymond of Aguilers reckoned that the crusaders had surpassed the Maccabees; which wasn't to say that they were more courageous, just that God had intervened on their behalf to greater effect.[29] The crusaders after all were 'Christ's soldiers' (*Christi milites*). The fact that they were Christians was emphasized, embedding the concept of *Christianitas* and the identity of Christianness firmly within the thinking of the age: it's been estimated that Albert of Aachen used the word 'Christians' (*christiani*) more than 210 times to describe the first crusaders.[30]

Monks at war?

At the same time that they were distanced from the Israelites, the early crusaders were brought into close proximity with the monks. It's easy to see why this happened. We've seen that many crusading nobles had close ties with religious houses and relied heavily on their support in money and prayers. The most sophisticated historians of the First Crusade were monks and it came naturally to them to dress the whole crusading experience up in monastic clothes. Guibert of Nogent for example wrote that the crusaders 'lived in continual and great need, leading the lives not of knights but of piously impoverished monks'.[31] This applied to fighting as well as to lifestyle. Like monks, the crusaders were fighting God's war (*bellum dei*), the difference being that a metaphysical and spiritual conflict waged in choir and cell had transformed into a literal and fleshly one fought on battlefields and town walls. Hence an entire language of combat between good and evil that had been developed in Europe's cloisters was transposed to the battlefields of the East.[32] This dialectic between the interior and the exterior found its resolution in the 1120s in the foundation of the Order of the Temple. Its members were skilled and tough fighters who were also practising religious. For St Bernard this synthesis of knight and monk was both proper and praiseworthy: 'his soul is protected by the armour of faith just as his body is protected by armour of steel'.[33] It could be said that it was a synthesis waiting to happen.

But while it was superficially attractive and certainly proved useful for the Templars, depicting crusade as temporary monasticism was always a clumsy construct. Over the long term neither monks not crusaders found that it suited them. There are signs that for some twelfth-century monks this intrusion of the values of warfare into a zone of life marked above all by peace was an atrocious trespass that should be resisted. Crusading was a splendid idea as a form of monastic 'outreach' to the laity; but allowing crusading to rebound back into the precious sanctuary of the monastic order was another thing altogether. The differences were just too glaring. As one historian of the Third Crusade put it, 'How distant, how different is the life of contemplation and meditation among the columns of the cloister from that dreadful exercise of war!'[34] Some religious never accepted that the Templars were *bona fide* monks.[35] As for crusaders, they knew very well what the difference was between pilgrimage and the monastic vocation and they'd signed up for the former.[36]

'Where his feet trod' – fighting for the Holy Land

It's likely that what gained St Bernard's support for the cause of the early Templars, as well as for crusading, was the end for which they fought:

the recovery and defence of sites that were sacred to Christendom. Bernard rhapsodized lyrically about the holy places of Palestine in the publicity tract that he wrote for the Templars, *In Praise of the New Knighthood* (*De laude novae militiae*). As penitential pilgrims the crusaders naturally expressed veneration for the Holy Land's shrines. But the shrines also gave a firm location and rationale to the warfare that they were waging. They were fighting a holy war at God's command (*deus lo vult*, as the crowd shouted at Clermont) and in his name, but they did so in order to win control over certain specific locations, pre-eminent among which were Christ's tomb and Calvary.

The association of combat with the freeing of the Holy Sepulchre, and the talismanic power of the Cross whose sign all crusaders displayed, were made explicit on numerous occasions in the *Gesta Francorum*. The source matters because historians are increasingly viewing the *Gesta Francorum* as the First Crusade's 'foundation text', so it's highly likely that any themes that are dominant in it reflect reality. Fighters at the battle of Dorylaeum were urged to trust 'in Christ and in the victory of the Holy Cross'.[37] An early conquest was to be held 'in fealty to God and the Holy Sepulchre'.[38] The count of Flanders was 'armed with the sign of the Cross'.[39] At Antioch the crusaders were exhorted to 'fight valiantly for God and the Holy Sepulchre', while Bohemund was 'protected on all sides by the sign of the Cross'.[40] The Turks were defeated 'by the power of God and the Holy Sepulchre'.[41] At the battle of Antioch the crusaders fought 'in the name of Jesus Christ and of the Holy Sepulchre'.[42] The crusaders triumphed 'by the help of God and the Holy Sepulchre'.[43] Their battle cry when things looked bad was 'God help us' (*deus adjuva*).[44]

The endless reiteration of phrases like these hammered home the message that crusading combat was spiritual in character.[45] In much the same way, Pseudo-Ansbert repeatedly called Barbarossa's host on the Third Crusade 'the army of the holy cross',[46] and when the Germans went into action against Malik Shah they sang a war song calling on God for aid.[47] When Richard I charged the Turks at the battle of Arsuf he shouted three times 'God and the Holy Sepulchre, help us!',[48] while during the Fifth Crusade the Templars responded to Muslim blasphemy by calling on 'Christ, the Holy Cross, the Holy Sepulchre and St George' to come to their aid.[49] Nor was it just on the battlefield that such incantations reinforced the sense of common purpose. A touching passage in the *Itinerarium peregrinorum* recounts that during the siege of Acre in 1190–1 the crusading army engaged in a collective appeal to the Holy Sepulchre for help every night before settling to sleep. A crier shouted, 'Holy Sepulchre, help us!', and the cry was repeated by the entire army three times.[50]

Liturgy and collective devotion

This passage forms a rare insight into devotional activity of which all too much has been lost to us, because it assumed a liturgical form that the chroniclers largely took for granted. It's unusual to learn the details of when Joinville heard his daily mass when he was living in the Holy Land,[51] or that when Stephen Valence experienced a vision of Christ in June 1098 he was instructed to make sure that the responsory *Congregati sunt* (Ps. 47:5) was sung in the daily Office, as prescribed by the Reims pontifical.[52] On occasion, however, specifics of time and place combine and devotional contours become visible. The author of the *Historia peregrinorum* gave an account of how the German crusaders celebrated the feast of Pentecost during their march on Iconium in May 1190. The circumstances were grim and his description makes poignant reading. Coincidentally, the Germans were granted a welcome break from their 'daily clashes' with the Turks, though they received reliable news that a substantial Turkish force was approaching and would attack them the following day. The army's elite, an exhausted and hungry band of brothers, gathered to hear a morale-rousing sermon by Bishop Godfrey of Würzburg about the significance of Pentecost and its relevance to their own task and sufferings. The emperor added a few words encouraging his followers to fight bravely, the gathering 'sang a war song in the German fashion', then the men dispersed to their tents to dine frugally.[53]

A much more renowned example of liturgical celebration occurred on 15 July 1099 when the first crusaders took Jerusalem. It's Raymond of Aguilers who gives the most compelling account of the celebrations on this day of all days:

> With the fall of the city, it was a delight to see the devotion of the pilgrims before the Lord's Sepulchre: how they rejoiced, exulting and singing a new song to the Lord, for their mind offered to the victorious and triumphant God sacrifices of praise which they could not express in words. A new day, new gladness, new and everlasting happiness, the completion of labour and devotion, demanded new words and new songs from everyone. I say that this day, to be famous in all ages to come, turned all our sorrows and labours to joy and exultation.

The emphasis here, unusually for a medieval text, is on novelty, but it's been pointed out that Raymond went on to remark that the priests, himself included, sang the Office for Easter Day, thereby giving the celebrations a solid liturgical earthing.[54] That said, the devotion of July 1099 was undoubtedly frenzied. An understated contrast is formed by events that occurred during the Palestinian phase of the Fifth Crusade in November 1217. The crusaders found themselves on the shore of the Sea of Galilee with three days to explore its sacred sites. Oliver of Paderborn recalled:

> wandering through places in which Our Saviour deigned to work miracles, and conversed with men in His corporal presence. We looked upon Bethsaida, the city of Andrew and Peter, then reduced to a small casale; places were pointed out to us where Christ called His disciples, walked on the sea with dry feet, fed the multitudes in the desert, went up into the mountain alone to pray, and the place where He ate with His disciples after the resurrection.

It's a classic and moving statement of the *ubi steterunt* theme ('where his feet trod . . .') and could easily come from a pilgrimage text,[55] but in reality this short period of contemplation occurred at the close of a raid from Acre which must have involved the usual quota of danger, fear and stress.[56]

Sacred soil – devotion for the Holy Land's shrines

The veneration that crusaders felt for Jerusalem is, unsurprisingly, most strongly evident when their armies approached the city itself, first in 1099 and then in 1190–2. The army of the First Crusade experienced a surge of self-confidence and renewed solidarity during the march southwards from Arqa that grew as it got closer to Jerusalem. The absence of resistance at places like Tripoli, Beirut and Acre helped, and in the last days of their march the crusaders were passing through locations familiar to them from scripture, many of them pilgrimage shrines. They experienced at first hand the holiness of the Holy Land.[57] The siege of the city was fuelled by their urgent desire to complete their pilgrimage; as the *Gesta Francorum* put it, 'our leaders then decided to attack the city with engines, so that we might enter it and worship at our Saviour's Sepulchre'.[58] Almost a century later, in December 1191, the army of the Third Crusade experienced similar feelings as it advanced towards Beit Nuba. Despite storms that ruined their food and spoiled their armour, 'they hoped that they were very soon going to visit the Lord's Sepulchre, for they had an indescribable yearning to see the city of Jerusalem and complete their pilgrimage'.[59] Richard's decision to abandon the march, in January 1192, was therefore a devastating blow and, without the sustaining hope of recovering Jerusalem, the retreat to Ramla and Ascalon in severe winter weather was a terrible ordeal. 'Our people were so weighed down with anxiety and overwhelmed with grief at going back that an enormous number almost abandoned the Christian faith.'[60]

Proximity to Jerusalem reinforced the identity of crusaders as pilgrims and it may have acted as a social leveller. According to Guibert of Nogent

31 Godfrey of Bouillon and Baldwin I, the first rulers of crusader Jerusalem and much praised for their piety.

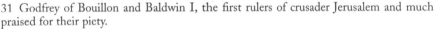

earth that was excavated during the siege of Arqa in the spring of 1099 was carried away by 'women and the wives of the nobles, even on holidays, in flowing robes or tunics'.[61] During the siege of Jerusalem a few weeks later everybody worked together to construct siege towers, 'all worked with a singleness of purpose, no one was slothful, and no hands were idle'.[62] The same spirit re-emerged at the rebuilding of Ascalon in 1192, which became a sort of substitute for the abandoned attempt to recover Jerusalem. 'You would have seen everyone working together, chiefs, nobles, knights, squires, and men-at-arms passing stones and rocks from hand to hand. There was no distinction between clergy and laity, noble and commoners, servants and princes.'[63]

The text that more than any other orchestrates the central theme that the Christians were fighting in and for a holy land is our main account of the Hattin campaign, the *Libellus de expugnatione Terrae Sanctae*. The roll-call of Saladin's conquests in 1187 made for telling propaganda, as evidenced by their dramatic citation in the letter that the Patriarch Eraclius sent to the West as the sultan approached Jerusalem in September. The thirty-four captured sites, which Eraclius listed one after the other without comment, read like the tolling of a funeral bell.[64] The funeral, unless help came quickly, would be that of the Christian Holy Land: for an audience in the West the impact would have been profound. But the author of the *Libellus* made even more astute use of the conquests. As he narrated Saladin's incursions and conquests over the course of 1187, he repeatedly expounded and eulogized the scriptural associations of the threatened or captured sites, Mount Tabor, Tiberias, Nazareth and Bethany among others.[65] There was no better way of bringing home the full sacred cargo that was at stake.

Time, like space, could be sacred. It was considered appropriate that Jerusalem fell to the first crusaders on 15 July because this was the feast-day of the dispersal of the Apostles. The coincidence enabled Raymond of Aguilers to observe that 'on this day the sons of the apostles reclaimed for God and the fathers the city and homeland'.[66] In their devotional practices crusaders paid strong regard to feast-days. This was especially the case with days which had associations with the Holy Land, since they strengthened the sense of common purpose. Peril could result given that the Muslims detected this tendency and launched attacks on feast-days when their enemies were likely to be at worship.[67] On Palm Sunday 1219 the Muslims attacked the crusaders outside Damietta in a fierce onslaught that lasted from before dawn until nightfall, and 'on that day, we were not given the opportunity of carrying palms other than crossbows, bows, and arrows, lances and swords and shields'.[68]

Martyrs for the faith

Integrating warfare into devotional activities that laid stress on the actuality of the sacred, especially in terms of place and time, was a good way to give holy war a stamp that was emphatically Christian. Another way was to celebrate fallen crusaders as martyrs. It's one of crusading's most idiosyncratic religious features that from the start participants insisted that their dead comrades were martyrs – that is, that they died bearing witness to their faith. The author of the *Gesta Francorum* put down a clear marker when he commented of those 'popular' crusaders from Germany and Italy who were killed by the Turks in 1096 that 'these men were the first to endure blessed martyrdom for the Name of our Lord Jesus'.[69] These were individuals whose undisciplined behaviour and quarrelling had received unfavourable comment just a few lines earlier in the text. Following the crusade's first major success, the capture of Nicaea, the *Gesta Francorum* makes an even stronger reference to martyrdom:

> Many of our men suffered martyrdom there and gave up their blessed souls to God with joy and gladness, and many of the poor starved to death for the Name of Christ. All these entered Heaven in triumph, wearing the robe of martyrdom which they have received, saying with one voice, 'Avenge,

O Lord, our blood which was shed for thee, for thou art blessed and worthy of praise for ever and ever.'[70]

Once implanted in this way, the conviction that men and women who perished while crusading had died as martyrs was like an article of faith, one that was constantly reiterated. The church attached to the cemetery where English crusaders who died at Lisbon in 1147 were buried was called St Mary of the Martyrs.[71] Even the Würzburg annalist, who regarded the origins of the Second Crusade with visceral hostility, believed that captured crusaders who were put to death when they refused to convert were straightway carried by angels to Abraham's bosom.[72] The brethren of the Military Orders who perished at Hattin got similar treatment: 'a ray of celestial light shone down clearly on the bodies of the holy martyrs during the three following nights, while they were still lying unburied'.[73] After Hattin the Christian cause needed such heroic martyrs badly and Peter of Blois dutifully penned an extraordinary Passion for Reynald of Châtillon, whom Saladin had personally executed and who, so Peter claimed, had originally gone to the Holy Land as a crusader.[74] Those who died at the siege of Acre were 'martyrs and confessors of the Faith', and people who perished during the gruelling advance to Jerusalem in the winter of 1191–2 'should be especially regarded as martyrs'.[75] Richard I supposedly anticipated martyrdom at Jaffa in August 1192: 'This is the wages for our labours, and the end of our life and our battles.'[76] Oliver of Paderborn wrote of those who died in Egypt that 'many martyrs for Christ, more confessors of Christ, being delivered from human cares at Damietta, went to the Lord'.[77] Another Fifth Crusade text recounted how a German on his deathbed experienced a vision in which a large man accompanied by a host of angels sang one of the most popular martyrdom passages in Scripture, Revelation 7:14, over the corpses of the crusaders who had died in a military encounter on 29 August 1219.[78]

It looks like this was a grass-roots phenomenon. No attempt seems to have been made to have the names of dead crusaders officially inscribed among the Church's martyrs; indeed given the numbers involved that wasn't a viable proposition. What was at stake was not formal acknowledgement of their status, but a collective mindset that insisted on the purity of those comrades who had died. Perhaps they foresaw some clerical criticism of their behaviour, and were making a pre-emptive strike against it. The trend didn't originate with pilgrimage and while there could be no suggestion that fighting in itself merited the status of martyrdom, it's probably best interpreted as part of the movement to christianize holy war by bringing it as fully as possible into a traditional framework regarding the deceased. It's especially noteworthy that those who died in 1219 were elsewhere described as 'companions' (*socii*) for St John the Baptist, because many of them were beheaded by the Muslims: 29 August was the feast-day of the saint's decapitation.[79]

Papal legates on campaign

So the more reflective crusaders constructed their own version of Christian holy war. That said, we need to remember that this was happening during expeditions which had been preached by the Church, and which many clerics accompanied to the East. It's been established that at least ten bishops, two archdeacons and five abbots set out on the First Crusade, and on later crusades it's almost certain that the high clergy was equally well represented. Some high-ranking clerics, especially those who were sent as papal representatives or legates, exerted a firm imprint on the character and conduct of

32 Adhemar of Le Puy leads the barons on the First Crusade: a strikingly assertive portrayal of the role that the first crusading legate played.

crusades. This applied above all to Adhemar of Monteil, the bishop of Le Puy, on the First Crusade and Cardinal Pelagius Galvani of Oporto on the Fifth.

In a letter which he wrote a matter of weeks after preaching at Clermont Urban II described Adhemar as 'leader [*dux*] in our place of this journey and labour, whose commands should be obeyed by those who decide to embark on this path as if they were our own'.[80] This was a powerful commission and while Adhemar doesn't seem to have interpreted it as a formal position of command in a military or political sense, his voice was always listened to. It's likely that the author of the *Gesta Francorum* struck the correct note when he described him in a short obituary as the 'ruler and shepherd' of the crusaders, 'a helper of the poor and a counsellor of the rich'.[81] To the visionary Stephen of Valence Adhemar was the nearest thing the crusaders had to a single leader.[82] It would be going too far to say that he held the crusade together, but it was no coincidence that his death at Antioch on 1 August 1098 was followed by the greatest crisis that the first crusaders encountered. Had he lived it's possible that he would have constituted the sort of respected authority required to settle the bitter dispute over who would possess captured Antioch. He would certainly have played the key role in making the highly sensitive series of appointments to episcopal sees that became necessary from this point onwards; indeed he'd already started to do so.[83]

We've already seen that Adhemar was particularly noted for his attention to the sufferings of the poor, and that he preached to the knights that they had a duty to defend their more vulnerable fellow pilgrims in exchange for their prayers.[84] It's tempting to detect in this 'social contract' message a reflection of Urban II's approach, though this is conjectural. Any attempt to place a firm interpretation on Adhemar's exercise of the commission that he'd received is hindered by his early death and by the sheer novelty of crusading at this point: few historians would now argue that Urban had a clear blueprint for his invention.[85] All we can say is that Adhemar represented the pope, so that not long after his death it was judged appropriate for the leaders of the crusade to write a joint letter to Urban asking him to come in person to the East to replace his deceased representative (*tuus vicarius*).[86]

Cardinal Pelagius – control and controversy

Cardinal Pelagius's exercise of his legation was both more forceful and more contentious. The legates who accompanied twelfth-century crusades were an undistinguished bunch with a low profile. The powers of a legate *a latere* (that is, sent from the pope's side or court) were sweeping and to a large extent they'd been developed in the context of the peace-making that formed an essential preliminary to a crusade.[87] But using these powers effectively hinged on each legate's personality and the specific circumstances of his crusade. Peter Capuano's role on the Fourth Crusade formed one extreme: judging that the crusade had slipped out of control by attacking Zadar, Peter washed his hands of it and sailed for Acre.[88] Pelagius was the exact opposite. When he arrived in Egypt in September 1218 he overruled the authority of John of Brienne, the king of Jerusalem, who'd been elected as commander at Acre, and asserted a decision-making leadership that no previous crusading legate had attempted. A combination of factors enabled Pelagius to do this: the lack of status enjoyed by John of Brienne; the esteem in which the legate was held by Pope Honorius III and his great predecessor, Innocent III; his access to plentiful supplies of cash; above all, the constant expectation of Frederick II's arrival.

But we shouldn't underestimate the importance of Pelagius's own assertive temperament. It's too ideological to view him as the personification of a 'papal programme' of dominance and control; rather, Pelagius recognized an opportunity (Heaven-sent, in his eyes) to fashion events and he seized it with both hands. His approach misfired badly, with the result that he became the natural target for people who were trying to explain failure. It would be wrong to attribute the military disaster in 1221 to the assumption of military command by a man who lacked the training for it and whose decisions sprang from theological rather than practical considerations. Assertive as he was, Pelagius always acted with the counsel of others, and the fact is that even a Bohemund of Taranto or a Richard I might well have found the strategic situation facing the crusaders after Damietta's fall to be an intractable one. The disastrous decision to advance into the Mansurah triangle in July 1221 derived principally from Pelagius, it's true, but it can't plausibly be attributed either to military naivety or to a clerical worldview. Such blunders happen all the time in history and if Pelagius placed his hope in God, so too did all crusaders.[89]

Clerical crusaders

It makes sense to view Pelagius's role on the Fifth Crusade less as a high-water mark in clerical assertions of leadership than as the product of chance. By contrast, Adhemar of Le Puy's well-judged combination of pastoral and moral guidance provided a constructive behavioural model for clerical crusaders, one that remained fruitful throughout the twelfth and thirteenth centuries.[90] Tasks normally carried out by beneficed clerics in the West, like celebrating mass, hearing confession and organizing processions and fasts, naturally fell to clerics who had taken the cross. They were trained to take the temperature of God's displeasure with his people and to set in motion the appropriate placatory measures.[91] One of the most famous such occasions was the procession around the walls of besieged Jerusalem on 8 July 1099. Raymond of Aguilers reported that 'it was publicly commanded that . . . the clergy should lead the procession with crosses and relics of the saints, while the knights and all able-bodied men, with trumpets, standards and arms, should follow them, bare-footed'. Typically, this was enjoined on the army by the ghost of Adhemar of Le Puy, in an appearance to the visionary Peter Desiderius. In addition to the need to regain God's favour by doing penance, the procession was couched in peace-making terms: 'let each one become reconciled to his brother whom he has offended, and let brother graciously forgive brother'.[92]

Nor did the pastoral assistance of the clerics stop when fighting began: they then made up a 'clerical militia' that offered up prayers for the success of military ventures at the same time that the army went into action. At the battle of Antioch they lined the city's walls, 'calling upon God to defend his people',[93] and when the crusaders left Jerusalem to fight the Fatimid army at Ascalon, 'Peter the Hermit stayed in Jerusalem to admonish and encourage all the Greek and Latin priests and the clerics to go in procession devoutly to the honour of God, and to pray and give alms, so that God might grant his people victory.'[94] And Oliver of Paderborn, eyewitness and cleric, described how, during the assault on the bridge tower at Damietta, 'the Patriarch [of Jerusalem] lay prostrate in the dust before the wood of the Cross; the clergy, standing barefoot, garbed in liturgical robes, cried out to heaven'.[95]

In these ways clerical crusaders acted as the bridge between God and his people, emphasizing the covenant that underpinned crusading as a collective enterprise. There were points, however, at which the planned activities of crusading armies appeared to throw this covenant into question, and when moral guidance was required. In this respect also Adhemar of Le Puy had established a clear precedent, but on later crusades his example was followed less by the legates than by a mixture of high-ranking clerics, bishops and abbots in particular. Their advice gained weight not from their official authority but from their personal standing and reputation. There are some excellent examples of this for the Second and Third Crusades. The first was the lengthy and learned counsel that Bishop Peter of Oporto gave to the Anglo-Norman and Low Countries crusaders, to the effect that they could and should assist in a Portuguese attack on Lisbon.[96] Another was the more down-to-earth and strident lobbying by Bishop Godfrey of Langres for an assault by Louis VII's army on the walls of Constantinople.[97] Similarly, when the German crusaders started to indulge in pillaging at Nish in 1189 they were harangued by the bishop of Würzburg, who warned them that they would forfeit God's support just as the Israelites had done.[98]

But it was during the Fourth Crusade's hotly disputed diversions that clerical advice was at its most influential. During the debate about the legitimacy of assaulting Zadar, the discussion that followed on Corfu, and above all the talks about attacking Constantinople in the spring of 1204, the opinions of clerics played a big role. These were complex debates. They were shaped by the interaction of legality, the nature of crusaders' religious vows, and their various logistical and military needs. It was inevitable that the views of trained and experienced prelates of the Church would carry particular weight. The problem was that the clerics on the Fourth Crusade were as divided in their views about what should be done as their lay audience was. The only occasion when they spoke with a single voice was in April 1204, when the failure of the first assault on Constantinople's walls sparked off a wave of moral panic. The situation was desperate; and faced with the disintegration of the whole venture a group of the high-ranking clergy led by the bishops of Halberstadt, Soissons and Troyes acted with unanimity and resolve. As Robert of Clari put it, on 11 April 'the bishops and the clergy of the host consulted together and gave judgement that the battle was a righteous one and that they were right to attack them'.[99] The expedition's religious framework was rigorously affirmed through confession and communion, and by expelling prostitutes from the camp the clerics isolated the cause of God's anger and thus gave hope that a renewed attack would receive his backing. Their astute moves succeeded in restoring morale and on the next day the walls were breached.

Providence – God's will in action

The crisis of confidence that afflicted the crusading army at Constantinople in April 1204 sprang from military failure. In this instance it was aggravated by the contested course of events that led up to it, but there was no inherent difference between the soul-searching carried out by the crusaders before the walls of Constantinople and the many other occasions in crusading history when setbacks and disasters provoked introspection. In a society dominated by a providential worldview any military defeat carried religious overtones, but crusading was an enterprise embarked on at God's command. So it took this outlook to extremes not experienced in other forms of war. By its nature it encouraged behavioural excesses as the response to both success and failure. The remarkable outburst of triumphalism that followed the fall of Jerusalem in 1099 was thus echoed, and quite possibly imitated, by the paean of joy with which both Count Baldwin of Flanders and Pope Innocent III greeted the capture of Constantinople in 1204. For both men the victory was marvellous proof of God's will: 'This was done by the Lord, and it is a miracle above all miracles in our eyes';[100] 'God produces this mystery through your ministry not as if it were by fortuitous chance but, to be sure, by an exalted plan.'[101] The outbursts of 1099 and 1204 were linked in a more tangible sense by the suggestion advanced by Baldwin to Innocent III that the capture of Constantinople could become the providential mechanism for turning the tide that had set against the Christian cause in the Holy Land in 1187.[102]

Given what had happened there were of course good reasons for Baldwin to take this line, but it's interesting that the pope not only seized on the idea with alacrity but went much further in his own interpretation of events. In an extraordinary letter written in January 1205 Innocent expressed his hope that with the help of the Greeks not only Jerusalem but Antioch and Alexandria – the other lost eastern patriarchates – could be recovered. The mission to convert pagan Livonia, the recent return to the Catholic Church of the Armenians, negotiations with the schismatic Bulgars and Vlachs, all were construed as elements in a pattern that pointed towards the imminent triumph of Catholic Christianity: and, by implication, the extinction of Islam.[103] Shortly afterwards Innocent commented wistfully that if the conquest of Constantinople had only happened earlier, the disastrous losses in the Holy Land might have been avoided.[104] The pope was evidently excited by this point, for unusually much of his January letter is written in the first person. His mood dissolved when accurate and appalling news reached him of what had been done at Constantinople.[105] None the less, his letters at this time represent a brief return of the post-1099 euphoria, and there's no reason not to think that his mood of exultation was felt just as keenly by the crusaders at Constantinople.

'Our sins have caused it' – God's loving chastisement

Defeat was different. Not only was it much more of a constant in crusading history, it was throughout interpreted very largely in terms of the sinfulness of the crusaders themselves. 'Our sins have caused it' (*peccatis exigentibus*) was the dominant religious response to disaster, inevitably given the synthesis of a providential outlook with the sense of sinfulness felt by crusaders, who after all were penitents.[106] Henry of Huntingdon thought that the root cause of the French and German defeats on the Second Crusade lay in fornication, looting 'and all kinds of crimes'; he contrasted them with the proper behaviour of the crusaders who took Lisbon, most of whom, he smugly claimed, were English.[107]

In his account of the Fifth Crusade Oliver of Paderborn displayed an especially acute sense of the crusaders' unworthiness to act as God's soldiers. Repeatedly their idleness, dissolute behaviour and greed undermined the enterprise's chances of success. On previous crusades, Oliver wrote, God had operated through human agency; but on this one 'he alone was magnified'.[108]

The sufferings that crusaders endured were a form of trial in which God tested their worth. So even when Oliver's comrades were 'pleasing to the Lord', after a three-day fast at the end of November 1218, 'it was necessary that temptation should prove them' in the form of the storms that tore their camp apart and the scurvy-like illness that ensued.[109]

But, however severe the failings of crusaders were, they were engaged on God's cause and their actions were inherently meritorious. Oliver of Paderborn took care to point this out towards the end of his account of the Fifth Crusade. The surrender of Damietta was both painful and deserved: 'The enormity of our evil deeds and the vast number of our crimes were compelling the vengeance of divine decision.' But 'although we may be sinners, nevertheless, carrying His Cross we have left homes or parents or wives or brothers or sisters or sons or fields for the sake of Him'. Hence God tempered his judgement with mercy: the army was saved from destruction and a portion of the True Cross was restored, in exchange for a city which couldn't in any case have been held against a Muslim counter-attack. In this convoluted way the humiliating defeat suffered in Egypt was reconciled with the propriety of crusading in the mind of a man who'd been one of its most effective and enthusiastic preachers.[110] Other chroniclers of the Fifth Crusade took much the same approach as Oliver on this issue. Sinfulness led to disaster as surely as night follows day: to James of Vitry the panicky flight of the crusaders who had set out to conquer Tanis motivated by greed caused some of them to die 'solely out of terror, driven crazy by the just but hidden judgement of God'.[111] On the other hand, one author commented that losses suffered by the crusaders were less than their sins deserved.[112]

In this regard, as in so much else, the historians of the Fifth Crusade were revisiting themes that had first been developed during the First Crusade. The author of the *Gesta Francorum* expressed it in a way that has the ring of truth: the crusaders found consolation in the knowledge that 'their god fights for them every day, and keeps them day and night under his protection, and watches over them as a shepherd watches over his flock'.[113] The same chastising but ultimately loving God watched over his people during the German march through Anatolia in 1190,[114] and at the siege of Acre during the Third Crusade: 'The Lord, who does not abandon those who hope in Him, regarded our people and saw that they had been made perfect by purification in the fire of long tribulation and severe trials which had pierced them to their very souls.'[115] And as at Acre, so too in the gruelling encounter at Arsuf: 'How great must their sin have been, when they needed such a great fire of tribulation to purify them?'[116] Peter of Blois put it best: God raised up the Muslims so that they could be brought down, but he brought down the Christians so that they could be raised up. For the one consumption, for the other consummation.[117]

33 A dagger clenched between his teeth, Christ himself leads crusaders into battle against the enemies of His faith.

Apocalypse now?

The evidence is overwhelming that this view of God's direct involvement in the military fortunes of crusaders was widely shared and persistent. Robert of Reims even argued that the only historical events that could bear comparison with the First Crusade were the creation of the world and Christ's crucifixion and resurrection, 'for this was not the work of men: it was the work of God'.[118] When the leaders of the First Crusade were mired in the dispute about Antioch's future, the radical and wholly impracticable suggestion was made that the expedition should proceed to Jerusalem with Christ alone as leader.[119] The author of one account of Barbarossa's crusade described God as a leader (*dux*) of the German army alongside the emperor and Frederick of Swabia.[120] To this extent crusaders held an eschatological view of what they were doing – that is, they believed that their operations formed part of a divine plan that included all the events that were recorded in both the Old and the New Testaments. At its strongest this gave powerful assurance of victory, as in the comment by the author of the *Gesta Francorum* that 'before they are even ready to join battle, their god, mighty and powerful in battle, together with his saints, has already conquered all their enemies'.[121] Did it also foster a belief that the end of history was imminent? After all, in the Gospels Christ stated that God's plan for his creation would culminate in his own return and the Last Judgement, and in both Mark 8:34–9 and Matthew 16:24–8 the call to take up the cross and follow Christ was followed by an explicit reference to his second coming (*parousia*).

It's impossible to be sure how many crusaders held to the literal interpretation of this sequence of events and became overtly apocalyptic in their expectations of what would happen after they'd achieved victory in the East. In the case of the First Crusade apocalypticism certainly featured in the preaching and influenced the ideas of many crusaders right through to the conquest of Jerusalem. In the early eleventh century Ralph Glaber commented that the growth in popularity of pilgrimage to Jerusalem was seen by some as portending the appearance of Antichrist, evil's protagonist in the apocalyptic drama.[122] A similar idea was incorporated by Guibert of Nogent into his account of Urban's sermon at Clermont. Guibert showed the pope arguing that the crusaders had the job of restoring the Christian position in the Holy Land so that Antichrist 'may find some nourishment of faith against which he may fight'.[123] Expressed in such a roundabout and pedantic way, it was hardly likely to fill his audience with enthusiasm.

In the preaching that followed Urban's at Clermont, an expectation of the *parousia* was encouraged. It may even have been the dominant viewpoint among some of the bands that made up the initial wave of crusaders.[124] The trouble is that none of these early groups got further than the area around Constantinople before being wiped out. This meant that their apocalyptic outlook didn't have time to develop fully, and the narrative sources for their ideas are much sparser than the ones that we have for the later armies. In these armies apocalyptic ideas make rarer appearances, and any argument that the crusaders didn't expect to return has to contend with the careful provisions that many made for the well-being of their lands and families at home. Why would they bother to do this if they expected their arrival in Jerusalem to usher in the end of human history? It's likely that a lot of crusaders expected to perish on the crusade and some, like pilgrims before them, may have hoped that they would end their days in Jerusalem, but the evidence for any expectation of a more sublime or mystical form of death is rather meagre.[125] Convictions that the *parousia* was imminent are less in evidence on the Second and Third Crusades than on the First. It's true that some participants in the Third Crusade said that 'they had only wished to live until the Christians gained Jerusalem' but this comment was made in 'the terrible sorrow' of the abandoned march on the city at the end of 1191,[126] and it's highly unlikely that it represented one of the crusade's major themes.

Prophecy and crusade

But a scarcity of developed apocalyptic thinking isn't the same as saying that crusaders failed to subscribe to an eschatological viewpoint, with its emphasis on the power of prophecy. Many crusaders were intrigued by the idea that the momentous events that they were helping to shape could be predicted, partly because of curiosity and partly because it could offer them consolation in difficult times or even help to find a way out of strategic dilemmas.

The most revealing 'encounters' between crusaders and prophecy occurred during the Third and Fifth Crusades. In the autumn of 1190 one of the most curious encounters of the entire Middle Ages took place when Richard I of England enjoyed a conversation with Abbot Joachim of Fiore at Messina. Joachim was already celebrated for his claim that he could interpret down to a fine degree of detail what the Bible had to say about the future. He provided a schematic model of the past and the future that was highly seductive, and he would exert an unparalleled influence on thinking about eschatology for centuries to come.[127] His message to Richard was comforting. He identified Saladin as the sixth of seven great persecutors of the Church, and he prophesied the sultan's defeat at Richard's hands. After this the seventh persecutor would be Antichrist himself, who would be elected pope and rule for three-and-a-half years. The meeting was written up at some length by Roger of Howden and it seems that Richard was genuinely interested in the topic rather than simply filling his leisure hours. When Joachim explained the timing of Saladin's defeat the king was concerned that it was some time away – 'In that case why have we come here so early?' – and he took issue with the abbot about the origins of Antichrist.[128] There are no signs that anything Joachim told Richard had any impact on the strategy that the king pursued in the Holy Land; surely if he'd been that impressed we could expect him to have persisted with his march inland on Jerusalem.

The impact of eschatological prophecy on the Fifth Crusade was more tangible and arguably detrimental. In his interpretation of what happened at Constantinople in 1204 Pope Innocent III quoted two passages from Joachim of Fiore's *Exposition on the Apocalypse*;[129] but it's impossible to know whether the crusaders who fought at Constantinople shared the pope's views. In the spring of 1221, on the other hand, we know that a number of prophetic texts were circulating and caused a lot of excitement in the crusaders' camp outside Damietta. One text, in Arabic, claimed to contain revelations that had been made by Christ to St Peter, and passed on by Peter to his own disciple Clement, who succeeded him as pope. It prophesied the arrival in Egypt of two kings who would come from the East and from the West. Pelagius ordered this manuscript to be translated and read aloud to the army.

At this point the crusaders were divided about whether they should accept the attractive peace terms offered by Sultan al-Kamil, start an advance southwards, or wait for the arrival of the Emperor Frederick II. It can't be said that the prophetic texts secured the victory of any one party in these disputes, but they probably assisted in the eventual triumph of the party that argued for an advance.[130] This at least was Oliver of Paderborn's view.[131] James of Vitry was particularly impressed by the texts and he transcribed two of them. For him the prophecies of Islamic doom were given credibility by the accuracy with which their author described the victories of Saladin, the Third Crusade's recovery of Acre and the capture of Damietta by the Fifth, 'as if he had seen them with his own eyes'. James admitted that some people were sceptical about the texts, but he argued for their authenticity and claimed that the overall effect of the prophecies on the crusaders was invigorating: 'And so the Lord's people, amid the many labours and shortages which it endured for Christ, was more cheered than we can describe, and strengthened in Christ's service.'[132]

It would be rash to build too much on these sources, but the Fifth Crusade had been launched on a wave of eschatological hope. *Quia maior*, the bull with which Innocent III called for a new expedition in 1213, had commented that 'the Lord . . . has already given us a sign that good is to come, that the end of this beast is approaching, whose number, according to the Revelation of St John [13:18], will end in 666 years, of which already nearly 600 have passed'.[133] It's likely that this passage reflected broader feelings on this point, and the hopes that Innocent's successor Honorius III placed in such readings of the future, in the context of both crusade and missionary work, have been well established. The crusade of the *pueri* of 1212 had been the most significant outburst of eschatological, and maybe even apocalyptic, excitement since the First Crusade.[134] Moreover, the crusaders in Egypt received confused news about Chinggis Khan's advance which allowed optimists like Oliver of Paderborn and James of Vitry to perceive the Mongols as the prophesied force that would come to their assistance from the East.[135]

'Wonderful to relate' – the miraculous

It's not just the popularity of these prophetic texts that shows the importance that crusaders attached to being able to 'read' God's will. A lot of importance was also attributed to signs in the sky and other natural phenomena. There were an unusual number of these before and after the council of Clermont: among others a meteor shower in April 1095, an eclipse of the moon in February 1096 and again in August, a 'sign in the sun' in March 1096, a comet in the autumn of 1097 and an eclipse of the sun in December 1098.[136]

The precise significance pinned on such events depended on their context. Following Hattin a sequence of solar and lunar eclipses that had led up to the disaster were construed as divine warnings to the Christians of Syria to mend their ways.[137] In contrast, a contemporary noted that the natural signs of 1095–6 were seen as proof of 'God's will and pleasure to free the Holy Sepulchre', intended 'to sharpen the minds of Christians so that they should want to hurry there'.[138] Their continuation in 1097–9 helped to maintain the morale of the crusaders as they made their way through hostile territory.[139] Miraculous signs were plentiful on later expeditions, for instance German crusaders witnessed a blood-red appearance of the cross in the night sky while performing the vigil for the Purification of the Virgin in February 1190.[140] Oliver of Paderborn recorded a mixed bag of 'signs in the heavens' during his preaching of the Fifth Crusade in the Low Countries.[141]

A more dramatic and practical form of divine intervention was the despatch of bellicose saints and angels to assist the crusaders in their combat with the Muslims. Saints George, Demetrius, Theodore and Blaise were reported as helping the crusaders in 1097–8.[142] The *Gesta Francorum* observed that at the battle of Antioch in 1098 '[there] appeared from the mountains a countless host of men on white horses, whose banners were all white. When our men saw this, they did not understand what was happening or who these men might be, until they realized that this was the succour sent by Christ, and that the leaders were St George, St Mercurius and St Demetrius.'[143] The importance of this manifestation was underscored by the next sentence in the text: 'This is quite true, for many of our men saw it'; we've seen that the decision to meet Kerbogha in battle was a make-or-break gamble and confidence in divine support was crucial for its success.[144] When the crusaders reached Palestine an increasing emphasis on St George became natural because of the proximity of his tomb at Lydda to Jerusalem, and its prominent position on the pilgrim road that connected Jaffa with the holy city. The saint's cult synthesized with exceptional clarity the military and devotional aspects of crusading, so it's not surprising that he featured a good deal in later artistic representations of the expedition.[145]

Angels and saints, above all St George, became dependable allies in later crusades. A strange being, clothed in white and riding a white horse, which helped the Germans against the Turks in 1190 was interpreted by some as St George and by others as an angel.[146] One source reported that Barbarossa vowed to endow a church dedicated to St George if the saint helped the crusaders in battle.[147] A popular way to counter scepticism about such appearances was to call on eyewitness testimony by the enemy. Defeated Turks in 1190 were alleged to have been demoralized by the appearance of 7,000 white-clad horsemen.[148] In August 1218 Muslims who had been captured in the

chain-tower at Damietta ingenuously asked who their white-clad opponents
had been. The tower's assailants were summoned to appear before the
Muslims, like a police line-up of suspects. But the captives weren't able to
identify their enemies, who'd apparently been 'the swiftest and strongest of
men', kitted out with supernatural powers. The crusaders deduced that Christ
had sent his angels to storm the tower and that St Bartholomew had also
fought for them, because the encounter took place on his feast-day.[149] On one
occasion the devil himself was brought in to witness to the assistance that the
Virgin gave to crusaders. When an exorcism was in progress at her shrine at
Tortosa in 1249, he obligingly told the exorcist not to bother asking for her
help because she was busy helping the French to disembark at Damietta.[150]

The visionaries

Through sightings of comets and eclipses, or angels and saints, God's will could
be affirmed and mobilized. The author of the *Itinerarium peregrinorum* devoted
no fewer than ten chapters to describing the various miracles that happened at
the siege of Acre, raging from a stone 'of immense size' bouncing off a man's
back without doing him any harm, to the Turk who urinated on the cross being
shot through the groin.[151] The voice of God never made an appearance, but
individual crusaders did experience visions in which Christ, the saints and their
own dead comrades-in-arms gave them useful advice as well as encouragement.

Never was this more the case than during the First Crusade, and in particular during its later stages, from the siege of Antioch onwards. It's been pointed
out that southern France and Provence were veritable nurseries of visionaries,
including a priest called Peter Desiderius who had six visions and a layman
called Peter Bartholomew who had thirteen.[152] Christ and his mother appeared
in several visions but it's the number of appearances by St Andrew that's most
notable.[153] The message that they gave to the crusaders through their chosen
intermediaries was a mixed one, part rebuke, part consolation and part direction. St Andrew strayed into the field of strategy and even politics; when this
happened the visionaries were listened to with attention and respect, but as with
the texts that circulated during the Fifth Crusade, their specific directions
weren't necessarily acted on.

As with all charismatics, the fortunes of the visionaries were volatile, and
Peter Bartholomew's career was a dramatic demonstration of fortune's wheel
in motion. His greatest coup was the vision that he experienced which led to
the discovery of the Holy Lance, the very spear used to pierce Christ's side on
the cross, in the cathedral at Antioch on 14 June 1098. The circumstances
behind the excavation of the lance, or more likely lance-head, are always
going to be obscure, but whatever happened that day the lance was considered

34 Adhemar bishop of Le Puy carries the Holy Lance into battle at Antioch, 28 June 1098.

a major find. We've seen that the relic was catalytic in raising morale throughout the crusading army to the level at which battle could be ventured a fortnight later. It also gave Peter Bartholomew a degree of authority which he proceeded to abuse, creating a backlash that threatened both him and the popularity of the relic whose guardian he became. When Peter's credibility was challenged he allowed himself to be manoeuvred into undergoing an ordeal by fire, which he spectacularly and fatally failed on 8 April 1099. The Holy Lance's prestige also suffered a setback and it became exclusively associated with the Provençal contingent, with which Peter Bartholomew himself had become all too closely connected.[154]

This headline case was exceptional, and it would be wrong to use Peter Bartholomew and the fate of the Holy Lance as evidence that the first crusaders were hopelessly gullible, as Muslim commentators on the affair came to believe.[155] It would be just as wrong to go to the other extreme and deduce that the crusaders set aside their religious views when they interfered with the hard facts of a military or political scenario. Neither approach does full justice to the situation. Visions of saints or revenants were deeply embedded in the religious world of the crusaders, and it's not surprising that they came to the fore in the stressful circumstances of 1097–9.

What *is* surprising is that this plethora of visions on the First Crusade was a one-off. There was plenty of stress on later crusades and the miraculous was constantly deployed to combat it. Something as banal as a flock of white birds could be construed as a sign from God when the German crusaders were at their lowest ebb in Anatolia in 1190.[156] Yet detailed visions rarely recurred. The best explanation seems to be that the high-ranking churchmen present were more willing to offer the sort of spiritual guidance that on the First Crusade came via its visionaries. It's been noted that, although there were some high-ranking clerics on the First Crusade, with the exception of Adhemar of Le Puy they made little imprint on it. This left the field clear for the visionaries. There are signs that some clerics thought the visionaries were muscling in on their territory: it was Robert of Normandy's chaplain, Arnulf of Chocques, who outmanoeuvred Peter Bartholomew on the issue of the Holy Lance's authenticity. On the other hand there was a regional as well as a professional rivalry at play in this instance because the northern French generally had come to resent the way the lance was being hijacked by the Provençals.

Sacred relics

The careers of the Holy Lance and its 'successor', the True Cross, were so spectacular that they've tended to overshadow the many other relics that featured in crusading. The lance was credited at the time with playing a central role in winning the battle of Antioch in June 1098, and after it had been discredited by the ordeal of April 1099 its loss as a symbol of unity seems to have been deeply felt. For obvious reasons relics from the crucifixion held a particular potency for crusaders; Alexios I was acting cannily when he incorporated those held at Constantinople into the oaths that were sworn there by the leaders in 1096–7.[157] So there was much excitement when the new patriarch of Jerusalem, the same Arnulf who had engineered Peter Bartholomew's fall from power, rediscovered a fragment of the True Cross on 5 August 1099. Like the lance this was carried into battle; in fact at the battle of Ascalon in August 1099 both relics were used in this way, the True Cross being carried by the patriarch Arnulf while the Provençals brought along the Holy Lance.[158]

The lance was probably lost in Asia Minor during the crusade of 1101, but the True Cross enjoyed a long history of devotion conjoined with its talismanic use in battle. Militarily it had an early run of successes, being present at four major victories over the Egyptians between 1099 and 1105.[159] As the author of the *Itinerarium peregrinorum* rhapsodized, it was 'the life-giving wood of the Cross of Salvation, on which our Lord and Redeemer hung, down whose trunk flowed the pious blood of Christ, whose image angels adore, humans venerate, demons dread, [and] through whose help our people had always won the victory in war'.[160] Between 1099 and 1187 there was a steady westwards migration of splinters from the True Cross, which helped to spread devotion for the relic; as early as 1109 a canon of the Holy Sepulchre reckoned that twenty known pieces of the cross were in existence.[161]

After the loss of the cross at Hattin its recovery remained a constant hope among the Christians on the Third and Fifth Crusades. At least one commentator seems to have been more deeply affected by the loss of the cross than by that of Jerusalem,[162] and Peter of Blois rolled out no fewer than twenty-two metaphors explaining its religious significance.[163] Baha' al-Din was impressed, and maybe bemused, by the behaviour of Richard I's envoys in 1191: 'The Holy Cross was brought to them and they looked upon it and reverenced it, throwing themselves to the ground and rubbing their faces in

the dust. They humbled themselves in a manner the like of which had never been seen.'[164] There were other fragments of the True Cross in Christian hands, and they were deeply revered, but they were no substitute for what seems to have been a substantial piece of wood.[165]

The importance of two artefacts that were so central to Christ's redemptive Passion can't be gainsaid, and there are grounds for arguing that there was a deep-rooted psychological need among crusaders for emblematic relics like these. Hence the extraordinary distress felt at the loss of the True Cross, shared devotion to which resembled an umbilical cord connecting the settlers in the East with their co-religionists in Catholic Europe. From another point of view, though, both lance and cross are significant because they stand for numerous other

35 A reliquary.

relics that enjoy at best a fleeting mention in the sources. For together with intercession and the liturgy, relics formed the chief means by which fear, isolation and self-doubt were combated. Crusaders brought with them relics on whose efficacy they had come to depend; and they collected relics throughout their journey to the East.[166] Relics were among their chief acquisitions, for many crusaders their only ones.

During the sack of Constantinople in particular the seizure of relics was as conspicuous as that of material riches. The sack generated no fewer than three *translatio* texts, in which the relics seized were described and their theft laboriously justified.[167] The most revealing text is that by Gunther of Pairis, who recorded the exploits of his abbot, Martin. Gunther's description of Martin's behaviour has come to symbolize the extraordinary rapacity practised by the crusaders in April 1204.[168] In Martin's eyes the relics that he bullied the Greeks into handing over, and frantically stored away in the folds of his habit, were 'more desirable . . . than all the riches of Greece'.[169] It's easy to share the almost sensory pleasure with which Gunther, like the other two authors of these *translatio* texts, listed his abbey's new relics one after the other.[170]

A shared religious world

In their obsession with relics crusaders reaffirmed their affinity with the religious lives of their relatives, dependants and ancestors back home; we've seen that two centuries before Abbot Martin's raid on Constantinople's shrines, Fulk Nerra of Anjou had bitten off part of the Holy Sepulchre at Jerusalem with his teeth to bring it home.[171] Battles like Antioch and Ascalon, and conquests like that of Constantinople, exposed the crusaders to extraordinary levels of stress and heights of triumph, but the spiritual armoury with which they overcame the former and achieved the latter contained no element that would have seemed either incongruous or novel to their contemporaries. Before the battle of Antioch in 1098, for example, the crusaders fasted for three days, prayed, confessed, and went from church to church with bare feet: none of this was unusual, though with a pitched battle in prospect it was audacious to engage in such a protracted fast.[172]

It won't come as a surprise that the one area in which crusaders *can* be seen broaching new ground was their attempts to conceptualize the warfare they were taking part in. In this they could be radical. Crusading generated not just a theology of Christian holy war but also a set of religious responses by participants that shaped their attitudes towards their enemies, which we'll look at next, and their fallen comrades, as well as their perceptions of themselves. But the fact remains that in most respects the devotion of participants, while certainly extreme at times, was neither deviant nor innovative.

For these reasons, and because it's so well evidenced, the practice of crusading functions as an excellent mirror for many of the religious beliefs held by Catholics at the time. It's possible to see devotional shifts happening as the changing ideals associated with new religious orders like the Cistercians and mendicants exerted an impact on the content and delivery of the crusading message, and then on the devotional behaviour of crusaders while on campaign.[173] And it's been argued that the growing emphasis in thirteenth-century preaching on Christ's suffering combined with a new strategic approach that took crusaders to theatres of conflict other than Palestine to create a devotional migration from sepulchre to cross.[174] This may be the case, but more significant is the persistence throughout the period of a solid bedrock of Catholic belief in its various doctrinal, sacramental and devotional aspects: the central value of penance, the physical 'location' of the sacred and the varied functions of relics, the celebration of martyrdom, the diverse roles of churchmen as mediators, teachers and advisers, the embrace of eschatology and the possibility of 'reading' the future that was planned by God, and the transmission of the divine will through signs and visions.[175]

8

❖

SARACENS

Difference and hostility

In 1290, after almost two centuries of crusading to the East and just months before Acre fell, a European author known as 'the Clerk of Enghien' wrote that 'in foreign nations they are not a bit like they are here. You know truly that the Oriental is quite otherwise than we are.'[1] This perception of difference runs through nearly all descriptions of the Muslim enemy. At times attempts were made to find parallels for what was observed, but they sprang from the hope of understanding the radically unfamiliar by reconfiguring it in terms of the well-known. A good example was the common belief that the caliph was 'the Saracens' pope' and that he had the same power to remit sins.[2] True, some artistic representations of the Muslims show them as all but indistinguishable in their arms and armour from their Christian opponents, but this was usually because the artist didn't know about the differences, and probably wasn't much interested in them anyway.[3] Abundant written and visual evidence shows that crusaders expected to encounter the 'Other' in the men against whom they fought.

This association of Islam with strangeness was seamlessly blended with an assumption of hostility. Any Muslim who refused the grace of baptism was an actual or potential enemy. Albert of Aachen believed that advice was accepted that all the Muslims in the captured city of Jerusalem in July 1099 should be killed so that they couldn't rise up against the Christians at the same time that the crusaders faced attack by a Fatimid army; as a result 'girls, women, noble ladies, even pregnant women, and very young children' were indiscriminately slaughtered.[4] Historically Albert's account is almost certainly inaccurate, because the massacre happened on the same day that Jerusalem fell, not three days later, but his story does capture a mentality.[5] Hence the sharp divergence of approach that took root almost immediately after Jerusalem's capture between crusaders who were planning to return home and those who decided to settle in the East. For the second group only Muslims who took up arms

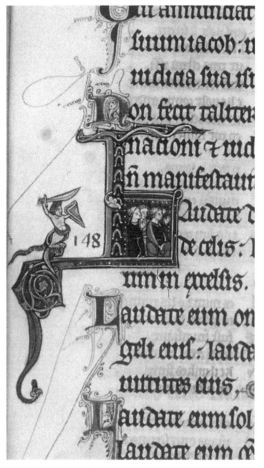

36 A group of peacefully praying Christians is treacherously attacked by a rampaging Saracen monster.

against them were enemies. All the others, peasants and artisans, traders and neighbouring rulers willing to live in peace, were viewed neutrally and even, in the case of the last group, treated with respect.

This difference in approach helped to trigger the final fall of Acre. At the same time that the Clerk of Enghien was writing, a body of Italian crusaders arrived at Acre in response to an appeal for help from Pope Nicholas IV. By killing a peaceful group of Muslim peasants and merchants the newcomers provided the sultan with an excuse to attack the city.[6] The incident fits the stereotypical image of the violently xenophobic crusader, and the crusading response to Islam can easily appear to be one of simple antagonism. Yet that would be a mistaken assumption. It will become clear in this chapter that, once we drill through

a bedrock of antagonism that was undeniably solid, the range of views that
crusaders formed of Islam and the Muslims was diverse. In many cases the
perception of difference led to exploration and in some instances, though sadly
fewer than has sometimes been supposed, it engendered appreciation.

Preconceptions and contact

Before we look more closely at this spectrum of views it's useful to ask what
initial picture crusaders had of the Muslims. Crusaders setting off for the East
already had an image of their enemy, though it's far from easy to recapture it
in detail. Their culture had a discordant view of the Muslim world, one that's
revealed by the most common term that was used in crusading sources to
describe the Muslim. 'Saracen' was etymologically muddled. Most medieval
Christians believed that it derived from Abraham's wife Sarah despite the
fact that the Arabs were thought to be descended from Abraham's illegitimate
offspring by Sarah's handmaid Hagar. To add to the confusion, Hagar
provided another term commonly used for Muslims, 'Agarenes'.[7] This conflation of religion with ethnicity was characteristic: in one English romance the
'sowdan of Damas' turned white when he was baptized,[8] and homiletic writers
like Paulinus of Nola couldn't resist the temptation to interpret black skin as
the result of sin.[9] For crusaders who came from areas that were far from both
Iberia and Sicily, the chances of their having even met a Muslim were slim,
and since relatively few Spaniards or Sicilians went on crusade to the East,
they weren't able to spread their knowledge of Islam more widely. In the
absence of such first-hand information initial views derived from sources like
miracle stories, imaginative literature and sermons.[10] They spread by word of
mouth and didn't gain in accuracy as they did so.

The composite picture that resulted was almost wholly denigratory.
Saracens were depicted as brutal, sadistic, greedy and lascivious people who
captured, enslaved and tortured Christians. The atrocity stories that featured
in crusade sermons and the like drew liberally on such themes. Some of them
were interwoven, especially when it allowed horror to be heaped on horror.
An excellent example is Guibert of Nogent's inclusion in his account of the
First Crusade of a prurient letter that purported to come from the Byzantine
emperor Alexios I. Sacrilege (the conversion of churches into stables and
brothels) was combined with sexual violence (the gang-rape of mothers in
front of their daughters and vice versa) and unnatural vice (the sodomising of
captured men, including a bishop).[11] Sexual violence recurs in one of Albert
of Aachen's strangest anecdotes, when a beautiful Christian woman is
captured by the Muslims and gang-raped before being killed.[12] Peter the
bishop of Oporto was almost certainly mimicking sources like these when he

tried to persuade the northern crusaders to fight against the Moors in 1147 by describing the latter cutting off the Church's arms and slashing her face.[13] It's pointless to expect such texts to yield any genuine information. At best they led crusaders to expect that they would encounter people who were flawed by defects that sprang from both perverse religious beliefs and a genetic programming which rendered them inescapably malicious. It's an unanswerable question whether they expected the Saracens to *look* loathsome, though there's not much evidence that they did. Their monstrosity resided not in their appearance, like the imagined Saracens of the cartographers and sculptors,[14] but in their behaviour.[15]

Once they arrived in the East the crusaders came across real Muslims, though the depth of their encounters varied a good deal from crusade to crusade. The French and German armies of the Second Crusade, and Barbarossa's host on the Third, were largely destroyed in Anatolia amid fighting that was confused and gave them little opportunity to learn much about the opposition; hunger, thirst, exhaustion and disease inflicted more harm than the Turks, whom many of these crusaders saw fleetingly at best.[16] On the First Crusade, it's no coincidence that descriptions of the battle of Dorylaeum, the first major engagement with the Turks and a lengthy one, include reflective commentaries on the enemy. From this point onwards contact was frequent, and it was particularly close during the siege of Antioch and the march southwards to Jerusalem. Sieges generated much contact between the fighting men on both sides, and this was certainly a characteristic of the prolonged siege of Acre during the Third Crusade. The two sides also had many opportunities to observe each other closely during the military operations that followed the Christian recovery of the port. Throughout the two crusades in Egypt exchanges with the Muslims were frequent and St Louis' crusade offers one of the finest perspectives of all in the captivity narrative that was written up, much later, it has to be added, by Joinville. In all these texts the enemy being observed was predominantly the Turks. The Fatimid intervention in the First Crusade was belated and short lived, and the finest troops in the Ayyubid armies under Saladin and his successors were of Turkish origin. We shall see, though, that the crusaders did show some awareness of the ethnic diversity among their enemies.

Demonization and its influence

The temptation existed to caricature the Muslims, indeed to go beyond caricature by demonizing them – that is, robbing them of their humanity. The logical corollary to the crusaders' perception of themselves as an army summoned by God to wage his war, a host of penitent sinners fighting to defend Christ's land, was a depiction of their enemy as the devil's army, men dedicated to spreading evil and fighting to destroy Christ's faith by annihi-lating its most sacred shrines.[17] 'We are protected by faith, they are enveloped by error.'[18] Even while on the march the Muslims passed the time by 'blaspheming the name of Christ and the cross of our redemption with their gabbling and polluted mouths'.[19] The attraction of working in terms of such opposites ran deep. One of the strategies adopted by the Church in its attempt to 'place' Islam as a faith was to denigrate Muhammad as a seducer who'd fashioned his great heresy around the embrace of life's easy options – carnality instead of spirituality, licentiousness instead of abstinence.[20] The Muslims had got everything wrong in both senses of the word. For Peter the Venerable in the mid-twelfth century Islam was 'the error of errors', the sewer into which the waste of all previous heresies flowed.[21]

From this viewpoint Muhammad's followers loathed everything Christian, from buildings to doctrines, because they stood for the righteous opposite of their own perverse creed. Only Christianity or Islam could prevail. The preaching of the First Crusade was disastrous for Christian–Islamic relations because it set this oppositional view in stone; there was no way to raise fresh armies to defend the Holy Land other than by constantly repeating the same message. Not that many churchmen were disposed to resist the trend. After all, messengers and reports arriving in a depressingly steady stream from their co-religionists and relatives in the East portrayed the military threat posed by Islamic rulers from Zengi onwards in terms that were all too graphic and urgent. In his *De predicacione crucis*, written in the 1260s, Humbert of Romans could hardly bring himself to mention the name of Muhammad and resorted to scatological abuse no different from that used a century earlier by Peter the Venerable.[22]

The question remains of how far this official demonization of Islam, its founder and adherents shaped the attitudes of crusaders once they were on campaign. There's certainly no scarcity of evidence for the constant denigration of the enemy along lines that echoed pretty closely the language, images and ideas of the sermons that crusaders had heard back in their homelands, and presumably continued to hear from the crusading clerics in their armies. It's interesting that Muslim sources were less passionate in their denunciation of Christianity than crusading ones were of Islam; in this respect they mirrored the outlook of the Christian settlers as opposed to the crusaders. Some Muslims showed appreciation of Christian embellishments of the holy places that were common to both religions. Following the recovery of Jerusalem by Saladin, the sultan's companion al-Fadel wrote, 'Islam received back a place which it had left almost uninhabited, but which the care of the unbelievers had transformed into a Paradise garden.'[23] But, as we've seen, crusaders believed that God intervened frequently and dramatically on behalf of 'his' people, and this was bound to reinforce their belief that the Muslims were God's enemies. 'In the eyes of God and humanity,' one commentator noted laconically, 'the Turks certainly deserved their fate because of their destruction of churches and slaying of people.'[24] Such dismissal all too easily spawned dehumanization – the Turks weren't fellow humans whose souls might be saved, but irredeemable agents of the devil. It was best to despatch them as soon as possible to 'the burning and sulphurous lake' of Hell and perpetual damnation.[25]

When the Turks didn't appear as the deserving victims of God's vengeful wrath they were the perpetrators of the devil's work, and in that capacity stereotypes that had already become familiar before 1095 were reiterated and reinforced. Apostasy worked especially well as a vehicle for the oppositional theme. James of Vitry wrote that it was hard for Saracen deserters to get used to strict Christian ways because they were used to complete licentiousness ('do what you want'); but Christians went over to the other side precisely so that they *could* enjoy a life of unbridled 'feasting, luxury and obscene pleasures'.[26] And in a letter that he was represented as despatching to the Seljuq authorities in Iran, Kerbogha of Mosul encouraged his co-religionists to 'enjoy yourselves, rejoicing with one accord, and fill your bellies, and let commands and injunctions be sent throughout the whole country that all men shall give themselves up to wantonness and lust, and take their pleasure in getting many sons who shall fight bravely against the Christians and defeat them'.[27]

The practice of war in Europe and the East

So far so straightforward. It's much harder to declare with confidence that this incessant flow of denigration influenced the behaviour of the crusaders, especially in terms of their fighting. We've seen that they rarely absorbed the Church's teaching without customizing it, making it cohere with their own, distinctively lay, view of the world. What was judged too astringent or inconvenient to follow in full – such as the ban on tournaments – was either paid token observance or tacitly brushed aside. So the obvious way to approach the question would be to ask whether crusaders waged war in accordance with the norms that shaped their fighting back home in the West. It's reasonable to expect that a thoroughgoing demonization of the enemy would create an ethos of 'total war', in which quarter was neither asked nor given.

Unfortunately this question isn't easily answered. In western Europe in the late Middle Ages the laws of war (*ius in bello*) were made subject to codes of behaviour governing the treatment of captives and civilians, though they weren't always observed.[28] But in the twelfth and thirteenth centuries such codes were rudimentary, if they existed at all. Learned contemporaries were starting to show an interest in who had the right to wage war (*ius ad bellum*) as definitions of government hardened; and this did influence their attitudes towards crusade.[29] But once swords had been drawn interest in the lawfulness of what happened dwindled. In the generation that followed the First Crusade a few commentators, notably the great chronicler Orderic Vitalis, were conscious that there existed a custom (*mos*) and practices (*rites*) that were normally adhered to across the span of the Anglo-Norman world that they were describing, but it's striking that on one of the occasions when Orderic used these terms he was writing about custom being breached.[30] More emphatic and legal words like *lex* and *ius* weren't employed much.[31] The most that can be said about the period before 1200 is that a combination of Christian humanity, reciprocal self-interest and aristocratic fellow

37 A European non-combatant pleads with a soldier not to burn her house.

feeling placed some constraints on the worst excesses. In this respect the crusaders' homelands were less advanced than the eastern Mediterranean lands. For example, the Muslims and Byzantines expected to ransom their captured soldiers and they already possessed quite sophisticated procedures for doing so.[32]

It follows that, while there were certainly occasions when crusaders behaved towards captured Muslims and non-combatants with shocking brutality, it doesn't take much effort to find equivalents or worse in wars fought between Christian lords and rulers in western Europe. Indeed, Walter the Chancellor held back from supplying too much detail about the tortures that were inflicted by the Turks on their Christian captives because he was worried that their techniques might be borrowed by his Christian readers, 'since kings, princes and other powerful people of the world . . . inflict many different punishments on their prisoners to extort money'.[33] Around 1100 Robert of Bellême and Thomas of Marle, a veteran of the First Crusade, became notorious for their cruel behaviour,[34] and in 1194–9 the war between Richard I and Philip II, more returned crusaders, was noted for the savagery used by both sides.[35] Richard I's decision to massacre his 2,700 Muslim prisoners at Acre in 1191 clearly exerted a negative impact on the Muslims: during the Fifth Crusade 'what they did at Acre' was recalled.[36] But the king's order was eagerly carried out by soldiers who were frustrated by Saladin's double-dealing on the return of the True Cross, or who wished 'to take revenge for the deaths of the Christians whom the Turks had killed with shots from their bows and cross-bows'.[37] And it's hard to believe that news of what happened at Acre caused many eyebrows to rise among Richard's contemporaries in the West.

In any sort of conflict, what we've come to regard as war atrocities were commonplace. Some derived from strategy, like William the Conqueror's 'harrying of the north' in 1069–70, the cold-blooded creation of a famine in which many thousands of non-combatants perished. The systematic ravaging of territory to suppress rebellion or bring an enemy ruler to heel was so deeply rooted in the practice of war that even Orderic Vitalis couldn't bring himself to condemn it.[38] Other atrocities were reprisals. Probably the first atrocity committed by the princely armies during the First Crusade was Raymond of Toulouse's blinding and mutilation of captured prisoners in Dalmatia in order to stop raids on his host, and these people, it has to be noted, were fellow Christians.[39] Cruelty and reprisals went hand in hand. When the crusaders besieging the port of Silves in Portugal in 1189 killed a Muslim prisoner before the eyes of his comrades-in-arms, the besieged responded by suspending three captured Christians from the city walls and hacking them to death. This was so familiar that it may be doubted whether attitudes towards the enemy were much affected by it. The crusaders at Silves wept with frustration 'and we were the more aroused to fight', but in general they displayed less contempt for the Moors than for their Portuguese allies, who 'neither worked nor fought, taunting us by saying that our labours were a waste of time because the fortress was impregnable'.[40] Our sense of fairness is affronted by the most fundamental custom relating to siege warfare, the 'right of storm'. This placed the lives and belongings of all the civilians in a besieged town at the mercy of the besiegers if its garrison decided to resist.[41] So, when Frederick of Swabia's crusaders massacred all the Turks whom they found in Iconium in May 1190, they weren't breaking the rules of war even for operations against fellow Christians.[42]

On the other hand, it's clear that for the most part the crusaders and their Muslim opponents created regulatory practices that represented a symbiosis of their different approaches towards waging war, especially in terms of ransoms and the conduct of sieges. During the disaster that overcame Louis IX's army in the Nile delta in 1250, the lives of Joinville and his fellow barons hinged on their claims to be men of substance.[43] One Christian commentator who was bitterly hostile towards Saladin admitted that the sultan forbade his troops to inflict harm on the captured populace of Acre and their possessions in July 1187.[44] Four years later, the terms of surrender that Saladin offered Jaffa's garrison were impressively concise: 'A horseman for a horseman, a *turcopole* [lightly armed cavalryman] for his equivalent and a foot-soldier for a foot-soldier. For any that cannot manage this, the Jerusalem tariff [the one used at its recovery in October 1187] applies.'[45] And the author of

38 Crusaders hurling Muslim heads into besieged Nicaea, 1097.

the *Itinerarium peregrinorum* portrayed the Muslims referring to the right of storm (*ius belli*) when discussing the likely outcome of the siege of Acre. Like all passages in which discussions among the enemy are depicted, this one has to be treated with caution. In particular, its reference to a lord's obligation to do his best to secure decent surrender terms for a garrison that had carried out its orders loyally but couldn't be relieved may have reflected Christian rather than Muslim practice. But the specific reference to Muslim law shows that the author of the *Itinerarium* believed that this practice was embedded among the Muslims too.[46]

So in practice crusading, even during the unusually harsh circumstances of the First Crusade, rarely took the form of 'total war'. But this isn't to say that it was perceived as being no different from warfare in the West. For contemporaries the identity of the enemy counted for a lot. Writing about the threatened German invasion of France in 1124, Abbot Suger of St Denis referred to the French being in a position to cut the enemy off, after which they could 'attack, overthrow, and slaughter them without mercy as if they were Saracens'.[47] It's an interesting phrase to use, perhaps showing that the massacres carried out in the East had made their mark on the consciousness of the literate elite in France. Certainly it demonstrates that commentators like Suger thought war against Saracens was different in kind.

As the century progressed a scale of values was created, in which some Christian enemies, in particular the Scots raiding northern England, and the detested mercenaries (*routiers*) who terrorized whole swathes of southern France, came close to being equated with the Muslims. For Richard of Hexham the Scots were 'more atrocious than the whole race of pagans, neither fearing God nor regarding man'.[48] It was emphasized that the Scots and *routiers* killed or enslaved non-combatants, and treated their prisoners poorly, as a matter of course, at a time when such practices had become unusual, and were starting to be frowned on, in other theatres of warfare. The diatribes of Henry of Huntingdon and Richard of Hexham against the Scots included accusations that exceeded those levelled against the Saracens, among them sacrilege.[49] Towards the century's end the spread of heretical beliefs added another factor to the equation. The Albigensian Crusade against the cathars and their supporters was waged with great savagery, possibly more than was customary by this point in crusading against Muslims in the East. Some of the worst massacres in crusading history were committed in southern France.[50]

Massacre – inducements and constraints

It's worth staying with massacres, and adding the even grimmer topic of cannibalism. Both can be instructive, though they're easily misconstrued. Most of the massacres perpetrated by crusaders in the East lose much of their ability to shock when they're examined in detail. This is because Christian and Muslim sources shared a tendency to exaggerate the losses that were suffered. Common sense tells us that when a town was taken by storm there were limits to the amount of killing that could be done by men who were usually exhausted and armed with pre-gunpowder weapons. The scale of the most infamous of all crusading massacres, that in Jerusalem in July 1099, has now been reduced to about 3,000 victims, coincidentally about the same number that were killed at Acre by Richard I's command in 1191.[51] For a long time it was thought that the figure was many times that, mainly because the event was the subject of a tidal wave of hyperbole on both sides of the religious divide. For the crusaders it would have seemed incongruous if a vengeful God, whose cause they'd faithfully served throughout their three-year ordeal, had failed to exact a just price from those whose sinful hands had polluted his churches and shrines. Their sense of that pollution was extremely strong. A generation previously the reforming cleric Peter Damian had written about the sexual activities of clerics: 'As you lay your hands on someone the Holy Spirit descends upon him; and you use [that] hand to touch the private parts of harlots.'[52] If this could be said about the sacraments we can readily imagine how uncontrollable tempers could become when confronted with the defeated enemy in the very midst of Christendom's most sacred shrines.

Hence the emphasis in Raymond of Aguilers and other sources on what sounds like a bizarre process of decontamination through bloodshed, with the crusaders echoing scripture by riding in blood 'up to their knees and their horses' bridles'.[53] The letter that the victorious crusaders wrote to the pope following Jerusalem's capture repeated Raymond's claim and like him it rejoiced in the massacre; it was a clear sign that they believed that this shedding of Muslim blood would be pleasing to the papal court.[54] For Muslims on the other hand the massacre became emblematic of a crusade that they viewed as a protracted act of bloody violence committed against Islam. So the restraint that was displayed by Saladin when he recovered the city in 1187 was trumpeted as the exact opposite of crusading behaviour in 1099, affirming both the superior values of Islam and the self-control of its soldiers. And this entailed emphasizing the horrors committed in 1099: in the early thirteenth century Ibn al-Athir claimed that more than 70,000 were massacred in the al-Aqsa mosque.[55]

Raymond of Aguilers wasn't the only cleric to get excited by the thought of Muslim blood being shed. Men hundreds of kilometres from the front came very close at times to preaching that killing a Muslim was a redemptive process in itself, rather than being coincidental to the expression of a crusader's penance. When St Bernard wrote that 'the Christian glories in the death of the pagan, because Christ is glorified',[56] and Pope Innocent II (1130–43) praised the Templars for 'consecrating their hands to the Lord in the blood of unbelievers',[57] they were playing with fire. They came close to validating sacred violence, acts of violence possessing spiritual value in themselves rather than as the means to an end. At different times the crusaders embraced this notion and rejected it. Nor is it surprising that they embraced it most eagerly when they were caught up in the excitement of combat and triumph (as in 1099); and that they rejected it when faced by the cooler choices of strategy and settlement over the long term.

In some instances we can see a divide opening up among crusaders between followers and leaders. A notable example occurred in July 1099 when Tancred tried to sell his protection to a group of Muslims in Jerusalem whose lives were threatened by the triumphant crusaders. Rank-and-file crusaders resented this intervention and they found a way to slaughter the Muslims anyway, much to Tancred's irritation. One interesting aspect of the incident is that the crusaders carried out their murderous raid on their victims early in the morning following the fall of Jerusalem, when we might expect simple blood-lust to have cooled down overnight.[58] This cruelty is shocking, but there's no need to view it as obedience to some sort of ideological imperative: and the underlying motivation for the attack could well have been the prospect of gain. This would make the incident a clash over the proper division of booty, like those that we looked at in chapter six.

Earlier in the same passage the writer took note of the frenzied pillaging of captured Jerusalem by the victorious crusaders, and Fulcher of Chartres recorded that the hope of gain caused some crusaders to slit open the stomachs of dead Turks in the hope of finding coins that they'd swallowed for safe keeping.[59] This raises the intriguing but slippery subject of attitudes towards the enemy's bodies.[60] It's apparent that the crusaders didn't regard their foes with physical abhorrence. They enjoyed sexual relations with Muslim women in all the towns that they captured from the First Crusade onwards. The mainly clerical chroniclers were horrified and it's clear that the 'paganism' of the women aggravated the sinfulness involved.[61] In the vision of the priest Stephen reported by the author of the *Gesta Francorum*, Christ himself complained bitterly about the crusaders' sexual congress with Christians and Muslims, from which 'a great stench goes up to heaven'.[62] But it's hard to read anything into this behaviour other than the obvious point that the libido of those who indulged themselves was stronger than the injunctions of the clerics in their armies.

Cannibalism as a behavioural extreme

In much more extreme encounters with enemy flesh, the first crusaders cannibalized Turkish dead during the famines of the First Crusade.[63] Again it's wise to be cautious. Rather than indicating dehumanization,[64] it could simply reveal the severity of starvation, coupled with an understandable preference for consuming the enemy's dead rather than the bodies of deceased comrades-in-arms. It might even be regarded as an extreme example of pillaging. Reprisals also have to be taken into account. When the Christians recovered Jaffa in July

1192 they deliberately mixed the cadavers of their dead foes with those of pigs, because they were well aware of the Islamic taboo on pigs. This looks like a gratuitous insult to the dead, but it fact it was a response to the fact that the Turks had earlier thrown together dead pigs and Christian corpses.[65]

Such examples reinforce the danger of generalizing. Every instance when extremes of behaviour were in evidence calls for precision. As a final example, take the notorious passage in the *Gesta Francorum* describing the crusaders' treatment of the enemy when they had captured Maarrat al-Numan in December 1098:

> Our men all entered the city, and each seized his own share of whatever goods he found in houses or cellars, and when it was dawn they killed everyone, man or woman, whom they met in any place whatsoever. No corner of the city was clear of Saracen corpses, and one could scarcely go about the city streets except by treading on the dead bodies of the Saracens ... While we were there some of our men could not satisfy their needs, either because of the long stay or because they were so hungry, for there was no plunder to be had outside the walls. So they ripped up the bodies of the dead, because they used to find bezants hidden in their entrails, and others cut the dead flesh into slices and cooked it to eat.[66]

Such carnage, followed by the desecration and cannibalization of corpses, add up to a picture of behavioural extremes, but, as at Jerusalem some months later, they needn't have derived from any ideological stance. As the author makes plain, these were desperately famished men. This brings the danger of distortion because the points of closest and most abrasive contact between crusaders and their Muslim enemies were associated with the most stressful periods in their stay in the East: pitched battle; protracted siege, usually accompanied by food shortages; and the capture of fortified sites. We don't need to ascribe what we have since come to regard as atrocities to ideological hatred: there were more than enough more immediate circumstances that could have generated them. The point to emphasize is that the dominant, and officially sanctioned, view that was held of the Muslim foe did nothing to rein in behaviour that was rooted in desperation and fury. On the contrary, to our eyes one of the most unsettling documents produced in the First Crusade is the letter written by its leaders to the pope, in which they made a point of emphasizing, and it seems exaggerating, the scale of the massacre perpetrated at Jerusalem.[67] A modern analogy would be Stalin writing to the United Nations boasting of the number of German civilians killed by the Red Army during its capture of Berlin in 1945. It's an inconceivable idea that establishes the sheer scale of the ideological change that occurred between 1095 and 1945.

Getting to know the enemy

So far this is a somewhat depressing portrayal of relations between the faiths. But it doesn't constitute the whole picture because, as stressed at the start of the chapter, the crusaders' view of their foe was far from monochromatic. In no respect is this truer than their information about the enemy. In the course of what amounted to a 200 years' war it was inevitable that a corpus of knowledge about Islam and the Turks in the Middle East would be assembled by Catholic Europeans. The greatest chronicler of the Latin East, who was born and lived in the crusader states, William of Tyre, provides a large amount of reliable detail about contemporary Islam.[68] In the next generation, Pope Innocent III made a point of asking the authorities in the East to forward information about the situation among the Muslims.[69] And during the decades leading up to the fall of Acre fact-finding became a fixed feature of crusade planning as enthusiasts grasped its importance to prevent Christian armies repeating past errors. Writers like the Dominican William of Tripoli and the Franciscan Fidenzio of Padua placed a good deal of reasonably accurate information about the Muslims before the papal court.[70]

The problem was that the wider dissemination of this information was subject to a whole cluster of practical and cultural constraints. It's certainly the case that the majority of crusaders had neither access to texts like these nor the ability to read them. But it has to be added that they wouldn't have wanted to anyway. Crusading to the Holy Land spanned many generations, but for individual crusaders the experience had a duration of years if not months; and they were there not because of concern about Islam as a religion but because of anxieties about their chances of salvation, linked to an acute sense of the Holy Land's importance to Christianity. In addition, the oppositional view of Islam that fed into crusade sermons and vernacular literature set up serious barriers against the absorption of such genuine knowledge. Jarringly inaccurate stereotypes of the enemy became so crucial a part of the crusading self-image that they overrode reality's claims. Two such stereotypes, significant because they could so easily have been disproved, were Muslim lasciviousness and polytheism. These were clung to by crusaders even though they could scarcely avoid coming into contact with a mass of evidence testifying to the emphasis that devout Muslims placed on personal asceticism, and to a monotheism that was even more rigorously defended by Muslims than it was by Christians.[71]

On some occasions when Muslims do move into the foreground, it transpires that they are little more than puppets, used to add depth to the experiences that the Christians are undergoing. One of the most fascinating passages in the *Gesta Francorum* is an imaginary dialogue between the lord of Mosul, Kerbogha, and his mother. This long conversation comes as a surprise in a text

39 Muslims shown (bottom right) worshipping an idol. This pollutes Jerusalem, the scene of Christ's passion and goal of Christian pilgrims, leading Urban II to preach the First Crusade.

whose author has up to this point shown relatively little interest in the Muslims; and it quickly becomes apparent that its main purpose is to heap praise on the crusaders and to stress their enjoyment of God's support. That said, there are hints of information about Islam, including the status of Aleppo, Muslims' interest in astrology and their possession of sacred books, which give the passage some verisimilitude and take us, for a few pages at least, beyond simple denigration.[72] Another key First Crusade narrator, Raymond of Aguilers, retained the gist of the passage but replaced Kerbogha's mother with a Turk called Mirdalin.[73] The consolatory (for the crusaders) theme appears of prophecies circulating among the Muslims about the fall of Islam, and this constantly recurred, especially during the Fifth Crusade.[74]

It was tempting to set the Muslims up for a fall by making them guilty of over-confidence, as when Kerbogha, shortly before his encounter with his mother, is shown mocking the poor quality of the crusaders' arms: 'Are these the warlike and splendid weapons which the Christians have brought into Asia against us, and with these do they confidently expect to drive us beyond the furthest boundaries of Khorasan, and to blot out our names beyond the rivers of the Amazons?'[75] Similarly, the Turks who attacked Barbarossa outside Iconium in 1190 were portrayed as 'so certain of victory that they brought chains with them rather than swords',[76] while the sultan during the Fifth Crusade was shown urging his troops on with prophecies of world domination and the rich spoils that were to be found in the tents of their enemies.[77]

Vanquished Muslims could be shown bewailing their losses. After his defeat at Ascalon in 1099 the Fatimid emir laments that 'I have been beaten by a force of beggars, unarmed and poverty-stricken, who have nothing but a bag and a scrip',[78] while Ambroise has Saladin exclaiming after his setback at Arsuf, 'Where are the great defeats which we find in the writings were inflicted by our ancestors, which are recounted to us daily, defeats which they used to inflict upon the Christians?'[79] On other occasions Muslims would be shown marvelling at miracles that frustrated their designs, as when Saladin tried to burn the True Cross and it leapt from the flames undamaged.[80] Behind many such passages there lurk biblical and classical themes such as hubris and vanished glories, especially in authors like Ambroise who were strongly influenced by the epic tradition.[81] As rhetorical devices they form a counterpoint to the righteous jubilation and triumphalism of the crusaders. What isn't on display is an inherent interest in the enemy, though by showing them reflecting on events the process at least has the effect of raising them above the level of mere diabolic agents.

Events dictated that it was usually the Christians who lamented their defeat. Jubilant Muslims were then shown taunting the Christians with an adapted quotation from Ps. 115:2, 'Where is the God of the Christians?'[82] This was firmly rooted in the Church's goal of shaming Christians into taking action, but occasionally the context for it was more reflective and humane. Joinville narrated how Louis IX's master of ordnance, a man called John the Armenian, travelled to Damascus in 1250–1 to buy horn and glue for cross-bows. It's interesting in itself that such a journey for such a purpose didn't seem odd to Joinville. In the bazaar John encountered an old Muslim who commented on Islam's recent successes – 'through your sins, you have been brought so low that we take you in the fields just as if you were cattle'. John's angry riposte was that Christian sins were nothing compared with those committed by Muslims, to which the Muslim replied that the sins committed by Christians offended God more because they were dearer to Him. God knew that He couldn't expect much from people as ignorant and blind as the Muslims.[83]

As we can infer from this unlikely self-denigration, there are hints of topos in the encounter; and one of the most popular texts of the late Middle Ages, *Mandeville's Travels*, would include a fictional dialogue in which the sultan of Egypt made much the same point to that text's eponymous narrator.[84] There's rather more plausibility in Joinville's story, not least because it reminds the reader of other intelligent and considered Muslim commentary that dated from his period of captivity in Egypt. It's not improbable that historically aware Muslims who were conversing with Christians would make reference to their antagonists' providential worldview. But even if the core of Joinville's story rings true, he still wheels in a non-believer to add colour to a familiar message about what's gone wrong in the Holy Land and, by implication, what has to be done to set things right again.

Much the same applies to the corpus of knowledge that the crusaders built up about their enemies' political profiles and military resources. The objective was to accumulate information so that the tide of Muslim conquest could be turned. It's impressive that the leaders of the First Crusade, perhaps as a result of Byzantine tutorials, quickly came to grasp the hostility that existed between the Seljuq Turks and the Fatimid Arabs.[85] But this information was deployed to try to enlist the alliance of the Fatimids on the basis that 'the enemy of my enemy is my friend'. There's a fascinating snapshot of the situation that had been reached by March 1098 in the second letter that Stephen of Blois wrote home to his wife Adela. The picture it presents is a mixed one. Stephen was an inquisitive and well-informed man, one of the most interesting of the crusade's leaders. He made a stab at naming the crusade's chief adversaries and got most of them almost right. He appreciated the significance of the arrival in camp of the envoys from Egypt. He was familiar with the term emir and tried to define it as 'a prince and a lord'. There's a degree of sophistication in all this. But like others Stephen enjoyed reeling off a list of the enemy contingents that jumbled together ethnic, religious and geographical groups of peoples. He referred to 'the Turks and pagans', which raises the question of what the Turks were in Christian eyes if not *pagani*. And in common with many other commentators Stephen saw nothing wrong in the practice of celebrating success by bringing back to camp the heads of dead Turks, 'more than 200 heads, so that Christ's people could rejoice together over what had been done'.[86] Nor was it only on the Christian side that information-gathering served a narrowly functional purpose: the Muslim crew of a vessel that sailed from Beirut in 1189 to break the blockade of Acre managed to get past Christian patrol vessels because the crew shaved off their beards, flew crosses and kept a menagerie of pigs prominently on deck.[87]

The bone of contention – Jerusalem and the rival faiths

It's not difficult to demonstrate that even when views of the Muslims got
further than demonization, the resulting image sprang largely from perceptions of self and/or the overriding concern with defeating the enemy's military might. This applies even to the appreciation that Christians at times
showed for the Muslim veneration of Jerusalem. This was an advance on the
simpler model of pollution and desecration, but it just served to emphasize
the difficulty of the military situation that faced the Christians. It didn't act
as the preamble to a novel solution of the conflict over the city. In particular,
it's a mistake to construe Frederick II's treaty of Jaffa of 1229, which acceded
to the partition of Jerusalem and opened the city up to adherents of
Christians and Muslims alike, as a breach in the crusading position. For
both sides it was a tactical step, a way for the emperor to secure an 'exit
strategy' from his ill-fated crusade which would enable him to return home
with glory. It's been pointed out that because there was no provision in the
treaty for returning to the canons of the Holy Sepulchre the property
and rents that had been dispersed after 1187, it simply wasn't practicable for
them to return to administer the religious complex.[88] An accurate and
bleak assessment of the conflict over Jerusalem appeared in Baha' al-Din,
when Saladin is made to state with brutal clarity the intractability of the
situation.

> Jerusalem is ours just as much as it is yours. Indeed, for us it is greater
> than it is for you, for it is where our Prophet came on his Night Journey
> and the gathering place of the angels. Let not the king imagine that we
> shall give it up, for we are unable to breathe a word of that amongst
> the Muslims. As for the land, it is also ours originally. Your conquest of it
> was an unexpected accident due to the weakness of the Muslims there at
> that time.[89]

For the Christians, the equivalent position was well put by the author of the
Itinerarium peregrinorum in describing the response to the preaching of the
Third Crusade, 'Summoned by their devoted fervour, from everywhere famous
champions had come for your consolation, Jerusalem! Look, already the whole
globe fights for you, to fulfil what was said through Isaiah the prophet [Isaiah
43:5–6].'[90] Even when a glimmer of appreciation was shown of the position
stated by Saladin, as by Walter von der Vogelweide in his 'Palestine song'
('Palästinalied') written *c.* 1228, it was followed by an emphatic vindication of
the Christian claim: 'Christians, Jews and also heathen / Claim this heritage
as theirs. / May God make the right to triumph / By the threefold name he

40 The Dome of the Rock, completed in 691 and the oldest surviving Islamic building in the world.

bears. / All the world comes here to fight; / But to us belongs the right. / God defend us by his might!'[91] It was a visceral fear of the Christians that because both faiths placed such a premium on the possession of Jerusalem, the Muslims might be tempted to destroy the principal Christian shrines 'so that there will no longer be any memorial of the Lord for the people of the Franks to seek'.[92]

Admiration for the enemy

The conviction that their Muslim opponents were in the wrong didn't stop crusaders admiring their fighting qualities. The first unambiguous expression of praise followed the battle of Dorylaeum in July 1097, which the author of the *Gesta Francorum* summarized in memorable terms:

> What man, however experienced and learned, would dare to write of the skill and prowess and courage of the Turks, who thought that they would strike terror into the Franks, as they had done into the Arabs and Saracens, Armenians, Syrians and Greeks, by the menace of their arrows? Yet, please God, their men will never be as good as ours. They have a saying that they are of common stock with the Franks, and that no men, except the Franks and themselves, are naturally born to be knights. This is true, and nobody can deny it, that if only they had stood firm in the faith of Christ and holy

Christendom . . . you could not find stronger or braver or more skilful soldiers; and yet by God's grace they were beaten by our men.[93]

What's remarkable about this passage is that the three key aspects of crusader praise for the Turks are already fully formed. In the first place, admiration focused on their abilities as fellow soldiers whose attributes of training, courage and ingenuity could be applauded. Secondly, the principal explanation given for this was an ethnic one – the Turks who had been encountered at Dorylaeum came of sound stock, and had been able to defeat all their opponents, including the Christian Byzantines, until they met their match in the Franks. The unwarlike Egyptians, by contrast, could only hope to prevail through sheer numbers, and by using captured crusaders for purposes of breeding, 'so that the lords of Babylon might then have warlike families of the race of the Franks'.[94] And thirdly, what stopped the Turks from overcoming the Franks was their false religion: no amount of skill and bravery could prevail in the face of God's wrath. This was a coherent overall position to take up and it required comparatively little further development. Indeed, the same position surfaced in the West almost immediately after the First Crusade in *The Song of Roland*. The Moorish enemies of the Franks in Spain were accorded very much the same profile. 'From Balaguet there cometh an Emir / His form is noble, his eyes are bold and clear, / When on his horse he's mounted in career / He bears him bravely armed in his battle gear, / And for his courage he's famous far and near; / Were he but Christian, right knightly he'd appear.'[95]

During the Third Crusade fairly similar views were expressed by each side about the fighting prowess of the other. On the Christian side, we have the testimony of the *Itinerarium peregrinorum*: 'What should be said about that unbelieving people who guarded [Acre]? They certainly ought to be admired for their valour in war and their integrity. If only they had held the right faith, there would be none better.' The dichotomy was affirmed when Acre's garrison filed out of the city following its surrender. The watching crusaders were filled with admiration for men whose 'fierce appearance made it seem that they had won the victory', though 'their superstitious rite and the miserable error of idolatry perverted and corrupted these strengths'.[96] Thanks to their denigration of Islam crusading commentators couldn't view their enemies' courage as a reflection of their devotion, but the more dispassionate Muslims could: Baha' al-Din, whose generous praise of the steadiness under fire that was shown by the Christian infantry was noted in an earlier chapter, also wrote that 'those on either side gave their lives to purchase the next world's peace and valued this world's existence as nothing beside eternal life'.[97]

Two points need to be made about this *topos* of admirable but fatally flawed Turkish fighting prowess. The first is that it was the child of circumstances.

Those crusaders who reflected on the military background to their presence in the East were bound to appreciate that their adversaries possessed extraordinary fighting skills; it was these which had brought the Turks to the Holy Land and the neighbouring regions, and which facilitated the rise of the house of Zengi, the hegemony of Saladin and the Ayyubid clan, and the ascendancy of the Mamluks: in other words, the variety of reasons why crusading was necessary. Individual crusaders who fought the Turks on battlefields, in raids, in assaults on town and castle walls, were similarly bound to appreciate these skills irrespective of whether they had gone through any such process of reflection. In either case, denigrating their fighting skills would have been both counter-productive and self-defeating: it would have made the task of defeating the Muslims harder and it would have caused the crusaders' own military successes to be belittled by their contemporaries. Unlike Muslim religious beliefs and practices, the enemy's fighting ability presented the crusaders with no ideological tensions, provided that the caveat of their ultimate defeat was always added. Hence the popularity of showing doom prophecies circulating among the Muslims: what better way of placing an expectation of defeat among the enemies themselves?

Muslim ethnicity

The other point to make about the crusaders' admiration for their enemy is that the contrast created between the evils of Islam and the fighting skills of the Turks was generally couched in ethnic terms. Christians were aware that Muhammad had been an Arab and many of Islam's vices, especially its lasciviousness and cruelty, were associated with Arabic culture and with the Middle East's oppressively hot climate, which among other things was held to encourage sexual licence. It was argued that genetically the Turks shared fewer of these vices, though they'd been pretty thoroughly infected with them by their adopted religion.[98]

This second point has to be advanced with caution, because it's by no means obvious that even by 1200, after a full century of crusading, the implications of the ethnic diversity that the crusaders faced had sunk in. During the First Crusade the lists of names that are usually given for the enemy leave the impression that clear distinctions were made relatively rarely. Names derived from ethnicity, geography, history and scripture jostled side by side. Thus: 'Turks, Persians, Paulicians, Saracens and Agulani, with other pagans, not counting the Arabs';[99] and 'Turks, Arabs, Saracens, Paulicians, Azymites, Kurds, Persians, Agulani and many other people who could not be counted'.[100] The mystery and exoticism associated with the orient only made the situation more confused. Guibert of Nogent's learning and concern for accuracy were relatively advanced,[101] but he still included in his description of Kerbogha's army outside

Antioch a strange tale about female archers. They were supposed to have given birth during their stay near Antioch and to have cast their tiny infants to one side during their headlong flight after Kerbogha's defeat.[102] Even the author of the *Libellus de expugnatione Terrae Sanctae*, a settler who must have known the enemy pretty well, couldn't resist the appeal of the catalogue when describing Saladin's army in 1187, listing a total of thirteen groups.[103]

The diversity of Muslim ethnicity aroused some curiosity. During the Third Crusade the appearance among the Muslim ranks not just of the Bedouin but also of Negroes from the Sudan was noted. It was a sign that the enemy's troops were being scrutinized in some detail. The comments made on Saladin's Sudanese troops by the author of the *Itinerarium peregrinorum* come close to racial stereotyping: 'a fiendish race, forceful and relentless, deformed by nature and unlike other human beings, black in colour, of enormous stature and inhuman savageness'. But the emphasis was always less on the ethnic differences that were observed than on the military challenge that was presented, as in this case: 'Instead of helmets they wore red coverings on their heads, brandishing in their hands clubs bristling with iron teeth, whose shattering blows neither helmets nor mailshirts could resist.'[104] Much the same applied to the Bedouin, 'savage and darker than soot, the most redoubtable infantrymen, carrying bows and quivers and round shields. They are a very energetic and agile race.'[105]

The entry of the 'noble Saracen' into the corpus of western imaginative literature undoubtedly owed something to the genuine encounters that took place in the Middle East, but few ideas could be more misguided than that this new image broke down pre-existing stereotypes. It would be more accurate to say that it demonstrated the diversity of the crusading experience. This included combat, in which glory could be earned by the display of leadership and courage in defeating a worthy foe; but it was also driven and characterized by zeal to release God's land from the grip of unbelieving and polluting pagans. The noble but flawed Turk and the cruel Saracen rubbed shoulders, because both were the product of fundamentally western viewpoints.

Saladin – an image and its evolution

This brings us to Saladin, for if any individual Muslim leader attracted admiration as well as interest it was he. Gervase of Canterbury summed him up well as 'a pagan man but a distinguished knight'.[106] Reading Ambroise, who fought on the Third Crusade, it's impossible not to be impressed by the depth of characterization given to the sultan as well as to his brother Saphadin. The two were portrayed as rounded human beings possessing both virtues and vices, incomparably more so than predecessors like Kerbogha,

Zengi and Nur ed-Din. The perceptions of Saladin's ability as a leader of men, his chivalric generosity (*largesse*) and courtesy (*courtoisie*), and his good faith that came to dominate his image in western Europe were constructs that were reflected if not created in the midst of combat in Palestine. It's clear that a lot of the crusaders who fought against Saladin's troops were aware that their opponents' commander had these qualities. Indeed historians have tended to attribute the transformation of Saladin's reputation from demonic persecutor into admirable foe to stories brought back to the West by returning crusaders.[107]

We can observe the change in Saladin's image happening over quite a short period of time, for example between the early (1191–2) and later (1217–22) versions of the *Itinerarium peregrinorum*, and between William of Tyre (died *c.* 1185) and the Old French continuations of William's history known as *Eracles* (early thirteenth century).[108] Not only were the sultan's positive qualities increasingly emphasized, but attempts were made to 'appropriate' him for the Christian cause by means of strategies which dated back almost to the time of the First Crusade. The belief circulated that he'd been dubbed as a knight by the Franks,[109] that, like Zengi before him, he was actually of Frankish descent,[110] and that he was sympathetic to Christianity, or even – the ultimate wish-fulfilment – had converted to it in secret.[111]

Much of the detail in this 'valorization' of Saladin occurred in the mid-thirteenth century or even later, but the seeds of the change can be seen in texts that were rooted in the crusading experience. For example, the early version of the *Itinerarium peregrinorum* already contained a passage in which Saladin was dubbed by Humphrey of Toron 'in accordance with the rite of the Franks'.[112] Baha' al-Din almost certainly came close to reporting the views of many on the Christian side when he quoted Richard I as commenting on Saladin's *coup de main* at Jaffa in 1191, 'This sultan of yours is a great man. Islam has no greater or mightier prince on earth than him . . . By God, I did not imagine that he could take Jaffa in two months. How did he take it in two days?'[113] Saladin was a man who honoured his word, proving receptive to the argument that 'the Turks ought to keep good faith with people of any nation, no matter what their beliefs'.[114]

Worthy adversaries – Saladin and Richard I

Comparing Baha' al-Din with the Christian sources that were most favourable towards Richard I, it's hard to avoid the sense of a parallel process of valorization going on. Just as a great Richard needed a worthy Saladin, a great Saladin required a noble as well as a highly capable opponent in the shape of the English king. The inconclusive outcome of the crusade may have reinforced this tendency, because both sides had to account for it without detracting from their own leader's renown. For a pro-Richard author like Ambroise there was the added advantage that Philip Augustus could be shown behaving worse than an infidel.[115] Thanks to western Europe's vicious politics this became a three-cornered contest, a fact that emerges amusingly in Richard of Devizes. He has Saphadin giving voice to an extravagant and bizarrely unlikely paean of praise for Richard, even alluding to the reputation of his father Henry II, before concluding, 'but, thank God, he was burdened with the king of the French and held back by him, like a cat with a hammer tied to its tail'.[116]

Setting aside the French complication, and following a tradition as old as the *Iliad*, it was tempting to depict the Third Crusade as a duel between the two commanders, so it's unsurprising that the myth of man-to-man combat between the two became popular in the West. It found expression in tiles used in English houses as well as a wall painting commissioned by Henry III in 1251 for the Antioch chamber in his palace at Clarendon.[117] But the breakthrough in individual characterization resulted not just from Saladin's own qualities or indeed those of Richard, but also from the length of time that Saladin was militarily active. By the time of the Third Crusade the sultan had been a much discussed as well as a stereotypically evil figure in Christian lands for well over a decade. We've seen that the tax levied for the crusade was named after him, and his deeds naturally played a big role during the preaching of the crusade, for example in Peter of Blois' hagiographic text about Reynald of Châtillon, the

41 Single combat between Richard I and Saladin: tiles from Chertsey Abbey.

Passio Reginaldi (1187–8).[118] Most crusaders who arrived at Acre would already have possessed a strong idea of Saladin's importance when they disembarked, and for all the negativity of the preaching that they'd heard, they may well have sensed his greatness. No thirteenth-century Islamic leader, not even Baybars, came near to matching this extraordinary impact. As for Saphadin, he was subjected to the familiar lament: 'a very noble and munificent man, who would have been worthy to be compared with the best of men if he had not rejected the creed and faith of the Christian religion'.[119]

Lessons of the prison cell

Third Crusade texts show crusaders and Muslims interacting to a remarkable degree, but it's likely that the closest contact of all occurred in 1250, when almost the entire French army was taken prisoner in the Nile delta. Joinville dealt with this traumatic series of events at length in his memoir, and his captivity narrative is unrivalled among crusading sources for the detail that it gives about the Muslims from a perspective of unsought but unavoidable intimacy. The picture is convincing precisely because it's such a varied one. The Muslims aren't shown exclusively in a good light, but the well-worn condemnations of earlier crusading texts are largely absent.

Following his capture Joinville records several acts of consideration and kindness. Some were probably motivated by the need to keep rich captives alive until they could be ransomed, but others may have stemmed from the Islamic obligation to show charity towards the unfortunate.[120] When Joinville inadvertently ate meat on a Friday a high-ranking Muslim advanced the common-sense argument, later reiterated by the papal legate, that God would know that he had no idea what day it was.[121] On the other hand, many of the French who could neither be ransomed nor sold as slaves, including Joinville's priest and his cleric, were casually killed during the chaotic circumstances of the round-up made of the crusaders.[122] Torture inflicted on the patriarch of Jerusalem in an attempt to force the king to agree to the conditions offered for his release was recounted in lurid detail,[123] and in one particularly vivid passage Joinville wrote of a rush into the prison tent by young warriors armed and ready to slaughter the prisoners, who seem to have been restrained from doing so by a reflective old Muslim.[124]

These events were chronicled in a text that's also full of information about the Ayyubid regime and its workings, especially its military strengths.[125] Much of this is accurate, though allowance has to be made for the continuing attraction of the 'exotic East', and for Joinville's love of a good story, a memorable example being his account of how the sultan of Homs frustrated an attack by the sultan of Cairo by bribing one of his rival's servants to spread poison on his chess mat.[126] Like the Third Crusade texts, Joinville revealed the full extent of the parallels that existed between the aristocratic ways of the Christians and those of their enemies. He described a chivalric encounter between a Genoese knight called Giannone and some Muslims outside Acre that was 'witnessed by the leading citizens in Acre and all the women who had gathered on the walls of the city to watch the fight'.[127] Writing about 'this valiant Turk' Fakhr ad-Din (Scecedin), the Ayyubid vizier in Egypt, Joinville commented that he was 'the most highly esteemed of any in the pagan world'. Fakhr ad-Din was allegedly accompanied by a banner that sported his arms, which included those of the Emperor Frederick II, 'who had made him a knight', together with the insignia of the sultans of Aleppo and Cairo. His name, 'son of the sheikh', indicated that he was accorded particular reverence by the Turks. Noble, knightly, valiant and respected, Fakhr ad-Din, like Saladin and Saphadin before him, seems to have been prevented from crossing the threshold of assimilation only by his religious beliefs.[128]

The Bedouin and the Assassins

Joinville also gave his reader fascinating insights into the knowledge that inquisitive crusaders in the mid-thirteenth century could acquire about the Shi'a Bedouin and Assassins. He described the way of life of the Bedouin, their distinctive clothing, their nomadic pastoralism and the tribute payments that they had to make to Christian and Muslim rulers alike.[129] In these respects the Bedouin were unusual though not without parallels in the West. The Assassins, noted above all for their practice of specific, and most likely suicidal, missions to kill, were another matter. In reality they were an Ismaili Shi'a sect based at the Iranian stronghold of Alamut, which acted as a constant thorn in the flesh of the Seljuq Turks from the time of their arrival in the region in the late eleventh century. They also captured fortresses in northern Syria from which they became a disruptive force in the politics of the region, but their most dramatic intervention in the affairs of the Christians in the Holy Land occurred in 1192 when, for reasons that have never been explained, two of them murdered Conrad of Montferrat in Tyre. When the author of the *Itinerarium peregrinorum* wrote about the Syrian Assassins in the context of Conrad's murder he had little specific to say. His knowledge of their religious beliefs was generalized – 'their creed is extremely cruel and obscure' – and the passage is characterized by the fanciful detail that their leader the sheikh al-Jezrel ('the Old Man of the Mountain'), 'gives each of them a horribly long sharp knife in order to carry our [their assigned assassination]'.[130]

With Joinville's account of the Assassins we enter a different world. When Louis IX was at Acre following his release from captivity the Old Man underestimated the king's status, demanding tribute to spare his life; in Mafia-like style, this demand was accompanied by the presentation to Louis of a winding-sheet 'for his burial if he refused'. Louis was unimpressed. He referred the envoys to the masters of the Military Orders, who coldly informed them of the extent of their lord's miscalculation. They withdrew and came back laden with exquisite gifts from an apologetic Old Man. Joinville not only described the gifts in detail, but made himself familiar with the report later made by an Arabic-speaking friar called Yves le Breton, whom Louis sent as his own envoy to the Old Man. This enabled Joinville to provide a reasonably accurate account of how Shi'a beliefs differed from those of Sunni Islam; he used their alleged belief in the transmigration of souls to help explain their willingness to face death so readily. Joinville was no less attracted by the bizarre side of the Assassins than the author of the *Itinerarium peregrinorum* had been. He included an anecdote about the Old Man being preceded when he went out riding by an escort carrying an elaborate axe studded with knives, an emblem of his murderous authority; but such picturesque details were anchored in the information that he gathered from his own observations and from Fr. Yves's report.[131] Joinville's understanding of Islam may have been far from complete, but his memoir shows that he possessed the intelligence and natural empathy to have made it so if circumstances had permitted.

Crusade and conversion

Nobody could doubt that in Joinville's narrative, and on occasion in earlier crusading texts, the Muslims went through a metamorphosis from diabolic agents to fully rounded human beings, albeit ones whom for inescapable religious reasons it was essential to fight and defeat. It's logical to assume that the more 'humanized' the Muslims became, the more the crusaders would give thought to converting them, recognizing that they possessed souls that could and should be saved. The desirability of Muslim conversion was a recurrent theme in crusading sources. It's arguable that the crusaders went beyond what the papal court and crusade preachers had asked for, since with the possible exception of the Fifth Crusade the idea of using crusade as a means to convert rarely cropped up in texts that emanated from the Church in the West. But the assumption that the crusaders' occasional attempts to convert their enemy sprang from a more 'liberal' view, one born of contact, is questionable. The exact opposite could be argued: that conversion was enmeshed with a sweepingly triumphalist outlook associated with denigration rather than appreciation.

So while much has been made of the attempts to convert that took place in 1097–9,[132] detailed inspection shows that they were unsystematic and circum-stantial episodes. In June 1098, in what looks like an attempt to buy time, the leaders of the First Crusade despatched Peter the Hermit with an interpreter called Herluin to offer conversion to Kerbogha.[133] This was a game that two could play. When Tancred sent six envoys to Duqaq, the emir of Damascus, in 1100 to demand that the emir either convert or abandon Damascus, the insulted Duqaq responded by offering them conversion to Islam or death.[134] It wasn't the only occasion that this grim choice was offered. In July 1098 at Tell-Mannas a Provençal lord called Raymond Pilet offered Muslim peasants the choice between baptism and death.[135] It's difficult to regard this as benign. In fact we seem to be back in the spring of 1096, when the same alternatives were forced on the Jews of the Rhineland, though this comparison merely highlights how seldom forced conversion, which after all was contrary to the dictates of canon law, cropped up during encounters with Muslims.

Some of the first crusaders seem to have made an *ad hoc* association between recovering Jerusalem and spreading the faith. It may even have been reinforced by the coincidence that they captured the holy city on 15 July, the feast-day of the Apostles' dispersal from Jerusalem to convert the gentiles. But the key association of the date, as stated for example by Raymond of Aguilers, was that of the Christians' own exile and return.[136] During later crusades conversion attempts were less conspicuous though they occasionally cropped up. The most famous example occurred in August 1219 during the Fifth Crusade, when St Francis made a brief visit to the army in an abortive attempt to try to convert the Ayyubid sultan al-Kamil.[137] A similar attempt to facilitate the baptism of a Muslim ruler, the Hafsid amir Muhammad, and by so doing bring about that of his subjects, may have been behind Louis IX's diversion of his second crusade to Tunis in 1270. It's hard to explain why he went there otherwise.[138] This targeting of Muslim rulers from Kerbogha of Mosul through to Muhammad of Tunis sprang from the fact that attempting the systematic conversion of the population was totally impracticable at the same time as conducting a tough military campaign. Conversion also carried the danger of being 'seduced' by the enemy's faith: after all, Muhammad had been history's great seducer, the Don Juan of religion. It was better, as Louis IX once remarked to Joinville, to leave disputing about the faith to the theologians and just run argumentative non-believers through with the sword.[139]

Christians, Muslims and crusading

The crusaders faced an enemy whose religion was, in more respects than most of them realized, similar to their own, and whose fighting skills were extraordinary. Of these two facets of the Islamic world, they distorted the religion to the point of caricature, while staying respectful of the skills. For the most part, what lay behind this two-fold response was purpose. The crusaders

42 St Vincent suffers disembowelment at the hands of Saracens, from a Book of Hours painted in Hainault *c.* 1300.

weren't fighting in the East to save the souls of unbelievers or to extend the bounds of the Christian religion. They fought to win salvation for themselves and to recover or defend sites that were sacred to their faith. The enemy's beliefs were misrepresented but in general he wasn't dehumanized. A comment on the crusaders' massacre of their opponents in the Muslim camp outside Mansurah in 1250 sums up the situation well: 'It was sad indeed to see so many dead bodies and so much blood spilt, except that they were enemies of the Christian faith.'[140]

Systematic dehumanization has been a feature of conflicts driven by ethnic rather than religious violence: it was always open to the cornered Muslim to escape death by converting. That said, an official ideology that verged on hatred combined with the casual brutality that characterized most medieval warfare, and the harsh circumstances of most crusading, to produce what we've since come to condemn as atrocities. Crusaders did recognize individuality in their enemy, and they acknowledged that the Muslims' most prominent and greatest leader was a man of honour as well as extraordinary talents. Few of them went further than this, and in the case of those that did the argument that deeper knowledge subdued hostility is for the most part wrong. It's open to debate whether Christianity and Islam could have enjoyed better relations if it hadn't been for crusading. What's certain is that it did nothing to help.

9

❖

BRAVE NEW WORLD

Geographical and mental horizons

Travelling for its own sake had a poor reputation in the Middle Ages. It was associated with fickleness and vanity, and a charge constantly laid at the door of pilgrims and crusaders alike was that their real motive wasn't devotion but restless curiosity born out of idleness, a notorious ploy of the devil. Inhabitants of the cloister in particular distrusted travel, seeing it as an insidious temptress working on their fellow religious.[1] The anonymous annalist of Würzburg was probably not alone in disparaging people who went on the Second Crusade 'for the sake of learning about strange lands'.[2] In reality it's likely that the overwhelming majority of the men and women who took the cross did so primarily out of a sense of religious commitment rather than from any burning desire to experience the novel. For all sorts of reasons they would have preferred not to travel hundreds of miles to defend the Holy Land. But while they were discharging their vows they couldn't help but come into contact with the unfamiliar.

Crusaders responded to the new in a variety of ways which tell us a great deal about the medieval Christians' view of their world; in this they resembled pilgrims both before and after them. In the case of crusading, though, there were additional dimensions that sprang from their potent perception of themselves as Christ's elect, and from their engagement with an arduous military task. In their encounters with eastern Christians who weren't fellow Catholics, and in their tense relations with the Byzantine court, they can be seen wrestling with the inherent tension between Catholic triumphalism and Christian brotherhood or ecumenism. Arguably this tension was resolved mainly by pragmatic considerations, until the massive act of violence perpetrated in 1204 cut the Gordian knot. Then in the thirteenth century the epistemological ground shifted. Horizons were dramatically broadened, in part because fresh strategic approaches were adopted towards the Holy Land's military dilemma, but also as a result of much increased knowledge of the lands and peoples that lay to its east. We're bound to ask whether crusading as a religious and cognitive experience was tied to a worldview that was bounded by time and place, one that was created by the narrow educational parameters of the early medieval ages, and was brought to an end by the dramatic changes imposed by the westwards surge of Mongol power in the 1200s.

Prior knowledge and assumptions

We can't hope to know what knowledge most crusaders had of the lands they visited in the East. But we can work out what information they *could* have gathered from the sources available to them. Surviving texts from the ancient world had fused with reports written by pilgrims and other travellers to form a body of knowledge that could have equipped a crusader to be surprised by little that they came across. This was increasingly the case once relevant information came to be recorded from 1099 onwards. Shortly before the battle of Hattin an unknown author wrote a detailed treatise about the Holy Land called *A Treatise about the Sites and Condition of the Holy Land* (*Tractatus de locis et statu suncte terre*). Anybody who set out on the Third Crusade after reading the *Tractatus* would have been well briefed, if they could remember it all[3] – even more so their successors, who had access to James of Vitry's informative and lively, albeit opinionated, *History of the East* (*Historia orientalis*).[4] But to a large extent the same point would apply even to the first crusaders. To take an obvious example, they anticipated severe summer heat, knowing that the Middle East lay towards the southern edge of the world's northern temperate zone. So Stephen of Blois observed with some surprise in a letter home during the First Crusade that winter temperatures at Antioch were much like those at home.[5]

The key texts for collecting information were those of Pliny the Elder (d. 79 CE), Solinus (fl. 238), Orosius (fl. 417) and Isidore of Seville (d. 636).[6] Pliny's *Natural History*, which he completed shortly before his death, provided a level-headed and fairly comprehensive descriptive account of the world's regions and their flora and fauna. Bede used Pliny's text when writing his commentary on *The Song of Songs*, noting in passing that his residence in northern Europe stopped him gaining first-hand knowledge of the biblical lands. The *Natural History* became a standard textbook at Laon, it was read in the early schools at Oxford, and through the conduit of Thomas of Cantimpré and Bartholomew of England it influenced Vincent of Beauvais' great encyclopaedia, his *Speculum Mundi* of c. 1244.[7]

Cartographically too even the earliest crusaders were better placed than might be supposed. A crusader who studied the Anglo-Saxon (Cotton) map of *c.* 1050 while preparing to set out in 1095–6 would have formed a reasonable idea of what would be involved in marching to the Holy Land. It's been speculated that Stephen of Blois may have consulted a map before setting out on the First Crusade: he was certainly prepared to estimate how long it would take to cover specific distances.[8] The impact of instruction by experienced Italian merchants, veteran Jerusalem pilgrims and helpful Byzantine officials can't be assessed with any precision, but it surely helped to combat ignorance. A century on and Roger of Howden provided a detailed and objective travelogue about the sea route taken by the English fleet on the Third Crusade.[9] And a century after Howden the maps that were drawn for Marino Sanudo's advisory treatise about crusading were similarly accurate. The map of Acre that Sanudo commissioned, or possibly drew himself, is painstakingly naturalistic, giving the impression of being done from memory.[10] In these contexts mistakes could cost lives: Roger of Howden was writing about navigation and Sanudo about the reconquest of the Holy Land. Pietro Vesconte, the prime candidate for Sanudo's unknown cartographer, drew the first surviving signed and dated marine chart in 1311.[11]

There are some important caveats to this rosy picture. The first is that all information was viewed through a scriptural lens and in some cases this proved extraordinarily unhelpful to accuracy. Maps of the world (*mappaemundi*) were overtly didactic, the continents of Europe, Asia and Africa converging to form a 'T' that represented the cross, with Jerusalem lying at its centre. The compiler of the *Tractatus* voiced a truism when he wrote at the start of his text that 'the land of Jerusalem is situated at the centre of the world'.[12] Cartographic depictions of the Holy Land were dominated by the need to fit in all twelve tribes of Israel, while maps of Jerusalem showed it as a circular city. It wasn't until Vesconte's time that the Levant's coastal cities were depicted in a detail that was largely accurate, and Jerusalem was given a more realistic portrayal. This wasn't a major problem though. Since contemporary knowledge of the world excluded the Americas, the T maps didn't call for a dramatic misreading of known geography. Nor did a circular Jerusalem introduce much distortion. A group of crusaders would have been perfectly capable of finding their way around Jerusalem with the plan given in the St Omer codex, for example.[13]

The second caveat is that contemporaries were enthralled by the fantastic. This doesn't mean that they treated observed reality in a cavalier way: Stephen of Blois pointed out that, contrary to what he'd heard, crossing the Bosphorus wasn't dangerous, any more than crossing the Marne or the Seine,[14] and at least two visitors to the Holy Land pointed out that it was untrue that no rain fell on Mount Gilboa.[15] The novel was measured against the familiar, as when crusaders from Germany noted that Silves in Portugal was about the size of Goslar, and Iconium that of Cologne, while the mouth of the Tagus was about as broad as

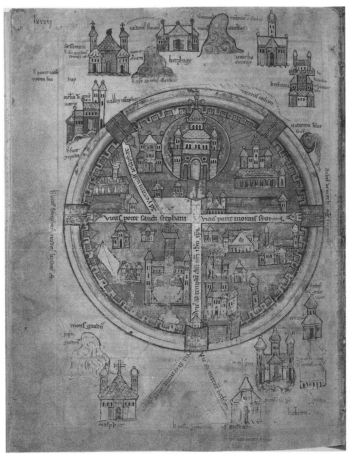

43 The thirteenth-century Uppsala map of Jerusalem, a highly accurate portrayal of the city and its surroundings.

that of the Elbe at Stade.[16] But while they respected the difference between truth and fantasy, crusaders were also happy to let gaps in their knowledge be filled up with imaginary animals, eccentric topography, spurious behaviour and bizarre natural phenomena.[17] This was an ancient trend that had been reinforced by Solinus and Isidore, in some cases because it lent itself to Christian didacticism. James of Vitry, an insightful observer who dismissed racial stereotypes, still devoted twenty-five pages in his _History of the East_ to a selection of the monstrous races, using information culled exclusively from his reading.[18] And the most popular of the thirteenth-century continuations of William of Tyre included thirteen chapters taken verbatim from _Li Fet des Romains_, a runaway bestseller of the time that combined anecdote, natural history and geographical lore in a concoction designed equally to amaze and amuse the reader.[19]

The third, and most significant, caveat is that while the geographical extent of the ancient world combined with the intellectual dominance of scripture to create a full and largely accurate picture of Palestine, Egypt, Syria and Asia Minor, the lands further to the east were scarcely charted at all. This made them a particularly fertile area for planting monsters, dog-headed people and the like, causing considerable disappointment when India and the Far East were visited and observations recorded.[20]

Fulcher of Chartres – crusader, historian and naturalist

Much of this can be observed in the first detailed account that was written about the Holy Land by a crusader. Fulcher of Chartres followed his narrative of the First Crusade with a history of the kingdom of Jerusalem up to 1127. He was well equipped to write it. As King Baldwin I's chaplain he was ideally placed to gain access to any information that was available in Jerusalem, and to compare what he observed and heard about with what he'd read in Solinus and Latin translations of the Jewish historian Flavius Josephus; and he quoted from a variety of other classical works.[21] Fulcher was alert and inquisitive and his interests were broad, including antiquity, geography and both animal and vegetable life. He took passing note of the quality of the Roman fortifications at Jarash (Gerasa),[22] and provided much detail about the history of Tyre.[23] He was willing to admit his mistake in identifying Arsuf with the Philistine city Azotus.[24] Seas, lakes and rivers seem to have fascinated him,[25] so it's not surprising that the Dead Sea and its shores attracted his particular interest. He testified to its bitterness from personal experience, and confirmed Josephus' observation that the lake's salinity stopped people submerging themselves in it.[26] When Baldwin I returned from a reconnaissance journey to the Red Sea in 1116 Fulcher questioned him eagerly about its salinity.[27]

Fulcher was struck by the fact that while a snake's bite could be lethal, the antidote for it could include the animal's own body.[28] He recorded the appearance of a cloud of locusts in the spring of 1114,[29] and another three years later: 'you could see them advance like an army of men in good order as if they had previously arranged it in council'.[30] A plague of rats in 1127 received similar attention.[31] He described Nile crocodiles and hippopotami, and what sound like giraffes,[32] and he noted absences: 'in Palestine I have seen neither a whale nor a lamprey, nor among the birds a magpie or warbler . . . Among the trees, I have seen neither the poplar, the hazel, the elder, the butcher's broom, nor any maple.'[33] Not that Fulcher was without his limitations. Locusts like Saracens he saw principally as God's punishment for men's sinfulness.[34] The main lesson to be drawn from observing nature was the wonder of God's creativity: 'if any [of God's works] seem ugly in our sight nevertheless they are to be praised because the Creator of all made them'.[35] Scripture shaped his interest rather more than history did, so Aleppo was noted as the location where Abraham pastured his cattle *en route* for Canaan.[36] He frankly admitted padding out his chapter on animal life with information taken from Solinus, while another dedicated to serpents is little more than a rehash of Solinus.[37] But when all's said and done there's a refreshing curiosity in Fulcher's description of his new surroundings. It really is an encounter between West and East.

Other close observers

The same combination of excitement, creative conjecture and bibliocentricity can be found in numerous texts written by crusaders and their associates in the decades that followed. Roger of Howden took note of flying fish and provided details on the shipworms whose damage to the English ships during their passage through the Mediterranean in 1190–1 necessitated substantial refitting.[38] The author of the *Itinerarium peregrinorum* described unpleasant encounters with tarantulas north of Caesarea; nocturnal attacks by the spiders were driven off with the help of loud noise.[39] At Bethgibelin in June 1192 the crusading army was tormented by tiny flies called *cincenelles* whose stings caused painful swellings.[40] This author was also struck by the speed of camels. He said they were faster than deer, which he could expect his readers to be familiar with.[41] Joinville gave a remarkable description of Norwegian crusaders hunting lions near Caesarea, diverting their attention with old bits of cloth while their comrades brought them down with arrows.[42] James of Vitry was another strong observer. In a letter written in September 1218 he commented on various wonders of the Nile delta, including the river's rise and fall, the practice of incubating chicks in ovens, and the habits of crocodiles.[43] Oliver of Paderborn wrote a number of chapters on the geography of Egypt including a garden on the outskirts of Cairo where rare balsam trees were cultivated. He observed that the trees were tended by both Christians and Muslims, whereas the author of the *Tractatus* reported didactically that they only yielded fruit for the former.[44]

Oliver's reference in this chapter to the church dedicated to the Virgin at a point where she paused during her flight to Egypt is typical of a tendency to emphasize Egypt's sacred geography so as to give devotional depth to the new strategy of attacking the delta. John of Tulbia noted the tradition that Moses had been born at Damietta and the prophet Jeremiah on a nearby island.[45] For this author, as for Oliver of Paderborn, Damietta's capture constituted the recovery of a lost Christian city, which John compared to the return of the prodigal son in Luke 15.[46] The tendency became programmatic in James of Vitry's letter, where the wealth of Egypt's Christian heritage was outlined in terms of Christ's stay there, the writings of the Church Fathers, and the region's substantial Christian population.[47] This was less a new development than an extension to Egypt of a reverence for holy places that was everywhere apparent in crusader descriptions of Palestine. For every crusader the encounter with the Holy Land was in a sense a homecoming, for the sites they visited were deeply familiar to them and the value of the novel lay in earthing their devotion in the visible, aural, olfactory and above all tangible world. In this respect there was no major difference between their attitudes and those of pilgrims, and an account like that of John of Würzburg would easily have been written by a crusader.[48]

Urban splendour at Acre and Antioch

Something that was new, and couldn't be assimilated to Scripture, was the size and grandeur of some of the cities that crusaders encountered in the eastern Mediterranean. It must be admitted that some of their responses are disappointingly meagre. One such is the remark by the author of the *Itinerarium peregrinorum* that 'Caesarea is a city of enormous extent and its buildings are of astonishing construction and workmanship,' a banal summary that he followed with a misidentification of the port with the inland Caesarea visited by Christ.[49] Curiously Acre, which during its boom period around 1200 must have presented a tumultuous and impressive spectacle to visiting crusaders, generated little comment except for pejorative remarks about its inhabitants' corruption. For James of Vitry it was 'a second Babylon' where murder was commonplace, poison could be bought on the open market and high-ranking clerics rented out their property to prostitutes.[50] Oliver of Paderborn described it as 'a sinful city and one filled with all uncleanness', preferring to bestow his descriptive power and admiration on the newly fortified Château-Pélerin at Athlit.[51] Joinville recalled the prophetic outburst of the papal legate accompanying Louis IX's army: 'No one knows as well as I do of all the mean and treacherous sins committed in Acre. That is why God will have to exact such vengeance for them that Acre shall be washed clean in the blood of its inhabitants and other people come to live there in their place.'[52] Thus was the scene set for the blame that many commentators attached to the inhabitants of Acre for the Mamluk conquest of the port in 1291.[53]

The city of Rhodes was the opposite of Acre. It had been one of the great ports of the ancient world, but by the time of the crusades had been in decline for centuries. So while the author of the *Itinerarium peregrinorum* deduced from the size of its site that its population had once been very large ('not much unlike Rome'), he could only note the 'remarkable and wonderful workmanship' of the ruins that remained.[54] Two cities that could hardly fail to impress, for reasons

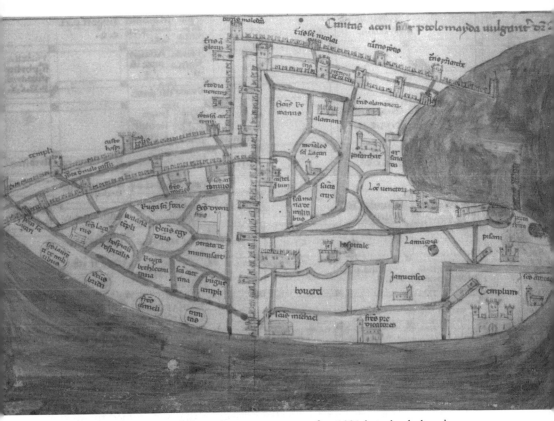

44 Marino Sanudo's map of Acre, drawn some years after 1291 but clearly based on a sound knowledge of the city's streets, walls and markets.

quite separate from religious ones, were Antioch and Constantinople. Antioch was founded by one of Alexander the Great's generals, Seleucus I Nicator, and it already had more than 1,400 years of history behind it when the crusaders arrived in 1097. It had been one of the greatest Roman cities, at its height the third largest city in the world, with a population that in the first century CE reached half a million. Its population had shrunk and conflicts between the Byzantines and the Arabs and Turks for control of the city and region had damaged many of Antioch's buildings, but the city remained an extraordinary sight. Stephen of Blois described it as 'great beyond belief'.[55] For the author of the *Gesta Francorum* it was 'the royal city of Antioch, capital of Syria',[56] and he devoted a short but very informative chapter to its description. His appreciation is apparent: 'the city of Antioch is a very fine and distinguished place'.

Understandably he picked out for special mention the strength of its defences, including its alleged 450 towers. Its topography was spectacular, for its south-eastern sector rose high into the mountains. But equally noteworthy was the fact that the major buildings lining Antioch's Seleucid gridiron town plan had been reasonably well maintained. 'Everything about this city is beautiful.' It wasn't only the strategic key to ruling over northern Syria – 'the door to the land' as Anselm of Ribemonte put it[57] – but also a city of charm and gravitas, 'the centre of great authority'.[58]

The queen of cities – Constantinople

Even Antioch, however, couldn't compare with Constantinople. The capital of the Byzantine empire was far larger than any city in western Europe. Including its sprawling suburbs, Constantinople was home to a population of several hundred thousand, compared with about 20,000 in twelfth-century London. It was defended by strong sea walls along the shores of the Golden Horn and Sea of Marmara, and by the triple set of Theodosian walls that ran for six-and-a-half kilometres (four miles) along the city's landward side. The city's marvels included the sixth-century Church of the Holy Wisdom (Hagia Sophia), the Great Palace (Bucoleon), the enormous hippodrome, the forums of Constantine and Theodosius, and the avenue, known as the Mese and eleven kilometres (seven miles) long, that ran almost the full length of the city from the Augusteum to the Golden Gate.

There are significant descriptions of Constantinople by crusaders who took part in the First, Second and Fourth Crusades. The first crusaders' encounter with the city was overshadowed by the difficulties that surrounded the working out of a viable relationship between Alexios Komnenos and the expedition's leaders. Peter the Hermit's followers went on the rampage in the city's suburbs and inflicted a good deal of damage, causing the emperor to move them quickly across the Hellespont.[59] Like schoolchildren in sweetshops, the crusaders were only allowed into the city in small and manageable groups, five or six an hour according to Fulcher of Chartres. Once inside they were understandably aston-ished by the city's sights, though both Fulcher and the author of the *Gesta Francorum Iherusalem expugnantium*, who rhapsodized about what they saw, are annoyingly short on specifics.[60]

Odo of Deuil was more forthcoming for the Second Crusade. Once again vandalism caused the Greeks to place strict controls over crusaders entering the city, but Odo accompanied Louis VII and he was even able to describe the banquet which Manuel hosted in the king's honour. Odo had a good eye for both topography and detail. He was particularly struck by the Blachernae Palace, the complex of buildings situated where the Theodosian wall approached the Golden Horn, and which under the Komnenoi became the main imperial residence. He noted its marble floors, abundance of gold decorations and unequalled location, which gave 'the triple pleasure of looking out upon sea, fields, and city'. Yet, as Odo observed, the palace's walls weren't strong, and they constituted a weak point in the defences which the crusaders were to exploit in 1204.[61] He commented too on the contrasting magnificence and squalor of the city, where palaces rubbed shoulders with hovels and crime was widespread and went unpunished. But he was impressed by Constantinople's numerous churches, their beauty and, of course, a huge attraction for the crusaders, their collections of relics.[62]

The circumstances of the Fourth Crusade were naturally different. The two major eyewitness accounts, by Geoffrey of Villehardouin and Robert of Clari, were both written after events had taken their momentous turn and their descriptions of the city were inevitably influenced by its conquest. A great prize had been won and its assessment was bound to be shaped by that fact. This is apparent from Geoffrey of Villehardouin. His description of the sight that met the eyes of the crusaders as they approached by ship from the Sea of Marmara isn't radically different from Fulcher or Odo: high walls, lofty towers, rich palaces, tall churches. This was the familiar reaction of the traveller gaping open-mouthed at the marvels that greeted him. But what follows marks a sudden shift in gear, the intrusion into this *topos* of a rhetoric derived from the epic. 'There was indeed no man so brave and daring that his flesh did not shudder at the sight. Nor was this to be wondered at, for never before had so grand an enterprise been carried out by any people since the creation of the world.'[63]

Robert of Clari doubled up the wonder, having the crusaders marvel at the size of the city while its inhabitants, from their vantage points on the sea wall, marvelled at the beauty of the Venetian fleet as it sailed by.[64] Once the city had been taken Robert came into his own. He provided an extraordinarily detailed account of its treasures and wonders. Relics naturally dominated his description but there was much else. His comments on the Great Palace brilliantly express the number, size and splendour of its mosaic-filled rooms, while the white marble pavement of the chapel of the Blessed Virgin of the Pharos is said to have been 'so smooth and clear that it seemed to be of crystal'.[65] He was impressed by the volume of gold, silver and precious stones that were evident in the columns, high altar and chandeliers of Hagia Sophia. The church's columns cured people of illnesses when they rubbed themselves against them, each column having its medical speciality; while a tube housed in the church door's great silver handle extracted poison from anybody who put it to their mouth.[66]

Like a lot of pilgrims to Rome, Robert was either mistaken or bemused about the identity and meaning of much of what he saw, such as the equestrian statue of Justinian in the Augusteum, the 'Golden Mantle' gate, and two sculpted columns, modelled on Trajan's column in Rome, that were located in the forums of Theodosius and the Xerolophos.[67] He had to admit defeat; 'if anyone should recount to you the hundredth part of the richness and the beauty and the nobility that was found in the abbeys and in the churches and in the palaces and in the city, it would seem like a lie and you would not believe it'.[68] Robert wasn't setting out to be elegiac, and this makes his account of what was destroyed, pillaged or damaged beyond repair in 1204 as telling, in its understated way, as the desperate lamentations of Niketas Choniates.[69]

Crusaders and Greeks

It's impossible to uncouple the crusaders' response to the sights of Constantinople from their attitude towards its inhabitants and imperial rulers. The relationship between the crusaders and the Greek Orthodox Church and Byzantine empire was hardly less problematic that that with Islam and the Turks. Just as an initial response of demonization was tempered in the case of the latter by elements of admiration, so close contact with the Greeks fractured and eventually shattered the myth of Christian solidarity. Like most generalizations this one proves vulnerable to close analysis, and in the case of Byzantine–crusader relations it's imperative to set aside the seductive and debilitating spell cast by the conquest and sack of 1204. It's all too easy to adopt one of two models that both amount to a deterministic reading of events.

One is a 'conflict model' that leads us to emphasize instances of collision.[70] These occurred partly for religious reasons, as the crusaders commented negatively on the doctrinal and liturgical differences between the Catholics and the Orthodox Church, above all the different version of the Nicene creed that the Greeks used.[71] Other clashes were of a military and political nature. It's undeniable that the passage of crusading armies through Byzantine lands caused more and more friction, while territorial rivalries, especially over Antioch, and the divergence of strategic aims between crusaders and Byzantines, became increasingly troublesome. The problem is that we tend to view these disagreements as cumulative, reaching their natural (for which read inevitable?) conclusion in the Fourth Crusade.

The other, even more sweeping model is that of a 'clash of civilizations'.[72] This views the many collisions as symptoms of something deeper, a gulf in comprehension between western Europe and the eastern empire that had developed over the course of centuries and that suddenly mattered because the West, as it were, had arrived on the East's doorstep. Viewed from this angle, constructive relations were impossible not just because of a multitude of divergent goals and expectations, but because the mental outlooks of the protagonists were shaped by cultural and educational backgrounds that were incompatible. As Niketas Choniates put it in relation to the Fourth Crusade, Byzantines and westerners 'had not a single thought in common'.[73] Taking the most obvious example, the practice of crusading itself was incomprehensible to the Greeks because all of the religious, social and military forces that created it, with the possible exception of pilgrimage, were unfamiliar to them. As we've already noted when looking at crusading motivations, the description of the First Crusade by Anna Komnena, Alexios Komnenos's daughter and biographer, is no more enlightened than that of Muslim commentators.[74] This comparison is significant, because taken to its extreme the second model creates the impression that the events of 1204 weren't just 'bound' to happen, but expressed an antagonism between Latins and Greeks that had become no less deeply rooted and universal than that between Latins and Muslims.

A mixed message – Byzantium and the First and Second Crusades

The antidote to these models is to look in detail at the sources, and when we do so it becomes clear that there was a major shift in western reactions towards the Greeks in the last two decades of the twelfth century. During the First and Second Crusades disparagement and appreciation were constantly rubbing shoulders.[75] There was certainly no lack of the former, but it has to be handled with care. This is because in the years immediately after the First Crusade Bohemund of Taranto mounted an extensive and imaginative propaganda campaign against Alexios Komnenos which included circulating a 'doctored' version of the *Gesta Francorum*. The main point of the revised text was to support Bohemund's claim to possess Antioch, but it also incorporated a host of derogatory phrases about the emperor's handling of the crusaders. We've already seen that the *Gesta Francorum* was one of the keystone narratives for the crusade, so the results of Bohemund's work seeped into a whole group of other influential texts. These included Robert of Reims's chronicle, which turned out to be the most popular of them all.[76]

There's another document that enjoyed wide circulation and bears the stamp of Bohemund's propaganda. This is a letter allegedly sent by Alexios to Count Robert of Flanders appealing for western help against the Turks. The letter placed the appeal of Constantinople's wealth alongside the Turkish atrocities and the city's many relics as reasons for the Franks to head east. 'Come quickly with all your forces and fight with all your might to prevent such a treasure falling into the hands of the Turks and Petchenegs.'[77] Guibert

45 The mosaic portrait of Alexios I Komnenos from Hagia Sophia, Constantinople.

of Nogent knew this letter and he shows signs of suspecting its authenticity. He poured scorn on Alexios's offer of Greek women, 'as though the beauty of Greek women were so great that they would be preferred to the women of Gaul, and for this reason alone, the Frankish army would march to Thrace'.[78] But Guibert allowed his natural scepticism and scholarly methods to be overridden by his Grecophobia, which caused him to view Alexios's offer of women as typical of Greek degeneracy.[79] Other commentators, and some leading participants like Stephen of Blois, were more appreciative of the assistance that Alexios had provided to the crusaders.[80] It's clear that opinion was divided, and certain episodes, like the fate of Nicaea's spoils in 1097, can still be used as litmus tests for contemporaries' attitudes towards the Greeks.[81]

The trouble was that the pro-Greek lobby was never coherent and organized enough to counter Bohemund's assiduous spin-doctoring, while from the Greek perspective the establishment during and after the first crusaders' conquest of the Holy Land of a church that was staffed entirely by Latin clerics did nothing to rescue the ideal of Christian fraternity.[82] It's a moot question whether the crusaders and settlers might have appointed Orthodox priests to important jobs if Byzantine military assistance during the expedition had been more impressive. The answer is probably no, given that they felt more comfortable with individuals who came from their own ethnic stock. More importantly, Orthodox priests would have neither welcomed nor been able to cope with the range of responsibilities in government and warfare that had to be shouldered by high-ranking clerics in a feudal context, above all in the embattled circumstances of the crusader states. But political and military relations were another matter entirely: it's salutary to be reminded, especially by an anti-Byzantine author like Raymond of Aguilers, that when the crusaders arrived at Constantinople in 1096 some of them not only expected Alexios I to become their expedition's leader, but assumed that he would take the cross as well.[83]

There's no doubt that the hostility towards the Greeks shown by our principal narrative source for the Second Crusade, Odo of Deuil, would have warmed Bohemund's heart. Odo criticized the Greeks constantly and from almost every angle. He embraced the familiar stereotyping of the Greeks as full of flattery, deceitful and unmanly.[84] He denounced their religious doctrines and observances as heretical, claiming that the extent of the divergence had become common knowledge among the crusaders and that 'because of this they were judged not to be Christians, [so] the Franks considered killing them a matter of no importance'.[85] Most significantly, he attributed the catastrophes that befell both the German and the French armies in Anatolia to Greek treachery and demanded vengeance: 'To us who suffered the Greeks' evil deeds . . . divine justice, and the fact that our people are not accustomed to endure shameful injuries for long, give hope of vengeance.'[86]

But although Louis VII referred just as overtly as Odo to Byzantine treachery during the crusade,[87] it's important to take into account the gratitude that Conrad III expressed towards Manuel both for his medical support and for the succour that he gave to the remnants of the German army at Constantinople: 'he showed us more honour than we hear of being afforded to any of our predecessors'.[88] Even Odo, in his fairer moments, admitted that there were faults on both sides. 'It was not held against the Greeks that they closed the city gates to the throng, since it had burned many of their houses and olive trees, either for want of wood or by reason of arrogance and the drunkenness of fools.'[89] In one telling phrase Odo acknowledged that the root problem with crusader–Byzantine relations lay in a different approach towards diplomacy: 'in general they really have the opinion that anything which is done for the holy empire cannot be considered perjury'.[90] As for ethnic stereotyping, this was standard practice in the twelfth century and, if Odo was severe in his judgement of the Greeks, the English chroniclers showed no more charity in their views about the French performance on the Third Crusade. Indeed relations between the English and French became so strained during the siege of Acre that they had to be kept apart. 'For the king of France and his people slandered the king of England and his people, and vice versa.'[91]

The more closely historians have examined the massive demands that were posed by provisioning and the maintenance of law and order during the long marches through the Balkans and Anatolia, the more they've appreciated the overall success with which, up until 1187, needs were met and peace preserved. Much of the credit for this has been attributed to the Byzantine court.[92] Of course it's possible, though unlikely, that the scale of this achievement wasn't grasped by the crusaders themselves, or that it was overshadowed by their perceptions of inadequate military support against the Turks or even of deliberate deception. The fact remains, however, that while the views expressed about the Greeks before the Third Crusade were mixed, they were far from being wholly hostile. There was as yet no formal split or schism between the two Churches, though talks about union had proved disappointing. A key factor in shaping relations was one of the paradoxes of crusading: the ideological justification for the First Crusade was the defeat that the Byzantines had suffered at Turkish hands at Manzikert in 1071, and their subsequent need for western military help. Yet the crusade's greatest achievement, the conquest of Jerusalem, from the start proved precarious and its defence against Muslim counter-attacks hinged on Byzantine support. For understandable geopolitical reasons this was never that impressive. Attempts were made at combined naval operations against Egypt between Jerusalem and Constantinople, but they never met expectations and they ended with the death of the pro-western Manuel I in 1180.

From disdain to conquest

After Manuel's death things went downhill fast. The deterioration of relations is clearly shown in the hostility that William of Tyre displayed towards the Greeks towards the end of his chronicle.[93] Then came Hattin, and the cards increasingly came to be stacked against any chance of a positive relationship. At Constantinople political stability and continuity of policy alike collapsed.[94] Isaac II Angelos (1185–95) forged an alliance with Saladin.[95] The crisis of 1187 in the Holy Land and the West's massive response foregrounded the dismal fact that the Byzantine court had become overtly aligned against the crusading cause. If all the armies of the Third Crusade had made their way to the East by sea the consequences might have been relatively restrained: just Richard I's clashes with the ethnically Greek population of Messina (denigrated as 'Griffons' by English chroniclers like Richard of Devizes and the author of the *Itinerarium peregrinorum*),[96] and the king's conquest of Cyprus from Isaac Komnenos, a great-nephew of Manuel I.[97] But Barbarossa's decision to march through the Balkans brought him into direct and sharp conflict with Isaac II. On this occasion the German sources leave no room for doubt: the Greeks were both condemned for their open opposition to the crusaders and despised for their constant double-dealing.[98] In Barbarossa's eyes the Greeks had shown themselves to be as much 'God's enemies' as the Saracens, and it was only Isaac's good sense in coming to terms during the winter of 1189–90 that saved his capital from an armed assault by land and sea the following spring.[99] Pseudo-Ansbert claimed that 'the whole army of Christ was yearning to conquer the city'.[100]

Given that Barbarossa's army was the last that tried to march the entire distance to the Holy Land, the question arises as to whether it might have been possible for the Byzantine empire simply to have disappeared off the radar of crusaders once the Germans had managed to cross into Anatolia in 1190. After all, in both geographical and military terms the empire was shrinking. Isaac Komnenos's seizure of control over Cyprus was typical of the way the court's grip over the provinces was failing. And it's been plausibly argued that, far from a build-up of hostility occurring in the late twelfth century, Byzantium actually meant less and less to western Europe once Manuel I's attempt to embrace western ways and to integrate his lands into the European political system had expired with him.[101] But for all its troubles the empire, above all Constantinople itself, presented too many attractions and remained too significant a force in the politics of the eastern Mediterranean for it to escape the attentions of crusaders. It's not necessary to argue for a planned diversion of the Fourth Crusade to take the line that given Constantinople's magnetic pull and the bloody chaos that was Byzantine court politics under the Angeloi emperors, what happened in 1203–4 went with the natural grain of events. The initial conquest of the city on behalf of Alexios IV Angelos was after all no more than Barbarossa was planning for in 1190: clearing the path, literally in 1190, financially in 1203, for the crusade to push onwards to its planned destination. Alexios IV's repudiation of his allies, and his deposition by Mourtzouphlos early in 1204, wrecked this plan and necessitated the second siege and capture.

The sources for these events are relatively plentiful, facilitating attempts to pinpoint a shift in the crusaders' attitudes towards the inhabitants of

Constantinople and its suburbs between 1203 and 1204.[102] For the Greeks this would have entailed a change of status from bystanders in a dynastic conflict, to opponents in a war that the crusaders considered to be both just, because of Alexios IV's binding undertakings to them, and holy, thanks to the assurances given by their prelates that fighting the Greeks would earn them salvation. The weakness of this argument is that it relies on sources that postdate the second conquest, when some writers were using every available idea to justify events retrospectively. It would be truer to say that the combination of legal rectitude and the inescapable bind of the situation facing the crusaders was sufficient in itself to validate the conquest of Constantinople in the combatants' eyes. In other words they were pushed. Of course there were 'pull' factors as well, and they extended beyond the obvious attraction of booty and relics. When the army's bishops had to rally the crusaders in the face of defeat in April 1204 they resorted to violent rhetoric, attacking the Greeks as 'the enemies of God'.[103] The more reflective crusaders may also have been reassured by the arguments of their clerics that the Greeks were schismatics who were being brought back to the fold by force for their own good.[104] The smug and self-righteous Gunther of Pairis would later weave together this and similar arguments to create a providentially based apologia for the West's triumph at Constantinople.[105] But there are no stronger grounds for associating Gunther's views with those of the crusaders than there are to believe that the first crusaders were the stained-glass heroes depicted by the monastic chroniclers of the early twelfth century. Overall, it's hard to argue convincingly that the western combatants in 1203–4 entertained deep-seated feelings of hostility towards their Greek enemy. It's likely that they viewed the Greeks not as agents of the devil but as well-heeled, misguided and shifty cousins; above all, they had come to be the key element in a quagmire of delay, disappointment and anxiety from which the only escape was their subjugation.

Schism and heresy – the eastern Churches

In terms of its authority and traditions the Greek Orthodox Church constituted the most powerful Christian presence in the Middle East. But it was far from being the only one encountered by the crusaders. One of the most interesting sections of the *Tractatus* described the full spectrum of ethnic and religious groups that inhabited the Holy Land. The treatise's author was well aware that the Christians were divided into 'various sects' and he gave thumbnail sketches of the Latins, Greeks, Syrians, Armenians, Georgians, Jacobites and Nestorians.[106] Other visitors, such as Wilbrand of Oldenburg in 1212, James of Vitry and Thietmar in 1217, and Oliver of Paderborn during the Fifth Crusade, showed an awareness of the confessional diversity that existed among their fellow Christians.[107] The Jacobites of Syria and the Copts of Egypt were Monophysites, a name that derived from their belief that Christ's nature was solely human or solely divine. The Nestorians also differed from Catholics on the christological issue, believing that Christ possessed two natures but that they were separate rather than unified.

All these groups were considered to be not just schismatic but heretical too. The Jacobites for example were banned from entering the Church of the Holy Sepulchre, though they were allowed into its precincts.[108] The divide between Catholicism and the Armenian and Georgian Churches was less severe, revolving around a mix of liturgical practices and questions of authority; unlike the Nestorians and Jacobites these were 'national' Churches whose development was influenced as much by ethnicity as by doctrine. Much the same can be said of the Maronites, who lived almost exclusively in the Lebanon.[109] The groups with which the crusaders came into closest contact were the Armenians, whose lands they crossed when they made the overland journey through Anatolia, the Maronites, and the Orthodox and Jacobite Syrians. The Christian population of Syria was substantial and it constituted Armenians, Orthodox and Jacobites. In Palestine there were fewer Christians and they tended to cluster around the shrines at Bethlehem, Nazareth and Mount Tabor.[110]

The attitude of the crusaders towards these various groups was formed in part by religious considerations and in part by practical ones. Their relations with the Armenians were certainly the best. The Armenians had settled in Cilicia, southern Anatolia, during the late eleventh century, and for army after army in the first three crusades their arrival here represented the end of an awful march, usually a fighting one, through Turkish territory. From 1097 onwards they could be assured of a welcome and access to plentiful supplies.[111] Tancred and Baldwin of Boulogne enjoyed the support of the Armenians in the conquests that they made from the Turks in Cilicia and Mesopotamia in 1097–8. Their gains proved to be the catalyst for the emergence of Armenian principalities.[112] The author of the *Itinerarium peregrinorum* commented on the Germans in 1190 that 'everyone was delighted because they had left an enemy kingdom and arrived in a Christian country';[113] Pseudo-Ansbert commented movingly on their joy when they once again encountered crosses, a sign of fellow believers.[114] Armenian relations with the German court were very close, and when Leon II was crowned as king of Armenia at Tarsus in 1198, the imperial chancellor Conrad of Hildesheim was present and the royal insignia had been brought from Germany by the archbishop of Mainz. Conrad of Mainz was papal legate and Leon's vigorous westernization of his kingdom included religious union with Rome. This proved to be largely window-dressing, but religious differences were less important than the common cause of Catholics and Armenians in the face of resurgent Muslim power and the military resources that the Armenian princes and kings of Cilicia could bring to bear. The author of the *Tractatus*, for example, noted that the Armenians were 'quite well practised in the use of arms'.[115]

The Syrian Christians were the other main separated group that crusaders encountered and their relations with them, Orthodox and Jacobite alike, weren't benign. The *Gesta Francorum* presented a negative picture of their reaction to the First Crusade during the siege of Antioch. It's true that Christian women within the city are depicted secretly applauding a defeat inflicted on the Turks;[116] but in other passages Armenians and Syrians alike are shown as motivated solely by the hope of gain, and displaying no consistent loyalty to either one side or the other.[117] Guibert of Nogent embroidered on this theme.[118] This formed the background to a perplexing passage in the letter that the leaders of the First Crusade wrote to Urban II from Antioch in September 1098. They exhorted the pope to come east to join their expedition: 'For we have defeated the Turks and pagans; the heretics, however, Greeks and Armenians, Syrians, and Jacobites, we cannot overcome.'[119] This was an extraordinary descent into bellicosity for an expedition that had been preached as a means of bringing aid to the eastern Church. If these groups had indeed been 'overcome' there would have been no Christians left to help. It's possible that, although it purported to come from all the crusading princes, the letter was actually dictated by Bohemund and formed part of his policy of whipping up hostility towards Byzantium.[120] Yet if that was the case it was a foolish, and therefore uncharacteristic, approach for a man who wanted above all else to rule over a city containing so many people from the very groups mentioned.

In practice, both at Antioch and in the kingdom of Jerusalem, a *modus vivendi* was followed throughout the twelfth century that didn't sharply disfavour Syrian Christians even when their beliefs and practices would have caused them to be condemned as heretics in the West.[121] James of Vitry gave a fascinating picture of the situation in the Holy Land in 1216–17 in a letter that he sent to friends back home. James had conflicting feelings about the remarkable mixture of races, languages and practices that he encountered among the Christians. He tried preaching to the Jacobites of Acre in their own church with the help of an interpreter who translated his Latin into Arabic. But his congregation wilfully misinterpreted his attempt to win them away from their monophysitism, and in James's remark that the Syrians were 'traitors and very corrupt men' there's an echo of their negative portrayal in the *Gesta Francorum*. It was even harder to practise such outreach in the case of the Nestorians, Georgians and Armenians because they had no official Church structure. Although James claimed some successes it was an uphill struggle; nothing similar seems to have been attempted previously; indeed the calibre of the clergy in twelfth-century Palestine wouldn't have been up to it.[122]

Prester John – salvation from the East?

In spite of these difficult experiences James of Vitry remained convinced that heretical and schismatic Christians would become Catholics, while Muslims would embrace Christianity if they could only hear the Gospel message preached properly. James's letter of 1216–17 demonstrates that like many contemporaries he expected the eagerly awaited forces of the Fifth Crusade to facilitate the conversion of the Muslims as well as recovering the Holy Land.[123] It was typical of James that he went out of his way to purchase and baptize Muslim children who were captured at the fall of Damietta.[124] His optimism had other causes, for, as the letter reporting his experiences at Acre shows, he believed that if the full global weight of religious allegiance could be mobilized it would assist the Catholic Church's cause and compensate for the many military failures of the past. In addition to sketching divisions among the Muslims, James communicated his belief that Christians living among the Muslims actually outnumbered the latter. There were Christian kings ruling in the East 'as far as to the land of Prester John', and they would come to support the Fifth Crusade.[125]

46 Cynocephali (dog-headed people) depicted on the tympanum at Vézelay (left of Christ's head).

Like most medieval geography this idea combined a modicum of fact with large doses of conjecture and wishful thinking. By James's time Catholic Europeans had become familiar with the existence of Christian Georgia, and they nourished the hope that its people might function as a sort of eastern equivalent of the Armenians: the author of the *Tractatus* gave the Georgians a higher rating than the Armenians in military terms.[126] East of Iran (Khurasan), however, the imagination could roam at will. In 1122 an Indian archbishop visited the papal court, almost certainly the first time that a Christian from India had reached the medieval West. His visit confirmed that despite the rise of Islam there were still Christians living in Asia, and twenty years later reports began to circulate of a Christian king called Prester John. According to what Bishop Hugh of Jabala told Otto of Freising in 1145, the king was a descendant of the Magi. He'd defeated the Persians and then had 'advanced to the help of the church of Jerusalem', but he couldn't cross the Tigris so had to turn back.[127]

Almost certainly Prester John's alleged victory derived from a real defeat that was inflicted on the Seljuq sultan Sanjar in 1141 by a nomadic people called the Qara-Khitan. They were Buddhist but the West conflated Buddhism with Christianity. In the 1160s a forged letter purporting to be from Prester John put flesh on the bones of his supposed existence. In it he promised to assist his co-religionists in their struggle against Islam: 'it is our intention to visit the Lord's Sepulchre with a very large army, as befits the glory of our majesty, to crush the enemies of Christ's cross and exalt his blessed name.'[128] Pope Alexander III went to the trouble of trying to establish contact with Prester John, and given the resurgence of Muslim power under Zengi and Nur ed-Din it's not hard to imagine the psychology that gave rise to his supposed offers of help.[129]

For reasons that are hard to fathom, the image of Prester John wasn't conjured up during the crisis years that followed Hattin, but during the Fifth Crusade the waves of rumour and speculation about the king from the East reached their height. In 1221 one of the various texts that circulated among the crusaders, called the *Relatio de Davide rege*, narrated the supposed victories over the Muslims of a 'King David'. He was friendly to the Christian cause, to the extent of releasing Christians whom his troops had captured. James of Vitry saw this as proof that the prediction he'd made in 1217 had come to pass. He deduced that King David must be the son or grandson of Prester John, and he vigorously rebuffed the doubts of sceptics.[130] Oliver of Paderborn was similarly impressed. He linked the news of David's westwards advance with the prophecies contained in an early Christian text that had been discovered by the legate Pelagius. Eschatology and rumour thus converged, and their impact was strengthened by a third element, the constant expectation of Frederick II's arrival; so 'mention is made of two kings, one of whom, it is claimed, will come from the East, the other from the West, to Jerusalem in that year when Easter will be on the third of April [1222]'.[131] If this meeting was to occur then Egypt would be conquered in 1221, a train of thought which encouraged the advocates of an advance southwards from Damietta.

As in the 1140s, 'King David' wasn't wholly imagined. His campaigns were a distant echo of Chinggis Khan's devastating onslaught against the Khwarazmshah Muhammad in 1218–25. News of this was almost certainly filtered through to the crusaders in the Nile delta by Nestorians. The Mongols seem to have encouraged rumours that they were Christians in order to catch their Christian opponents in Asia and Europe off-guard, and though they were presumably ignorant of the Prester John legend, this sly ruse might well have consolidated their association with it.[132] As it transpired, Chinggis Khan's campaigns did nothing to assist the cause of the Fifth Crusade; instead, their destruction of the Khorezmian empire sent westwards large bands of Turks who'd been dislocated – like snakes driven from their holes, as one contemporary put it. We've already seen that one consequence was their capture of Jerusalem from the Christians in 1244.[133] Appropriately enough, Joinville believed that the Mongols included Prester John's kingdom among the list of their victims.[134] Displaced from the imagined East, Prester John began what's been termed the 'continental drift' that ended with his kingdom being relocated in Ethiopia in the fourteenth and fifteenth centuries.[135]

A changing world – the Mongols

In contrast to Prester John, the Mongols were all too real. Their conquests forced a radical reconfiguration of European views about what lay to the east of the Holy Land, and about the balance of power between Christianity and Islam. In the course of a series of missions to the Mongols, the mendicant friars John of Piano Carpini, Andrew of Longjumeau and above all William of Rubruck provided their fellow Catholics with a clearer and more accurate idea than they had ever possessed of the extent and nature of the central Asian landmass, the Buddhist religion and the civilization of China.[136] During his journey of 1253–5 William of Rubruck discovered no evidence for 'the monsters or human freaks who are described by Isidore and Solinus' and he questioned their existence.[137] Instead there were real people, in particular the Mongols themselves, whose ways the travelling missionaries described in illuminating detail.[138]

Familiarity didn't engender appreciation. William of Rubruck, who knew the Mongols better than most, despised their arrogance and would willingly have preached a crusade against them.[139] If anything they were demonized even more than the Saracens had been, with a new emphasis on primitivism that carried an echo of Isidorean monstrosity. Matthew Paris described the Mongols as 'inhuman and of the nature of beasts, rather to be called monsters than men, thirsting after and drinking blood, and tearing and devouring the flesh of dogs and human beings'.[140] Given the Mongols' ambitions and their savage techniques of conquest, the West had good reason to be alarmed. Thinking up a 'remedy against the Tatars' was one of the several items placed on the agenda at the second council of Lyons in 1245 alongside the desperate condition of the Latin East.

But in practice the Mongols didn't impinge very much on crusading efforts to defend and recover the Holy Land.[141] This was because the major thrust that the Mongols sent into Palestine, in 1260, was decisively repelled by the Mamluks at the battle of Ain Jalut. At that point the threat that the Mongols posed was considered to be so severe that the rulers of the kingdom of Jerusalem came close to fighting alongside the Muslims and did provide them with supplies.[142] Ironically the Muslims shielded what remained of the crusader states from the rampages of the Mongols, a taste of which they experienced in the Mongol sack of Sidon. But Ain Jalut gave the Mamluk regime of Egypt an ascendancy as great as that enjoyed by Saladin, and more enduring. The result was that the Mongols were soon viewed in a different light, as disagreeable but necessary allies against expulsion by the Muslims. Even before 1260 Mongol rulers and generals had dangled the idea of an alliance before the Christians, and once they'd grasped how difficult it would be to defeat the Mamluks by themselves they made a series of similar overtures.[143] Nine years following the fall of Acre, great excitement was generated in the West when the Mongol ruler of Persia, Ghazan, briefly conquered Syria from the Mamluks and offered the Holy Land to the Christians in exchange for their military help.[144]

Expanding world, contracting hope?

This added up to a complex and volatile situation, and from about 1240 onwards most intelligent and reflective crusaders who made their way east to the Holy Land must have been aware that the strategic scenario there had been transformed by the arrival of the Mongols, even if they weren't sure exactly how. Such awareness pervades Rutebeuf's poem 'La Complainte de Constantinople' (1262), a deeply troubled lament for the condition of the crusading cause throughout the eastern Mediterranean region. The people of Acre should lay out a large cemetery because they were going to need it.[145] There's no doubting that much more knowledge of all kinds was available in Rutebeuf's day than had been the case a century earlier. We've seen that since c. 1200 the papal court had grasped the importance of gathering as much information as possible about the political, religious and military situation in the Middle East. Operations in the Nile delta afforded the opportunity for Europeans to become well informed at first hand about most aspects of Egypt's social, economic and religious life. It might seem logical to infer that crusading attitudes had fundamentally altered now that the confined world-view held by the early crusaders had been radically opened out. The world was more complicated than Catholics had once thought and it was harder to be confident that Jerusalem lay at its centre. At the same time most commentators on demography in the late thirteenth century argued that Christians were heavily outnumbered, by ten or even twenty to one.[146] Some conspiracy theorists maintained that the rumours in circulation about Mongol conversion to Christianity were planted to try to sustain Christian morale and encourage people to go on taking the cross.[147]

It's tempting to argue that pessimism about the strategic situation facing the Christians, globally and in the Middle East in particular, caused Jerusalem's devotional centrality to Catholics to be eroded at the same time as its geographical one. But the relationship between epistemological change and faith was not a simple one. To Peter of Blois, comparing the Holy Land's smallness with the vastness of its hostile neighbours proved how wonderfully God had protected it thus far against Muslim attack.[148] We've seen that Fulcher of Chartres' generation was far from ignorant about its world, while incessant tangles with the Greeks had shown that the range of political and military issues facing crusaders had never been straightforward. As with 1204, our hindsight knowledge of what happened in 1291 isn't helpful. It's become clear to us that the arrival of the Mongols proved to be disastrous for the crusader states because it drove the Mamluks to accelerate and complete their conquests. But for contemporaries there seemed to be opportunities as well as threats, whether they took the form of an alliance with the Mongols or just exploiting Muslim weaknesses: William of Rubruck for one believed that 'not one man in ten' in Anatolia was a Muslim, the rest being Greeks and Armenians.[149] There was a widespread perception of how dangerous this newly revealed world was, but for many Christians, up to 1291 and indeed well beyond, it was a reason for greater resolution rather than despair.

10

❖

REMEMBRANCE OF THINGS PAST

A vow fulfilled?

'What man of spirit can hesitate for a moment to undertake this journey when, among the many hazards involved, none could be more unfortunate, none could cause greater distress, than the prospect of coming back alive?' This bit of 'up and at 'em' bravado was allegedly voiced by a Welsh nobleman and crusader called Gruffydd on the eve of the Third Crusade.[1] It was in tune with the machismo that often accompanied recruitment, but, as we've seen, this August 1914 mood of adventure soon gave way to deep homesickness. Some crusaders may have viewed their venture in apocalyptic terms that ruled out the prospect of returning to mundane reality; but in most cases crusaders yearned for the time when they'd see homes and loved ones again. The Church's response to their yearning was ambivalent. Preachers and clerical chroniclers enjoyed nurturing the idea that people who'd taken the cross had their hearts and thoughts single-mindedly fixed on the Holy Land, but canon lawyers accepted that the crusader's status was temporary and they set their minds to teasing out the issues surrounding return.

Two questions in particular taxed the brains of the canonists. How to be sure that individual crusaders who claimed to have discharged their vows had actually done so? And how to verify reports of a crusader's death in the East? These questions mattered because of the value adhering to the status of crusader and the interests that were tied up with it, especially those of relatives and creditors. It wasn't just the consequences of sin that fell away when crusaders carried out their vows: their juridical status as 'temporary monks', with its whole battery of legal and financial privileges and exemptions, also came to an abrupt end.[2] There was even a symbolic ritual copied from pilgrims, the trip to the Jordan river to bathe and collect a palm to carry back home, which acted as the counterpart to taking the cross;[3] and some evidence exists to show that homecoming crusaders moved their cloth cross from their shoulder to their chest.[4]

This assumed that crusaders were free agents, which most of them weren't. They belonged to social and military groups that were usually arranged hierarchically. Just as we can rarely be sure how many participants made a decision to go on crusade which we would now regard as 'individual', so the decision to return was usually made by a social superior, a lord or king. It was impracticable to remain in the East if the necessary framework of leadership and support had been removed. And if sufficient pressure could be exerted from below this process could work in the opposite direction, as in 1099 when Raymond of Toulouse's position in the jockeying for power at Jerusalem was subverted by his fellow Provençals. They were desperate to return home and wanted their count to come with them, for the sake of his leadership and financial means.[5]

Sometimes there emerged a shared sense that the military venture which everybody had signed up for had reached its natural conclusion, for better or worse. In the First Crusade the turning point wasn't the capture of Jerusalem but the battle of Ascalon; the decisive defeat of the Fatimid army confirmed the Christian tenure of the holy city, enabling the majority of the crusaders to return confident that they'd not just fulfilled their vows but done all that they reasonably could to leave a secure military scenario behind them.[6] In the Second and Third Crusades the turning point occurred when the presiding kings, Louis VII, Conrad III and Richard I, accepted that there was nothing more they could do with the military forces available to them, following the débâcle at Damascus and the peace of Jaffa. The two expeditions had effectively run their course. The Muslims knew about their opponents' votive obligations and occasionally they played on them to grease the wheels of departure. In 1192 crusading vows were discharged, and the crusade's failure to some extent disguised, by Saladin's sanctioning of a series of unarmed pilgrimages to Jerusalem.[7] This offer of free access to Jerusalem's shrines as a means of demilitarizing crusade had first been attempted in 1099 by the Fatimids.[8] On that occasion the crusaders had laughed at it, but in 1192 circumstances were very different. In the end the 'fatigue of pilgrimage' wore everybody down – even Richard I who, as one admirer put it, 'did more and stayed longer than anyone else'.[9]

The crusaders who fought in the Nile delta in 1218–21 returned home when military disaster robbed them both of their strength and of their all-important base at Damietta. In the case of St Louis' crusade, the king himself wanted to carry on after his ransom had been negotiated, but his preference was defied by the majority of the barons who'd accompanied him to Acre. The debate was closely argued and emotional: France would suffer if they stayed, the Holy Land if they went. It's very revealing that for all the importance that the French barons vested in Louis' leadership and the respect that they paid to him personally, this

47 Sculpture of a returning crusader with his wife.

was a crusade, not a royal campaign, and their assent couldn't be taken for granted. They had to be won around. Understandably given all that they'd suffered, the collective will of the surviving crusaders in 1250 was that enough was enough.[10] Most idiosyncratic was the Fourth Crusade, which didn't achieve 'closure' in the same way as these other expeditions. Pope Innocent III argued that following the capture of Constantinople the crusaders should go on to assist the Holy Land, but in practice they either put down roots in the conquered lands or returned to their homes in the West. In a sense the Fourth Crusade never came to a formal end; instead it metamorphosed into the protracted and ultimately hopeless defence of the conquered city against the attacks of the westerners' various enemies, above all of course the displaced Byzantines.[11]

What's undeniable is that in the case of all these ventures, with the sole exception of the First Crusade, the circumstances of return were those of men and women bowing to the inevitable rather than rejoicing in a task completed. It's hard not to sympathize with their plight, demonstrated for example in Oliver of Paderborn's strained attempt to put a positive spin on the situation that the Fifth Crusade confronted in 1221. Whether or not the vows taken in happier times had been fulfilled was a question that the Church, out of tact or embarrassment, seldom chose to address. Roger of Howden commented on Philip II's meeting with Pope Celestine III in 1191 that 'although they had not fulfilled their vow, he gave palms to them and hung crosses on their necks, declaring that they were pilgrims'.[12] There wasn't much else that Celestine could have done, but the Church's evasion or silence on this issue formed an emphatic contrast to the zeal with which it often hounded those *crucesignati* who had failed to set out or deserted the armies en route. Clearly defeat moved the agenda on: it was more important to address the issue of what could be done next to help the beleaguered Latin East.

Crusade and settlement

In the late autumn of 1099, just weeks after the battle of Ascalon, Bohemund of Taranto and Baldwin of Boulogne made their way southwards from Antioch and Edessa to worship at Jerusalem's shrines. Fulcher of Chartres, Baldwin's chaplain, was present and he portrayed the journey in terms of their belated fulfilment of their crusade vows. The pilgrimage was a revealing event from several angles. Fulcher's lengthy apologia for the fact that Bohemund and Baldwin had stayed in Syria and Mesopotamia earlier, and his emphasis on the sufferings that they endured on their way to Jerusalem, surely reflect a public perception that the two leaders were guilty of neglecting their vows. This was irrespective of the strategic importance that some people attached to the cities that they were holding against the Muslims.[13] More generally, the incident opens up the question of the relationship between crusade and settlement. For it's evident that the decision to return home didn't just signify an individual's belief that the devotional act of pilgrimage was complete, or even a resolution on the part of leaders and/or the collective will that a military venture had run into the sand; it also represented a rejection of the alternative, which was to remain permanently in the Holy Land.

The consequences of this rejection became clear in the immediate aftermath of the First Crusade when all the settlements faced an acute shortage of manpower. It was described with eloquence by Fulcher of Chartres, for whom their very survival was God's work.

> Truly it is manifest to all that it was a wonderful miracle that we lived among so many thousands of thousands and as their conquerors made some of them our tributaries and ruined others by plundering them and making them captives. But whence came this virtue? Whence this power? Truly from Him whose name is the Almighty.[14]

Because so many subsequent expeditions failed, the problem didn't recur in the same way, though diversions like the capture of Cyprus and Constantinople indirectly aggravated the Holy Land's demographic problem by siphoning off scarce resources. But if Edessa or Damascus had been taken by the Second Crusade, or Jerusalem by the Third, it's questionable whether the settlers in the East would have managed to hold on to any of them. Barbarossa was aware that manpower shortages ruled out his holding on to captured Iconium in 1190,[15] and the issue of how to garrison a recaptured Jerusalem taxed the leaders of the Third and Fifth Crusades almost as much as that of how to recover the city. It's arguable that Louis IX was forced to march on Cairo in 1249 because the alternative strategy of capturing the great port of Alexandria would have presented him with the near impossibility of defending both it and Damietta, once he and his crusaders had returned to France.[16]

Addressing the demographic deficit

Contemporaries could hardly fail to be aware of this central flaw in the character of crusading. Roger Bacon put it succinctly: 'If the Christians are victorious, no one stays behind and defends the occupied lands.'[17] We've already seen in Chapter 4 how it arose in the contexts of desertion and the stalemated Third Crusade, manifesting itself in the most destructive way during the regular departures that punctuated the Fifth Crusade's operations. There's fascinating evidence of an early attempt to address the issue in two appeals for reinforcements that Simeon, the Greek patriarch of Jerusalem, sent to the West in 1097–8 when the crusading army was besieging Antioch. In his first letter Simeon and his co-author Adhemar of Le Puy pointed out that the Turks outnumbered the crusaders and they begged for assistance, especially from those who hadn't followed up their vows.[18] Simeon wrote again some weeks later and this letter, which survives in no fewer than thirty-two manuscripts, is more revealing than its predecessor. With much exaggeration Simeon claimed that the bulk of the fighting had now been done and that the need was for garrisons to hold the forty cities and 200 [sic] fortresses that the crusaders had captured. His appeal was couched firmly in terms of permanent settlement by men who were best able to fight, with a scriptural reference to 'the land flowing with milk and honey and abounding in all good things', and the sensible proposal that for the moment only men should come east, with their womenfolk following later.[19]

It's surely significant that this attempt to steer crusading strategy in the direction of armed settlement originated with a Greek cleric who was both familiar with the circumstances of Palestine and knew that he'd be expected to share the responsibility for its defence once Jerusalem had been conquered. Pope Urban II seems to have made no such explicit reference to settlement, though Robert of Reims, writing a decade later, echoed Simeon's argument fairly closely in his version of the pope's Clermont sermon; Robert even included the same quotation from Exodus 3:8.[20] But Simeon was handicapped by the votive framework that the pope had established for crusading. Like others he referred at the end of his letter to the need to focus attention on those who hadn't yet fulfilled their vows. Even if these delinquents could be dragooned into coming to the East, they'd only return home later which wouldn't solve the problem faced by Simeon. When the Third Crusade was being preached Ralph Niger reiterated Simeon's approach, treating the recovery and resettlement of the Holy Land as separate issues. Ralph argued that women shouldn't go east until the military job was completed, but he didn't address the question of how they could then be persuaded to go.[21]

We don't know what Urban II's plans were for the defence of the recovered Jerusalem. The most likely scenario is that he pinned his hopes on collaboration with the Byzantine Greeks, which Simeon's letter in a sense represents, combined with some leaders of high status, like Raymond of Toulouse, making the welcome decision to remain in the East. Urban knew that if they did so they would retain reasonable numbers of troops through the operation of ties of vassalage, kinship and paid support. There would of course always be some crusaders from the ranks of the lesser knights who didn't possess strong family ties or attractive prospects at home. Such men would embrace the opportunities that presented themselves in the East.[22] It was only to be hoped that both these princes and their armed followers would act out of piety rather than greed. If this was Urban's approach, it was consistent with the optimistic attitude that we've seen the Church adopting towards crusading throughout. It wasn't altogether wishful thinking, for a number of knights did stay in the East after 1099 out of devotion, a pattern of behaviour that contributed to the foundation of the military religious orders a few decades later.[23]

It's highly unlikely that either Urban II or any of his contemporaries believed that there would be a mass migration to the Holy Land, so they wouldn't have been surprised when most crusaders decided to return home in 1099.[24] This approach never changed, nor indeed could it given that, despite all the developments that occurred within crusading, its essential foundation in pilgrimage was never challenged.[25] In 1200 Innocent III instructed the archbishop of Canterbury that craftsmen and farmers should be allowed to go on crusade. This sounds radical but the pope wasn't tackling the vexed issue of depopulation; rather his concern was with crusaders who couldn't support themselves while they were in the East. They would be like students taking part-time jobs while studying for their degrees. It's clear that Innocent expected such people to come back home; in fact he feared that the craftsmen would find themselves short of work in the Holy Land because its permanent population was so small.[26] The idea of getting them to solve this problem by staying doesn't seem to have occurred to the pope. Or if it did he rejected it: for the sad reality was that by this point, just a century after the triumph of the First Crusade, it was common knowledge that nobody would voluntarily stay in the Holy Land. So the only way the Church could actively promote settlement there was through a policy of transporting criminals; and if we can believe the poet Rutebeuf this proved counter-productive because such riff-raff apostatized and fought for the Muslims.[27]

By the late thirteenth century commentators were constantly wringing their hands in despair about the Holy Land's chronic under-population. There was an inescapable and painful contrast with the stereotype of lusty Muslims whose rulers could draw on bottomless reserves of manpower: following Hattin, Saladin's troops were described as swarming over the whole region from Tyre to Jerusalem like 'innumerable ants'.[28] It's been suggested that this imbalance between the human resources available to Christians and Muslims was one of the principal ways in which demographic issues began to impinge on European consciousness around 1300, a legacy of crusading that's tended to escape attention in the past. In the early fourteenth century the commentator Peter Dubois for one considered that a programme of managed immigration was the only way to deal with the problem. His contemporary Peter of La Palud toyed with the idea of allowing polygamy in the Holy Land, though he shied away from it on the ground that it would breach natural law.[29]

Westward bound

There's not much evidence for the return of most crusaders, though thanks to the ever reliable Joinville Louis IX's sea voyage forms a vivid exception to the rule.[30] Joinville apart, the scarcity of detail springs from the fact that there was no longer any need for groups of crusaders to assemble and travel in large forces. Indeed supply issues became much more manageable if people travelled in small parties, and this made it harder for narratives to give return journeys a coherent treatment. There was a natural lack of interest in the aftermath (often disappointing) of the great expeditions, and in the case of many thousands who'd set out from their homes there was no story to tell anyway: they'd either died in the East or passed into the shadow-life of slavery. This was the fate in particular of the majority who took part in the crusade of 1101, the Second Crusade and Barbarossa's great host. Out of ten named companions of Leopold of Austria on the Third Crusade, nine perished in the East.[31] Captives usually pass from our sight completely, just as they did from that of their loved ones. But Germans who were captured during the Second Crusade trickled home years later, their mutilated bodies bearing tragic testimony to the brutal conditions of their enslavement.[32] And in one poignant passage Richard of Devizes described crusaders observing the plight of the enslaved when they visited Jerusalem under licence in 1192: 'Misery indeed was to be seen there . . . Chained together in companies, their feet ulcerated [and] their backs scourged, they carried material to the stonemasons to make Jerusalem impregnable against the Christians.'[33] Physical deprivations were aggravated by the mental distress of knowing that they were making their former comrades' job harder.

The return of the first crusaders is poorly documented, though many seem to have made use of the ships that were increasingly arriving in the conquered seaports.[34] It's likely that the largest group accompanied Robert of Normandy and Robert of Flanders, who travelled to Constantinople on ships which were provided by the Byzantine governor of Cyprus.[35] Some crusaders stayed until Easter 1100 but after that date, as the patriarch of Jerusalem complained in an appeal to the Germans for financial help, substantial outlays in wages and gifts were needed to garrison the captured towns.[36] There's a distinct absence of specifics here that recurs in later crusades. The *Itinerarium peregrinorum* is typical in its generalizations about the Third Crusade:

> As the people had discharged their vow of pilgrimage, they prepared ships to go home. With favourable winds they set the sails and each committed themselves to their planned voyages. At once they were separated by a variety of winds and carried in different directions. The pilgrims were thrown far away through the tracts of the sea. Some of them were thrown out into various harbours, and escaped unharmed; others were scattered and endangered by shipwreck; others died in the sea on the voyage, and their allotted cemetery was the vastness of the sea. Others were infected by incurable disease and never regained their health, even in their homeland.[37]

In the case of the leaders there were naturally complications that arose from the often unsatisfactory outcomes and bitter disputes that had characterized their crusades. Immediately following the débâcle at Damascus in the summer of 1148 Conrad III sailed for Thessalonica, where he received an invitation to spend Christmas at the court of Manuel Komnenos at Constantinople. The occasion was used to create a solid alliance between the western and eastern empires, directed against King Roger of Sicily. Louis VII, by contrast, only left Palestine the following summer. He travelled on a Sicilian ship and landed in Calabria, where he pursued an alliance with Roger based among other things on their shared hostility towards the Emperor Manuel. The journeys home undertaken by the two monarchs therefore helped to consolidate the new political configuration that the crusade's disastrous events had shaped.[38]

But it was the political fall-out from the Third Crusade that exerted the greatest impact on the return journeys of western leaders. When Philip II sailed from Tyre in August 1191 he was seething with fury at the way he'd been treated by Richard I. He determined to do all that he could both to blacken Richard's reputation as a crusader and to exploit Richard's continued absence in the East to undermine his security in England and overrun his lands in France. Philip even attempted, brazenly and without success, to secure papal support for his planned encroachment on Angevin territory.[39] The results were a substantial misrepresentation of Richard's actions (above all his negotiations with Saladin), the seizure of power by John, and the creation of a scenario in which Richard's own return couldn't be less than perilous. Through his alliances in Europe and his actions in the East Richard had paved the way for Philip's machinations, for he'd managed to antagonize a lot of important people – the king of France, the Holy Roman Emperor Henry VI, Leopold duke of Austria, Count Raymond of Toulouse and the family and friends of Conrad of Montferrat.

When Richard sailed from Jaffa in October 1192 it was all but impossible for him to reach his lands except incognito, and when he tried this his lavish expenditure caught him out, leading to his arrest by Duke Leopold's men near Vienna. As Henry VI candidly put it in a letter to Philip II, 'we know that this news will bring you great happiness'. The king's ransom was set at 150,000 marks of silver, an extraordinary sum to find after a crusade which itself had been very expensive to finance.[40] Richard was set free in February 1194; Philip alerted John to the news with the dramatic message, 'Look to yourself, the devil is loosed.' Never was the fragility of the protection that the Church guaranteed to crusaders more clearly exposed. Leopold was left to God's punishment, which took the form of an agonizing death from gangrene following a fall from a horse at the end of 1194.[41]

Celebration and recrimination

The returning first crusaders were hailed as heroes. Like pilgrims before them, they were dubbed 'the Jerusalemites' (*Jerosolimitani*). It was a label that they applied to themselves during the expedition,[42] and it seems to have stuck for the rest of their lives. The celebrity status enjoyed by Bohemund of Antioch was such that he was able to capitalize on it when he toured France recruiting for a follow-up expedition in 1106. Many nobles asked him to become godfather to their children.[43] In the case of most later expeditions homecomings were considerably less ecstatic. Conrad III summed up the Second Crusade thus: 'we set out on a journey to liberate the Christians, but on account of our sins we had little success and after adoring the relic of the living and salvatory cross in Jerusalem we returned to our own land'.[44] It's not hard to imagine the subdued homecomings of Conrad and his fellow crusaders. The writer of one song from the time of the Third Crusade predicted that its survivors would be honoured on their arrival home,[45] but in practice the author of the *Itinerarium peregrinorum* reported that returning Third crusaders encountered derision, 'saying how little the pilgrims had achieved in the country of Jerusalem since they had not yet recovered Jerusalem'. Feeling sensitive, perhaps, about the issue of Jerusalem, the author countered this criticism by emphasizing the suffering and piety of the crusaders.[46] In this he followed the lead of Otto of Freising, who'd underlined the gains of the Second Crusade in terms of the souls that had been saved.[47]

48 St George's intervention on behalf of the crusaders at the battle of Antioch in 1098 is commemorated above the door of the church dedicated to the saint at Fordington in Dorset.

But military setbacks couldn't be circumvented this easily. As defeat followed defeat contemporaries increasingly picked out individuals and groups whom they could blame for failure. Following the Fifth Crusade there was substantial criticism of Cardinal Pelagius, whose misguided decisions were reckoned to be the more reprehensible because they resulted from a churchman meddling in military matters. 'When the clergy have the task of leading knights,' grumbled the Norman cleric William le Clerc in 1226/7, 'certainly that is contrary to the law.'[48] This hostile reaction to the legate's errors compounded criticism that was already being levelled against the clerical hierarchy for allowing individuals who took the cross to redeem their vows for cash instead of going to Egypt. The process smacked of fraud and was particularly painful at a time when captured crusaders were languishing in Muslim gaols. The poet Huon of St Quentin accused the Church of selling short the crusading cause, 'stealing from Acre and Bethlehem what the crusaders had promised to give to God'. For Huon the Church's behaviour was akin to Ganelon's celebrated betrayal of Roland in *The Song of Roland*. As for those who had redeemed their vows, the *décroisés*, like Judas they would forfeit Paradise.[49]

The outcome of Frederick II's visit to Palestine in 1229 created scandal for different reasons, notably his agreement to a truce that gave Christians access to Jerusalem but excluded them from the Temple Mount. Frederick's expedition was so mired in polemic that any assessment of its success or failure hinged largely on whether you were a supporter or opponent of the emperor.[50] Some crusaders believed that the leaders of the 'barons' crusade' of 1239–40 were taking backhanders from their Muslim opponents,[51] and the anonymous author of a polemical song that attacked the expedition's leadership predicted a shameful homecoming if things didn't improve.[52] The humiliation of an unavenged defeat was the main argument put forward by one poet against Louis IX returning to France in 1250.[53] Gone were the days when returning crusaders could expect to bask in glory, like Bohemund in 1106. Indeed, during the last fifty years or so before the fall of Acre in 1291 anybody committing themselves to a crusade must have been well aware that the odds were solidly stacked against success.

The tasks and pleasures of homecoming

Irrespective of the reaction of their contemporaries to what they'd done in the East, the first task facing crusaders following their journey home was usually sorting out serious problems that had arisen while they were away. Richard of Devizes provided a poetic but accurate summary of England's fate during Richard I's absence on the Third Crusade: 'As the earth shudders at the absence of the sun, so the face of the realm was altered at the king's departure. Certain nobles became busy; castles were strengthened; towns were fortified, and moats were dug.'[54] Few others faced crises on the scale that confronted Richard after his release from captivity in Austria, but there were many cases that replicated at local or regional level the dual challenge that the king faced from his brother John and Philip II of France. This applied in particular to the first crusaders, who lived in an age when the protection of lands and loved ones depended on personal action rather than interventions from any higher authorities.[55] In the summer of 1098 Anselm of Ribemonte foresaw the need to rescue 'churches and the poor' from 'the hands of tyrants'; since he died at Arqa in February 1099 it was a task that Anselm never had to face.[56]

One-and-a-half centuries later, when attacking the person and belongings of a crusader was supposed to be punished by Church and government alike, leaving home was still fraught with peril. When Joinville was pressurized by Louis IX to join him on his second crusade, he refused to do so because of the harm that his dependants had suffered at the hands of royal officials during his absence in 1248–54 (it should be added that this was an unusually long absence). Joinville had his answer ready to those who accused him of turning a deaf ear to Christ's call to 'take up his cross and follow him' (Mark 8:34). In the same way that Christ died to save his people, he wrote, it was in the best interests of Joinville's people that he should stay to defend them.[57] By this point it's likely that Joinville's reply had become gratingly familiar to preachers of the crusade.

The task of recovering lands and rights that had been seized can't have been made any easier by the simultaneous need to pay off debts, given that the crusader's moratorium had come to an end. In the letter that the leaders of the First Crusade wrote home after the battle of Ascalon they asked that their co-religionists pay their debts for them in exchange for a share in their spiritual rewards, but there's little evidence that their request did them any good.[58] As the Fourth Crusade moved towards its last act in 1203, Hugh count of St Pol wrote of his anxiety about how he'd repay his debts when he got back to France.[59] In his masterpiece *The Seventh Seal* Ingmar Bergman depicted a homecoming crusader struggling to escape the clutches of Death, but in practice they had more to fear from their creditors. Nor did they bring back much in the form of specie or precious metals that would help them repay their debts. In fact, the desire that many crusaders felt to make donations to religious houses as thank-offerings for their safe return from the East only added to the expenses associated with their return. One first crusader, Guigo of 'Mara', gave a whole church to the house of St Julien of Tours, where he rested during his journey home.[60] Many crusaders had to honour vows that they'd made to the saints at moments of extreme peril in the East, to the effect that if they survived they'd give money or lands to their shrines.[61]

Amid all these difficulties and expenses there was one set of rituals that in the case of the veterans of the First and Fourth Crusades must have given great satisfaction to many homecomers. This was the bestowal of relics, for it was relics that constituted the 'wealth' of most returning crusaders. Their collection began early; Robert of Flanders sent home relics that he acquired in southern Italy while on his way to the East.[62] But the majority of the gifts clearly accompanied the returning crusaders, and the overall harvest amounted to an unprecedented addition to Catholic Europe's sacred treasures. It's reasonable to infer that in deciding where to place them, their donors were inspired by a 'spiritual strategy', in which they either consolidated existing ties of patronage or created desirable new ones; and there may well have been associated economic benefits. Among those artefacts that made their way to the West after the fall of Jerusalem there were fragments of the two most famous relics that had been discovered by the first crusaders, the Holy Lance and True Cross. There was also a portion of the arm of St George, which was donated by Robert of Flanders to the abbey of Anchin. The arm's history was strange and unsettling: one after another of its custodians died or fell ill during the later stages of the expedition.[63]

In volume at least, no group of relics that were brought back from the First Crusade could compare with the 'triumphal spoils of holy plunder' that Abbot Martin of Pairis collected at Constantinople in 1204. According to Gunther of Pairis, the spiritual aura generated by the freight of sacred baggage that Martin brought back home with him was so powerful that pirate ships 'turned tame and gentle, hailing [his vessel] with every peaceful salute'.[64] The same happened in the case of bandits during the journey overland from Venice to Basel. Martin was generous with his gifts at Basel but he didn't hand out any of his many relics: these were carefully hoarded for his own abbey church. Here they were placed on the high altar on St John's Day (24 June) 1205. The whole exercise had been a triumph of abbatial management by Martin, acting 'in grand style but with the great humility of piety', as Gunther described it, getting the best of both worlds.[65]

Transformed lives?

For most crusaders the lodging of their relics with religious houses was the final act in the devotional process that had begun with their assumption of the cross. But a minority went further. A few of the survivors of the First Crusade embraced the monastic life. Odo Arpin, a participant in the crusade of 1101, was captured by the Muslims at the battle of Ramle in 1102 and imprisoned at Cairo; after his eventual return to France he entered Cluny. And as part of his dealings with the abbey of St Jacques de Liège in preparing for the Second Crusade, Maurice of Glons specified that if he came back from the crusade he should be allowed to join its community.[66] The heart of Odo of Nevers, who died in the East in 1266, was brought home and deposited at Cîteaux.[67]

Most surviving crusaders of course remained laymen and women, but some exhibited proof in their way of life that they had been changed fundamentally by their experiences in the East. The outstanding example was Louis IX of France. According to some sources the king expressed the desire to give up the crown and enter a religious house but was dissuaded by his wife Margaret.[68] Louis had always been pious and his way of life after his return to France wasn't transformed, but it was a lot more ascetic than it had been before his crusade. As Joinville put it:

After the king's return from oversea he lived with such a disregard for worldly vanities that he never wore ermine or squirrel fur, nor scarlet cloth, nor were his stirrups or his spurs gilded ... He had such sober tastes in food that he never ordered any special dish for himself, but took what his cook prepared, and ate whatever was put before him ... He always took care to see that his poor were fed and, after they had eaten, sent money to be distributed among them.[69]

Much of the king's government was concerned with tackling sinful practices such as games of chance, prostitution and usury. In this, given the limited bureaucracy at his disposal and the many opportunities for evasion, Louis was at best partially successful. In external affairs he became famous as a peacemaker, a ruler who could be relied upon to arbitrate fairly on the basis of his conviction that all war between Christians was evil.[70] He was in fact much less partisan and bellicose than the contemporary popes, who in the decades following Frederick II's death in 1250 became entangled in seemingly endless disputes about the disposition of the emperor's legacy with a variety of great lords and self-governing towns in Germany and Italy.[71]

Remarkable though Louis' devotional life between 1254 and 1270 was, not much can be inferred from it about the response of the majority of crusaders to what they'd gone through in the East. The king's status was after all exceptional, and he had good luck: France faced no major internal or external threats in the mid-thirteenth century, so Louis enjoyed freedom of action to an unusual degree. By way of comparison, it's very hard to tell if and how his grandfather Philip II was 'marked' by his participation in the Third Crusade.[72] Many returning crusaders, certainly during the first century of crusading, didn't have the option of creating a radically different way of life for themselves outside the cloister. Irrespective of their own preferences, the imbroglios that they confronted about landholding, feudal duties and kinship obligations meant that they had to plunge back into secular affairs and sometimes resort to violence. Few of them would have had the leisure to engage in the sort of metaphysical reflections which preoccupy Bergman's knight in *The Seventh Seal*. This spoiled the neat symmetry beloved of the clerics, whereby the departure of infamous troublemakers on crusades both saved their souls and brought peace to their neighbours.[73]

A dispute that erupted in 1107 between Hugh II of Le Puiset and Rotrou of Perche illustrates this particularly well. Rotrou had erected a fortification on land that was contested between the two lords. The complications included the fact that Hugh II had taken the cross, presumably to join Bohemund of Taranto's new expedition; the leading canonist Ivo of Chartres expressed his uncertainty about the proper legal process to pursue. What's striking is that Rotrou himself was a first crusader, so one might expect to find some community of interest and sympathy between him and Hugh. But, if such a tie did exist, family rights and honour took priority. And there were veterans of the First Crusade who were more vicious in their behaviour than Rotrou. Raimbold Croton, a hero of Antioch and Jerusalem, castrated a monk within a year or two of his arrival home. Thomas of Marle, another of the expedition's heroes and a combatant at Nicaea, Dorylaeum, Antioch and Jerusalem, went on to become one of the most notorious war-captains in northern France until his unlamented death in 1130.[74]

Of course it's necessary to make some allowance for the slanted way in which the military exploits of men like Thomas of Marle were narrated, usually by monks who had wearily resumed the role of being their principal victims. At the same time that a distinguished group of Benedictine historians were writing narratives that described the first crusaders exhibiting quasi-monastic behaviour during their march to Jerusalem, their fellow religious were painting the predatory exploits of some crusaders after their return to the West in colours that were much more in tune with the charters and chronicles of the eleventh century. Yet when all allowance is made for the distorted character of the evidence, these behavioural extremes do fit our knowledge of the society that these people belonged to. It was precisely because sin was unavoidable that crusading enjoyed its popularity. Even when a greater measure of social peace had been imposed, enabling homecomers to fit back into their communities with relative ease, evidence that crusading changed its participants for the better in religious terms is hard to come by outside the pages of Joinville.

This can hardly have been surprising given that it had always been the case with pilgrimage. In the early eleventh century it had been glaringly demonstrated by Fulk Nerra's bizarre oscillation between sin and contrition. The best that could be said about Fulk when he returned from Jerusalem in 1003 was that 'for a time he moderated his customary ferocity'.[75] It followed that as a rival devotional practice, Europe's religious houses didn't have much to fear from crusading. In the early thirteenth century the Cistercians even believed that the pope allowed anybody who had taken the cross to enter their order instead, because it would be better for their souls. It was 'more whole-some to impress a long cross upon his mind than to sew a short cross for a brief period to his garment'.[76] This explains why crusading was able to flourish in centuries that witnessed the creation of more than fifty new religious orders.[77] Recurrent sinning (recidivism) continued to represent the clinching argument in favour of the monastic vocation, because the only sure way to escape the snares of the world's temptations was to quit it for the cloister.

'We shall talk of this day' – crusading remembered

Though crusading didn't transform the lives of most of its participants, the experience stayed lodged in their minds. True, some were traumatized by their ordeals and, living at a time that possessed minimal understanding of how to deal with trauma, they just subsumed their terrors. This is partly why we have so few narrative sources for the Second Crusade. To the German author of one charter written in 1148 the expedition was 'marvellous more by its start than its end'.[78] This was a masterly understatement. Many participants surely shared the view expressed by Otto of Freising that it would be depressing to recall the terrible things that had happened to them.[79] On the other hand, the character and scale of Barbarossa's impressive preparations for his crusade in 1188–9 show that he didn't forget his earlier sufferings,[80] and even the Second Crusade bequeathed some memories to cherish, like the capture of Lisbon which German crusaders in 1189 knew had been captured 'by our pilgrims'.[81]

Most crusaders expected to look back on what they did. In a famous passage in his memoir, Joinville narrated how the count of Soissons dismissed the frenzied shouting of the Turks at the battle of Mansurah: 'Seneschal, let these dogs howl as they will. By God's bonnet, we shall talk of this day yet, you and I, sitting at home with our ladies.'[82] Such memories could last a long time. In the 1330s John of Le Vignay inserted into a translation that he was making of Primat's Latin chronicle a crusading reminiscence of his father that dated back eighty years.[83] The urge to remember and record was surely all the stronger when the returning crusader's family already possessed a corpus of crusading memories which would be added to. So a lot of individual homecomers felt the need to establish reference points for what they'd experienced. In addition to which there was a strong collective impetus to construct ways of remembering that had happened. The crusaders after all had been supported by their families; the whole Catholic world had prayed for them; and they'd fought on behalf of Christendom. It's not inappropriate to summarize the spectrum of associations and reflections that resulted under the word 'remembrance'.

Acts of commemoration

Surviving rituals of remembrance, what we would now regard as acts of commemoration, are rare. Given the religious character of the enterprise this comes as a surprise and it's hard to explain. One twelfth-century text that was rich in crusading resonances, the *Pseudo-Turpin*, proposed an annual commemoration of all Christians who'd fallen in Spain or in Jerusalem from the time of Charlemagne onwards, on the basis that they were martyrs.[84]

49 Holy Sepulchre Church at Northampton, built by Simon of Senlis after his return from the First Crusade.

As we've seen, this was in line with the feelings of crusaders themselves about their deceased comrades. But reality fell short of this. At Jerusalem itself the commemoration of those who died liberating the city in 1099 was incorporated into the feast-day of Jerusalem's liberation (*Laetare Ierusalem*), which was celebrated each year on the anniversary of the city's recovery, 15 July.[85] Thanks to the popularity of pilgrimage to Jerusalem before Hattin many thousands of westerners would have witnessed this commemoration. Conveniently it occurred about halfway between the spring passage, when many of them arrived, and the autumn passage when most left.[86] In one sermon that was composed to be given on this occasion, probably at the very spot where the crusaders first entered the city, the author heaped praise on those who had 'sweated their way to Jerusalem'.[87]

We have the texts of two sermons that were delivered by Odo of Châteauroux, one of the great preachers of the thirteenth century, to commemorate those who fell at the battle of Mansurah in February 1250. The dead crusaders included the king's brother Robert of Artois, and in addition to praising them Odo took the opportunity to engage in theological speculation about the vexing issue of why God had allowed the catastrophe at Mansurah to happen. These were refined and complex sermons, given by a high-powered theologian who was almost certainly preaching before the king himself during the Palestinian phase of his crusade, perhaps at Acre on the battle's first anniversary in 1251. It's possible that similar texts delivered on other anniversaries have been lost, but it's also conceivable that Odo's sermons were created for a unique set of circumstances: a king who was still resident in the East, experienced particularly strong grief for his dead brother, and could call on the services of a preacher of Odo's calibre.[88] It's not easy to cite parallels to Odo's sermons in the West. In 1190 the Cistercian General Chapter associated fallen crusaders with the dead who were commemorated in the daily Mass for the Dead in every Cistercian house.[89] But this is an isolated case and to find similar religious occurrences we have to go beyond 1291.

It's very noticeable that the massive mobilization of efforts by the Church to secure the launching and success of its crusades appears to have lacked a parallel in the large-scale commemoration of those who perished on them. In the twelfth century the task of praying for the dead fell in piecemeal fashion to the religious houses with which fallen crusaders had possessed ties of patronage, and which so often had both contributed to and benefited from their crusading efforts.[90] When the Church at large started to plant the needs of crusading in its liturgical formulae, following Hattin, the emphasis was understandably on the provision of spiritual and material assistance for the defence or recovery of the Holy Land. It looked to the future rather than to the past.[91]

Confraternity

The chief way in which veterans chose to memorialize their crusading past was through confraternity with the various religious corporations that were closely associated with the Holy Land. When the Patriarch Eraclius called for the assistance of the West as Saladin's army approached Jerusalem's walls in 1187, he promised to anybody who answered his appeal that 'all such benefactors, helpers and contributors will be included in our prayers and confraternity, enjoying the same status as our *confratres*'.[92] It was an astute offer, because by this point confraternity with the Church of the Holy Sepulchre was in vogue in the West. A community of Augustinian canons was established to administer the church's services by Patriarch Arnulf in 1114, and the order acquired the right to serve the shrine churches at an impressive cluster of other devotional sites including the Temple of the Lord, Mount Sion, Bethlehem, Nazareth and Hebron. King Baldwin II bestowed kudos on the order by dying in 1131 in the habit of a canon.[93]

Fraternity with the military orders of the Hospital and Temple was at least as important. In large measure confraternity was driven by the personal benefit that was gained from being taken into an order's devotional embrace, 'so that we may be regarded by God as participants in the prayers, fasts, masses, almsgiving, punishments and all holy works which the brothers of the order perform', as a donor to the Hospitallers expressed it;[94] but it could result from first-hand experience of the order's work in the East and most likely it reflected sympathy with that work. A natural follow-up to confraternity was late entry into one of the orders and generous legacies to them on the point of death. William Marshal, who spent two poorly documented years in the Holy Land in the mid-1180s, took the robe of a Templar on his deathbed in 1219.[95]

Commemorating in stone and glass

It wasn't hard to find physical reminders of the Holy Land. The relics brought back by veterans acted as a constant spur to its memory, and there was a trend to build churches that were dedicated to the Holy Sepulchre and in some cases copied its architecture. The parish church dedicated to the Holy Sepulchre at Northampton was almost certainly built by Earl Simon of Senlis on his return from the First Crusade. The Round Church at Cambridge was one of a number of churches that were built by lay confraternities of the Holy Sepulchre, and it's hardly surprising that the dedicatory and imitative trend was especially strong in the case of churches that fell into the hands of the Hospitallers and Templars.[96]

In this, as in most things, crusaders developed a tradition that was already in place because of the pious actions of returning pilgrims. Fulk Nerra, for example, had founded the abbey of Beaulieu-les-Loches 'in honour of the Holy Sepulchre', reputedly to house a relic of the cross that he brought back with him from his first pilgrimage to the Holy Land.[97] Neuvy-Saint-Sépulcre in Berry knits together pilgrimage and crusade. It was probably founded by Odo Le Roux in 1042 following a pilgrimage in 1027, from which Odo brought back many fragments of the Holy Sepulchre. Albert of Aachen believed that Peter the Hermit started his preaching of the First Crusade at Neuvy-Saint-Sépulcre, and the viscount of Berry, Odo Arpin, took part in the 1101 expedition. Odo of Châteauroux donated some drops of Christ's blood together with more stones from the Holy Sepulchre when he came back in 1254.[98] The town of Huy in the Low Countries acquired not just a church dedicated to the Holy Sepulchre but a Constantinople gate and a tower of Damietta.[99]

The most spectacular piece of devotional architecture possessing crusading associations was Louis IX's Sainte-Chapelle on the Île de la Cité in Paris. Louis built the chapel to provide an appropriate setting for his collection of relics of the passion, in particular the Crown of Thorns, which he bought in 1238 from the impoverished Latin emperor of Constantinople. The chapel was consecrated in April 1248 and architecturally it's a radical departure from the tradition of copying the Holy Sepulchre, which had faded by this time. None the less, its association with royal commitment to crusading was strong from the start. The chapel's original windows depicted the king as a barefoot pilgrim wearing pilgrim's clothes, directly mirroring the message conveyed by the narrative sources, and its consecration was postponed so that it could take place just before Louis' departure for the East. In addition to the pomp of consecration, it's likely that the display of the chapel's passion relics was inserted into the various ceremonies that marked Louis's departure.[100]

In the years after the king's return this exquisite, soaring building and its holy contents were bound to form a constant reminder to Louis of the sanctity and critical state of the Holy Land. When Joinville was summoned to Paris in the spring of 1267 and didn't know why, the mystery was solved when he went to the Sainte-Chapelle and saw the king supervising the removal from its casing of his cherished fragment of the True Cross. 'Never believe me again', he heard one member of the royal council saying to another, 'if the king doesn't take the cross here in this chapel.' Which was precisely what happened on the following day, the Feast of the Annunciation (25 March).[101] As in 1248 the chapel's relics featured in the ceremonies marking departure, for Louis presented a gift from them to the bishop of Clermont in December 1269.[102] Decades later the association was reiterated when Louis' great-grandson Philip VI of Valois summoned his barons to meet in the Sainte-Chapelle in 1332, to launch a crusade that was moulded in the tradition of his ancestor's two expeditions. Not only was the chapel symbolically appropriate as the setting for such an occasion, but its relics acted as a guarantee for the politically vital oaths that the king made his leading barons and prelates swear, that in the event of Philip's death on crusade they would crown his son as his successor.[103] Devotion, dynasty and crusade converged.

By the time Louis IX took the cross in 1267 there was little danger that any king or high-ranking nobleman who'd been on crusade would be allowed to forget the fact. Like universities targeting their rich and famous alumni, the Holy Land's rulers and the papal court focused their appeals for help on Europe's most influential crusade veterans. Paradoxically, Louis' assumption of the cross caused consternation at the papal court, because of the poor state of the king's health and the fact that the pope was a former royal servant – he was well aware of the dangers that could afflict the kingdom during Louis' absence.[104] Nor was another general passage under royal command considered to be the best way for the French to help the Holy Land. Since 1254 Louis had maintained a garrison of troops at Acre, initially comprising just one hundred knights, and they'd come to be a vital element in the defence of the residual Christian settlements.[105] The pope and other well-informed contemporaries were starting to see the best hope of staving off Mamluk attacks as lying in the regular reinforcement of the Latin East through mercenaries, money and supplies rather than in another big crusade. Coming back to the alumni comparison, they thought that a sustained pattern of giving was better than a single big donation.

Whatever form it took, some assistance was certainly hoped for from former crusaders of Louis' status. Edward Plantagenet went on Louis' second crusade, and following the French king's death and Edward's succession to the throne of England, it was he who was looked to first and foremost for assistance. Edward I never forgot the seventeen months that he spent in Palestine in 1271–2. Given his rivalry with Philip IV of France it made political sense for the king to respond positively to pleas for his assistance by taking the cross in 1287. But there's enough evidence for a heartfelt commitment to support the argument that Edward really did yearn to return. Needless to say, as king he didn't possess the freedom of action that he had enjoyed as heir to the throne. It's possible that he viewed his financial support for the expedition that was led in 1291 by the Savoyard knight Otto of Grandson as a sort of surrogate venture: Otto had been one of his comrades-in-arms twenty years earlier.[106]

Collective remembrance: creating the history of the First Crusade

Thus far the patterns of remembrance that we've looked at had two things in common: they were predominantly individual, and they revolved around the desire to maintain links with the Holy Land. For collective acts, focusing more on what crusaders had *done* while they were in the East, we have to look to more reflective processes, and this comes down to attempts to construct a historical perspective on crusading. In written accounts of what had been achieved a plethora of individual experiences and reports were woven together to form unified narratives, though we always have to be mindful that these narratives both emanated from and were read by the literate minority. For a number of reasons it's the recording of the First Crusade that forms the best example of the process. Its scale and achievements were of course momentous, but above all there was its unprecedented character. It overshadowed its age and most intellectually alert contemporaries were fascinated by it.

It took a lengthy sequence of discovery, reflection and debate to absorb in full the events of 1095–9, and it helps to divide the sequence into three phases. The initial phase constituted a series of narratives written by four participants, the anonymous author of the *Gesta Francorum*, Raymond of Aguilers, Fulcher of Chartres and Peter Tudebode. Of course all of these narratives were to some degree tendentious – that's to say, their authors wrote with purposes other

50 Godfrey of Bouillon, hero of the First Crusade, leads his troops into battle.

than the simple recording of events. Fulcher sought to vindicate the decision made by his lord Baldwin of Boulogne to divert his following to Edessa, while Raymond openly stated at the start of his narrative that he wrote in order to recover the crusade from the mythologizing of those deserters who had disseminated a false picture of what happened.[107] Not that this consideration invalidates Fulcher or Raymond. Indeed, if we only possessed this first layer of narrative accounts we'd still be in a strong position not just to establish the expedition's events but also to reconstruct the thinking of its participants. It's a substantial bonus that their authors belonged to some of the leading ethnic groups that took part in the crusade, the south Italian Normans, Provençals and northern French.[108] The high value that contemporaries placed on these

eyewitness accounts is shown by the fact that the texts by Fulcher and
Raymond were added to Walter the Chancellor's *History of the Antiochene
Wars* to make up a package intended for liturgical use.[109]

The second phase in the First Crusade's reception comprised the wave of
more sophisticated narratives composed in western Europe during the first
half of the twelfth century. We've already seen that a cluster of these accounts
were written in northern France by learned Benedictine monks, Baldric of
Bourgueil, Robert of Reims and Guibert of Nogent. It's likely that all three
had completed their works by 1111. Guibert's explanation of why he
composed his history focused on the shortcomings of the eyewitness narratives that he'd read: the speed with which these accounts circulated in the
West was extraordinary and it probably owed much to the 'follow-up' crusades
that took place in the early twelfth century.[110] The style of the *Gesta
Francorum* was too banal for Guibert's taste, 'woven out of excessively simple
words, often violating grammatical rules . . . it may often bore the reader with
the stale, flat quality of its language'.[111] Fulcher's style, on the other hand, was
too grandiose, with its 'swollen, foot-and-a-half-long words'. Fulcher was
something of a whipping boy for Guibert, whose temper was probably not
helped by the fact that Fulcher's work only came to his attention when he'd
already finished his own history.[112] He accused Fulcher of making misleading
judgements, as in his scepticism about the Holy Lance. 'Was the worthy
bishop of Puy so foolish,' Guibert clinically retorted, 'as to have carried a lance
of questionable authenticity with such reverence when he went out to fight
Kerbogha?'[113]

Guibert was aware of the subtext in Fulcher's history: 'while our men were
suffering from starvation at Antioch, [he] was feasting at ease in Edessa'.[114]
In a long passage Guibert was coldly critical of some of the flights of fancy
that he'd come across. Sarcastically, he remarked that the woman who supposedly had followed a goose at the start of the crusade would have been better
off cooking it for her supper.[115] He displayed common sense on the question
of numbers, scaling down the vast estimates afforded by Fulcher on the
ground that 'I would be surprised if all the land this side of the Alps, indeed
if all the kingdoms of the West, could supply so many men.'[116] Such remarks
as these, together with Guibert's careful sifting and comparison of all the
known sources for the expedition, including some of the letters written home,
make him appear notably modern at times. Yet this can be misleading,
because Guibert, Baldric and Robert had their own axes to grind and they
were as rooted in their preconceptions as any of their contemporaries. All
were French and they emphasized the 'Frankish' nature of the crusade. This
applied above all to Robert of Reims and may account for the extraordinary
popularity of his history, which survives in more than 120 manuscripts.[117]

Guibert recorded a quarrel that he'd had with the archdeacon of Mainz who'd insulted the French. 'If you think them so weak and languid,' Guibert retorted, 'tell me upon whom did Pope Urban call for aid against the Turks?'[118] Their chief intellectual concern was to make sense of what had happened in the East in terms of contemporary theology. We've seen that their key contribution, potentially a misleading one, was to place the crusaders' devotional lives within a monastic worldview.[119]

Other writers in this second phase had different perspectives. Above all there was Albert of Aachen, whose history of the crusade and its aftermath was completed around 1130 and was the longest at 120,000 words.[120] Albert drew heavily on the reminiscences of veterans who'd fought alongside Godfrey of Bouillon; he gave the German and imperial point of view and tended to be conservative in his outlook. The terminology he used about the First Crusade was at times old-fashioned compared with that used by the north-French Benedictines.[121] Albert was also more willing than they were to include anecdotes for their own sake: it's probable that Guibert would have placed Albert on his blacklist together with Fulcher. This has created a reputation for garrulity and unreliability, but it could well be construed as a strength, bringing Albert closer to the lived experience of crusaders, among whom rumour was surely rife.[122]

But arguably the most significant divergence between Albert and his north-French contemporaries related to the crusade's origins. For Guibert and his fellow religious the crusade started when it was preached at Clermont by the pope. Albert, reflecting the views of his informants, attributed the crusade to Peter the Hermit, who preached it in response to his personal experience of the sufferings that were inflicted on pilgrims to Jerusalem by the Turks.[123] Hard though it is to believe, it seems to be the case that people who fought their way through to Jerusalem side by side held very different opinions about how their great venture had originated. It's quite possible that some of Godfrey of Bouillon's followers, like the duke himself, had fought against Urban II during the papal–imperial dispute that preceded the First Crusade. They wouldn't have taken kindly to Urban being given a prominence that in their eyes he didn't deserve.[124] Even more remarkably, there was no reconciliation of this divergent picture in the twelfth century: the 'Urbanist' view is apparent, for example in the opening of *Quantum praedecessores*, the bull with which Eugenius III launched the Second Crusade in 1146.[125] On the other hand, a modified version of the 'Petrine' view became enshrined in the chronicle of William of Tyre, which was completed in the 1180s.[126] Because of William's reputation it passed into many other works in the thirteenth century and beyond.[127]

By the time William of Tyre wrote, the formation of views about what had happened on the First Crusade had passed into its third and most eclectic phase. Myth creation and imaginative reworking now jostled for attention with real events.[128] Few Christians living in Europe at the time of the battle of Hattin could have been unaware that a century earlier an armed pilgrimage had taken place that had captured first Antioch and then Jerusalem. The central fact of Jerusalem's recovery in 1099 was brought home to many through the chanting of the liturgy on the feast-day of the city's liberation.[129] But much of the remainder of what contemporaries believed about the First Crusade was actually wrong. There was a general belief that the great emperor Charlemagne had carried out a pilgrimage to Jerusalem; indeed, Guy of Bazoches argued that the First Crusade should really be called the Second 'because Charlemagne made the first one'.[130] Local myths associated with crusading exploits were starting to form.[131] The people of Cambrai may still have been told the story of the goose.[132] And it's quite possible that people whose primary source of information about the crusade was the central tympanum at Vézelay could have harboured the mistaken belief that the expedition's goal was not the recovery of Jerusalem but the conversion of the gentiles.[133]

At the same time the series of vernacular crusade epics was in gestation, starting with Graindor of Douai's version of *The Song of Antioch* (*La Chanson d'Antioche*) (*c.* 1180).[134] These built on and enhanced popular curiosity about the First Crusade while generating confusion about it: for the author of the *Itinerarium peregrinorum* the events narrated in *The Song of Antioch* were to be taken as fact, providing fuel for an unfavourable comparison between the participants of the First and Third Crusades.[135] It was probably due to the popularity of the *chansons* that Godfrey of Bouillon's reputation rose, so that he came to be viewed as a commander rivalling Bohemund. *The Song of Antioch* portrayed Godfrey winning his victories using the same sword that had been wielded by Vespasian.[136] For a number of reasons accuracy and consistency were vain hopes. Historical recollection served a host of functions, including commemoration, exhortation, didacticism and entertainment, and this meant that it was marked by diversity and at times contradiction. Its impact on contemporaries depended on levels of literacy, rank, geographical location and personal inclinations. Crusading was a general Christian undertaking, belonging to no single religious order, dynasty or nation, so the narrative traditions that shaped its recording were diffuse; they reflected the tensions as well as the creativity that typified the European twelfth century. These included national antagonisms. According to John of Würzburg, who visited Jerusalem in *c.* 1170, Franco-German rivalry relating to the capture of Jerusalem was so strong that it had caused the defacing of an epitaph to a prominent member of Godfrey's household, a hero called Wicher.[137]

51 This fifteenth-century illustrator of Urban II's Clermont sermon depicts the pope's audience sedately seated in a church.

Past and future crusading

There was no reason why this bustling conflation of truth, inaccuracy and legend should change.[138] After the death of Louis IX of France the legend took root that the king had himself brought back to France the relics that were housed in the Sainte-Chapelle.[139] Humbert of Romans included in his *De predicacione sanctae crucis* references to Roncesvalles and Roland,[140] while Rutebeuf wove Roland, Godfrey of Bouillon and the contemporary hero Geoffrey of Sergines into a seamless tapestry of Christian chivalry.[141] The view that was held of the First Crusade by the master of the Hospitallers, Fulk of Villaret, a few years after the fall of Acre in 1291, contained inaccuracies that were potentially dangerous, because he let them mould his opinions about the best way a future crusade should be organized.[142]

Yet, as this example indicates, misinformation didn't just derive from the ample room that was allowed for error by low levels of literacy and poor communication. It resulted also from the fact that on many if not most of the occasions when people's attention was drawn to past crusading, whether it was by histories, letters, treatises, sermons, poems and songs or artistic representations, the context was less what we would regard as remembrance than an attempt to renew past efforts by mobilizing enthusiasm. When a knight from the Auvergne called Grassegals presented Louis VII with a manuscript

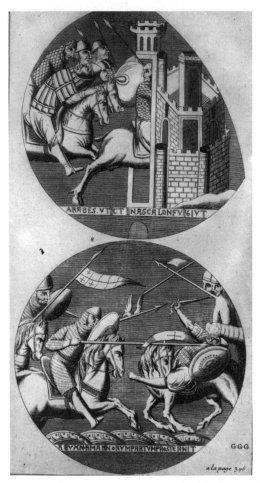

52 Memory and exhortation converge in this portrayal of the battle of Ascalon, 1099, in the (now lost) First Crusade windows of St Denis.

containing three narrative accounts of the First Crusade and its aftermath, probably at Christmas 1137, he exhorted the king to imitate the great deeds of his ancestors Hugh of Vermandois and Robert of Flanders: Grassegals himself was a veteran of the expedition.[143] Recruiting for the Third Crusade was almost certainly one of the goals of Graindor of Douai in compiling *The Song of Antioch*.[144] Humbert of Romans listed 'the example of those who went before' among the reasons to be advanced for taking the cross.[145] His fellow preacher Odo of Châteauroux also appealed to the precedent of the First Crusade,[146] and the reason why Rutebeuf summoned up the images of Godfrey, Bohemund and Tancred in 1277 was that he hoped to retrieve the desperate situation in the East.[147]

It's appropriate to bring this book to a close in the early Gothic interior of the great shrine church of St Denis. The church's links with French crusading surpassed even those of the Sainte-Chapelle and Vézelay. We've seen that it was in St Denis that Louis VII received his pilgrim insignia in 1147 and Louis IX in 1248. From the mid-twelfth century onwards visitors to the church's ambulatory could admire fourteen panels of stained glass, unfortunately since destroyed, that either Abbot Suger or his successor Odo of Deuil placed there in honour of the First Crusade. It's highly likely that the idea behind commissioning the panels was as much exhortation as commemoration or instruction. The window was a sermon in glass. By depicting the battle of Ascalon, the last four panels in the sequence seem to have made the point that the struggle for the Holy Land was still in progress. We saw earlier that it was after their victory at Ascalon that the first crusaders felt free to return home. Far from being the end of the story, however, the recovery of Jerusalem represented a sacred and ongoing commitment for the faithful.[148] Suger himself had commented that 'in recollecting the things that have occurred we show the things that will happen'.[149] In this way, it was hoped, the past could be mobilized to serve the future. There would be more Ascalons to be fought and won. For this reason it was only when the need and urge to crusade in the East had finally faded that the task of giving crusading its place in history could be addressed in full. Until then crusading belonged too much to the present to be allowed an existence that lay wholly in the past.

ABBREVIATIONS

AA	Albert of Aachen, *Historia Ierosolimitana*, ed. and tr. S. B. Edgington (Oxford, 2007).
Ambroise	Ambroise, *Estoire de la guerre sainte*, ed. M. Ailes and M. Barber, tr. M. Ailes, 2 vols (Woodbridge, 2003).
Andrea	A. J. Andrea, ed. and tr., *Contemporary Sources for the Fourth Crusade* (Leiden, 2000).
APC	M. Balard, ed., *Autour de la première Croisade* (Paris, 1996).
Baha' al-Din	Baha' al-Din Ibn Shaddad, *The Rare and Excellent History of Saladin*, tr. D. S. Richards (Aldershot, 2001).
BC	Bernard of Clairvaux, *Letters*, ed. B. Scott James, 2nd edn (Stroud, 1998).
Bédier and Aubry	J. Bédier and P. Aubry, eds, *Les Chansons de croisade* (Paris, 1909).
CIR	Riley-Smith, L. and J., trs, *The Crusades: Idea and Reality, 1095–1274* (London, 1981).
CSEPBH	J. France and W. G. Zajac, eds, *The Crusades and their Sources: Essays Presented to Bernard Hamilton* (Aldershot, 1998).
De expugnatione	C. W. David., ed., *De expugnatione Lyxbonensi* (New York, 1936).
EBTT	R. Allen, ed., *Eastward Bound: Travel and Travellers, 1050–1550* (Manchester, 2004).
ECWA	M. Bull and N. Housley, eds, *The Experience of Crusading*, 1: *Western Approaches* (Cambridge, 2003).
Edbury	P. W. Edbury, ed., *The Conquest of Jerusalem and the Third Crusade: Sources in Translation* (Aldershot, 1996).
EHR	*English Historical Review.*
'Epistola'	'Epistola de morte Friderici imperatoris', in A. Chroust, ed., *Quellen zur Geschichte des Kreuzzuges Kaiser Friedrichs I.* (Berlin, 1928), 173–8.
FC	Fulcher of Chartres, 'Historia Iherosolymitana', in *RHC, Historiens occidentaux*, vol. 3, tr. F. R. Ryan, ed. H. S. Fink as *A History of the Expedition to Jerusalem, 1095–1127* (Knoxville, TN, 1969).
FCOI	J. Phillips, ed., *The First Crusade: Origins and Impact* (Manchester, 1997).
'Gesta cruc.'	'Gesta crucigerorum rhenanorum', in R. Röhricht, ed., *Quinti Belli Sacri Scriptores Minores* (Geneva, 1879), 27–56.
'Gesta obsid.'	'Gesta obsidionis Damiatae', in R. Röhricht, ed., *Quinti Belli Sacri Scriptores Minores* (Geneva, 1879), 71–115.
GF	R. Hill, ed. and tr., *Gesta Francorum* (repr. Oxford, 1972).

GN	Guibert of Nogent, 'Gesta Dei per Francos', in *RHC, Historiens occidentaux*, vol. 4, tr. R. Levine as *The Deeds of God through the Franks* (Woodbridge, 1997).
GP	A. J. Andrea, ed. and tr., *The Capture of Constantinople: The 'Hystoria Constantinopolitana' of Gunther of Pairis* (Philadelphia, PA, 1997).
GW	Gerald of Wales, 'Itinerarium Kambriae', in J. F. Dimock, ed., *Giraldi Cambrensis Opera*, vol. 6 (RS, London, 1868), 1–152, tr. L. Thorpe as *The Journey through Wales and The Description of Wales* (Harmondsworth, 1978).
Hagenmeyer	H. Hagenmeyer, ed., *Die Kreuzzugsbriefe aus den Jahren 1088–1100* (Innsbruck, 1901), partially tr. A. C. Krey in *The First Crusade: The Accounts of Eye-Witnesses and Participants* (repr. Gloucester, MA, 1958).
Haymar	Haymar, 'De expugnatione civitatis Acconensis', in Roger of Howden, *Chronica*, ed. W. Stubbs, 4 vols (RS, London, 1868–71), vol. 3, preface, appendix I, pp. cv–cxxxvi.
HC	K. M. Setton, gen. ed., *A History of the Crusades*, 6 vols (Madison, WI, 1969–89).
'Historia'	'Historia peregrinorum', in A. Chroust, ed., *Quellen zur Geschichte des Kreuzzuges Kaiser Friedrichs I.* (Berlin, 1928), 116–72.
Huygens	R. B. C. Huygens, ed., *Lettres de Jacques de Vitry* (Leiden, 1960).
IP	W. Stubbs, ed., *Itinerarium peregrinorum et gesta regis Ricardi* (RS, London, 1864), tr. H. J. Nicholson as *Chronicle of the Third Crusade* (Aldershot, 1997).
JMH	*Journal of Medieval History*.
Joinville	John of Joinville, *Vie de Saint Louis*, ed. and French tr. J. Monfrin (Paris, 1995), English tr. M. R. B. Shaw as *Joinville & Villehardouin: Chronicles of the Crusades* (Harmondsworth, 1963).
JT	John of Tulbia, 'De domino Iohanne rege Ierusalem', in R. Röhricht, ed., *Quinti Belli Sacri Scriptores Minores* (Geneva, 1879), 117–40.
KC	N. Housley, ed., *Knighthoods of Christ: Essays on the History of the Crusades and the Knights Templar, Presented to Malcolm Barber* (Aldershot, 2007).
LWAC	J. H. Pryor, ed., *Logistics of Warfare in the Age of the Crusades* (Aldershot, 2006).
Lyon Continuation	M. R. Morgan, ed., *La Continuation de Guillaume de Tyr (1184–1197)* (Paris, 1982), tr. in Edbury, 11–145.
Maier	C. T. Maier, ed. and tr., *Crusade Propaganda and Ideology: Model Sermons for the Preaching of the Cross* (Cambridge, 2000).
MGHS	*Monumenta Germaniae Historica, Scriptores*
MP	Matthew Paris, *Chronica maiora*, ed. H. R. Luard, 7 vols (RS, London, 1872–83), tr. J. A. Giles as *Matthew Paris's English History, from the Year 1235 to 1273*, 3 vols (London, 1852–4).
'Narratio'	C. W. David, ed., 'Narratio de itinere navali peregrinorum hierosolymam tendentium et Silviam capientium, AD 1189', in *Proceedings of the American Philosophical Society* 81 (1939), 591–676 (alternative edition in A. Chroust, ed., *Quellen zur Geschichte des Kreuzzuges Kaiser Friedrichs I.* [Berlin, 1928], 179–96).
OD	Odo of Deuil, *De profectione Ludovici VII in orientem*, ed. and tr. V. G. Berry (New York, 1948).

OP	Oliver of Paderborn, 'Historia Damiatina', in H. Hoogeweg, ed., *Die Schriften des kölner Domscholasters, späteren Bischofs von Paderborn und Kardinal-Bischofs von S. Sabina Oliverus* (Tübingen, 1894), 159–280, tr. J. J. Gavigan in E. Peters, ed., *Christian Society and the Crusades, 1198–1229* (Philadelphia, PA, 1971), 49–138.
'Ordinacio'	'Ordinacio de predicacione S. Crucis in Anglia', in R. Röhricht, ed., *Quinti Belli Sacri Scriptores Minores* (Geneva, 1879), 1–26.
Outremer	B. Z. Kedar, H. E. Mayer and R. C. Smail, eds, *Outremer: Studies in the History of the Crusading Kingdom of Jerusalem* (Jerusalem, 1982).
OV	Orderic Vitalis, *Historia aecclesiastica*, ed. and tr. M. Chibnall, 6 vols (Oxford, 1969–79).
PA	Pseudo-Ansbert, 'Historia de expeditione Friderici imperatoris', in A. Chroust, ed., *Quellen zur Geschichte des Kreuzzuges Kaiser Friedrichs I.* (Berlin, 1928), 1–115.
PJ	C. F. Beckingham and B. Hamilton, eds, *Prester John: The Mongols and the Ten Lost Tribes* (Aldershot, 1996).
PL	J. P. Migne, ed., *Patrologiae cursus completus, Series Latina*, 221 vols (Paris, 1844–64).
RA	Raymond of Aguilers, 'Historia Francorum qui ceperunt Iherusalem', in *RHC, Historiens occidentaux*, vol. 3, tr. A. C. Krey in *The First Crusade: The Accounts of Eye-Witnesses and Participants* (repr. Gloucester, MA, 1958).
RaC	Ralph of Caen, 'Gesta Tancredi', in *RHC, Historiens occidentaux*, vol. 3, tr. B. S. and D. S. Bachrach as *The 'Gesta Tancredi' of Ralph of Caen: A History of the Normans on the First Crusade* (Aldershot, 2005).
RC	Robert of Clari, *The Conquest of Constantinople*, ed. and tr. E. H. McNeal (repr. Toronto, 1996).
RD	Richard of Devizes, *Chronicle*, ed. and tr. J. T. Appleby (London, 1963).
RHC	*Recueil des historiens des croisades* (Paris, 1841–1906).
RH, *Chronica*	Roger of Howden, *Chronica*, ed. W. Stubbs, 4 vols (RS, London, 1868–71).
RH, *Gesta*	Roger of Howden, *Gesta Henrici II et Ricardi I*, ed. W. Stubbs, 2 vols (RS, London, 1867).
RR	Robert of Reims, 'Historia Iherosolimitana', in *RHC, Historiens occidentaux*, vol. 3, tr. C. Sweetenham as *Robert the Monk's History of the First Crusade* (Aldershot, 2005).
Rothelin	Rothelin, 'Continuation de Guillaume de Tyr de 1229 à 1261, dite du manuscrit de Rothelin', in *RHC, Historiens occidentaux*, vol. 2, tr. J. Shirley as *Crusader Syria in the Thirteenth Century* (Aldershot, 1999).
RS	Rolls Series
Rutebeuf	Rutebeuf, *Oeuvres complètes*, ed. E. Faral and J. Bastin (Paris, 1959).
SCH	Studies in Church History.
TRHS	*Transactions of the Royal Historical Society.*
Villehardouin	Geoffrey of Villehardouin, *La Conquête de Constantinople*, ed. and French tr. E. Faral, 2 vols (Paris, 1973), English tr. M. R. B. Shaw as *Joinville & Villehardouin: Chronicles of the Crusades* (Harmondsworth, 1963).

NOTES

1. Crusading in the East, 1095–1291

1. For more detailed accounts of crusading in the East see J. Riley Smith, *The Crusades: A History*, 2nd edn (London and New York, 2005); H. E. Mayer, *The Crusades*, 2nd edn (Oxford, 1988); J. Richard, *The Crusades, c. 1071–c. 1291* (Cambridge, 1999); K. M. Setton, ed., *A History of the Crusades*, 2nd edn, 6 vols (Madison, WI, 1969–89). The classic study by S. Runciman, *A History of the Crusades*, 3 vols (Cambridge, 1951–4) is very readable but shows its age now. The fullest recent treatment is C. Tyerman, *God's War: A New History of the Crusades* (London, 2006).

2. The call to crusade

1. PA, p. 111.
2. Maier, pp. 108–9.
3. Ibid., pp. 106 7.
4. Bédier and Aubry, p. 22.
5. J. Le Goff, *The Birth of Purgatory*, tr. A. Goldhammer (London, 1984).
6. Bédier and Aubry, p. 297.
7. OV, bk 8, ch. 17, 4.236–51.
8. R. Bartlett, *England under the Norman and Angevin Kings, 1075–1225* (Oxford, 2000), pp. 604–7, incl. fig. 15.
9. Generally see C. S. Watkins, 'Sin, penance and Purgatory in the Anglo-Norman realm: the evidence of visions and ghost stories', *Past & Present*, 175 (2002), 3–33.
10. A point stressed by M. Bull, *Knightly Piety and the Lay Response to the First Crusade: The Limousin and Gascony, c. 970–c. 1130* (Oxford, 1993), pp. 196–201. This and similar comments are evidence that the road-show witnessed by Walchelin was from the embryonic Purgatory rather than Hell.
11. B. Hamilton, *Religion in the Medieval West* (London, 1986), chs 12–13.
12. AA, bk 1, ch. 22, pp. 44–5; S. Schein, *Gateway to the Heavenly City: Crusader Jerusalem and the Catholic West (1099–1187)* (Aldershot, 2005), p. 22.
13. 'Epistolae Sugerii', in *Recueil des historiens des Gaules et de la France*, 24 vols (Paris, 1737–1904), 15.483–532, no. 13, p. 488, no. 19, p. 491, no. 62, p. 507.
14. PA, p. 69. Cf. R. Hiestand, ' "Precipua tocius christianismi columpna": Barbarossa und der Kreuzzug', in A. Haverkamp, ed., *Handlungsspielräume und Wirkungsweisen des staufischen Kaisers* (Sigmaringen, 1992), pp. 51–108, at pp. 102–3.
15. Andrea, p. 106.
16. Joinville, chs 5, 735 (*pelerinage de la croix*).

17. Maier, pp. 210–11.
18. Ibid., pp. 106–7.
19. Ibid., pp. 212–13 (Humbert of Romans).
20. *De expugnatione*, pp. 72–3.
21. PA, p. 23.
22. J. Riley-Smith, *The Crusades: A History*, 2nd edn (London and New York, 2005), pp. 149–50.
23. Maier, pp. 136–7, 204–7; K. J. Brahney, ed., *The Lyrics of Thibaut de Champagne* (New York, 1989), pp. 226–7, 234–5; Rutebeuf, pp. 463, 473–4, 508.
24. 'Ordinacio', p. 4.
25. Odo of Châteauroux: P. Cole, *The Preaching of the Crusades to the Holy Land, 1095–1270* (Cambridge, MA, 1991), p. 181.
26. This was true of those who took the cross for the East: the crusading movement was exceptionally broad-based geographically. See N. Housley, *Contesting the Crusades* (Oxford, 2006), ch. 1.
27. PA, p. 1; Peter of Blois, 'Passio Reginaldi principis olim Antiocheni', in *PL*, 207.957–76, at col. 958. See also Y.-M.-J. Congar, 'Église et cité de Dieu chez quelques auteurs cisterciens à l'époque des croisades', in *Mélanges offerts à Étienne Gilson* (Toronto, 1959), 173–202, esp. pp. 191–2.
28. C. Morris, *The Sepulchre of Christ and the Medieval West, from the Beginning to 1600* (Oxford, 2005), ch. 2.
29. RH, *Chronica*, 3.131.
30. A. Linder, 'The liturgy of the liberation of Jerusalem', *Mediaeval Studies* 52 (1990), 110–31.
31. E.g. Bédier and Aubry, p. 297.
32. *IP*, bk 1, ch. 17, tr. p. 47.
33. 'De expugnatione Terrae Sanctae per Saladinum, libellus', in *Radulphi de Coggeshall Chronicon Anglicanum*, ed. J. Stevenson (RS, London, 1875), 209–62, at p. 226.
34. AA, bk 6, ch. 28, pp. 438–9.
35. N. Jaspert, 'Zwei unbekannte Hilfsersuchen des Patriarchen Eraclius vor dem Fall Jerusalems (1187)', *Deutsches Archiv für Erforschung des Mittelalters* 60 (2004), 483–516, at pp. 515–16.
36. Rothelin, ch. 41, tr. p. 64.
37. MP, 4.337–44, tr. 1.522–8.
38. Ibid., 5.3–5, tr. 2.253–4.
39. Ibid., 4.456–62, tr. 2.86–91.
40. Ibid., 4.502–3, tr. 2.127–8.
41. Ibid., 4.489, tr. 2.117.
42. Ibid., 5.427, tr. 2.452. See also M. Barber, 'The crusade of the shepherds in 1251', in J. F. Sweets, ed., *Proceedings of the Tenth Annual Meeting of the Western Society for French History* (Lawrence, KS, 1984), 1–23; W. C. Jordan, *Louis IX and the Challenge of the Crusade: A Study in Rulership* (Princeton, NJ, 1979), pp. 113–16; G. Dickson, *The Children's Crusade: Medieval History and Modern Mythistory* (Basingstoke, 2008), pp. 147–51.
43. MP, 5.249, tr. 2.453.
44. Barber, 'Crusade', p. 10.
45. GW, bk 2, ch. 13, tr. p. 204.
46. Cf. Henry of Albano in Germany a few months earlier: PA, p. 10.
47. GW, bk 1, ch. 11, tr. p. 141; Gerald of Wales, 'De rebus a se gestis', in J. S. Brewer, ed., *Giraldi Cambrensis Opera*, vol. 1 (RS, London, 1861), 1–122, at pp. 75–6. See also P. W. Edbury, 'Preaching the crusade in Wales', in A. Haverkamp and H. Vollrath, eds, *England and Germany in the High Middle Ages* (Oxford, 1996), 221–33, at p. 224.

48. GW, bk 1, chs 2, 4–8, bk 2, chs 2, 4, 6, 7, 10, 12, tr. pp. 80, 109, 114, 121, 126, 132, 172, 178, 184, 186, 196, 202.
49. Ibid., bk 2, ch. 13, tr. p. 204.
50. Peter of Blois, 'De Hierosolymitana peregrinatione acceleranda', in *PL*, 207.1057–70, at col. 1057.
51. Edbury, 'Preaching', p. 232.
52. J. Riley-Smith, *The First Crusaders, 1095–1131* (Cambridge, 1997), pp. 75–6.
53. C. T. Maier, *Preaching the Crusades: Mendicant Friars and the Cross in the Thirteenth Century* (Cambridge, 1994).
54. BC, no. 391, pp. 460–3.
55. Bédier and Aubry, p. 21 (I've used the translation by Schein, *Gateway*, pp. 122–3).
56. Maier, pp. 118–19.
57. Ibid., pp. 114–15.
58. Ibid., pp. 220–1.
59. Maier, *Preaching*, p. 122.
60. GW, bk 1, ch. 2, tr. p. 80.
61. Brahney, ed., *Lyrics*, pp. 226–7.
62. GW, bk 2, ch. 6, tr. p. 185.
63. *IP*, bk 1, ch. 17, tr. p. 48.
64. GW, bk 2, ch. 2, tr. p. 172.
65. Edbury, 'Preaching', p. 227.
66. Gerald of Wales, 'De rebus', p. 75.
67. GW, bk 2, ch. 7, tr. p. 186.
68. Ibid., bk 2, ch. 12, tr. p. 201.
69. BC, no. 391, pp. 460–3.
70. Peter of Blois, 'De Hierosolymitana', col. 1059.
71. Andrea, pp. 12–13. The Spanish were included in the list of humiliated nations because of Castile's disastrous defeat at Alarcos in 1195.
72. *IP*, bk 1, ch. 5, tr. p. 33 and cf. A. Murray, 'Mighty against the enemies of Christ: the relic of the True Cross in the armies of the kingdom of Jerusalem', in *CSEPBH*, 217 38, at p. 225.
73. G. Dickson, 'The genesis of the Children's Crusade (1212)', in his *Religious Enthusiasm in the Medieval West: Revivals, Crusades, Saints* (Aldershot, 2000), study IV, p. 36.
74. *Audita tremendi*, the bull proclaiming the Third Crusade in 1187, is unusual in containing a fairly detailed description of the battle of Hattin, presumably because this was so catastrophic an event that it demanded such treatment.
75. Baha' al-Din, tr. p. 125. For context see C. Morris, 'Picturing the crusades: the uses of visual propaganda, c. 1095–1250', in *CSEPBH*, 195–216, esp. p. 197.
76. Maier, pp. 126–7 and see too pp. 56–7, 98–9.
77. Bédier and Aubry, p. 8 (God's fiefs), p. 10 (tournament, vengeance), pp. 20–1 (God's lordship), p. 33 (shame), p. 34 (God's inheritance), p. 71 (God's land), p. 79 (vengeance). Crusade as tournament recurs ibid., p. 290.
78. For what follows see Cole, *Preaching*; Maier, *Preaching*; S. Lloyd, *English Society and the Crusade, 1216–1307* (Oxford, 1988), chs 1–2; A. Linder, *Raising Arms: Liturgy in the Struggle to Liberate Jerusalem in the Late Middle Ages* (Turnhout, 2003).
79. 'Ordinacio', pp. 24–5. See too RH, *Gesta*, 2.22.
80. 'Ordinacio', p. 12.
81. Maier, *Preaching*, p. 118.
82. E.g. ibid., pp. 121–2.
83. It's notable how many people claimed to have heard Urban preach, though there's always the danger that they did this to strengthen an argument: E. Siberry, *Criticism of Crusading, 1095–1274* (Oxford, 1985), pp. 39–40.

84. Riley-Smith, *First Crusaders*, pp. 56–60.
85. GN, bk 2, ch. 8, tr. p. 48.
86. J. Flori, *Pierre l'Ermite et la première croisade* (Paris, 1999).
87. G. Constable, 'The Second Crusade as seen by contemporaries', *Traditio* 9 (1953), 213–79, at pp. 244–7 (emphasizing the importance of the saint's letters about the crusade), and pp. 276–8.
88. OD, bk 1, tr. pp. 8–9.
89. BC, no. 323, p. 399.
90. S. Runciman, *A History of the Crusades*, 3 vols (Cambridge, 1951–4), 2.256.
91. Villehardouin, chs 1–2, tr. p. 29.
92. Ralph of Coggeshall, 'Chronicon Anglicanum', in J. Stevenson, ed., *Radulphi de Coggeshall Chronicon Anglicanum* (RS, London, 1875), 1–208, at p. 83 (I've used the translation by Cole, *Preaching*, p. 91).
93. M. R. Gutsch, 'A twelfth-century preacher – Fulk of Neuilly', in L. J. Paetow, ed., *The Crusades and Other Historical Essays* (repr. Freeport, NY, 1928), pp. 183–206.
94. OP, ch. 9, tr. p. 60.
95. Le Goff, *Birth*, p. 298.
96. Huygens, p. 77.
97. Ibid., pp. 92–3.
98. P. Cole, D. L. d'Avray and J. Riley-Smith, 'Application of theology to current affairs: memorial sermons on the dead of Mansurah and on Innocent IV', *Historical Research* 63 (1990), 227–47.
99. A. Linder, 'The loss of Christian Jerusalem in late medieval liturgy', in L. I. Levine, ed., *Jerusalem: Its Sanctity and Centrality to Judaism, Christianity, and Islam* (New York, 1999), 393–407, at pp. 404–5.
100. Maier, pp. 96–7 (James of Vitry).
101. Ibid., pp. 196–7.
102. Rutebeuf, pp. 470–8, 'La disputaison du croisé et du décroisé'.
103. There are strong echoes in Odo of Châteauroux's model sermons: Maier, pp. 136–7, 140–1.
104. Ibid., pp. 194–5 (Gilbert of Tournai).
105. Cole, *Preaching*, pp. 147–8.
106. Borrelli de Serres, 'Compte d'une mission de prédication pour secours à la Terre Sainte (1265)', *Mémoires de la Société de l'histoire de Paris et de l'Île-de-France* 30 (1903), 243–61.
107. Cole, *Preaching*, pp. 192–3.
108. Rutebeuf, pp. 428, 475, 504.
109. Cole, *Preaching*, p. 202.
110. Ibid., pp. 34–6, 55, 91.
111. Ibid., pp. 91, 148.
112. *IP*, bk 1, ch. 17, tr. p. 48, and cf. PA, p. 15.
113. Bédier and Aubry, p. 34.
114. J. H. and L. L. Hill, *Raymond IV Count of Toulouse* (Syracuse, NY, 1962). On the *fideles S. Petri* see Riley-Smith, *First Crusaders*, pp. 44–7.
115. Riley-Smith, *First Crusaders*, pp. 156–7.
116. B. S. Bachrach, *Fulk Nerra, the Neo-Roman Consul, 987–1040: A Political Biography of the Angevin Count* (Berkeley, CA, 1993), p. 248.
117. GW, bk 1, ch. 5, tr. p. 114, and cf. bk 1, ch. 10, tr. p. 140 on the twelve murderous archers of St Clears.
118. Joinville, chs 277–8, tr. p. 234.
119. See Bull, *Knightly Piety*, passim.
120. Lyon Continuation, ch. 77, tr. p. 79.

121. The evidence is reviewed in C. Smith, *Crusading in the Age of Joinville* (Aldershot, 2006), pp. 57–8.
122. E.g. G. Constable, 'Medieval charters as a source for the history of the crusades', in P. W. Edbury, cd., *Crusade and Settlement* (Cardiff, 1985), 73–89, at p. 76.
123. Maier, p. 113, and cf. p. 165 (Odo of Châteauroux).
124. Bull, *Knightly Piety*, p. 186 and ch. 4 passim.
125. Joinville, ch. 733, tr. p. 345.
126. Riley-Smith, *First Crusaders*, p. 88.
127. Ibid., p. 87; Lloyd, *English Society*, p. 80.
128. J. A. Brundage, 'A note on the attestation of crusaders' vows', *Catholic Historical Review* 52 (1966), 234–9.
129. A. Gottlob, *Kreuzablass und Almosenablass* (Stuttgart, 1906), p. 308.
130. *GF*, pp. 89–90.
131. E.g. Morris, *Sepulchre*, p. 178 (a good early example); M. Phillips, 'The thief's cross: crusade and penance in Alan of Lille's *Sermo de cruce domini*', *Crusades* 5 (2006), 143–56, at p. 148; *GF*, p. 2 (though cf. p. 7, *in dextra vel inter utrasque scapulas*).
132. *GF*, p. 7.
133. Morris, *Sepulchre*, p. 202.
134. N. Kenaan-Kedar and B. Z. Kedar, 'The significance of a twelfth-century sculptural group: le retour du croisé', in M. Balard, B. Z. Kedar and J. Riley-Smith, eds, *Dei gesta per Francos: Études sur les croisades dédiées à Jean Richard* (Aldershot, 2001), pp. 29–44.
135. *CIR*, pp. 136–9. See also J. A. Brundage, *Medieval Canon Law and the Crusader* (Madison, WI, 1969), p. 120 and frontispiece illustration.
136. *CIR*, p. 139.
137. Huygens, p. 100.
138. FC, bk 1, ch. 4, tr. p. 68.
139. M. G. Pegg, *The Corruption of Angels: The Great Inquisition of 1245–1246* (Princeton, NJ, 2001), pp. 126–30.
140. Maier, pp. 180–1.
141. Ibid., pp. 124–5.
142. RA, ch. 14, tr. p. 214.
143. Maier, pp. 66, 172–3.
144. Hagenmeyer, p. 142, tr. p. 132.
145. Maier, pp. 200–1.
146. Ibid., pp. 122–3 (James of Vitry), 196–7 (Gilbert of Tournai).
147. Dickson, *Children's Crusade*, pp. 121–3.
148. Brundage, *Medieval Canon Law*, pp. 104–5.
149. Maier, *Preaching*, pp. 141–50.
150. *IP*, bk 2, ch. 4, tr. p. 144 (referring to Henry II, whose failure to keep his vow became notorious).
151. 'Historia', p. 169.
152. Brundage, *Medieval Canon Law*, p. 130.
153. H. E. Salter, ed., *Eynsham Cartulary*, 2 vols (Oxford, 1907–8), pp. 338–9.
154. Constable, 'Second Crusade', p. 269 and n. 288.

3. Signed with the cross

1. 'Epistolae Sugerii', no. 68, p. 509, and cf. PA, p. 5.
2. Peter of Blois, 'De Hierosolymitana', col. 1070, and see also R. W. Southern, 'Peter of Blois and the Third Crusade', in H. Mayr-Harting and R. I. Moore, eds, *Studies in Medieval History Presented to R. H. C. Davis* (London, 1985), pp. 207–18.

3. MP, 3.615, tr. 1.235.
4. GN, bk 2, tr. p. 47.
5. J. Riley-Smith, *The Knights of St John in Jerusalem and Cyprus, c. 1050–1310* (London, 1967), pp. 34–7.
6. E. Joranson, 'The great German pilgrimage of 1064–1065', in L. J. Paetow, ed., *The Crusades and Other Historical Essays* (repr. Freeport, NY, 1928), pp. 3–43.
7. FC, bk 1, ch. 6, first redaction (= *RHC, Historiens occidentaux*, 3.328 n. 19): *quod si vixerit, infra tres annos ad eam repatriabit*, i.e. including the return journey. Cf. A. Murray, 'Money and logistics in the forces of the First Crusade', in *LWAC*, 229–49, at p. 230; J. H. Pryor, 'Digest', ibid., 275–92, at p. 285.
8. OD, bk 2, pp. 28–30 (my translation).
9. Ibid., pp. 24–5.
10. Ibid., bk 5, pp. 94–5.
11. F. Hausmann, ed., *Die Urkunden Konrads III. und seines Sohnes Heinrich* (Vienna, 1969), no. 195, p. 354.
12. 'Historia', p. 126, and cf. Hiestand, ' "Precipua" ', p. 86; Murray, 'Money', pp. 231–2; Lloyd, *English Society*, p. 78. Other sources vary, but all specify either a sum or a period of time for which provision had to be made.
13. MP, 3.620, tr. 1.239.
14. Brundage, *Medieval Canon Law*, pp. 160–75.
15. Murray, 'Money', pp. 235–9 (though it's hard to see what Urban could have done to help matters).
16. PA, p. 17.
17. Brundage, *Medieval Canon Law*, ch. 6 passim.
18. Huygens, p. 74.
19. Brundage, *Medieval Canon Law*, pp. 176, 181, 184.
20. RH, *Gesta*, 2.32.
21. Brundage, *Medieval Canon Law*, p. 183.
22. C. Tyerman, *England and the Crusades, 1095–1588* (Chicago, 1988), pp. 196–7.
23. C. Marshall, *Warfare in the Latin East, 1192–1291* (Cambridge, 1992), pp. 74–5.
24. C. Tyerman, 'Who went on crusades to the Holy Land?', in B. Z. Kedar, ed., *The Horns of Hattin* (Jerusalem, 1992), pp. 13–26.
25. J. France, 'Patronage and the appeal of the First Crusade', in *FCOI*, 5–20.
26. GW, bk 2, ch. 5, tr. pp. 182–3.
27. J. Riley-Smith, 'The motives of the earliest crusaders and the settlement of Latin Palestine, 1095–1100', *EHR* 98 (1983), 721–36.
28. D. Crouch, *The Birth of Nobility: Constructing Aristocracy in England and France 900–1300* (Harlow, 2005), ch. 4.
29. G. Constable, 'The financing of the crusades in the twelfth century', in *Outremer*, pp. 64–88, at p. 87.
30. Riley-Smith, *First Crusaders*, p. 111.
31. GN, bk 2, tr. p. 46.
32. R. L. Crocker, 'Early crusade songs', in T. P. Murphy, ed., *The Holy War* (Columbus, OH, 1976), pp. 78–98, at p. 83.
33. J. Riley-Smith, *The First Crusade and the Idea of Crusading* (London, 1986), p. 43.
34. P. Spufford, *Money and its Use in Medieval Europe* (Cambridge, 1988), p. 98.
35. Murray, 'Money', pp. 240–1.
36. Riley-Smith, *First Crusaders*, pp. 125–6.
37. Constable, 'Financing', p. 67.
38. Spufford, *Money*, p. 99.
39. Andrea, p. 247.
40. Constable, 'Financing', p. 72.

41. Ibid., p. 86.
42. Riley-Smith, *First Crusaders*, pp. 114–15.
43. William of Newburgh, 'Historia rerum anglicarum', in R. Howlett, ed., *Chronicles of the Reigns of Stephen, Henry II, and Richard I*, 2 vols (RS, London, 1884–5), 1.306.
44. J. Gillingham, *Richard I* (New Haven, CT, 1999), pp. 117–22, surveys the issues.
45. RH, *Gesta*, 2.90; I've used the translation by Gillingham, *Richard I*, p. 117.
46. R. C. Stacey, 'Crusades, martyrdoms, and the Jews of Norman England, 1096–1190', in A. Haverkamp, ed., *Juden und Christen zur Zeit der Kreuzzüge* (Sigmaringen, 1999), 233–51, at p. 250.
47. PA, p. 98.
48. *IP*, bk 2, ch. 3, tr. p. 143.
49. Tyerman, *England*, pp. 82–3.
50. Ibid., pp. 80–1.
51. D. E. Queller and T. F. Madden, *The Fourth Crusade: The Conquest of Constantinople*, 2nd edn (Philadelphia, PA, 1997), pp. 11–12, pointing out that comparisons with other contracts from a few years previously reveal only minor differences.
52. Gillingham, *Richard I*, p. 129.
53. Joinville, ch. 109, tr. p. 191; MP, 5.93, tr. 2.323; Jordan, *Louis IX*, pp. 70–7.
54. M. Purcell, *Papal Crusading Policy, 1244–1291* (Leiden, 1975), pp. 55–6.
55. Huygens, p. 100.
56. The crusade's leading historian has suggested that this formed part of Pope Innocent III's strategic thinking: J. M. Powell, *Anatomy of a Crusade 1213–1221* (Philadelphia, PA, 1986), p. 92.
57. RH, *Gesta*, 2.104–5.
58. Gillingham, *Richard I*, ch. 13.
59. 'Epistolae Sugerii', no. 66, pp. 508, no. 69, pp. 509–10.
60. K. Jordan, *Henry the Lion: A Biography*, tr. P. S. Falla (Oxford, 1986), p. 188.
61. J. Richard, *Saint Louis: Crusader King of France*, tr. J. Birrell (Cambridge, 1983), pp. 316–17, 330–1.
62. C. Dyer, *Making a Living in the Middle Ages: The People of Britain, 850–1520* (New Haven, CT, 2002), p. 148.
63. W. C. Jordan, ' "Amen!" Cinq fois "Amen!". Les chansons de la croisade égyptienne de saint Louis, une source négligée d'opinion royaliste', *Médiévales* 34 (1998), pp. 79–91, at pp. 82, 89.
64. RH, *Gesta*, 2.31–2. Cf. Bartlett, *England*, p. 167; Gillingham, *Richard I*, p. 89.
65. RH, *Gesta*, 2.59.
66. Bédier and Aubry, pp. 45–6.
67. Cf. Hiestand, ' "Precipua" ', p. 86: 'erstaunlich wenig erfährt man über die nicht minder wichtige Frage der Finanzierung des Kreuzzuges'.
68. RD, pp. 47–8.
69. Purcell, *Papal Crusading Policy*, pp. 197–8; Riley-Smith, *Crusades*, pp. 212–13.
70. Jordan, *Louis IX*, ch. 4 passim.
71. W. E. Lunt, ed., *Papal Revenues in the Middle Ages*, 2 vols (New York, 1934); Spufford, *Money*, ch. 11.
72. Peter the Venerable, *Letters*, ed. G. Constable, 2 vols (Cambridge, MA, 1967), no. 130, 1.327–30.
73. Jordan, *Louis IX*, pp. 85–6.
74. Lloyd, *English Society*, esp. ch. 5; Tyerman, *England*, ch. 8.
75. For this and other specified examples see Lloyd, *English Society*, pp. 81, 149, 167–8, 183.
76. Cole, *Preaching*, pp. 205–6.
77. *CIR*, pp. 58–9.

78. RH, *Gesta*, 2.32.
79. *IP*, bk 2, ch. 13, p. 157.
80. Purcell, *Papal Crusading Policy*, p. 188.
81. Joinville, ch. 110, tr. p. 192.
82. Maier, pp. 174–5 (Odo of Châteauroux).
83. Constable, 'Medieval charters', p. 82.
84. Joinville, ch. 111, tr. p. 192.
85. Jordan, *Louis IX*, pp. 53–63.
86. Riley-Smith, *First Crusaders*, pp. 120–1.
87. Ibid., p. 118.
88. Ibid., pp. 119–20.
89. Linder, 'Loss', p. 404, and for the next four paragraphs see his *Raising Arms*, passim.
90. P. Geary, 'Humiliation of saints', in S. Wilson, ed., *Saints and their Cults* (Cambridge, 1983), pp. 123–40.
91. Linder, 'Loss', passim.
92. RH, *Chronica*, 3.23. Cf. RD, p. 73.
93. Huygens, pp. 109–11, and cf. ibid., p. 130.
94. Cf. Linder, 'Loss', p. 404.
95. *CIR*, pp. 123–4.
96. Ibid., p. 64.
97. A. Linder, '*Deus venerunt gentes*. Psalm 78 (79) in the liturgical commemoration of the destruction of Latin Jerusalem', in B.-S. Albert, Y. Friedman and S. Schwarzfuchs, eds, *Medieval Studies in Honour of Avrom Saltman* (Ramat-Gan, 1995), 145–71, esp. pp. 153–5.
98. Joinville, chs 120–2, tr. p. 195.
99. J. Le Goff, *Saint Louis* (Paris, 1996), pp. 184–6.
100. OD, bk 1, tr. pp. 16–18.
101. Maier, pp. 158–9 (Odo of Châteauroux).
102. Ibid., pp. 98–9 (James of Vitry).
103. Ibid., pp. 158–9, and cf. Peter the Venerable, *Letters*, 1.327, no. 130: 'devotione, oratione, consilio et auxilio'.
104. FC, bk 1, ch. 6, tr. p. 74.
105. C. T. Maier, 'The roles of women in the crusade movement: a survey', *JMH* 30 (2004), 61–82, at pp. 77–8.
106. *De expugnatione*, pp. 70–3.
107. OD, bk 1, pp. 18–19.
108. C. T. Maier, 'The *bible moralisée* and the crusades', in *ECWA*, 209–22, at pp. 212–16.
109. Maier, pp. 202–3 (Gilbert of Tournai).
110. *IP*, bk 2, chs 6–7, tr. pp. 148, 150.
111. Bédier and Aubry, p. 290.
112. Villehardouin, ch. 47, tr. p. 40.
113. Joinville, ch. 122, tr. p. 195.
114. Maier, pp. 98–9, 188–91.
115. *IP*, bk 1, ch. 17, tr. p. 48.
116. GW, bk 1, ch. 4, tr. p. 109.
117. M. Routledge, 'Songs', in J. Riley-Smith, ed., *The Oxford Illustrated History of the Crusades* (Oxford, 1995), pp. 91–111, at p. 99.
118. Bédier and Aubry, p. 113; I've used the translation by Routledge, 'Songs', pp. 102–3.
119. Bédier and Aubry, p. 32 (replicated by the castellan of Arras, ibid., p. 138), and cf. Crocker, 'Early crusade songs', pp. 84–5.
120. Bédier and Aubry, p. 33.
121. Ibid., pp. 284–5.

122. Brahney, ed., *Lyrics*, p. xxviii, and cf. M. Lower, *The Barons' Crusade: A Call to Arms and its Consequences* (Philadelphia, PA, 2005), p. 112.
123. Brahney, ed., *Lyrics*, pp. 230–1.
124. Ibid., pp. 234–5. There was a polemical edge here, because as noted above Pope Gregory IX had attempted to divert Thibald's crusade to Constantinople: Lower, *The Barons' Crusade*, pp. 112–14.
125. Brahney, ed., *Lyrics*, pp. 230–3.
126. Ibid., pp. 232–3. On Thibald's lyrics see also W. C. Jordan, 'The representation of the crusades in the songs attributed to Thibaud, count palatine of Champagne', *JMH* 25 (1999), pp. 27–34.
127. Bédier and Aubry, p. 9 (Louis VII and the Second Crusade).
128. Smith, *Crusading*, p. 65, points out that the 'separation motif' is also to be found in *The Song of Roland*.

4. Eastward bound

1. Marshall, *Warfare*, p. 26.
2. FC, bk 2, ch. 51, tr. p. 209. See also Riley-Smith, *Crusades*, pp. 112–16.
3. GW, bk 1, ch. 1, tr. pp. 77–8.
4. J. Sumption, *Pilgrimage: An Image of Medieval Religion* (London, 1975), ch. 11.
5. Hagenmeyer, pp. 136–7, tr. *CIR*, p. 38.
6. Andrea, p. 14; *CIR*, p. 125.
7. *CIR*, p. 125.
8. Siberry, *Criticism*, pp. 53–62.
9. Peter of Blois, 'Passio', col. 958, and see Southern, 'Peter of Blois', passim.
10. 'Historia', p. 126.
11. Villehardouin, ch. 57, tr. p. 42.
12. Baha' al-Din, tr. pp. 232–3, and see also Gillingham, *Richard I*, p. 220.
13. M. Hoch, 'The choice of Damascus as the objective of the Second Crusade', in *APC*, 359–70.
14. Huygens, p. 102.
15. Edbury, p. 181.
16. E.g. 'Gesta cruc.', p. 42.
17. E.g. OD, bk 7, pp. 130–3, on the debate at Adalia.
18. Riley-Smith, *First Crusaders*, p. 108.
19. B. S. Bachrach, 'Crusader logistics: from victory at Nicaea to resupply at Dorylaion', in *LWAC*, 43–62, at pp. 52–3.
20. R. Gertwagen, 'Harbours and facilities along the eastern Mediterranean sea lanes to *Outremer*', in *LWAC*, 95–118, at pp. 95–6.
21. *IP*, bk 1, ch. 20, tr. p. 55.
22. PA, p. 24.
23. Lyon Continuation, ch. 96, tr. p. 89.
24. Hiestand, ' "Precipua" ', pp. 75–6.
25. For the next two paragraphs see Joinville, chs 617–51, tr. pp. 318–27.
26. For similar vows see Constable, 'Financing', p. 82.
27. A well-contained fire was always kept lit in the hold.
28. RH, *Gesta*, 2.142.
29. 'Gesta cruc.', p. 38.
30. RH, *Gesta*, 2.116.
31. Huygens, p. 82.
32. Ibid., p. 78.
33. Cole, *Preaching*, p. 210.

34. B. Z. Kedar, 'The passenger list of a crusader ship, 1250: towards the history of the popular element on the Seventh Crusade', *Studi medievali*, 3rd ser. 13 (1972), 267–79, at pp. 269–70.

35. G. Hutchinson, *Medieval Ships and Shipping* (London, 1994), pp. 10, 16, 69–70, 73, 77–9, 82–3 has useful figures on length and beam, and see p. 54 for a telling illustration of the congestion.

36. A. L. Foulet, ed., *Lettres françaises du xiiie siècle: Jean Sarrasin, lettre à Nicolas Arrode (1249)* (Paris, 1924), para. x, p. 5.

37. Lloyd, *English Society*, pp. 78–9.

38. J. A. Mol, 'Frisian fighters and the crusade', *Crusades* 1 (2002), 89–110, at p. 95.

39. Cole, *Preaching*, p. 210.

40. Huygens, p. 78.

41. Brocardus, 'Directorium ad passagium faciendum', in *RHC, Documents arméniens*, vol. 2, 365–517, at p. 412.

42. Ibid., p. 414.

43. *IP*, bk 2, ch. 33, tr. p. 186; Gertwagen, 'Harbours', pp. 99–100; Pryor, 'Digest', p. 290. Joinville (ch. 125, tr. p. 196) graphically describes the caulking of the door used for equine embarkation, confining them to the hold until the next landfall.

44. Gertwagen, 'Harbours', passim.

45. B. Z. Kedar, 'Reflections on maps, crusading, and logistics', in *LWAC*, 159–83, at p. 179.

46. PA, pp. 96–7.

47. Rothelin, ch. 20, tr. p. 39.

48. Pryor, 'Digest', esp. pp. 288–9.

49. 'Narratio', p. 610 (= Chroust, p. 179).

50. R. W. Unger, 'The northern crusaders: the logistics of English and other northern crusader fleets', in *LWAC*, 251–73; J. H. Pryor, *Geography, Technology, and War: Studies in the Maritime History of the Mediterranean, 649–1571* (Cambridge, 1988), chs 1–3.

51. A. Forey, 'Cyprus as a base for crusading expeditions from the west', in N. Coureas and J. Riley-Smith, eds, *Cyprus and the Crusades* (Nicosia, 1995), pp. 69–70.

52. *IP*, bk 2, ch. 38, tr. p. 192, and cf. bk 2, ch. 42, p. 196 on the supply of essential foodstuffs.

53. J. France, *Victory in the East: A Military History of the First Crusade* (Cambridge, 1994), pp. 190–6.

54. Runciman, *History*, 2.21–4; Riley-Smith, *First Crusade*, pp. 129–30.

55. P. Jackson, ed. and tr., *The Mission of Friar William of Rubruck* (London, 1990), p. 278; it's hard to account for William's hostility towards Hungary in this passage.

56. 'Narratio', p. 636 (= Chroust, p. 193).

57. E.g. 'Narratio', p. 632 (= Chroust, p. 192).

58. Andrea, pp. 98–115.

59. Pryor, 'Digest', p. 279.

60. E.g. AA, bk 2, ch. 6, pp. 68–71.

61. Pryor, 'Digest', pp. 282, 287.

62. OD, bk 2, pp. 30–1, and cf. 'Epistolae Sugerii', no. 12, p. 487.

63. RA, ch. 1, tr. pp. 64–5; Hills, *Raymond IV*, p. 45.

64. *GF*, p. 23.

65. France, *Victory*, p. 186.

66. *GF*, p. 27.

67. Riley-Smith, *First Crusade*, pp. 129–31.

68. See Conrad III's succinct letter to Wibald reporting events, Hausmann, ed., *Die Urkunden*, no. 195, pp. 354–5.

69. 'Epistolae Sugerii', no. 36, pp. 495–6.

70. Ibid., p. 496.

71. OD, bk 6, pp. 118–19.

72. C. R. Glasheen, 'Provisioning Peter the Hermit: from Cologne to Constantinople, 1096', in *LWAC*, 119–29, at p. 121; J. Haldon, 'Roads and communications in the Byzantine empire: wagons, horses and supplies', ibid., 131–58, at p. 143; France, *Victory*, p. 171.

73. *GF*, pp. 11–12.

74. FC, bk 1, ch. 9, tr. p. 80.

75. Hagenmeyer, p. 145, tr. p. 130.

76. OD, bk 7, pp. 124–5.

77. Ibid., pp. 128–43 for the whole sequence of events.

78. PA, pp. 85–6 reels off the list of his conquests in Europe.

79. E.g. 'Historia', pp. 128, 131–2.

80. PA, p. 26.

81. Ibid., pp. 31, 57, 59; 'Historia', pp. 135, 149.

82. PA, p. 43.

83. Ibid., p. 71.

84. Ibid., p. 77; 'Epistola', pp. 174–6; 'Historia', p. 161.

85. 'Historia', p. 167.

86. Baha' al-Din, tr. pp. 115–16.

87. PA, p. 92.

88. Ibid., pp. 92–3: 'if you had seen the deaths that occurred there [at Acre] you would have believed that humankind had reached its end'.

89. E. N. Johnson, 'The crusades of Frederick Barbarossa and Henry VI', in *IIC*, 2. 87–122, at p. 92, 114.

90. Baha' al-Din, tr. p. 117, and cf. p. 126 on the horses.

91. Ibid., tr. p. 126.

92. It may not be coincidence that the first recorded use of the word *crucesignati* as a noun occurs in a passage describing the crusaders massacring Jews: AA, bk 1, ch. 26, tr. pp. 50–1.

93. R. Chazan, *European Jewry and the First Crusade* (Berkeley, CA, 1987), p. 248.

94. AA, bk 1, ch. 29, pp. 56–9. For Ekkehard see A. C. Krey, ed. and tr., *The First Crusade: The Accounts of Eye-Witnesses and Participants* (repr. Gloucester, MA, 1958), p. 53.

95. On all this see Chazan, *European Jewry*, passim; usefully summarized in idem, *The Jews of Medieval Western Christendom, 1000–1500* (Cambridge, 2006), pp. 74, 179–81, 186, 245, 280.

96. We have no first-hand sources for Rudolf's preaching, but see the account by Rabbi Ephraim of Bonn, in S. Eidelberg, ed. and tr., *The Jews and the Crusaders: The Hebrew Chronicle of the First and Second Crusades* (Madison, WI, 1977), pp. 121–2.

97. Chazan, *European Jewry*, p. 170, quoting Ephraim of Bonn, but concluding (p. 172) that Jewish losses were few.

98. William of Newburgh, 'Historia', 1.310.

99. Ibid., 1.311.

100. BC, no. 393, p. 466.

101. Bartlett, *England*, pp. 358–9.

102. Notoriously advocated by Peter the Venerable in 1146: *Letters*, ed. Constable, no. 30, 1.328–30.

103. Chazan, *The Jews*, p. 68 (Innocent III).

104. Maier, pp. 178–9.

105. Barber, 'Crusade', pp. 5–6.

106. Tyerman, *England*, pp. 61–4.

107. RH, *Gesta*, 2.129.
108. Hiestand, ' "Precipua" ', p. 104.
109. Ibid., p. 83.
110. Ibid., pp. 83–5.
111. PA, pp. 34–5.
112. *IP*, bk 1, ch. 22, tr. p. 60.
113. PA, pp. 46, 69, and cf. Hiestand, ' "Precipua" ', p. 81.
114. OD, bk 7, pp. 124–7.
115. *De expugnatione*, pp. 56–7. Constable, 'Second Crusade', p. 222, suggests the influence of St Bernard.
116. J. France, *Western Warfare in the Age of the Crusades, 1000–1300* (London, 1999), p. 125.
117. *De expugnatione*, pp. 98–9.
118. 'Gesta cruc.', p. 29; 'De itinere Frisonum', in R. Röhricht, ed., *Quinti Belli Sacri Scriptores Minores* (Geneva, 1879), pp. 57–70, at p. 59.
119. FC, bk 1, ch. 7, tr. pp. 75–6.
120. Ibid., ch. 8, pp. 76–7.
121. RA, ch. 20, tr. p. 254.
122. Hagenmeyer, p. 142, tr. p. 132.
123. Ibid., pp. 148–9, tr. pp. 143–4.
124. Ibid., p. 165, tr. p. 195.
125. *CIR*, p. 40.
126. Hagenmeyer, p. 176, tr. p. 265.
127. Ibid., p. 175, tr. p. 279.
128. Ibid., pp. 79–84, tr. pp. 153–5.
129. Ibid., pp. 165–7 (my translation). In Bruno's defence there's no evidence that he had taken the cross, though that raises the question of why he went east at all.
130. *GF*, p. 27.
131. Riley-Smith, *First Crusade*, p. 125.
132. GN, bk 5, tr. pp. 104–5, bk. 6, tr. p. 112.
133. Riley-Smith, *First Crusade*, p. 127.
134. Villehardouin, ch. 96, tr. p. 51.
135. Ibid., ch. 110, tr. p. 54.
136. Ibid., ch. 115, tr. p. 55.
137. OP, ch. 54, tr. p. 111.
138. Powell, *Anatomy*, p. 166.
139. OP, ch. 30, tr. p. 84.
140. Huygens, p. 101.
141. Ibid., p. 122.
142. 'Gesta obsid.', ch. 23, p. 90.
143. Andrea, pp. 15–16, 30–1, and cf. p. 24.
144. Marshall, *Warfare*, pp. 68–9, 77–83; J. Riley-Smith, 'The crown of France and Acre, 1254–1291', in D. H. Weiss and L. Mahoney, eds, *France and the Holy Land: Frankish Culture at the End of the Crusades* (Baltimore, MD, 2004), pp. 45–62.
145. Maier, pp. 116–17 (James of Vitry), pp. 150–1 (Odo of Châteauroux).
146. Baha' al-Din, tr. p. 224. Though, as he makes clear (pp. 195, 232), Saladin could be scarcely less bleak in his assessment of his own position.
147. Cf. 'De expugnatione', p. 260, a forged letter supposedly written by Saladin to Barbarossa: 'et si inter nos et eos quos nominastis Christianos mare est; inter Sarracenos, qui non possunt aestimari, non est mare inter eos et nos, nec ullum impedimentum veniendi ad nos.'

5. Crusading warfare

1. *CIR*, p. 43.
2. M. Angold, 'The Byzantine empire, 1025–1118', in D. Luscombe and J. Riley-Smith, eds, *New Cambridge Medieval History*, 4: *c.1024–c.1198, Part Two* (Cambridge, 2004), pp. 217–53; M. Brett, ' 'Abbasids, Fatimids and Seljuqs', ibid., pp. 675–720; C. Hillenbrand, 'The First Crusade: the Muslim perspective', in *FCOI*, pp. 130–41.
3. *GF*, p. 21.
4. C. Hillenbrand, *The Crusades: Islamic Perspectives* (Edinburgh, 1999), p. 513.
5. C. R. Bowlus, 'Tactical and strategic weaknesses of horse archers on the eve of the First Crusade', in *APC*, pp. 159–66, rightly emphasizes their vulnerability when they were so engaged.
6. France, *Victory*, p. 158.
7. Marshall, *Warfare*, p. 160.
8. Ambroise, ll. 5653–62; I've used the translation by Gillingham, *Richard I*, p. 174.
9. Ambroise, ll. 6232–3; Gillingham, *Richard I*, p. 176. Cf. 'Historia', p. 156.
10. France, *Victory*, pp. 246–51, 282–96.
11. 'Gesta obsid.', ch. 40, p. 103. Cf. OP, ch. 29, tr. p. 82.
12. Rothclin, ch. 23, tr. p. 43.
13. Marshall, *Warfare*, p. 161; idem, 'The use of the charge in battles in the Latin East, 1192–1291', *Historical Research* 63 (1990), pp. 221–6.
14. Y. Lev, 'Infantry in Muslim armies during the crusades', in *LWAC*, 185–207.
15. K. Caspi-Reisfeld, 'Women warriors during the crusades, 1095–1254', in S. B. Edgington and S. Lambert, eds, *Gendering the Crusades* (Cardiff, 2001), pp. 94–107; S. Geldsetzer, *Frauen auf Kreuzzügen, 1096–1291* (Darmstadt, 2003), pp. 122–8; Powell, *Anatomy*, p. 161.
16. E.g. *PL*, 216, col. 1262 (Innocent III, 1200).
17. PA, p. 52, who shows no sense of irony in describing them as 'excellent knights' (*egregii milites*).
18. Johnson, 'Crusades', pp. 119–20.
19. *IP*, bk 1, ch. 61, tr. pp. 118–19.
20. Andrea, p. 106.
21. Haymar, p. cxx.
22. RH, *Chronica*, 2.320, and cf. n. 2 (Ralph of Coggeshall).
23. RD, pp. 27–8.
24. Geldsetzer, *Frauen*, pp. 129–53.
25. *IP*, bk 3, ch. 7, tr. p. 209.
26. OP, ch. 25, p. 78.
27. FC, bk 1, ch. 11, tr. p. 85.
28. Baha' al-Din, tr. pp. 147–8.
29. Ibid., pp. 144–5.
30. GW, bk 1, ch. 8, tr. pp. 132–3.
31. 'Historia', p. 164.
32. PA, p. 84; 'Historia', p. 168. See also Hiestand, ' "Precipua" ', p. 72.
33. *GF*, p. 74 (*minuta gens, pauperes*).
34. Hagenmeyer, p. 175, tr. p. 279, and cf. p. 167, tr. p. 192 (both poor and women).
35. OD, bk 5, pp. 94–5.
36. GN, bk 1, tr. p. 28.
37. *GF*, p. 74.
38. OP, ch. 57, tr. p. 115.
39. Ibid., ch. 52, p. 108.
40. Ralph Niger, *De re militari et triplici via peregrinationis Ierosolimitane*, ed. L. Schmugge (Berlin, 1977), pp. 224, 227. See also Siberry, *Criticism*, pp. 25–46 for the whole issue.

41. 'De Hierosolymitana', cols 1067–8.
42. Maier, pp. 138–41, and cf. pp. 65–6. See also Dickson, *Children's Crusade*, pp. 126–7, for a Paris preacher's exhortation to imitate the *pueri* of 1212.
43. Maier, pp. 146–9.
44. *PL*, 216, col. 1261, and cf. Brundage, *Medieval Canon Law*, p. 104 n. 125.
45. Maier, pp. 146–7.
46. Huygens, p. 98.
47. France, *Victory*, p. 242.
48. OD, bk 7, pp. 132–3.
49. Riley-Smith, *First Crusade*, p. 65.
50. 'Epistola', p. 177. 'Historia', p. 168, specifies 1,000.
51. Haymar, p. cxii; Powell, *Anatomy*, p. 148.
52. Baha' al-Din, tr. p. 177; Muslim losses of horses at Arsuf were also heavy.
53. RC, tr. pp. 100–1.
54. Brahney, ed., *Lyrics*, pp. 226–7 (with American spelling).
55. 'Historia', pp. 158–9.
56. *IP*, bk 2, ch. 42, tr. p. 196.
57. Ibid., bk 4, ch. 30, tr. p. 271, and see also Gillingham, *Richard I*, p. 186.
58. Joinville, chs 174–6, tr. pp. 208–9.
59. Marshall, *Warfare*, pp. 177–81.
60. Rothelin, ch. 27, tr. p. 48.
61. Ibid., ch. 31, tr. p. 55 (also Bédier and Aubry, p. 233).
62. Bédier and Aubry, p. 252, and see also Jordan, ' "Amen!" '
63. Riley-Smith, *First Crusade*, pp. 133–4.
64. RA, ch. 7, tr. p. 141.
65. Bédier and Aubry, pp. 263–5.
66. Rothelin, ch. 26, tr. p. 46.
67. Ibid., ch. 64, tr. p. 95, and see M. Barber, *The New Knighthood: A History of the Order of the Temple* (Cambridge, 1994), pp. 148–50.
68. Baha' al-Din, tr. pp. 225–6.
69. *IP*, bk 4, ch. 28, tr. p. 267.
70. France, *Western Warfare*, pp. 64–76.
71. Marshall, *Warfare*, pp. 171–5.
72. Baha' al-Din, tr. p. 175.
73. Ibid., tr. p. 137.
74. 'De expugnatione', ed. Stevenson, pp. 213, 224–5.
75. OP, ch. 57, tr. p. 114.
76. Joinville, ch. 143, p. 200.
77. Foulet, ed., *Lettres*, para. vi, p. 3; cf. ibid., p. 20 (up to 3,000 knights of whom 1,900 came from France) and J. R. Strayer, 'The crusades of Louis IX', in *HC*, 2.487–518, at pp. 493–4.
78. Rothelin, ch. 64, tr. p. 97.
79. OP, ch. 48, tr. p. 106.
80. *IP*, bk 1, ch. 56, tr. pp. 110–11.
81. Ibid., ch. 57, tr. pp. 111–12.
82. OP, ch. 82, tr. p. 134; Mol, 'Frisian fighters', passim.
83. 'Gesta obsid.', ch. 26, pp. 91–2. For a similar arrangement practised on the Third Crusade see Baha' al-Din, tr. p. 137.
84. Marshall, *Warfare*, pp. 76–7.
85. *CIR*, p. 41.
86. E.g. Marshall, *Warfare*, pp. 89, 151.
87. RD, p. 81.
88. PA, p. 35, and cf. 'Historia', p. 139.

89. RH, *Gesta*, 2.95.
90. C. Marshall, 'The crusading motivation of the Italian city republics in the Latin East, 1096–1104', in *ECWA*, pp. 60–79.
91. Huygens, p. 77.
92. *Historia hierosolymitana abbreviata*, bk 1, ch. 67, tr. M.-G. Grossel as *Histoire orientale de Jacques de Vitry* (Paris, 2005), p. 193.
93. Pryor, *Geography*, pp. 113–20.
94. OP, ch. 49, tr. p. 107.
95. Hillenbrand, *Crusades*, p. 570.
96. Ibid., p. 572.
97. Ibid., p. 570.
98. Mangonels and petraries worked by torsion, trebuchets by counterweights.
99. Mantlets were light, portable wooden shelters used during an assault on the walls, cats more durable penthouses used while ramming or mining was in progress at their base.
100. OP, ch. 12, tr. p. 64, and cf. Haymar, p. cix.
101. R. Rogers, *Latin Siege Warfare in the Twelfth Century* (Oxford, 1992), esp. chs 1, 2, 6.
102. An engraving in Runciman, *History*, vol. 1, plate 3 facing p. 220, shows the precipitate ascent.
103. RA, ch. 5, tr. p. 128.
104. France, *Victory*, pp. 222–56, provides an in-depth account of these operations.
105. *GF*, pp. 44–8.
106. France, *Victory*, pp. 332–56; J. Prawer, 'The Jerusalem the crusaders captured: a contribution to the medieval topography of the city', in P. W. Edbury, ed., *Crusade and Settlement* (Cardiff, 1985), pp. 1–16.
107. *IP*, bk 1, ch. 32, tr. p. 83.
108. Ibid., ch. 25, tr. p. 69. Cf. 'De expugnatione', ed. Stevenson, p. 254.
109. Rogers, *Latin Siege Warfare*, pp. 212–36.
110. Baha' al-Din, tr. p. 105.
111. Ibid., p. 108; Haymar, p. cx.
112. Baha' al-Din, tr. pp. 120, 135, 142–3; Haymar, p. cxxii.
113. *IP*, bk 1, ch. 40, tr. p. 94.
114. 'De expugnatione', ed. Stevenson, p. 254. Haymar (pp. cxviii–cxix) was more sympathetic to the rank and file.
115. Baha' al-Din, tr. p. 141.
116. RD, p. 39.
117. *IP*, bk 3, ch. 2, tr. p. 202.
118. RC, tr. pp. 97–8.
119. OP, ch. 12, tr. p. 65.
120. 'Gesta cruc.', p. 40.
121. OP, ch. 39, tr. p. 96.
122. 'Gesta obsid.', ch. 29, p. 93.
123. Ibid., ch. 53, pp. 110–11.
124. OP, chs 15, 23, 29, tr. pp. 68, 76, 81; 'Gesta obsid.', ch. 39, p. 101.
125. France, *Victory*, p. 294.
126. *IP*, bk 2, chs 16, 41, tr. pp. 163, 195 (15 days); P. W. Edbury, *The Kingdom of Cyprus and the Crusades, 1191–1374* (Cambridge, 1991), pp. 5–7.
127. Baha' al-Din, tr. pp. 170–1.
128. OP, ch. 57, tr. pp. 114–15.
129. *IP*, bk 4, ch. 18, tr. p. 248.
130. RH, *Chronica*, 3.131, tr. Edbury, p. 180.
131. Baha' al-Din, tr. p. 174.
132. Rothelin, ch. 60, tr. p. 87 (32 years); Foulet, ed., *Lettres*, para. xiv, p. 7 (22 years), and see also Smith, *Crusading*, p. 137.

133. Foulet, ed., *Lettres*, para. xix, p. 9.
134. Rothelin, ch. 66, p. 103.
135. Joinville, ch. 218, tr. p. 219.
136. Ibid., ch. 235, tr. p. 222.
137. Ibid., ch. 242, tr. p. 225.
138. Ibid., ch. 243, tr. p. 225.
139. Ibid., ch. 377, tr. p. 257.
140. J. Prawer, *Crusader Institutions* (Oxford, 1980), ch. 18.
141. Marshall, *Warfare*, pp. 32–3, 93, 257–61.

6. The needs of the flesh

1. Cole, *Preaching*, p. 210.
2. 'Gesta obsid.', ch. 22, p. 90.
3. RD, p. 73, makes the point well.
4. K. Leyser, 'Money and supplies on the First Crusade', in his *Communications and Power in Medieval Europe: The Gregorian Revolution and Beyond*, ed. T. Reuter (London, 1994), pp. 77–95.
5. Hiestand, ' "Precipua" ', p. 79.
6. Jackson, ed., *The Mission*, p. 278; idem, *The Mongols and the West, 1221–1410* (Harlow, 2005), pp. 139–40.
7. S. Mennell, *All Manners of Food: Eating and Taste in England and France from the Middle Ages to the Present* (Oxford, 1985), pp. 40–61; C. M. Woolgar, D. Serjeantson and T. Waldron, eds, *Food in Medieval England: Diet and Nutrition* (Oxford, 2006). I'm grateful to Chris Dyer for these references.
8. *CIR*, pp. 174–5.
9. Joinville, ch. 131, tr. p. 197.
10. Ibid., chs 297, 502–4, tr. pp. 238, 291.
11. Ibid., ch. 487, tr. p. 286.
12. Bachrach, 'Crusader logistics', p. 50.
13. Hagenmeyer, pp. 168–9.
14. Haldon, 'Roads', pp. 148–9.
15. Hagenmeyer, p. 157, tr. p. 158.
16. RA, ch. 11, tr. p. 173.
17. Riley-Smith, *First Crusade*, p. 85.
18. France, *Victory*, p. 335.
19. *GF*, pp. 33, 62.
20. RA, ch. 6, tr. p. 139.
21. Hagenmeyer, p. 148, tr. p. 143.
22. RA, ch. 11, tr. p. 173.
23. AA, bk 4, ch. 34, pp. 300–1. Fans of Charlie Chaplin will fondly recall the scene in *The Gold Rush* when he eats his own boot.
24. RA, ch. 14, tr. p. 209.
25. *GF*, p. 80.
26. RA, ch. 14, tr. p. 213.
27. Cannibals had been burnt alive at Tournus in 1031/3: Rodulfus Glaber, *Historiarum libri quinque*, ed. and tr. J. France (Oxford, 1989), pp. 186–9.
28. AA, bk 6, chs 6–7, pp. 410–13.
29. PA, pp. 79, 81, 83, 86; 'Historia', pp. 155–7, 161, 165–6.
30. RH, *Chronica*, 3.21–2. For food shortages see Haymar, pp. cx–cxii.
31. Lyon Continuation, ch. 103, tr. 94, and cf. Edbury, p. 171.
32. *IP*, bk 1, chs 64–81, tr. pp. 125–37 (influenced but not invalidated by its author's anti-Conradian views); Haymar, pp. cxxi–cxxii, cxxx; RH, *Gesta*, 2.145.

33. Haymar, p. cxxix.
34. *IP*, bk 1, chs 67, 69, 72, tr. pp. 127–30.
35. Ibid., ch. 67, tr. pp. 127–8.
36. Ibid., ch. 69, tr. p. 129.
37. Ibid., ch. 73, tr. p. 131.
38. Ibid., chs 68, 73, tr. pp. 128, 131.
39. Ibid., bk 6, ch. 35, tr. pp. 379–80.
40. Edbury, pp. 172–4.
41. *IP*, bk 1, chs 74, 77, 80, tr. pp. 132, 134, 136–7.
42. RD, pp. 42–3.
43. RC, tr. pp. 45–6.
44. Andrea, p. 82.
45. RC, tr. p. 84; *IP*, bk 1, ch. 66, tr. p. 127.
46. Andrea, p. 302.
47. T. F. Madden, 'Food and the Fourth Crusade: a new approach to the "diversion question" ', in *LWAC*, 209–28.
48. Andrea, p. 107.
49. Powell, *Anatomy*, p. 130.
50. OP, ch. 22, tr. p. 75.
51. 'Gesta obsid.', ch. 18, p. 86.
52. OP, ch. 78, p. 130.
53. Joinville, ch. 293, tr. p. 237, and see also Rothelin, ch. 65, p. 99.
54. Joinville, ch. 291, tr. p. 237.
55. Riley-Smith, *First Crusade*, p. 75.
56. RaC, ch. 58, tr. p. 84.
57. Riley-Smith, *First Crusade*, p. 66.
58. Queller and Madden, *Fourth Crusade*, pp. 158–9.
59. J. Riley-Smith, *Hospitallers: The History of the Order of St John* (London, 1999).
60. Haymar, p. cxxii.
61. *GF*, p. 33.
62. Ibid., p. 43.
63. RA, ch. 20, tr. p. 258.
64. Ibid., ch. 16, tr. p. 224.
65. Hagenmeyer, p. 150, tr. p. 156.
66. RH, *Gesta*, 2.32.
67. *IP*, bk 1, ch. 78, tr. pp. 135–6; Haymar, p. cxxx.
68. *IP*, bk 4, ch. 15, tr. pp. 244–5.
69. Baha' al-Din, tr. p. 143.
70. M. Prestwich, *Armies and Warfare in the Middle Ages: The English Experience* (New Haven, CT, 1996), p. 303.
71. P. D. Mitchell, *Medicine in the Crusades: Warfare, Wounds and the Medieval Surgeon* (Cambridge, 2004), p. 243.
72. Hagenmeyer, p. 145, tr. pp. 129–30.
73. *IP*, bk 3, ch. 4, tr. p. 204.
74. Ibid., bk 1, ch. 70, tr. p. 129.
75. Baha' al-Din, tr. pp. 116–17, 138.
76. Mitchell, *Medicine*, pp. 185–6.
77. OP, ch. 20, tr. p. 72; 'Gesta obsid.', ch. 12, p. 83.
78. Huygens, p. 116.
79. Joinville, ch. 303, tr. p. 239.
80. Ibid., chs 299, 306, 310, tr. pp. 238–40.
81. 'Gesta cruc.', p. 41. Cf. 'Fragmentum de captione Damiatae', in R. Röhricht, ed., *Quinti Belli Sacri Scriptores Minores* (Geneva, 1879), pp. 167–202, at p. 170.

82. 'Les Gestes des Chiprois', in *RHC, Documents arméniens*, vol. 2, 651–872, partially tr. P. Crawford as *The 'Templar of Tyre': Part III of the 'Deeds of the Cypriots'* (Aldershot, 2003), p. 68.
83. Joinville, chs 323–4, tr. p. 244.
84. Ibid., chs 329–30, tr. pp. 245–6.
85. Mitchell, *Medicine*, pp. 19, 210.
86. 'Ordinacio', p. 25.
87. Joinville, ch. 175, tr. p. 208.
88. AA, bk 3, ch. 4, pp. 142–5.
89. Mitchell, *Medicine*, pp. 64–5, 84–5.
90. Marshall, *Warfare*, p. 165. Before 1187 the Hospitallers sent a mobile field hospital out on campaigns, but there is no evidence that it catered to the needs of crusaders.
91. E.g. *CIR*, p. 121.
92. RA, ch. 12, tr. p. 187.
93. Ibid., ch. 6, tr. p. 140.
94. AA, bk 3, ch. 52, pp. 220–1, and see also W. G. Zajac, 'Captured property on the First Crusade', in *FCOI*, 153–80, at p. 168.
95. Murray, 'Money', pp. 246–7.
96. RH, *Chronica*, 3.125.
97. Hagenmeyer, p. 149, tr. p. 131.
98. Riley-Smith, *First Crusade*, pp. 68–71.
99. 'Epistolae Sugerii', no. 37, p. 496, no. 52, pp. 501–2, no. 67, p. 508, no. 68, pp. 508–9.
100. RH, *Gesta*, 2.112.
101. *IP*, bk 4, ch. 1, tr. p. 227.
102. OP, ch. 57, tr. p. 115.
103. Ibid., ch. 28, tr. p. 80.
104. Rothelin, ch. 31, tr. p. 55 (also Bédier and Aubry, p. 232).
105. Joinville, ch. 136, tr. p. 198.
106. Rothelin, ch. 65, tr. pp. 99–100.
107. Prestwich, *Armies*, pp. 83–113; P. Contamine, *War in the Middle Ages*, tr. M. Jones (Oxford, 1984), pp. 90–101.
108. Andrea, p. 189.
109. A point well made by Murray, 'Money', pp. 248–9.
110. See Pryor, 'Digest', p. 291, and Constable, 'Second Crusade', p. 221 for the pillaging that accompanied early seaborne crusading.
111. Andrea, p. 186.
112. AA, bk 4, ch. 54, pp. 332–5 and bk 2, ch. 30, pp. 112–13 for Nicaea.
113. *GF*, pp. 19–20.
114. Rosalind Hill's translation and footnote don't help at this point, because given the preceding words it's far from certain that *divites* refers to material riches.
115. 'Historia', p. 168.
116. *GF*, p. 20.
117. Ibid., p. 70.
118. *IP*, bk 2, ch. 41, tr. p. 195.
119. Baha' al-Din, tr. pp. 118–19, and see Lyon Continuation, ch. 103, tr. pp. 94–5 for the background of desperation.
120. *IP*, bk 4, ch. 19, tr. p. 257.
121. Ibid., bk 6, ch. 4, tr. pp. 340, 342.
122. *GF*, p. 92.
123. Villehardouin, ch. 250, tr. p. 92.
124. RC, tr. p. 101.
125. Andrea, p. 166.
126. Zajac, 'Captured property', passim.

127. *GF*, p. 95.
128. RA, ch. 20, tr. p. 248, and cf. ch. 14, tr. p. 220.
129. FC, bk 1, ch. 29, tr. p. 123.
130. RA, ch. 20, tr. p. 263, ch. 21, tr. p. 268.
131. Zajac, 'Captured property', p. 171.
132. *De expugnatione*, pp. 176–7.
133. 'Narratio', pp. 627–32 (= Chroust, pp. 189–92); Ralph of Diceto, *Ymagines histori-arum*, ed. W. Stubbs, 2 vols (RS, London, 1876), 2.65–6; J. F. O'Callaghan, *Reconquest and Crusade in Medieval Spain* (Philadelphia, PA, 2003), p. 59.
134. 'Gesta cruc.', pp. 33–4.
135. *IP*, bk 2, ch. 9, tr. p. 151; Gillingham, *Richard I*, pp. 128, 145, 153–4.
136. Lyon Continuation, ch. 124, tr. pp. 106–7.
137. RH, *Gesta*, 2.181, 185; *IP*, bk 3, ch. 18, tr. p. 221.
138. RH, *Gesta*, 2.186; *IP*, bk 4, ch. 1, tr. p. 227.
139. RH, *Gesta*, 2.188.
140. *IP*, bk 3, ch. 23, tr. pp. 225–6.
141. Ibid., bk 6, ch. 3, tr. p. 338.
142. Queller and Madden, *Fourth Crusade*, pp. 12–13.
143. Ibid., pp. 175–6.
144. Ibid., p. 197.
145. RC, tr. pp. 100–2.
146. On this point see also the Anonymous of Soissons, Andrea, p. 233.
147. Ibid., pp. 212–21 (quote at p. 215).
148. JT, p. 139.
149. Huygens, p. 127.
150. OP, ch. 39, tr. p. 96.
151. Ibid., ch. 82, tr. p. 134. This could mean that the Church got less than Oliver reckoned was its proper share.
152. Ibid., ch. 39, tr. p. 96; Huygens, p. 128.
153. Powell, *Anatomy*, pp. 162–6.
154. JT, pp. 138–9.
155. OP, ch. 39, tr. p. 96.
156. Joinville, chs 167–9, tr. pp. 206–7.
157. Queller and Madden, *Fourth Crusade*, p. 198.
158. Anna Comnena, *The Alexiad*, tr. E. R. A. Sewter (Harmondsworth, 1969), p. 311.
159. Andrea, p. 173.
160. Phillips, 'The thief's cross', p. 154; M. Menzel, 'Kreuzzugsideologie unter Innocenz III.', *Historisches Jahrbuch* 120 (2000), pp. 39–79, at p. 54.
161. *De expugnatione*, pp. 134–5.
162. *GF*, p. 48.
163. Andrea, pp. 147–8.
164. Ibid., p. 167.
165. E.g. Innocent III, writing in 1200: *PL*, 216, col. 1262.
166. Andrea, pp. 67–8, citing Judges 8:4–17 and Luke 6:1–5.
167. *De expugnatione*, pp. 82–3.
168. Crocker, 'Early crusade songs', pp. 88–9 (orig. Bédier and Aubry, pp. 44–7).
169. Peter of Blois, 'De Hierosolymitana', col. 1064.
170. *CIR*, p. 37.
171. Hagenmeyer, p. 137, tr. *CIR*, p. 39.
172. 'Annales Herbipolenses', *MGHS*, 16.1–12, at p. 3.
173. RA, ch. 9, tr. p. 168.
174. Ibid., ch. 13, tr. p. 198.
175. PA, pp. 59–60.

176. *IP*, bk 4, ch. 9, tr. p. 235.
177. Ibid., ch. 27, tr. p. 265.
178. Ibid., bk 5, ch. 20, tr. p. 299.
179. OP, ch. 38, tr. p. 95.
180. Ibid., ch. 48, tr. p. 106.
181. Huygens, p. 129.
182. Ibid., p. 135.
183. *IP*, bk 1, ch. 65, tr. p. 126.
184. Andrea, p. 18.
185. Joinville, ch. 405, tr. p. 265.
186. Ibid., ch. 171, tr. p. 207.
187. AA, bk 3, ch. 46, pp. 208–11. See also J. A. Brundage, 'Prostitution, miscegenation and sexual purity in the First Crusade', in P. W. Edbury, ed., *Crusade and Settlement* (Cardiff, 1985), pp. 57–65, p. 59 and passim.
188. PA, p. 60; 'Historia', p. 148.
189. Joinville, ch. 505, tr. p. 292.
190. Huygens, p. 139.
191. FC, bk 1, ch. 15, tr. p. 95.
192. Huygens, p. 139.
193. RA, ch. 21, tr. p. 264.
194. *IP*, bk 6, ch. 8, tr. p. 346; Rothelin, ch. 31, tr. pp. 54–5. See also M. Strickland, *War and Chivalry: The Conduct and Perception of War in England and Normandy, 1066–1217* (Cambridge, 1996), p. 119.
195. Joinville, ch. 583, tr. pp. 310–11.
196. Ibid., chs 297–8, tr. p. 238.
197. 'Gesta obsid.', ch. 18, p. 87.
198. Brahney, ed., *Lyrics*, pp. 76–9.
199. Ibid., pp. 232–3, and see also Jordan, 'Representation', pp. 32–3.
200. *De expugnatione*, pp. 130–1.
201. Bédier and Aubry, pp. 103–4, and see also Smith, *Crusading*, p. 79.
202. Bédier and Aubry, p. 34.
203. *De expugnatione*, pp. 72–3.

7. *Storming Heaven*

1. Peter of Blois, 'De Hierosolymitana', col. 1067.
2. 'Ordinacio', p. 25.
3. *IP*, bk 1, ch. 50, tr. p. 106.
4. Maier, pp. 202–3 (Gilbert of Tournai).
5. Joinville, ch. 601, tr. pp. 314–15, has a mild example.
6. *IP*, bk 1, ch. 50, tr. p. 106.
7. Baha' al-Din, tr. pp. 149–50.
8. AA, bk 7, ch. 2, pp. 486–9; Runciman, *History*, 1.308.
9. Riley-Smith, *First Crusade*, pp. 49, 106, 122; Joinville, ch. 331, tr. p. 246.
10. PA, p. 79; 'Historia', pp. 161, 166.
11. *IP*, bk 1, ch. 74, tr. p. 132.
12. Baha' al-Din, tr. pp. 142–3. See also 'De expugnatione', ed. Stevenson, p. 235, for the lavish bribe that the sultan allegedly offered to apostates at Acre in 1187.
13. 'Gesta obsid.', p. 108.
14. Rothelin, ch. 65, tr. pp. 99–100.
15. Joinville, ch. 319, tr. p. 243.
16. Huygens, p. 130.

17. Joinville, chs 297–8, tr. p. 238.
18. E.g. Humbert of Romans in Maier, pp. 212–3.
19. 'Narratio', p. 615 (= Chroust, pp. 181–2).
20. E. R. Labande, 'Pellegrini o crociati? Mentalità e comportamenti a Gerusalemme nel secolo XII', *Aevum* 54 (1980), 217–30; Constable, 'Second Crusade', p. 237 and n. 130.
21. Hagenmeyer, p. 175, tr. p. 279.
22. PA, pp. 55, 57, 68, and cf. 'Historia', p. 116.
23. RH, *Chronica*, 3.201–2.
24. Andrea, p. 61, and cf. ibid., p. 42 where the Venetians appear to be cast as the thieves who robbed the traveller in Luke 10:30.
25. JT, ch. 10, p. 122.
26. Huygens, p. 109.
27. Maier, p. 55 and footnoted references to sermons.
28. GN, bk 7, tr. p. 124, bk 6, tr. p. 107.
29. RA, ch. 6, tr. p. 136.
30. Morris, *Sepulchre*, p. 222.
31. GN, bk 6, tr. p. 107.
32. B. H. Rosenwein, 'Feudal war and monastic peace: Cluniac liturgy as ritual aggression', *Viator* 2 (1971), 129–57.
33. Bernard of Clairvaux, 'In praise of the new knighthood', tr. C. Greenia in *The Works of Bernard of Clairvaux*, vol. 7 (Kalamazoo, MI, 1977), pp. 113–67, at p. 130.
34. *IP*, bk 4, ch. 19, tr. p. 254.
35. Barber, *New Knighthood*, pp. 38–63.
36. For more on these themes see G. Constable, 'The place of the crusader in medieval society', *Viator* 29 (1998), 377–403.
37. *GF*, pp. 19–20.
38. Ibid., pp. 25–6.
39. Ibid., p. 31.
40. Ibid., p. 37.
41. Ibid., p. 41.
42. Ibid., p. 70.
43. Ibid., p. 77.
44. RA, ch. 14, tr. p. 219.
45. Including the *Chanson d'Antioche*: S. B. Edgington, 'Holy Land, Holy Lance: religious ideas in the *Chanson d'Antioche*', in R. N. Swanson, ed., *The Holy Land, Holy Lands, and Christian History*, SCH 36 (Woodbridge, 2000), pp. 142–53, at p. 144.
46. PA, pp. 39, 45, 46, 53 and passim.
47. 'Historia', p. 164.
48. *IP*, bk 4, ch. 19, tr. p. 257.
49. 'Gesta obsid.', ch. 36, pp. 99–100.
50. *IP*, bk 4, ch. 12, tr. p. 240. In 1187 the besieged populace of Jerusalem appealed in their desperation to 'the holy True Cross and the Sepulchre of Jesus Christ's resurrection', to protect them: 'De expugnatione', ed. Stevenson, p. 242.
51. Joinville, ch. 501, tr. p. 291.
52. *GF*, p. 58.
53. 'Historia', pp. 162–3, and see Lyon Continuation, ch. 92, tr. pp. 86–7 on Bishop Godfrey.
54. Morris, *Sepulchre*, p. 186 with commentary.
55. E.g. ibid., pp. 56–7.
56. OP, ch. 2, tr. pp. 53–4.
57. J. Riley-Smith, 'Peace never established: the case of the kingdom of Jerusalem', *TRHS*, 5th ser. 28 (1978), 87–102, esp. p. 93.

58. *GF*, pp. 89–90.
59. *IP*, bk 4, ch. 34, tr. pp. 278–9.
60. Ibid., bk 5, chs 2–3, tr. pp. 284–6.
61. GN, bk 6, tr. p. 122.
62. RA, ch. 20, tr. p. 258.
63. *IP*, bk 5, ch. 6, tr. p. 288.
64. Jaspert, 'Hilfsersuchen', pp. 512–15, and cf. his letter to the pope, Edbury, pp. 162–3.
65. 'De expugnatione', ed. Stevenson, pp. 219, 220–1, 231, 240–1.
66. Morris, *Sepulchre*, p. 186.
67. 'Gesta obsid.', ch. 22, p. 89.
68. OP, ch. 25, tr. p. 78.
69. *GF*, p. 4.
70. Ibid., p. 17.
71. *De expugnatione*, pp. 132–5, and see p. 134 n. 1.
72. 'Annales Herbipolenses', p. 5.
73. *IP*, bk 1, ch. 5, tr. p. 34.
74. Peter of Blois, 'Passio', cols 957–76, with crusade ref. at col. 963. See also B. Hamilton, 'The elephant of Christ: Reynald of Châtillon', in D. Baker, ed., *Religious Motivation: Biographical and Sociological Problems for the Church Historian*, SCH 15 (Oxford, 1978), pp. 97–108.
75. *IP*, bk 1, ch. 31, tr. p. 83, bk 4, ch. 34, tr. p. 279. Cf. PA, pp. 79–80.
76. *IP*, bk 5, ch. 22, tr. p. 362.
77. OP, ch. 16, tr. p. 69.
78. 'Gesta obsid.', ch. 41, pp. 103–4.
79. JT, ch. 40, p. 132.
80. Hagenmeyer, pp. 136–7, tr. *CIR*, p. 38.
81. *GF*, p. 74.
82. RA, ch. 11, tr. p. 179.
83. FC, bk 3, ch. 34, tr. p. 268, and see also Riley-Smith, *First Crusade*, p. 80.
84. Ch. 5 at n. 37 = *GF*, p. 74.
85. J. Brundage, 'Adhemar of Puy: the bishop and his critics', *Speculum* 34 (1959), 201–12.
86. Hagenmeyer, p. 164, tr. pp. 194–5.
87. I. S. Robinson, *The Papacy, 1073–1198: Continuity and Innovation* (Cambridge, 1990), ch. 4, esp. pp. 169–70.
88. Queller and Madden, *Fourth Crusade*, p. 95.
89. For a balanced judgement on this see Powell, *Anatomy*, pp. 195–203.
90. E.g. Haymar's obituary for Archbishop Baldwin of Canterbury in 1190, p. cxxviii.
91. E.g. RA, ch. 6, tr. p. 140.
92. Ibid., ch. 20, tr. pp. 254–5.
93. Ibid., ch. 12, tr. p 188.
94. *GF*, p. 94.
95. OP, ch. 13, tr. p. 66.
96. *De expugnatione*, pp. 69–85: a rich text that has long been acknowledged as an epitome of crusading ideas in the mid-twelfth century, e.g. J. Phillips, 'Ideas of crusade and holy war in *De expugnatione Lyxbonensi*', in Swanson, ed., *The Holy Land*, pp. 123–41.
97. OD, bk 4, pp. 68–71.
98. PA, pp. 33–4 (with reference to Joshua 7); 'Historia', p. 138, and cf. pp. 162–3 and 167–8 on later preaching by the bishop.
99. RC, tr. p. 94.
100. Andrea, p. 107.

101. Ibid., pp. 125–6.
102. Ibid., pp. 108–9.
103. Ibid., pp. 132–9.
104. Ibid., p. 161–2.
105. Ibid., pp. 163–8, 171–6.
106. Siberry, *Criticism*, pp. 69–108.
107. Henry of Huntingdon, *Historia Anglorum*, ed. and tr. D. Greenway (Oxford, 1996), bk 10, ch. 27, pp. 752–3.
108. OP, ch. 17, tr. p. 70.
109. Ibid., ch. 19, tr. pp. 71–2.
110. Ibid., chs 78–80, tr. pp. 130–3.
111. Huygens, p. 129.
112. 'Gesta cruc.', p. 52.
113. *GF*, p. 53: the words are put into the mouth of Kerbogha's mother during their exchange before the battle of Antioch.
114. PA, pp. 76–7.
115. *IP*, bk 1, ch. 42, tr. p. 97, and cf. Haymar, p. cxxv.
116. *IP*, bk 4, ch. 19, tr. p. 257.
117. Peter of Blois, 'Passio', cols 961–2.
118. RR, prologue, tr. p. 77. Remarkably, Jewish commentators made similarly radical claims about the response of the Rhineland communities to crusading persecution: Chazan, *European Jewry*, pp. 256, 277.
119. RA, ch. 14, tr. p. 212.
120. 'Historia', p. 116.
121. *GF*, p. 54.
122. Rodulfus Glaber, *Historiarum*, p. 205.
123. GN, bk 2, tr. p. 44.
124. J. Flori, 'Une ou plusieurs "première croisade"? Le message d'Urbain II et les plus anciens pogroms d'Occident', *Revue historique* 285 (1991), 3–27.
125. For a balanced assessment see J. Rubenstein, 'How, or how much, to reevaluate Peter the Hermit', in S. Ridyard, ed., *The Medieval Crusade* (Woodbridge, 2004), pp. 53–79.
126. *IP*, bk 6, ch. 7, tr. p. 345.
127. M. Reeves, *The Influence of Prophecy in the Later Middle Ages: A Study in Joachimism* (Oxford, 1969).
128. RH, *Chronica*, 3.77–8; Gillingham, *Richard I*, pp. 138–9.
129. Andrea, pp. 116, 121–2, 123.
130. Powell, *Anatomy*, pp. 178–9.
131. OP, ch. 56, tr. pp. 113–14, and cf. ch. 35, tr. pp. 89–91.
132. Huygens, pp. 152–3.
133. *CIR*, p. 120.
134. Dickson, 'Genesis', passim.
135. Jackson, *Mongols*, p. 48.
136. Riley-Smith, *First Crusade*, pp. 33–4.
137. *IP*, bk 1, ch. 1, tr. p. 23.
138. Riley-Smith, *First Crusade*, p. 33.
139. Ibid., p. 92.
140. PA, pp. 62–3.
141. OP, ch. 9, tr. pp. 60–1.
142. Riley-Smith, *First Crusade*, p. 105.
143. *GF*, p. 69. See also Hagenmeyer, p. 147, tr. p. 143.
144. Robert of Reims ingeniously tied this in with a conversion narrative relating to Antioch's Turkish betrayer, Pirrus: RR, bk 5, chs 8–9, tr. pp. 141–3, and see

S. Throop, 'Combat and conversation: interfaith dialogue in twelfth-century crusading narratives', *Medieval Encounters* 13 (2007), 310–25.

145. Riley-Smith, *First Crusade*, pp. 105 and 193 n. 74; Morris, 'Picturing', pp. 204–5.
146. PA, p. 81, and cf. p. 83 on invocations of the saint; 'Epistola', p. 176; 'Historia', p. 165.
147. 'Historia', p. 167, and cf. n. 3.
148. PA, p. 82; 'Epistola', p. 176; 'Historia', p. 164.
149. 'Gesta obsid.', pp. 76–7.
150. Joinville, chs 597–8, tr. p. 314.
151. *IP*, bk 1, chs 47–56, tr. pp. 103–11.
152. Riley-Smith, *First Crusade*, p. 101.
153. See ibid., pp. 101–7 for a full analysis.
154. C. Morris, 'Policy and visions: the case of the holy lance at Antioch', in J. Gillingham and J. C. Holt, eds, *War and Government in the Middle Ages: Essays in Honour of J. O. Prestwich* (Woodbridge, 1984), pp. 33–45; W. Giese, 'Die "lancea Domini" von Antiochia (1098/99)', in W. Setz, ed., *Fälschungen im Mittelalter*, 6 vols (Hanover, 1988–90), 5.485–504.
155. Hillenbrand, *Crusades*, p. 314.
156. PA, p. 80.
157. RA, ch. 14, tr. p. 208.
158. Ibid., ch. 21, tr. p. 269; Murray, 'Mighty', p. 232.
159. Murray, 'Mighty', passim, esp. p. 221.
160. *IP*, bk 1, ch. 5, tr. p. 33.
161. Murray, 'Mighty', p. 221. Schein, *Gateway*, pp. 83–5, with article literature at p. 84 n. 98.
162. 'De expugnatione', ed. Stevenson, pp. 226–7, and see also P. Cole, 'Christian perceptions of the battle of Hattin (583/1187)', *Al-Masāq* 6 (1993), 9–39, esp. pp. 10–15, 25.
163. Peter of Blois, 'Passio', col. 959.
164. Baha' al-Din, tr. p. 163.
165. *IP*, bk 5, chs 36, pp. 53–4, tr. pp. 314, 333–4.
166. Riley-Smith, *First Crusade*, pp. 93–9.
167. Andrea, pp. 223–64 (the Anonymous of Soissons and the Deeds of the Bishops of Halberstadt); GP.
168. H. E. Mayer, *The Crusades*, tr. J. Gillingham, 2nd edn (Oxford, 1988), p. 203.
169. GP, ch. 19, tr. p. 111.
170. Ibid., ch. 24, tr. pp. 125–7; Andrea, pp. 235–7, 262.
171. Bachrach, *Fulk Nerra*, p. 248.
172. Hagenmeyer, p. 167, tr. p. 192.
173. For the mendicants see Maier, *Preaching*. A forthcoming study by William Purkis, *Crusading Spirituality in the Holy Land and Iberia, c. 1095–c. 1187* (Boydell) will be important for the Cistercian impact.
174. Morris, *Sepulchre*, pp. 269–71.
175. Hamilton, *Religion*, passim.

8. Saracens

1. D. B. Strickland, *Saracens, Demons, and Jews: Making Monsters in Medieval Art* (Princeton, NJ, 2003), p. 7.
2. E.g. 'Gesta obsid', ch. 27, p. 92; 'Liber duellii christiani in obsidione Damiate exacti', in R. Röhricht, ed., *Quinti Belli Sacri Scriptores Minores* (Geneva, 1879), pp. 141–66, at ch. 28, p. 153; Rothelin, ch. 18, tr. pp. 36–7. See also J. V. Tolan, *Saracens: Islam in the Medieval European Imagination* (New York, 2002), p. 122.
3. Strickland, *Saracens*, p. 188.

4. AA, bk 6, chs 29–30, pp. 440–3.
5. B. Z. Kedar, 'The Jerusalem massacre of July 1099 in the western historiography of the crusades', *Crusades* 3 (2004), 15–75, at pp. 22–3.
6. 'Les Gestes des Chiprois', chs 480–1, tr. pp. 101–2. See also Runciman, *History*, 3.409–10.
7. N. Daniel, *The Arabs and Medieval Europe*, 2nd edn (London, 1979), p. 53; Tolan, *Saracens*, pp. 10–12.
8. Strickland, *Saracens*, p. 169.
9. J. B. Friedman, *The Monstrous Races in Medieval Art and Thought* (Cambridge, MA, 1981), p. 65.
10. M. Bull, 'Views of Muslims and of Jerusalem in miracle stories, c. 1000–c. 1200: reflections on the study of first crusaders' motivations', in *ECWA*, 13–38.
11. GN, bk 1, tr. pp. 36–7.
12. AA, bk 3, ch. 46, pp. 208–11.
13. *De expugnatione*, pp. 78–9.
14. I think Strickland, *Saracens*, p. 159, is wrong to make this assumption. Friedman, *The Monstrous Races*, p. 67, refers to a tendency to depict Saracens with the heads of dogs (*cynocephali*) but this was rare.
15. M. Uebel, 'Unthinking the monster: twelfth-century responses to Saracen alterity', in J. J. Cohen, ed., *Monster Theory* (Minneapolis, MN, 1996), pp. 264–91.
16. Cf. 'Annales Herbipolenses', p. 5.
17. E.g. 'De expugnatione', ed. Stevenson, pp. 211, 231–2.
18. C. Kohler, 'Un sermon commémoratif de la prise de Jerusalem par les croisés attribué à Foucher de Chartres', *Revue de l'orient latin* 8 (1900–1), 158–64, at p. 162.
19. 'De expugnatione', ed. Stevenson, p. 239.
20. Tolan, *Saracens*, ch. 6 passim.
21. Uebel, 'Unthinking', p. 275.
22. P. Cole, 'Humbert of Romans and the crusade', in *ECWA*, 157–74, at p. 167.
23. Morris, *Sepulchre*, p. 191.
24. *IP*, bk 4, ch. 6, tr. p. 232.
25. 'De expugnatione', ed. Stevenson, p. 212.
26. Huygens, pp. 137–8.
27. *GF*, p. 52.
28. M. Keen, *The Laws of War in the Late Middle Ages* (London, 1965).
29. E.-D. Hehl, 'War, peace and the Christian order', in D. Luscombe and J. Riley-Smith, eds, *The New Cambridge Medieval History*, 4: *c. 1024–c. 1198, Part One* (Cambridge, 2004), pp. 185–228.
30. Strickland, *War*, pp. 202, 253.
31. Ibid., pp. 35–6.
32. Y. Friedman, *Encounter between Enemies: Captivity and Ransom in the Latin Kingdom of Jerusalem* (Leiden, 2002), ch 2.
33. Walter the Chancellor, *Bella Antiochena*, ed. H. Hagenmeyer (Innsbruck, 1896), tr. T. S. Asbridge and S. B. Edgington as *Walter the Chancellor's 'The Antiochene Wars'* (Aldershot, 1999), bk 2, ch. 15, tr. p. 166.
34. Strickland, *War*, pp. 199–200, and nn. 114, 116.
35. Ibid., p. 164.
36. JT, ch. 36, p. 130.
37. Haymar, p. cxxxvi (True Cross); *IP*, bk 4, ch. 4, tr. p. 231 (revenge).
38. Strickland, *War*, pp. 273–7, 286–7 and ch. 10 passim.
39. RA, ch. 1, tr. p. 65.
40. 'Narratio', pp. 623, 629–30 (= Chroust, pp. 186, 191).
41. Strickland, *War*, pp. 222–4.
42. PA, p. 85; 'Epistola', p. 177.

43. Joinville, chs 320, 322, 326, tr. pp. 243–5.
44. 'De expugnatione', ed. Stevenson, p. 235.
45. Baha' al-Din, tr. p. 220.
46. *IP*, bk 3, ch. 17, tr. pp. 218–19, and see also Strickland, *War*, pp. 35–6.
47. Suger, *Vie de Louis VI le Gros*, ed. H. Wacquet (Paris, 1929), tr. R. C. Cusimano and J. Moorhead as *Suger: The Deeds of Louis the Fat* (Washington, DC, 1992), ch. 28, tr. p. 129.
48. Strickland, *War*, p. 293.
49. Ibid., pp. 294–7.
50. M. Barber, 'The Albigensian Crusades: wars like any other?', in M. Balard, B. Z. Kedar and J. Riley-Smith, eds, *Dei gesta per Francos: Études sur les croisades dédiées à Jean Richard* (Aldershot, 2001), pp. 45–55.
51. Kedar, 'Jerusalem massacre', pp. 73–4. This was the figure given by Ibn al-Arabi for those killed in the al-Aqsa mosque; undoubtedly others died elsewhere, but all the figures are approximate.
52. K. G. Cushing, *Reform and the Papacy in the Eleventh Century: Spirituality and Social Change* (Manchester, 2005), p. 122.
53. RA, ch. 20, tr. p. 261.
54. Hagenmeyer, p. 171, tr. p. 277; the letter may have been written by Raymond.
55. Ibn al-Athir, *Chronicle for the Crusading Period Part 1*, tr. D. S. Richards (Aldershot, 2006), tr. p. 21.
56. Bernard of Clairvaux, 'In praise', ch. 3, tr. p. 134.
57. Morris, *Sepulchre*, p. 217.
58. *GF*, pp. 91–2.
59. FC, bk 1, ch. 28, tr. p. 122.
60. E.g. Uebel, 'Unthinking', a stimulating but at times conjectural approach.
61. RA, ch. 9, tr. p. 168.
62. *GF*, p. 58.
63. E.g. RA, ch. 14, tr. pp. 213–14; FC, bk 1, ch. 25, tr. p. 112.
64. M. Rouche, 'Cannibalisme sacré chez les croisés populaires', in Y.-M. Hilaire, ed., *La Religion populaire: Aspects du Christianisme populaire à travers l'histoire* (Lille, 1981), pp. 29–41.
65. *IP*, bk 6, ch. 17, tr. p. 358.
66. *GF*, pp. 79–80.
67. Hagenmeyer, p. 171, tr. p. 277: it's hard not to be chilled by the phrase *si scire desideratis* ('if you want to know') coyly inserted before the repetition of Raymond of Aguilers' reference to spilled blood reaching the knees of riders, though it's wrong to read too much into three words.
68. P. W. Edbury and J. G. Rowe, *William of Tyre: Historian of the Latin East* (Cambridge, 1988), ch. 9; R. C. Schwinges, *Kreuzzugsideologie und Toleranz: Studien zu Wilhelm von Tyrus* (Stuttgart, 1977).
69. Rothelin, ch. 15, tr. pp. 33–4.
70. Tolan, *Saracens*, pp. 203–13; A. Leopold, *How to Recover the Holy Land: The Crusade Proposals of the Late Thirteenth and Early Fourteenth Centuries* (Aldershot, 2000).
71. Thorough treatment in Tolan, *Saracens*, esp. pp. 105–34.
72. *GF*, pp. 53–6.
73. RA, ch. 12, tr. pp. 187–8.
74. Rothelin, chs 12–14, tr. pp. 29–33.
75. *GF*, p. 51.
76. *IP*, bk 1, ch. 23, tr. p. 63.
77. 'Gesta obsid.', ch. 44, p. 105.
78. *GF*, p. 96.
79. Ambroise, tr. 2.123.

80. Cole, 'Christian perceptions', pp. 10–11.
81. M. Jubb, *The Legend of Saladin in Western Literature and Historiography* (Lampeter, 2000), p. 151.
82. E.g. Innocent III in Andrea, p. 12.
83. Joinville, chs 446–8, tr. p. 275.
84. Mandeville, *Travels*, tr. C. W. R. D. Moseley (Harmondsworth, 1983), pp. 107–8.
85. T. S. Asbridge, 'Knowing the enemy: Latin relations with Islam at the time of the First Crusade', in *KC*, pp. 17–25.
86. Hagenmeyer, pp. 149–52, tr. pp. 131–2, 155–7.
87. Baha' al-Din, tr. p. 124; *IP*, bk 1, ch. 41, tr. p. 97.
88. Morris, *Sepulchre*, p. 259.
89. Baha' al-Din, tr. p. 186.
90. *IP*, bk 1, ch. 25, tr. pp. 68–9.
91. Morris, *Sepulchre*, p. iv.
92. RA, ch. 21, tr. p. 269.
93. *GF*, p. 21.
94. RA, ch. 21, tr. p. 268.
95. D. L. Sayers, tr., *The Song of Roland* (Harmondsworth, 1957), stanza 72, p. 87, and see Jubb, *Legend*, p. 91 for a similar passage in the *Chanson d'Aspremont*.
96. *IP*, bk 3, chs 15, 18, tr. pp. 216, 220.
97. Baha' al-Din, tr. p. 112.
98. For Catholic views of Muhammad see Tolan, *Saracens*, pp. 135–69.
99. *GF*, p. 20.
100. Ibid., p. 49. Guibert of Nogent was confused by this list: GN, bk 5, tr. p. 94.
101. As he himself boasted in his preface, GN, tr. p. 26.
102. GN, bk 5, tr. p. 103.
103. 'De expugnatione', ed. Stevenson, p. 210, and cf. p. 260.
104. *IP*, bk 1, ch. 35, tr. p. 90, and see also bk 4, ch. 18, tr. p. 247.
105. Ibid., bk 4, ch. 18, tr. p. 247.
106. Jubb, *Legend*, p. 174.
107. Ibid., p. 19.
108. Ibid., pp. 19–31.
109. Ibid., ch. 5.
110. Ibid., ch. 4.
111. Ibid., ch. 6.
112. *IP*, bk 1, ch. 3, tr. p. 27, following a paragraph describing Saladin's early career as Nur ed-Din's pimp; Jubb, *Legend*, pp. 67–8.
113. Baha' al-Din, tr. p. 223.
114. *IP*, bk 6, ch. 32, tr. p. 375.
115. Jubb, *Legend*, p. 153.
116. RD, pp. 75–8; the passage is reminiscent of Kerbogha's conversation with his mother in the *Gesta Francorum*.
117. Jubb, *Legend*, pp. 145–8.
118. Ibid., pp. 5–17, 90.
119. IP, bk 6, ch. 22, tr. p. 364. See also M. J. Ailes, 'The admirable enemy? Saladin and Saphadin in Ambroise's *Estoire de la guerre sainte*', in *KC*, pp. 51–64.
120. Joinville, chs 324–5, tr. pp. 244–5.
121. Ibid., chs 327–8, tr. p. 245.
122. Ibid., chs 329–30, tr. pp. 245–6.
123. Ibid., ch. 365, tr. p. 255.
124. Ibid., ch. 337, tr. p. 247.
125. Ibid., chs 280–6, tr. pp. 234–6.
126. Ibid., chs 144–5, tr. p. 200.

127. Ibid., chs 548–50, tr. pp. 302–3.
128. Ibid., chs 196, 198–9, tr. p. 214.
129. Ibid., chs 249–53, tr. pp. 227–8.
130. *IP*, bk 5, ch. 27, tr. pp. 306–7. Cf. the disappointing account given in the Rothelin continuation of William of Tyre: Rothelin, ch. 17, tr. pp. 35–6.
131. Joinville, chs 451–63, tr. pp. 277–80.
132. E.g. A. Cutler, 'The First Crusade and the idea of "conversion" ', *The Muslim World* 58 (1968), 57–71, 155–64.
133. Ibid., pp. 65–71; France, *Victory*, p. 280.
134. AA, bk 7, ch. 17, pp. 508–11, and see also Cutler, 'First Crusade', p. 163; Runciman, *History*, 1.311. The same procedure was followed by the Muslims in 1250: Joinville, ch. 334, tr. p. 246.
135. *GF*, p. 73, and see also Riley-Smith, *First Crusade*, pp. 110–11.
136. Morris, *Sepulchre*, p. 186.
137. Powell, *Anatomy*, pp. 158–9.
138. Richard, *Saint Louis*, pp. 319–24. When Louis took the cross in 1244 it was predicted that he would baptize the sultan of 'Turkey': Bédier and Aubry, p. 253.
139. Joinville, ch. 53, tr. p. 175.
140. Rothelin, ch. 64, tr. p. 95.

9. Brave new world

1. G. Constable, 'Opposition to pilgrimage in the Middle Ages', *Studia gratiana* 19 (1976), 125–46.
2. 'Annales Herbipolenses', p. 3.
3. B. Z. Kedar, 'The *Tractatus de locis et statu sancte terre ierosolimitane*', in *CSEPBH*, 111–33, esp. pp. 121–2 on influences.
4. Which survives in over a hundred MSS: J. Bird, 'The *Historia orientalis* of Jacques de Vitry: visual and written commentaries as evidence of a text's audience, reception, and utilization', *Essays in Medieval Studies* 20 (2003), pp. 56–74, at p. 56.
5. Hagenmeyer, p. 150, tr. p. 156.
6. B. Hamilton, 'The impact of the crusades on western geographical knowledge', in *EBTT*, 15–34, at pp. 15–16.
7. M. Chibnall, 'Pliny's *Natural History* and the Middle Ages', in T. A. Dorey, ed., *Empire and Aftermath: Silver Latin II* (London, 1975), pp. 57–78 passim.
8. Hagenmeyer, p. 140, tr. p. 109; Kedar, 'Reflections', esp. pp. 182–3.
9. RH, *Chronica*, 3.39–112.
10. E. Edson, 'Reviving the crusade: Sanudo's schemes and Vesconte's maps', in *EBTT*, 131–55, at p. 134, fig. 7.
11. Edson, 'Reviving', esp. p. 137.
12. Kedar, '*Tractatus*', p. 123.
13. C. Delano-Smith, 'The intelligent pilgrim: maps and medieval pilgrimage to the Holy Land', in *EBTT*, 107–30, esp. p. 120, fig. 5.
14. Hagenmeyer, p. 139, tr. p. 107, and cf. Kedar, 'Reflections', p. 182.
15. Kedar, '*Tractatus*', pp. 122 n. 35, 128.
16. 'Narratio', pp. 616, 619 (= Chroust, pp. 182, 184), though admitting that Goslar was less impressive than Silves; 'Epistola', p. 177.
17. Chibnall, 'Pliny's *Natural History*', pp. 70–2.
18. Friedman, *Monstrous Races*, pp. 42, 76–7; Bird, '*Historia orientalis*', p. 59.
19. Rothelin, chs 46–58, pp. 71–85 and see also M. R. Morgan, 'The Rothelin continuation of William of Tyre', in *Outremer*, 244–57.
20. Chibnall, 'Pliny's *Natural History*', p. 72.

21. See Fink's introduction to the English tr. of FC, pp. 36–46.

22. FC, bk 3, ch. 10, tr. p. 235.

23. Ibid., chs 29–30, tr. pp. 256–62.

24. Ibid., bk 2, ch. 3, tr. pp. 142–3. But he still misidentified Azotus as Ibelin (Jabneel): bk 2, ch. 13, tr. p. 160, bk 3, ch. 18, tr. p. 242.

25. Ibid., bk 2, chs 56–9, tr. pp. 215–18 (the Red Sea, Nile and Euphrates), bk 3, chs 51–2, tr. pp. 292–3 (streams near Raphaniya and Acre), bk 3, ch. 59, tr. pp. 299–300 (Mediterranean Sea).

26. Ibid., bk 2, ch. 5, tr. pp. 145–7.

27. Ibid., ch. 56, tr. pp. 216–17.

28. Ibid., bk 3, ch. 59, tr. p. 300.

29. Ibid., bk 2, ch. 52, tr. p. 210.

30. Ibid., ch. 60, tr. pp. 218–19.

31. Ibid., bk 3, ch. 62, tr. pp. 303–4.

32. Ibid., ch. 49, tr. pp. 284–8, 'the different kinds of beasts and serpents in the land of the Saracens'.

33. Ibid., ch. 48, tr. p. 284. This contrasted with the author of the *Tractatus*, who believed that the Holy Land was home to all of Europe's flora and fauna: Kedar, '*Tractatus*', p. 128.

34. FC, bk 2, ch. 60, tr. pp. 218–19.

35. Ibid., bk 3, ch. 59, tr. p. 300.

36. Ibid., ch. 38, tr. p. 273.

37. Ibid., ch. 49, tr. p. 288, ch. 60, tr. pp. 300–2.

38. RH, *Chronica*, 3.53, pp. 71–2.

39. *IP*, bk 4, ch. 13, tr. p. 241. Much in this passage is puzzling, not least its unconvincing depiction of the spiders attacking *en masse*.

40. Ibid., bk 5, ch. 44, tr. p. 322.

41. Ibid., bk 6, ch. 5, tr. p. 343.

42. Joinville, ch. 494, tr. p. 289.

43. Huygens, p. 104.

44. OP, ch. 60, tr. pp. 117–18; Kedar, '*Tractatus*', pp. 128–9.

45. JT, ch. 2, p. 119.

46. Ibid., ch. 55, p. 140; OP, ch. 33, tr. p. 88.

47. Huygens, pp. 102–3.

48. J. Wilkinson, with J. Hill and W. F. Ryan, eds, *Jerusalem Pilgrimage, 1099–1187* (London, 1988), pp. 244–73.

49. *IP*, bk 4, ch. 14, tr. p. 242.

50. Huygens, pp. 87–8, though this picture dramatically highlights the conversions that James achieved there.

51. OP, ch. 6, tr. pp. 57–8.

52. Joinville, ch. 613, tr. pp. 317–18.

53. S. Schein, *Fideles Crucis: The Papacy, the West, and the Recovery of the Holy Land, 1274–1314* (Oxford, 1991), pp. 129–32.

54. *IP*, bk 2, ch. 27, tr. pp. 176–7.

55. Hagenmeyer, p. 150, tr. p. 155.

56. *GF*, p. 27.

57. Hagenmeyer, p. 160, tr. p. 191.

58. *GF*, pp. 76–7 (*Status Urbis*).

59. Ibid., p. 3; Runciman, *History*, 1.127–8.

60. FC, bk 1, chs 8–9, tr. pp. 78–9 and 79 n. 1. On imperial policy see also RR, bk 1, ch. 6, tr. p. 84.

61. Queller and Madden, *Fourth Crusade*, p. 121.

62. OD, pp. 62–7.

63. GV, ch. 128, tr. pp. 58–9.
64. RC, tr. pp. 66–7.
65. Ibid., tr. pp. 102–3.
66. Ibid., tr. pp. 106–7.
67. Ibid., tr. pp. 107, 108, 110–11.
68. Ibid., tr. p. 112.
69. Queller and Madden, *Fourth Crusade*, pp. 139–40, 193–8.
70. Well characterized by S. Edgington, 'The First Crusade: reviewing the evidence', in *FCOI*, 55–77, at pp. 64–73.
71. S. Runciman, *The Eastern Schism* (Oxford, 1955) remains the best treatment of this.
72. See J. Harris, *Byzantium and the Crusades* (London, 2003), pp. xiv–xvi.
73. M. Angold, *The Fourth Crusade: Event and Context* (Harlow, 2003), p. 24.
74. Anna Comnena, *Alexiad*, tr. pp. 308–52.
75. For the situation before 1095 see J. France, 'Byzantium in western chronicles before the First Crusade', in *KC*, pp. 3–16.
76. RR, English tr., Introduction, p. 21.
77. Ibid., tr. pp. 221–2. For the letter's text see Hagenmeyer, pp. 130–6.
78. GN, bk 1, tr. p. 38.
79. Ibid., tr. pp. 36–9.
80. For Albert of Aachen see Edgington, 'First Crusade', pp. 64–73. Much the same could be said of Fulcher of Chartres, FC, Introduction, pp. 37–8. For Stephen of Blois' warm praise see Hagenmeyer, pp. 138–40, tr. pp. 100–1, 107–9.
81. E.g. Hagenmeyer, p. 140, tr. p. 109 (Stephen of Blois: pro); ibid., p. 145, tr. p. 107 (Anselm of Ribemonte: mixed); *GF*, p. 17, and RA, ch. 3, tr. p. 104: contra.
82. B. Hamilton, *The Latin Church in the Crusader States: The Secular Church* (London, 1980), esp. chs 2–3, 7.
83. RA, ch. 2, tr. p. 66.
84. OD, bk 2, pp. 26–7, bk 3, pp. 56–9.
85. Ibid., bk 3, pp. 56–7.
86. Ibid., bk 5, pp. 98–9. See also Constable, 'Second Crusade', pp. 217, 272–3.
87. 'Epistolae Sugerii', no. 36, pp. 495–6.
88. Hausmann, ed., *Die Urkunden*, no. 195, pp. 354–5.
89. OD, bk 4, pp. 66–7.
90. Ibid., bk 3, pp. 56–7.
91. RH, *Chronica*, 3.117, and cf. p. 114, where the members of the military orders are described as acting as umpires between them.
92. Most vigorously by Bachrach, 'Crusader logistics', passim.
93. Edbury and Rowe, *William of Tyre*, pp. 139–50.
94. Angold, *Fourth Crusade*, pp. 28–47 summarizes the situation well.
95. C. M. Brand, 'The Byzantines and Saladin, 1185–1192: opponents of the Third Crusade', *Speculum* 37 (1962), 167–81.
96. *IP*, bk 2, ch. 12, tr. pp. 155–6; RD, p. 20.
97. Edbury, *Cyprus*, pp. 3–7.
98. E.g. 'Historia', pp. 116, 132, 151.
99. PA, pp. 40–3.
100. Ibid., p. 68.
101. Angold, *Fourth Crusade*, pp. 50–71.
102. Notably by T. Madden, 'Vows and contracts in the Fourth Crusade: the treaty of Zara and the attack on Constantinople in 1204', *International History Review* 15 (1993), 441–68.
103. RC, tr. p. 94.
104. Ibid.
105. See Andrea's introduction to his translation.

106. Kedar, '*Tractatus*', pp. 124–5.
107. OP, chs 62–9, tr. pp. 118–22; Huygens, pp. 96–7; J. Prawer, 'Social classes in the crusader states: the "minorities" ', *HC*, 5.59–115, at pp. 59–60 and passim.
108. Hamilton, *Latin Church*, pp. 188–211, esp. p. 195.
109. Good synopsis in Hamilton, *Religion*, pp. 159–60.
110. Prawer, 'Social classes', pp. 66–9.
111. *GF*, pp. 26–7.
112. S. D. Nersessian, 'The kingdom of Cilician Armenia', in *HC*, 2.630–59, esp. pp. 635–51.
113. *IP*, bk 1, ch. 24, tr. p. 64.
114. PA, p. 89.
115. Kedar, '*Tractatus*', p. 124.
116. *GF*, p. 41.
117. Ibid., pp. 29, 33, 37, 43, 48.
118. GN, bk 4, tr. pp. 75, 78, 84.
119. Hagenmeyer, p. 164, tr. p. 195 (but with *expugnare* wrongly translated as 'expel').
120. Though as far as I'm aware no attempt has yet been made to include this letter in the corpus of anti-Byzantine propaganda concocted by Bohemund in 1106–7.
121. Prawer, 'Social classes', passim.
122. Huygens, pp. 83–5; Hamilton, *Latin Church*, pp. 113–36.
123. Huygens, p. 89.
124. Ibid., p. 128.
125. Ibid., p. 95.
126. Kedar, '*Tractatus*', p. 124: *armis plurimum exerciti* as opposed to *armis aliquatenus exerciti*. See also B. Hamilton, 'Continental drift: Prester John's progress through the Indies', in *PJ*, pp. 237–69, at pp. 241–2, on Innocent III's approach to the king of Georgia in 1211.
127. C. F. Beckingham, 'The achievements of Prester John', in *PJ*, pp. 1–22, at pp. 2–3, 7–8.
128. F. Zarncke, 'Prester John's letter to the Byzantine emperor Emanuel', in *PJ*, pp. 40–112, at p. 78.
129. For the political background to the letter see B. Hamilton, 'Prester John and the Three Kings of Cologne', in *PJ*, pp. 171–85.
130. Huygens, pp. 141–53.
131. OP, ch. 56, tr. pp. 113–14.
132. Jackson, *Mongols*, pp. 48–9.
133. MP, 4.337–44, tr. 1.522–8; above, ch. 2.
134. Joinville, chs 479–80, tr. pp. 284–5.
135. Hamilton, 'Continental drift', pp. 251–2 and passim.
136. See Jackson, Introduction to William of Rubruck, esp. pp. 47–51.
137. Jackson, ed., *The Mission*, p. 201.
138. C. Dawson, ed., *The Mongol Mission* (London, 1955); Jackson, ed., *The Mission*.
139. Jackson, ed., *The Mission*, p. 173.
140. MP, 4.76–8, tr. 1.312–14; Jackson, *Mongols*, pp. 135–64.
141. For a rare example of crusade preaching against the Mongols see Maier, pp. 9, 144–51; idem, *Preaching*, p. 85.
142. Rothelin, ch. 81, tr. pp. 118–19; Jackson, *Mongols*, pp. 117–18.
143. Jackson, *Mongols*, pp. 165–95.
144. S. Schein, '*Gesta Dei per Mongolos* 1300: the genesis of a non-event', *EHR* 94 (1979), 805–19.
145. Rutebeuf, pp. 424–30, esp. pp. 425–6.
146. P. Biller, *The Measure of Multitude: Population in Medieval Thought* (Oxford, 2000), pp. 244–9.
147. MP, 5.87, tr. 2.319.

148. Peter of Blois, 'Passio', col. 966, with the tuition in geography deriving from the patriarch Eraclius when he toured the West.
149. Jackson, ed., *The Mission*, p. 276.

10. Remembrance of things past

1. GW, bk 1, ch. 1, tr. p. 76.
2. Brundage, *Medieval Canon Law*, pp. 124–7; J. Riley-Smith, *What were the Crusades?*, 3rd edn (Basingstoke, 2002), p. 60.
3. E.g. FC, bk 1, chs 32, 34, tr. pp. 128, 133: 'as is customary' (*ut mos est*).
4. E.g. Phillips, 'The thief's cross', p. 148.
5. RA, ch. 13, tr. p. 263.
6. E.g. Hagenmeyer, p. 171, tr. p. 277.
7. *IP*, bk 6, chs 30–5, tr. pp. 373–9. Louis VII and Conrad III visited Jerusalem before the attack on Damascus.
8. RA, ch. 16, tr. p. 222. In Robert of Reims' account the same offer became the occasion for a fascinating critique of armed pilgrimage: RR, bk 5, ch. 1, tr. pp. 136–7.
9. PA, p. 101, and cf. p. 110.
10. Richard, *Saint Louis*, pp. 133–4. The debate was described in detail by Joinville, chs 419–42, tr. pp. 268–74, who probably exaggerated his own role in it (cf. Smith, *Crusading*, pp. 68–9). For a strong advocacy of staying see Rothelin, ch. 69, tr. pp. 107–8.
11. Andrea, p. 163.
12. RH, *Chronica*, 3.167, and see also Labande, 'Pellegrini', p. 220.
13. FC, bk 1, ch. 33, tr. pp. 128–33.
14. Ibid., bk 2, ch. 6, tr. pp. 148–50 (quote at p. 150).
15. 'Historia', p. 170.
16. Joinville, ch. 183, tr. p. 210, presents the two options.
17. Roger Bacon, *Opus maius*, ed. J. H. Bridges, 3 vols (repr. Frankfurt/Main, 1964), 3.121 and cf. p. 122: 'Christiani cruce signati etsi aliquando vincant, tamen facta peregrinatione ad propria revertuntur, et indigenae remanent et multiplicantur'. Cf. Humbert of Romans in the early 1270s: *CIR*, p. 113.
18. Hagenmeyer, pp. 141–2, tr. p. 132.
19. Ibid., pp. 146–9, tr. pp. 142–4.
20. RR, bk 1, ch. 1, tr. pp. 80–1. See ibid., tr. pp. 222–3 for the suggestion that Simeon's letter was used in Bohemund's propaganda campaign of 1106–7.
21. Ralph Niger, *De re militari*, p. 227.
22. France, 'Patronage', passim.
23. Riley-Smith, *First Crusaders*, pp. 157–9.
24. Idem, 'Motives', passim.
25. Y. Friedman, 'Immigration and settlement in crusader thought', in B.-S. Albert, Y. Friedman and S. Schwarzfuchs, eds, *Medieval Studies in Honour of Avrom Saltman* (Ramat-Gan, 1995), pp. 121–34. On this subject Ralph Niger was as radical as on many others: *De re militari*, p. 227.
26. *PL*, p. 216, col. 1261.
27. Rutebeuf, p. 427. Cf. the caustic comments of James of Vitry, *Historia*, bk 1, ch. 83, tr. pp. 236–8.
28. PA, p. 4, and cf. Peter of Blois, 'Passio', cols 962, 966.
29. Biller, *Measure*, pp. 239–44.
30. See ch. 4 at n. 25.
31. PA, pp. 97–8.
32. 'Annales Herbipolenses', p. 5.

33. RD, p. 84.
34. AA, bk 6, ch. 60, pp. 484–5; Riley-Smith, *First Crusaders*, pp. 147–8.
35. OV, bk 10, ch. 12, 5.270 81.
36. Hagenmeyer, p. 177.
37. *IP*, bk 6, ch. 35, tr. p. 379.
38. Runciman, *History*, 2.285–7. The argument that Louis and Roger planned a new crusade against Manuel has been discredited. See T. Reuter, 'The "non-crusade" of 1149–50', in J. Phillips and M. Hoch, eds, *The Second Crusade: Scope and Consequences* (Manchester, 2001), pp. 150–63.
39. RH, *Gesta*, 2.229.
40. A. L. Poole, *From Domesday Book to Magna Carta 1087–1216*, 2nd edn (Oxford, 1955), pp. 365–6.
41. Gillingham, *Richard I*, pp. 222–53.
42. E.g. Hagenmeyer, p. 161.
43. Riley-Smith, *First Crusaders*, pp. 78–9.
44. Hausmann, ed., *Die Urkunden*, no. 198, p. 358, and see also Riley-Smith, *First Crusaders*, p. 146. Conrad's comment in this charter is interesting largely for what it omits, which is any reference to betrayal by the local Christians: cf. his earlier letter to Wibald, Hausmann, ed., *Die Urkunden*, no. 197, pp. 356–7.
45. Bédier and Aubry, p. 71.
46. *IP*, bk 6, ch. 35, tr. pp. 379–80.
47. Otto of Freising, *Gesta Friderici*, tr. C. C. Mierow (repr., Toronto, 1994), bk 1, ch. 65, tr. pp. 105–6, and see also Constable, 'Second Crusade', p. 220.
48. Siberry, *Criticism*, p. 35.
49. Bédier and Aubry, p. 148.
50. E.g. Rothelin, ch. 19, tr. p. 37, and the texts tr. by E. Peters in his *Christian Society and the Crusades, 1198–1229* (Philadelphia, PA, 1971), pp. 162–70.
51. Rothelin, ch. 31, tr. p. 53.
52. Ibid., p. 54 (also in Bédier and Aubry, p. 232).
53. Bédier and Aubry, pp. 263–5.
54. RD, p. 30.
55. Riley-Smith, *First Crusaders*, pp. 145–6.
56. Hagenmeyer, p. 160, tr. p. 191, and see also Hagenmeyer, pp. 176, 412.
57. Joinville, ch. 735, tr. p. 346.
58. Hagenmeyer, pp. 173–4, tr. p. 278.
59. Andrea, pp. 186–7.
60. Riley-Smith, *First Crusaders*, p. 147.
61. Constable, 'Medieval charters', p. 79; idem, 'Financing', p. 82.
62. Hagenmeyer, pp. 142–3.
63. Riley-Smith, *First Crusaders*, pp. 150–2.
64. Andrea, ed., *Capture*, p. 123.
65. Ibid., pp. 123–5.
66. Riley-Smith, *First Crusaders*, pp. 154–5.
67. Rutebeuf, pp. 455–60 ('La complainte du comte Eudes de Nevers'), at pp. 457–8.
68. Richard, *Saint Louis*, pp. 151–2.
69. Joinville, ch. 667, tr. p. 331.
70. Richard, *Saint Louis*, pp. 155–210.
71. E. Jordan, *Les Origines de le domination angevine en Italie* (Paris, 1909), passim.
72. J. Bradbury, *Philip Augustus, King of France 1180–1223* (London, 1998), pp. 96–7.
73. 'Epistolae Sugerii', no. 3, pp. 484–5, with reference to Peter de Miliaco and the *pagus Belvacensis* during the Second Crusade.
74. Riley-Smith, *First Crusaders*, pp. 136, 156–7.
75. Rodulfus Glaber, *Historiarum*, pp. 60–1.

76. Siberry, *Criticism*, pp. 36–8.
77. Dickson, *Children's Crusade*, p. 27.
78. Constable, 'Medieval charters', p. 74.
79. Otto of Freising, *Gesta Friderici*, bk 1, ch. 47, tr. p. 79.
80. Cf. PA, p. 75 for knowledge of events on the Second Crusade at Ephesus.
81. 'Narratio', p. 616, and see also p. 642 (= Chroust, pp. 182, 196).
82. Joinville, ch. 242, tr. p. 225.
83. Smith, *Crusading*, p. 9. This was outdone by the Muslim who talked to one of Joinville's informants at Damascus in 1250–1 and claimed to have been at the battle of Montgisard in 1177: Joinville, ch. 446, tr. p. 275.
84. E. A. R. Brown and M. W. Cothren, 'The twelfth-century crusading window of the abbey of Saint-Denis: *praeteritorum enim recordatio futurorum est exhibitio*', *Journal of the Warburg and Courtauld Institutes* 49 (1986), 1–40, at p. 20 n. 90.
85. Schein, *Gateway*, pp. 29–31, vividly described by John of Würzburg *c.* 1170: Wilkinson, ed., *Jerusalem Pilgrimage*, pp. 263–4.
86. Linder, 'Liturgy', passim.
87. Kohler, 'Un sermon', esp. p. 163.
88. Texts in Cole, *Preaching*, pp. 235–43. See also Cole et al., 'Application', passim.
89. Linder, 'Loss', p. 393.
90. Constable, 'Financing', p. 81 n. 87; Bull, *Knightly Piety*, passim. Cf. Linder, 'Loss', p. 393, though his assertion that 'ceremonies [of remembrance] were undoubtedly performed in the usual way and on the appropriate dates in numerous churches throughout Europe' isn't substantiated.
91. Linder, *Raising Arms*, passim.
92. Jaspert, 'Hilfsersuchen', p. 516.
93. Morris, *Sepulchre*, pp. 210–13.
94. A. Forey, *The Military Orders: From the Twelfth to the Early Fourteenth Centuries* (Basingstoke, 1992), p. 104.
95. D. Crouch, *William Marshal: Court, Career and Chivalry in the Angevin Empire, 1147–1219* (London, 1990), pp. 51–2, 187.
96. Morris, *Sepulchre*, pp. 230–45.
97. Ibid., p. 155. See also Schein, *Gateway*, pp. 63–4.
98. Morris, *Sepulchre*, p. 160.
99. Ibid., p. 245.
100. Jordan, *Louis IX*, pp. 107–9.
101. Joinville, chs 730–4, tr. pp. 345–6; Richard, *Saint Louis*, pp. 303–5.
102. Jordan, *Louis IX*, p. 216.
103. N. Housley, ed. and tr., *Documents on the Later Crusades, 1274–1580* (Basingstoke, 1996), p. 67.
104. Richard, *Saint Louis*, p. 304.
105. Marshall, *Warfare*, pp. 77–83.
106. M. Prestwich, *Edward I* (London, 1988), pp. 326–33.
107. RA, preface, tr. p. 8.
108. Edgington, 'First Crusade', p. 57.
109. Linder, 'Liturgy', p. 128 n. 55.
110. Riley-Smith, *First Crusade*, pp. 135–6.
111. GN, preface, tr. p. 24.
112. Ibid., bk 7, tr. p. 155.
113. Ibid., tr. p. 157. The discordant treatments given to the lance remained contentious for centuries: J. Rubenstein, 'Putting history to use: three crusade chronicles in context', *Viator* 35 (2004), 131–68, at pp. 153–4 and n. 122.
114. GN, bk 7, tr. p. 157.
115. Ibid., tr. p. 156.

116. Ibid., tr. p. 162.
117. Edgington, 'First Crusade', p. 59.
118. GN, bk 2, tr. p. 41.
119. Riley-Smith, *First Crusade*, pp. 135–52.
120. S. Edgington, 'Albert of Aachen reappraised', in A. V. Murray, ed., *From Clermont to Jerusalem: The Crusades and Crusader Societies, 1095–1500* (Turnhout, 1998), pp. 55–67.
121. C. Morris, 'The aims and spirituality of the First Crusade as seen through the eyes of Albert of Aix', *Reading Medieval Studies* 16 (1990), 99–117.
122. For a good characterization of Albert see S. Edgington, 'Albert of Aachen and the *Chansons de Geste*', in *CSEPBH*, 23–37.
123. AA, bk 1, chs 2–5, pp. 2–9.
124. Edgington, 'First Crusade', p. 64.
125. *CIR*, p. 57. See also J. M. Powell, 'Myth, legend, propaganda, history: the First Crusade, 1140–ca. 1300', in *APC*, 127–41, at pp. 134–5.
126. Edbury and Rowe, *William of Tyre*, p. 47.
127. Ibid., pp. 3–5. See also Leopold, *How to Recover the Holy Land*, p. 171.
128. Powell, 'Myth', passim.
129. Schein, *Gateway*, p. 31, though note n. 54 on its limited diffusion.
130. Brown and Cothren, 'Crusading window', p. 15 n. 66; Morris, *Sepulchre*, p. 224. On Charlemagne's alleged crusade, see Leopold, *How to Recover the Holy Land*, pp. 23, 41, 92, 145, 171.
131. E.g. F. Cardini, 'Crusade and "presence of Jerusalem" in medieval Florence', in *Outremer*, 332–46.
132. GN, bk 7, tr. p. 156.
133. A. Katzenellenbogen, 'The central tympanum at Vézelay, its encyclopaedic meaning and its relation to the First Crusade', *The Art Bulletin* (1944), 141–51. See also Morris, 'Picturing', pp. 198–9.
134. See Smith, *Crusading*, pp. 30–5 for an excellent treatment of the *Chansons de croisade*.
135. IP, bk 6, ch. 8, tr. p. 346. See also Edgington, 'Holy Land', passim.
136. Powell, 'Myth', p. 139; Linder, 'Loss', p. 395.
137. Wilkinson, ed., *Jerusalem Pilgrimage*, pp. 264–5. Further on Wicher, see Riley-Smith, *First Crusaders*, p. 224.
138. See Smith, *Crusading*, pp. 126–31.
139. Jordan, *Louis IX*, p. 108.
140. Smith, *Crusading*, p. 91.
141. Rutebeuf, pp. 444–50 ('La complainte d'Outremer'), at pp. 446, 447, 449.
142. Housley, ed., *Documents*, p. 41.
143. Rubenstein, 'Putting history to use', passim.
144. Edgington, 'Holy Land', pp. 143, 153.
145. Maier, pp. 228–9.
146. Ibid., pp. 154–5.
147. Rutebeuf, pp. 497–509 ('La nouvelle complainte d'Outremer'), at p. 508.
148. Brown and Cothren, 'Crusading window', pp. 16–17, and see also the comments by Morris, 'Picturing', p. 198.
149. Brown and Cothren, 'Crusading window', p. 38 n. 155.

BIBLIOGRAPHY

Primary sources

Albert of Aachen, *Historia Ierosolimitana*, ed. and tr. S. B. Edgington (Oxford, 2007).

Ambroise, *Estoire de la guerre sainte*, ed. M. Ailes and M. Barber, tr. M. Ailes, 2 vols (Woodbridge, 2003).

Andrea, A. J., ed. and tr., *The Capture of Constantinople: The 'Hystoria Constantinopolitana' of Gunther of Pairis* (Philadelphia, PA, 1997).

Andrea, A. J., ed. and tr., *Contemporary Sources for the Fourth Crusade* (Leiden, 2000).

Anna Comnena, *The Alexiad*, tr. E. R. A. Sewter (Harmondsworth, 1969).

'Annales Herbipolenses', *MGHS*, 16.1–12.

Baha' al-Din Ibn Shaddad, *The Rare and Excellent History of Saladin*, tr. D. S. Richards (Aldershot, 2001).

Bédier, J., and P. Aubry, eds, *Les Chansons de croisade* (Paris, 1909).

Bernard of Clairvaux, *Letters*, ed. B. Scott James, 2nd edn (Stroud, 1998).

Bernard of Clairvaux, 'In praise of the new knighthood', tr. C. Greenia in *The Works of Bernard of Clairvaux*, vol. 7 (Kalamazoo, MI, 1977), 113–67.

Brahney, K. J., ed., *The Lyrics of Thibaut de Champagne* (New York, 1989).

Brocardus, 'Directorium ad passagium faciendum', in *RHC, Documents arméniens*, vol. 2, 365–517.

David, C. W., ed. and tr., *De expugnatione Lyxbonensi* (New York, 1936).

David, C. W., ed., 'Narratio de itinere navali peregrinorum hierosolymam tendentium et Silviam capientium, A.D. 1189', in *Proceedings of the American Philosophical Society* 81 (1939), 591–676 (alternative edition in A. Chroust, ed., *Quellen zur Geschichte des Kreuzzuges Kaiser Friedrichs I.* [Berlin, 1928], 179–96).

'De expugnatione Terrae Sanctae per Saladinum, libellus', in J. Stevenson, ed., *Radulphi de Coggeshall Chronicon Anglicanum* (RS, London, 1875), 209–62.

'De itinere Frisonum', in R. Röhricht, ed., *Quinti Belli Sacri Scriptores Minores* (Geneva, 1879), 57–70.

Edbury, P. W., ed., *The Conquest of Jerusalem and the Third Crusade: Sources in Translation* (Aldershot, 1996).

Eidelberg, S., ed. and tr., *The Jews and the Crusaders: The Hebrew Chronicle of the First and Second Crusades* (Madison, WI, 1977).

'Epistola de morte Friderici imperatoris', in A. Chroust, ed., *Quellen zur Geschichte des Kreuzzuges Kaiser Friedrichs I.* (Berlin, 1928), 173–8.

'Epistolae Sugerii', in *Recueil des historiens des Gaules et de la France*, 24 vols (Paris, 1737–1904), 15.483–532.

Foulet, A. L., ed., *Lettres françaises du xiiie siècle: Jean Sarrasin, lettre à Nicolas Arrode (1249)* (Paris, 1924).

'Fragmentum de captione Damiatae', in R. Röhricht, ed., *Quinti Belli Sacri Scriptores Minores* (Geneva, 1879), 167–202.

Fulcher of Chartres, 'Historia Iherosolymitana', in *RHC, Historiens occidentaux*, vol. 3, tr. F. R. Ryan, ed. H. S. Fink, as *A History of the Expedition to Jerusalem, 1095–1127* (Knoxville, TN, 1969).

Geoffrey of Villehardouin, *La Conquête de Constantinople*, ed. and French tr. E. Faral, 2 vols (Paris, 1973), English tr. M. R. B. Shaw as *Joinville & Villehardouin: Chronicles of the Crusades* (Harmondsworth, 1963).

Gerald of Wales, 'De rebus a se gestis', in J. S. Brewer, ed., *Giraldi Cambrensis Opera*, vol. 1 (RS, London, 1861), 1–122.

Gerald of Wales, 'Itinerarium Kambriae', in J. F. Dimock, ed., *Giraldi Cambrensis Opera*, vol. 6 (RS, London, 1868), 1–152, tr. L. Thorpe as *The Journey through Wales and The Description of Wales* (Harmondsworth, 1978).

'Gesta crucigerorum rhenanorum', in R. Röhricht, ed., *Quinti Belli Sacri Scriptores Minores* (Geneva, 1879), 27–56.

'Gesta obsidionis Damiatae', in R. Röhricht, ed., *Quinti Belli Sacri Scriptores Minores* (Geneva, 1879), 71–115.

'Les Gestes des Chiprois', in *RHC, Documents arméniens*, vol. 2, 651–872, partially tr. P. Crawford as *The 'Templar of Tyre': Part III of the 'Deeds of the Cypriots'* (Aldershot, 2003).

Guibert of Nogent, 'Gesta Dei per Francos', in *RHC, Historiens occidentaux*, vol. 4, tr. R. Levine as *The Deeds of God through the Franks* (Woodbridge, 1997).

Hagenmeyer, H., ed., *Die Kreuzzugsbriefe aus den Jahren 1088–1100* (Innsbruck, 1901), partially tr. A. C. Krey in *The First Crusade: The Accounts of Eye-Witnesses and Participants* (repr., Gloucester, MA, 1958).

Hausmann, F., ed., *Die Urkunden Konrads III. und seines Sohnes Heinrich* (Vienna, 1969).

Haymar, 'De expugnatione civitatis Acconensis', in Roger of Howden, *Chronica*, ed. W. Stubbs, 4 vols (RS, London, 1868–71) vol. 3, preface, appendix I, pp. cv–cxxxvi.

Henry of Huntingdon, *Historia Anglorum*, ed. and tr. D. Greenway (Oxford, 1996).

Hill, R., ed. and tr., *Gesta Francorum* (repr. Oxford, 1972).

'Historia peregrinorum', in A. Chroust, ed., *Quellen zur Geschichte des Kreuzzuges Kaiser Friedrichs I.* (Berlin, 1928), 116–72.

Housley, N., ed. and tr., *Documents on the Later Crusades, 1274–1580* (Basingstoke, 1996).

Huygens, R. B. C., ed., *Lettres de Jacques de Vitry* (Leiden, 1960).

Ibn al-Athir, *Chronicle for the Crusading Period, Part 1*, tr. D. S. Richards (Aldershot, 2006).

Jackson, J., ed. and tr., *The Mission of Friar William of Rubruck* (London, 1990).

James of Vitry, *Historia hierosolymitana abbreviata*, tr. M.-G. Grossel as *Histoire orientale de Jacques de Vitry* (Paris, 2005).

John of Joinville, *Vie de Saint Louis*, ed. and French tr. J. Monfrin (Paris, 1995), English tr. M. R. B. Shaw as *Joinville & Villehardouin: Chronicles of the Crusades* (Harmondsworth, 1963).

John of Tulbia, 'De domino Iohanne rege Ierusalem', in R. Röhricht, ed., *Quinti Belli Sacri Scriptores Minores* (Geneva, 1879), 117–40.

Kohler, C., 'Un sermon commémoratif de la prise de Jerusalem par les croisés attribué à Foucher de Chartres', *Revue de l'orient latin* 8 (1900–1), 158–64.

Krey, A. C., ed. and tr., *The First Crusade: The Accounts of Eye-Witnesses and Participants* (repr., Gloucester, MA, 1958).

'Liber duellii christiani in obsidione Damiate exacti', in R. Röhricht, ed., *Quinti Belli Sacri Scriptores Minores* (Geneva, 1879), 141–66.

Lunt, W. E., ed., *Papal Revenues in the Middle Ages*, 2 vols (New York, 1934).

Maier, C. T., ed. and tr., *Crusade Propaganda and Ideology: Model Sermons for the Preaching of the Cross* (Cambridge, 2000).

Mandeville, *Travels*, tr. C. W. R. D. Moseley (Harmondsworth, 1983).

Matthew Paris, *Chronica maiora*, ed. H. R. Luard, 7 vols (RS, London, 1872–83), tr. J. A. Giles as *Matthew Paris's English History, from the Year 1235 to 1273*, 3 vols (London, 1852–4).

Morgan, M. R., ed., *La Continuation de Guillaume de Tyr (1184–1197)* (Paris, 1982), tr. P. W. Edbury as *The Conquest of Jerusalem and the Third Crusade* (Ashgate, 1996), 11–145.

Odo of Deuil, *De profectione Ludovici VIII in orientem*, ed. and tr. V. G. Berry (New York, 1948).

Oliver of Paderborn, 'Historia Damiatina', in H. Hoogeweg, ed., *Die Schriften des kölner Domscholasters, späteren Bischofs von Paderborn und Kardinal-Bischofs von S. Sabina Oliverus* (Tübingen, 1894), 159–280, tr. J. J. Gavigan in E. Peters, ed., *Christian Society and the Crusades, 1198–1229* (Philadelphia, PA, 1971), 49–138.

Orderic Vitalis, *Historia aecclesiastica*, ed. and tr. M. Chibnall, 6 vols (Oxford, 1969–79).

'Ordinacio de predicacione S. Crucis in Anglia', in R. Röhricht, ed., *Quinti Belli Sacri Scriptores Minores* (Geneva, 1879), 1–26.

Otto of Freising, *Gesta Friderici*, tr. C. C. Mierow (repr. Toronto, 1994).

Peter of Blois, 'De Hierosolymitana peregrinatione acceleranda', in *PL*, 207.1057–70.

Peter of Blois, 'Passio Reginaldi principis olim Antiocheni', in *PL*, 207.957–76.

Peter the Venerable, *Letters*, ed. G. Constable, 2 vols (Cambridge, MA, 1967).

Pseudo-Ansbert, 'Historia de expeditione Friderici imperatoris', in A. Chroust, ed., *Quellen zur Geschichte des Kreuzzuges Kaiser Friedrichs I.* (Berlin, 1928), 1–115.

Ralph of Caen, 'Gesta Tancredi', in *RHC, Historiens occidentaux*, vol. 3, tr. B. S. and D. S. Bachrach as *The 'Gesta Tancredi' of Ralph of Caen: A History of the Normans on the First Crusade* (Aldershot, 2005).

Ralph of Coggeshall, 'Chronicon Anglicanum', in J. Stevenson, ed., *Radulphi de Coggeshall Chronicon Anglicanum* (RS, London, 1875), 1–208.

Ralph of Diceto, *Ymagines historiarum*, ed. W. Stubbs, 2 vols (RS, London, 1876).

Ralph Niger, *De re militari et triplici via peregrinationis Ierosolimitane*, ed. L. Schmugge (Berlin, 1977).

Raymond of Aguilers, 'Historia Francorum qui ceperunt Iherusalem', in *RHC, Historiens occidentaux*, vol. 3, tr. A. C. Krey in *The First Crusade: The Accounts of Eye-Witnesses and Participants* (repr, Gloucester, MA, 1958).

Richard of Devizes, *Chronicle*, ed. and tr. J. T. Appleby (London, 1963).

Riley-Smith, L. and J., trs, *The Crusades: Idea and Reality, 1095–1274* (London, 1981).

Robert of Clari, *The Conquest of Constantinople*, ed. and tr. E. H. McNeal (repr. Toronto, 1996).

Robert of Reims, 'Historia Iherosolimitana', in *RHC, Historiens occidentaux*, vol. 3, tr. C. Sweetenham as *Robert the Monk's History of the First Crusade* (Aldershot, 2005).

Rodulfus Glaber, *Historiarum libri quinque*, ed. and tr. J. France (Oxford, 1989).

Roger Bacon, *Opus maius*, ed. J. H. Bridges, 3 vols (repr. Frankfurt/Main, 1964).

Roger of Howden, *Chronica*, ed. W. Stubbs, 4 vols (RS, London, 1868–71).

Roger of Howden, *Gesta Henrici II et Ricardi I*, ed. W. Stubbs, 2 vols (RS, London, 1867).

Rothelin, 'Continuation de Guillaume de Tyr de 1229 à 1261, dite du manuscrit de Rothelin', in *RHC, Historiens occidentaux*, vol. 2, tr. J. Shirley as *Crusader Syria in the Thirteenth Century* (Aldershot, 1999).

Rutebeuf, *Oeuvres complètes*, ed. E. Faral and J. Bastin (Paris, 1959).

Salter, H. E., ed., *Eynsham Cartulary*, 2 vols (Oxford, 1907–8).

Sayers, D. L., tr., *The Song of Roland* (Harmondsworth, 1957).

Stubbs, W., ed., *Itinerarium peregrinorum et gesta regis Ricardi* (RS, London, 1864), tr. H. J. Nicholson as *Chronicle of the Third Crusade* (Aldershot, 1997).

Suger, *Vie de Louis VI le Gros*, ed. H. Wacquet (Paris, 1929), tr. R. C. Cusimano and J. Moorhead as *Suger: The Deeds of Louis the Fat* (Washington, DC, 1992).

Walter the Chancellor, *Bella Antiochena*, ed. H. Hagenmeyer (Innsbruck, 1896), tr. T. S. Asbridge and S. B. Edgington as *Walter the Chancellor's 'The Antiochene Wars'* (Aldershot, 1999).

Wilkinson, J., with J. Hill and W. F. Ryan, eds, *Jerusalem Pilgrimage, 1099–1187* (London, 1988).

William of Newburgh, 'Historia rerum anglicarum', in R. Howlett, ed., *Chronicles of the Reigns of Stephen, Henry II, and Richard I*, 2 vols (RS, London, 1884–5).

Secondary sources

Ailes, M. J., 'The admirable enemy? Saladin and Saphadin in Ambroise's *Estoire de la guerre sainte*', in *KC*, 51–64.

Angold, M., 'The Byzantine empire, 1025–1118', in D. Luscombe and J. Riley-Smith, eds, *New Cambridge Medieval History*, 4: *c. 1024–c. 1198, Part Two* (Cambridge, 2004), 217–53.

Angold, M., *The Fourth Crusade: Event and Context* (Harlow, 2003).

Asbridge, T. S., 'Knowing the enemy: Latin relations with Islam at the time of the First Crusade', in *KC*, 17–25.

Bachrach, B. S., 'Crusader logistics: from victory at Nicaea to resupply at Dorylaion', in *LWAC*, 43–62.

Bachrach, B. S., *Fulk Nerra, the Neo-Roman Consul, 987–1040: A Political Biography of the Angevin Count* (Berkeley, CA, 1993).

Barber, M., 'The Albigensian Crusades: wars like any other?', in M. Balard, B. Z. Kedar and J. Riley-Smith, eds, *Dei gesta per Francos: Études sur les croisades dédiées à Jean Richard* (Aldershot, 2001), 45–55.

Barber, M., 'The crusade of the shepherds in 1251', in J. F. Sweets, ed., *Proceedings of the Tenth Annual Meeting of the Western Society for French History* (Lawrence, KS, 1984), 1–23.

Barber, M., *The New Knighthood: A History of the Order of the Temple* (Cambridge, 1994).

Bartlett, R., *England under the Norman and Angevin Kings, 1075–1225* (Oxford, 2000).

Beckingham, C. F., 'The achievements of Prester John', in *PJ*, 1–22.

Biller, P., *The Measure of Multitude: Population in Medieval Thought* (Oxford, 2000).

Bird, J., 'The *Historia orientalis* of Jacques de Vitry: visual and written commentaries as evidence of a text's audience, reception, and utilization', *Essays in Medieval Studies* 20 (2003), 56–74.

Borrelli de Serres, 'Compte d'une mission de prédication pour secours à la Terre Sainte (1265)', *Mémoires de la Société de l'histoire de Paris et de l'Île-de-France* 30 (1903), 243–61.

Bowlus, C. R., 'Tactical and strategic weaknesses of horse archers on the eve of the First Crusade', in *APC*, 159–66.

Bradbury, J., *Philip Augustus, King of France 1180–1223* (London, 1998).

Brand, C. M., 'The Byzantines and Saladin, 1185–1192: opponents of the Third Crusade', *Speculum* 37 (1962), 167–81.

Brett, M., ''Abbasids, Fatimids and Seljuqs', in D. Luscombe and J. Riley-Smith, eds, *New Cambridge Medieval History*, 4: *c. 1024–c. 1198, Part Two* (Cambridge, 2004), 675–720.

Brown, E. A. R., and M. W. Cothren, 'The twelfth-century crusading window of the abbey of Saint-Denis: *praeteritorum enim recordatio futurorum est exhibitio*', *Journal of the Warburg and Courtauld Institutes* 49 (1986), 1–40.

Brundage, J. A., 'Adhemar of Puy: the bishop and his critics', *Speculum* 34 (1959), 201–12.

Brundage, J. A., *Medieval Canon Law and the Crusader* (Madison, WI, 1969).

Brundage, J. A., 'A note on the attestation of crusaders' vows', *Catholic Historical Review* 52 (1966), 234–9.

Brundage, J. A., 'Prostitution, miscegenation and sexual purity in the First Crusade', in P. W. Edbury, ed., *Crusade and Settlement* (Cardiff, 1985), 57–65.

Bull, M., *Knightly Piety and the Lay Response to the First Crusade: The Limousin and Gascony, c. 970–c. 1130* (Oxford, 1993).

Bull, M., 'Views of Muslims and of Jerusalem in miracle stories, c. 1000–c. 1200: reflections on the study of first crusaders' motivations', in *ECWA*, 13–38.

Cardini, F., 'Crusade and "presence of Jerusalem" in medieval Florence', in *Outremer*, 332–46.

Caspi-Reisfeld, K., 'Women warriors during the crusades, 1095–1254', in S. B. Edgington and S. Lambert, eds, *Gendering the Crusades* (Cardiff, 2001), 94–107.

Chazan, R., *European Jewry and the First Crusade* (Berkeley, CA, 1987).

Chazan, R., *The Jews of Medieval Western Christendom, 1000–1500* (Cambridge, 2006).

Chibnall, M., 'Pliny's *Natural History* and the Middle Ages', in T. A. Dorey, ed., *Empire and Aftermath: Silver Latin II* (London, 1975), 57–78.

Cole, P., 'Christian perceptions of the battle of Hattin (583/1187)', *Al-Masāq* 6 (1993), 9–39.

Cole, P., 'Humbert of Romans and the crusade', in *ECWA*, 157–74.

Cole, P., *The Preaching of the Crusades to the Holy Land, 1095–1270* (Cambridge, MA, 1991).

Cole, P., D. L. d'Avray and J. Riley-Smith, 'Application of theology to current affairs: memorial sermons on the dead of Mansurah and on Innocent IV', *Historical Research* 63 (1990), 227–47.

Congar, Y.-M.-J., 'Église et cité de Dieu chez quelques auteurs cisterciens à l'époque des croisades', in *Mélanges offerts à Étienne Gilson* (Toronto, 1959), 173–202.

Constable, G., 'The financing of the crusades in the twelfth century', in *Outremer*, 64–88.

Constable, G., 'Medieval charters as a source for the history of the crusades', in P. W. Edbury, ed., *Crusade and Settlement* (Cardiff, 1985), 73–89.

Constable, G., 'Opposition to pilgrimage in the Middle Ages', *Studia gratiana* 19 (1976), 125–46.

Constable, G., 'The place of the crusader in medieval society', *Viator* 29 (1998), 377–403.

Constable, G., 'The Second Crusade as seen by contemporaries', *Traditio* 9 (1953), 213–79.

Contamine, P., *War in the Middle Ages*, tr. M. Jones (Oxford, 1984).

Crocker, R. L., 'Early crusade songs', in T. P. Murphy, ed., *The Holy War* (Columbus, OH, 1976), 78–98.

Crouch, D., *The Birth of Nobility: Constructing Aristocracy in England and France 900–1300* (Harlow, 2005).

Crouch, D., *William Marshal: Court, Career and Chivalry in the Angevin Empire, 1147–1219* (London, 1990).

Cushing, K. G., *Reform and the Papacy in the Eleventh Century: Spirituality and Social Change* (Manchester, 2005).

Cutler, A., 'The First Crusade and the idea of "conversion" ', *The Muslim World* 58 (1968), 57–71, 155–64.

Daniel, N., *The Arabs and Medieval Europe*, 2nd edn (London, 1979).

Delano-Smith, C., 'The intelligent pilgrim: maps and medieval pilgrimage to the Holy Land', in *EBTT*, 107–30.

Dickson, G., *The Children's Crusade: Medieval History and Modern Mythistory* (Basingstoke, 2008).

Dickson, G., 'The genesis of the Children's Crusade (1212)', in his *Religious Enthusiasm in the Medieval West: Revivals, Crusades, Saints* (Aldershot, 2000), study IV.

Dyer, C., *Making a Living in the Middle Ages: The People of Britain, 850–1520* (New Haven, CT, 2002).

Edbury, P. W., *The Kingdom of Cyprus and the Crusades, 1191–1374* (Cambridge, 1991).

Edbury, P. W., 'Preaching the crusade in Wales', in A. Haverkamp and H. Vollrath, eds, *England and Germany in the High Middle Ages* (Oxford, 1996), 221–33.

Edbury, P. W., and J. G. Rowe, *William of Tyre: Historian of the Latin East* (Cambridge, 1988).

Edgington, S., 'Albert of Aachen and the *Chansons de Geste*', in *CSEPBH*, 23–37.

Edgington, S., 'Albert of Aachen reappraised', in A. V. Murray, ed., *From Clermont to Jerusalem: The Crusades and Crusader Societies, 1095–1500* (Turnhout, 1998), 55–67.

Edgington, S., 'The First Crusade: reviewing the evidence', in *FCOI*, 55–77.

Edgington, S., 'Holy Land, Holy Lance: religious ideas in the *Chanson d'Antioche*', in R. N. Swanson, ed., *The Holy Land, Holy Lands, and Christian History*, SCH 36 (Woodbridge, 2000), 142–53.

Edson, E., 'Reviving the crusade: Sanudo's schemes and Vesconte's maps', in *EBTT*, 131–55.

Flori, J., *Pierre l'Ermite et la première croisade* (Paris, 1999).

Flori, J., 'Une ou plusieurs "première croisade"? Le message d'Urbain II et les plus anciens pogroms d'Occident', *Revue historique* 285 (1991), 3–27.

Forey, A., 'Cyprus as a base for crusading expeditions from the west', in N. Coureas and J. Riley-Smith, eds, *Cyprus and the Crusades* (Nicosia, 1995), 69–70.

Forey, A., *The Military Orders. From the Twelfth to the Early Fourteenth Centuries* (Basingstoke, 1992).

France, J., *Victory in the East: A Military History of the First Crusade* (Cambridge, 1994).

France, J., 'Patronage and the appeal of the First Crusade', in *FCOI*, 5–20.

France, J., *Western Warfare in the Age of the Crusades, 1000–1300* (London, 1999).

France, J., 'Byzantium in western chronicles before the First Crusade', in *KC*, 3–16.

Friedman, J. B., *The Monstrous Races in Medieval Art and Thought* (Cambridge, MA, 1981).

Friedman, Y., *Encounter between Enemies: Captivity and Ransom in the Latin Kingdom of Jerusalem* (Leiden, 2002).

Friedman, Y., 'Immigration and settlement in crusader thought', in B. S. Albert, Y. Friedman and S. Schwarzfuchs, eds, *Medieval Studies in Honour of Avrom Saltman* (Ramat-Gan, 1995), 121–34.

Geary, P., 'Humiliation of saints', in S. Wilson, ed., *Saints and their Cults* (Cambridge, 1983), 123–40.

Geldsetzer, S., *Frauen auf Kreuzzügen, 1096–1291* (Darmstadt, 2003).

Gertwagen, R., 'Harbours and facilities along the eastern Mediterranean sea lanes to *Outremer*', in *LWAC*, 95–118.

Giese, W., 'Die "lancea Domini" von Antiochia (1098/99)', in W. Setz, ed., *Fälschungen im Mittelalter*, 6 vols (Hanover, 1988–90), 5.485–504.

Gillingham, J., *Richard I* (New Haven, CT, 1999).

Glasheen, C. R., 'Provisioning Peter the Hermit: from Cologne to Constantinople, 1096', in *LWAC*, 119–29.

Gottlob, A., *Kreuzablass und Almosenablass* (Stuttgart, 1906).

Gutsch, M. R., 'A twelfth-century preacher – Fulk of Neuilly', in L. J. Paetow, ed., *The Crusades and Other Historical Essays* (repr. Freeport, NY, 1928), 183–206.

Haldon, J., 'Roads and communications in the Byzantine empire: wagons, horses and supplies', in *LWAC*, 131–58.

Hamilton, B., 'Continental drift: Prester John's progress through the Indies', in *PJ*, 237–69.

Hamilton, B., 'The elephant of Christ: Reynald of Châtillon', in D. Baker, ed., *Religious Motivation: Biographical and Sociological Problems for the Church Historian*, SCH 15 (Oxford, 1978), 97–108.

Hamilton, B., 'The impact of the crusades on western geographical knowledge', in *EBTT*, 15–34.

Hamilton, B., *The Latin Church in the Crusader States: The Secular Church* (London, 1980).

Hamilton, B., 'Prester John and the Three Kings of Cologne', in *PJ*, 171–85.

Hamilton, B., *Religion in the Medieval West* (London, 1986).

Harris, J., *Byzantium and the Crusades* (London, 2003).

Hehl, E.-D., 'War, peace and the Christian order', in D. Luscombe and J. Riley-Smith, eds, *The New Cambridge Medieval History*, 4: *c. 1024–c. 1198, Part One* (Cambridge, 2004), 185–228.

Hiestand, R., ' "Precipua tocius christianismi columpna": Barbarossa und der Kreuzzug', in A. Haverkamp, ed., *Handlungsspielräume und Wirkungsweisen des staufischen Kaisers* (Sigmaringen, 1992), 51–108.

Hill, J. H. and L. L., *Raymond IV Count of Toulouse* (Syracuse, NY, 1962).

Hillenbrand, C., *The Crusades: Islamic Perspectives* (Edinburgh, 1999).

Hillenbrand, C., 'The First Crusade: the Muslim perspective', in *FCOI*, 130–41.

Hoch, M., 'The choice of Damascus as the objective of the Second Crusade', in *APC*, 359–70.

Housley, N., *Contesting the Crusades* (Oxford, 2006).

Hutchinson, G., *Medieval Ships and Shipping* (London, 1994).

Jackson, P., *The Mongols and the West, 1221–1410* (Harlow, 2005).

Jaspert, N., 'Zwei unbekannte Hilfsersuchen des Patriarchen Eraclius vor dem Fall Jerusalems (1187)', *Deutsches Archiv für Erforschung des Mittelalters* 60 (2004), 483–516.

Johnson, E. N., 'The crusades of Frederick Barbarossa and Henry VI', in *HC*, 2.87–122.

Joranson, E., 'The great German pilgrimage of 1064–1065', in L. J. Paetow, ed., *The Crusades and Other Historical Essays* (repr. Freeport, NY, 1928), 3–43.

Jordan, E., *Les Origines de le domination angevine en Italie* (Paris, 1909).

Jordan, W. C., *Louis IX and the Challenge of the Crusade: A Study in Rulership* (Princeton, NJ, 1979).

Jordan, K., *Henry the Lion: A Biography*, tr. P. S. Falla (Oxford, 1986).

Jordan, W. C., ' "Amen!" Cinq fois "Amen!". Les chansons de la croisade égyptienne de saint Louis, une source négligée d'opinion royaliste', *Médiévales* 34 (1998), 79–91.

Jordan, W. C., 'The representation of the crusades in the songs attributed to Thibaud, count palatine of Champagne', *JMH* 25 (1999), 27–34.

Jubb, M., *The Legend of Saladin in Western Literature and Historiography* (Lampeter, 2000).

Katzenellenbogen, A., 'The central tympanum at Vézelay, its encyclopaedic meaning and its relation to the First Crusade', *The Art Bulletin* (1944), 141–51.

Kedar, B. Z., 'The Jerusalem massacre of July 1099 in the western historiography of the crusades', *Crusades* 3 (2004), 15–75.

Kedar, B. Z., 'The passenger list of a crusader ship, 1250: towards the history of the popular element on the Seventh Crusade', *Studi medievali*, 3rd ser. 13 (1972), 267–79.

Kedar, B. Z., 'Reflections on maps, crusading, and logistics', in *LWAC*, 159–83.

Kedar, B. Z., 'The *Tractatus de locis et statu sancte terre ierosolimitane*', in *CSEPBH*, 111–33.

Keen, M., *The Laws of War in the Late Middle Ages* (London, 1965).

Kenaan-Kedar, N., and B. Z. Kedar, 'The significance of a twelfth-century sculptural group: le retour du croisé', in M. Balard, B. Z. Kedar and J. Riley-Smith, eds, *Dei gesta per Francos: Études sur les croisades dédiées à Jean Richard* (Aldershot, 2001), 29–44.

Labande, E. R., 'Pellegrini o crociati? Mentalità e comportamenti a Gerusalemme nel secolo XII', *Aevum* 54 (1980), 217–30.

Le Goff, J., *The Birth of Purgatory*, tr. A. Goldhammer (London, 1984).

Le Goff, J., *Saint Louis* (Paris, 1996).

Leopold, A., *How to Recover the Holy Land: The Crusade Proposals of the Late Thirteenth and Early Fourteenth Centuries* (Aldershot, 2000).

Lev, Y., 'Infantry in Muslim armies during the crusades', in *LWAC*, 185–207.

Leyser, K., 'Money and supplies on the First Crusade', in his *Communications and Power in Medieval Europe: The Gregorian Revolution and Beyond*, ed. T. Reuter (London, 1994), 77–95.

Linder, A., 'Deus venerunt gentes. Psalm 78 (79) in the liturgical commemoration of the destruction of Latin Jerusalem', in B.-S. Albert, Y. Friedman and S. Schwarzfuchs, eds, Medieval Studies in Honour of Avrom Saltman (Ramat-Gan, 1995), 145–71.

Linder, A., 'The liturgy of the liberation of Jerusalem', Mediaeval Studies 52 (1990), 110–31.

Linder, A., 'The loss of Christian Jerusalem in late medieval liturgy', in L. I. Levine, ed., Jerusalem: Its Sanctity and Centrality to Judaism, Christianity, and Islam (New York, 1999), 393–407.

Linder, A., Raising Arms: Liturgy in the Struggle to Liberate Jerusalem in the Late Middle Ages (Turnhout, 2003).

Lloyd, S., English Society and the Crusade, 1216–1307 (Oxford, 1988).

Lower, M., The Barons' Crusade: A Call to Arms and its Consequences (Philadelphia, PA, 2005).

Madden, T. F., 'Food and the Fourth Crusade: a new approach to the "diversion question" ', in LWAC, 209–28.

Madden, T. F., 'Vows and contracts in the Fourth Crusade: the treaty of Zara and the attack on Constantinople in 1204', International History Review 15 (1993), 441–68.

Maier, C. T., 'The bible moralisée and the crusades', in ECWA, 209–22.

Maier, C. T., Preaching the Crusades: Mendicant Friars and the Cross in the Thirteenth Century (Cambridge, 1994).

Maier, C. T., 'The roles of women in the crusade movement: a survey', JMH 30 (2004), 61–82.

Marshall, C., 'The crusading motivation of the Italian city republics in the Latin East, 1096–1104', in ECWA, 60–79.

Marshall, C., 'The use of the charge in battles in the Latin East, 1192–1291', Historical Research 63 (1990), 221–6.

Marshall, C., Warfare in the Latin East, 1192–1291 (Cambridge, 1992).

Mayer, H. E., The Crusades, tr. J. Gillingham, 2nd edn (Oxford, 1988).

Mennell, S., All Manners of Food: Eating and Taste in England and France from the Middle Ages to the Present (Oxford, 1985).

Menzel, M., 'Kreuzzugsideologie unter Innocenz III.', Historisches Jahrbuch 120 (2000), 39–79.

Mitchell, P. D., Medicine in the Crusades: Warfare, Wounds and the Medieval Surgeon (Cambridge, 2004).

Mol, J. A., 'Frisian fighters and the crusade', Crusades 1 (2002), 89–110.

Morgan, M. R., 'The Rothelin continuation of William of Tyre', in Outremer, 244–57.

Morris, C., 'The aims and spirituality of the First Crusade as seen through the eyes of Albert of Aix', Reading Medieval Studies 16 (1990), 99–117.

Morris, C., 'Picturing the crusades: the uses of visual propaganda, c. 1095–1250', in CSEPBH, 195–216.

Morris, C., 'Policy and visions: the case of the holy lance at Antioch', in J. Gillingham and J. C. Holt, eds, War and Government in the Middle Ages: Essays in Honour of J. O. Prestwich (Woodbridge, 1984), 33–45.

Morris, C., The Sepulchre of Christ and the Medieval West, from the Beginning to 1600 (Oxford, 2005).

Murray, A., 'Mighty against the enemies of Christ: the relic of the True Cross in the armies of the kingdom of Jerusalem', in CSEPBH, 217–38.

Murray, A., 'Money and logistics in the forces of the First Crusade', in LWAC, 229–49.

Nersessian, S. D., 'The kingdom of Cilician Armenia', in HC, 2.630–59.

O'Callaghan, J. F., Reconquest and Crusade in Medieval Spain (Philadelphia, PA, 2003).

Pegg, M. G., The Corruption of Angels: The Great Inquisition of 1245–1246 (Princeton, NJ, 2001).

Phillips, J., 'Ideas of crusade and holy war in *De expugnatione Lyxbonensi*', in R. N. Swanson, ed., *The Holy Land, Holy Lands, and Christian History*, SCH 36 (Woodbridge, 2000), 123–41.

Phillips, M., 'The thief's cross: crusade and penance in Alan of Lille's *Sermo de cruce domini*', *Crusades* 5 (2006), 143–56.

Poole, A. L., *From Domesday Book to Magna Carta 1087–1216*, 2nd edn (Oxford, 1955).

Powell, J. M., *Anatomy of a Crusade 1213–1221* (Philadelphia, PA, 1986).

Powell, J. M., 'Myth, legend, propaganda, history: the First Crusade, 1140–ca. 1300', in *APC*, 127–41.

Prawer, J., *Crusader Institutions* (Oxford, 1980).

Prawer, J., 'The Jerusalem the crusaders captured: a contribution to the medieval topography of the city', in P. W. Edbury, ed., *Crusade and Settlement* (Cardiff, 1985), 1–16.

Prawer, J., 'Social classes in the crusader states; the "minorities"', *HC*, 5.59–115.

Prestwich, M., *Armies and Warfare in the Middle Ages: The English Experience* (New Haven, CT, 1996).

Prestwich, M., *Edward I* (London, 1988).

Pryor, J. H., 'Digest', in *LWAC*, 275–92.

Pryor, J. H., *Geography, Technology, and War: Studies in the Maritime History of the Mediterranean, 649–1571* (Cambridge, 1988).

Purcell, M., *Papal Crusading Policy, 1244–1291* (Leiden, 1975).

Queller, D. E., and T. F. Madden, *The Fourth Crusade: The Conquest of Constantinople*, 2nd edn (Philadelphia, PA, 1997).

Reeves, M., *The Influence of Prophecy in the Later Middle Ages: A Study in Joachimism* (Oxford, 1969).

Reuter, T., 'The "non-crusade" of 1149–50', in J. Phillips and M. Hoch, eds, *The Second Crusade: Scope and Consequences* (Manchester, 2001), 150–63.

Richard, J., *Saint Louis: Crusader King of France*, tr. J. Birrell (Cambridge, 1983).

Riley-Smith, J., *The Crusades: A History*, 2nd edn (London and New York, 2005).

Riley-Smith, J., 'The crown of France and Acre, 1254–1291', in D. H. Weiss and L. Mahoney, eds, *France and the Holy Land: Frankish Culture at the End of the Crusades* (Baltimore, MD, 2004), 45–62.

Riley-Smith, J., *The First Crusade and the Idea of Crusading* (London, 1986).

Riley-Smith, J., *The First Crusaders, 1095–1131* (Cambridge, 1997).

Riley-Smith, J., *Hospitallers: The History of the Order of St John* (London, 1999).

Riley-Smith, J., *The Knights of St John in Jerusalem and Cyprus, c. 1050–1310* (London, 1967).

Riley-Smith, J., 'The motives of the earliest crusaders and the settlement of Latin Palestine, 1095–1100', *EHR* 98 (1983), 721–36.

Riley-Smith, J., 'Peace never established: the case of the kingdom of Jerusalem', *TRHS*, 5th ser. 28 (1978), 87–102.

Riley-Smith, J., *What were the Crusades?*, 3rd edn (Basingstoke, 2002).

Robinson, I. S., *The Papacy, 1073–1198: Continuity and Innovation* (Cambridge, 1990).

Rogers, R., *Latin Siege Warfare in the Twelfth Century* (Oxford, 1992).

Rosenwein, B. H., 'Feudal war and monastic peace: Cluniac liturgy as ritual aggression', *Viator* 2 (1971), 129–57.

Rouche, M., 'Cannibalisme sacré chez les croisés populaires', in Y.-M. Hilaire, ed., *La Religion populaire: Aspects du Christianisme populaire à travers l'histoire* (Lille, 1981), 29–41.

Routledge, M., 'Songs', in J. Riley-Smith, *The Oxford Illustrated History of the Crusades* (Oxford, 1995), 91–111.

Rubenstein, J., 'How, or how much, to reevaluate Peter the Hermit', in S. Ridyard, ed., *The Medieval Crusade* (Woodbridge, 2004), 53–79.

Rubenstein, J., 'Putting history to use: three crusade chronicles in context', *Viator* 35 (2004), 131–68.

Runciman, S., *The Eastern Schism* (Oxford, 1955).

Runciman, S., *A History of the Crusades*, 3 vols (Cambridge, 1951–4).

Schein, S., *Fideles Crucis: The Papacy, the West, and the Recovery of the Holy Land, 1274–1314* (Oxford, 1991).

Schein, S., *Gateway to the Heavenly City: Crusader Jerusalem and the Catholic West (1099–1187)* (Aldershot, 2005).

Schein, S., '*Gesta Dei per Mongolos* 1300: the genesis of a non-event', *EHR* 94 (1979), 805–19.

Schwinges, R. C., *Kreuzzugsideologie und Toleranz: Studien zu Wilhelm von Tyrus* (Stuttgart, 1977).

Setton, K. M., gen. ed., *A History of the Crusades*, 6 vols (Madison, WI, 1969–89).

Siberry, E., *Criticism of Crusading, 1095–1274* (Oxford, 1985).

Smith, C., *Crusading in the Age of Joinville* (Aldershot, 2006).

Southern, R. W., 'Peter of Blois and the Third Crusade', in H. Mayr-Harting and R. I. Moore, eds, *Studies in Medieval History Presented to R. H. C. Davis* (London, 1985), 207–18.

Spufford, P., *Money and its Use in Medieval Europe* (Cambridge, 1988).

Stacey, R. C., 'Crusades, martyrdoms, and the Jews of Norman England, 1096–1190', in A. Haverkamp, ed., *Juden und Christen zur Zeit der Kreuzzüge* (Sigmaringen, 1999), 233–51.

Strayer, J. R., 'The crusades of Louis IX', in *HC*, 2.487–518.

Strickland, D. B., *Saracens, Demons, and Jews: Making Monsters in Medieval Art* (Princeton, NJ, 2003).

Strickland, M., *War and Chivalry: The Conduct and Perception of War in England and Normandy, 1066–1217* (Cambridge, 1996).

Sumption, J., *Pilgrimage: An Image of Medieval Religion* (London, 1975).

Throop, S., 'Combat and conversation: interfaith dialogue in twelfth-century crusading narratives', *Medieval Encounters* 13 (2007), 310–25.

Tolan, J. V., *Saracens: Islam in the Medieval European Imagination* (New York, 2002).

Tyerman, C., *England and the Crusades, 1095–1588* (Chicago, 1988).

Tyerman, C., 'Who went on crusades to the Holy Land?', in B. Z. Kedar, ed., *The Horns of Hattin* (Jerusalem, 1992), 13–26.

Uebel, M., 'Unthinking the monster: twelfth-century responses to Saracen alterity', in J. J. Cohen, ed., *Monster Theory* (Minneapolis, MN, 1996), 264–91.

Unger, R. W., 'The northern crusaders: the logistics of English and other northern crusader fleets', in *LWAC*, 251–73.

Watkins, C. S., 'Sin, penance and Purgatory in the Anglo-Norman realm: the evidence of visions and ghost stories', *Past & Present*, 175 (2002), 3–33.

Woolgar, C. M., D. Serjeantson and T. Waldron, eds, *Food in Medieval England: Diet and Nutrition* (Oxford, 2006).

Zajac, W. G., 'Captured property on the First Crusade', in *FCOI*, 153–80.

IMPORTANT DATES

FIRST CRUSADE

1095 (27 Nov) Urban II calls for an armed pilgrimage to liberate Jerusalem at the council of Clermont
1096 wave of attacks on the Jews in Europe
1097 (1 Jul) crusaders defeat Turks at the battle of Dorylaeum
1097–8 siege of Antioch
1098 (28 Jun) crusaders defeat Kerbogha at the battle of Antioch
1099 (15 Jul) crusaders storm Jerusalem
1099 (12 Aug) crusaders defeat Fatimid army at battle of Ascalon
1101 crusaders coming to reinforce the settlers in Palestine wiped out in Anatolia

1107–8 Bohemund of Taranto organizes and leads crusade which initially attacks the Byzantine Greeks
1144 (24 Dec) Zengi captures Edessa

SECOND CRUSADE

1145 (1 Dec) Eugenius III issues the bull *Quantum praedecessores*, a call to arms to recover Edessa
1146 attacks on the Jews in the Rhineland
1147–8 German and French crusaders suffer devastating losses on their march through Anatolia
1147 (24 Oct) Lisbon captured by Portuguese with the help of crusaders on the way east
1148 (Jul) unsuccessful siege of Damascus by the crusaders

1169 Nur ed-Din seizes control of Egypt
1187 (3–4 Jul) Saladin destroys the army of the kingdom of Jerusalem at the battle of Hattin
1187 (2 Oct) Saladin reoccupies Jerusalem

THIRD CRUSADE

1187 (29 Oct) Pope Gregory VIII proclaims crusade in response to news of Hattin, with bull *Audita tremendi*
1188 Saladin tithe imposed in France and England to fund their crusading efforts
1189 (Aug) Guy of Lusignan lays siege to Acre

1189 (3 Sept) Silves falls to Portuguese, assisted by crusaders *en route* to the East
1190 (10 Jun) Frederick Barbarossa drowns in the Saleph river
1191 (Jun) Richard I seizes Cyprus
1191 (12 Jul) Acre's garrison capitulates to the Christians
1191 (7 Sept) Richard I defeats Saladin at the battle of Arsuf
1192 (2 Sept) treaty of Jaffa ends hostilities in Palestine

FOURTH CRUSADE

1198 (Aug) Innocent III proclaims new crusade to carry forward recovery of Holy Land
1202 (Nov) crusaders storm Dalmatian port of Zadar
1203 (Jul) crusaders and Venetians take Constantinople on behalf of pretender Alexios
1204 (Apr) crusaders and Venetians take Constantinople for themselves, and establish
   Latin empire there

1212 crusade of the *pueri* (so-called 'Children's Crusade')

FIFTH CRUSADE

1213 (Apr) Innocent III proclaims another crusade to bring assistance to the Holy Land
   with the bull *Quia maior*
1218 (May) crusaders lay siege to Damietta
1219 (Nov) crusaders capture Damietta
1221 (Aug) crusaders defeated at Mansurah

SIXTH CRUSADE

1228–9 Frederick II in the East
1229 (Feb) treaty of Jaffa restores most of Jerusalem to Christians

1239–41 'Barons' Crusade' makes gains in Palestine
1244 (Aug) Khorezmian Turks seize and sack Jerusalem
1244 (17 Oct) Christian settlers suffer heavy defeat at battle of Harbiyah

SEVENTH CRUSADE

1244 (Dec) Louis IX takes the cross
1248 (Aug) French army embarks at Aigues-Mortes
1249 (Jun) crusaders seize Damietta
1250 (8 Feb) battle of Mansurah
1250 (6 Apr) Louis capitulates to Muslims
1250–4 Louis IX resident in Palestine
1251 crusade of the *pastoureaux*

1258 Mongols sack Baghdad
1260 (3 Sept) Mamluks defeat Mongols at battle of Ain Jalut
1267 Louis IX takes cross for second time
1268 Antioch falls to Mamluks
1270 (25 Aug) death of Louis IX at Carthage
1291 (18 May) fall of Acre

INDEX